To My Family in the Three Americas

Frontispiece. Pablo Picasso, *Don Quichotte*

Contents

Acknowledgments

Versions of some material in this book have been published previously. The material on Hitchcock's *Rear Window* in chapter 1 was originally published in an article co-authored with Roberta Pearson (who has generously allowed me to include portions of it) entitled "Hitchcock's *Rear Window:* Reflexivity and the Critique of Voyeurism," in *Enclitic*, Vol. VII, no. 1 (Spring 1983). A variant version of the material on *Numéro Deux* was published in *Millenium Film Journal*, No. 3 (Winter/Spring 1979) under the title *"Numéro Deux:* Politics, Pornography, and the Media." The material on *Every Man for Himself* was published in *Millenium Film Journal*, Nos. 10/11 (Fall/Winter 1981–1982) under the title "Jean-Luc Godard's *Sauve Qui Peut/(la Vie).* A different version of chapter 4, "The Carnival of Modernism," appeared in *Wedge: An Aesthetic Inquiry*, Number 1 (Summer 1982) with the title "On the Carnivalesque." The material on *Jonah Who Will be 25 in the Year 2000* appeared in a slightly different version in *Jump Cut*, No. 15 (July 1977) under the title "The Subversive Charm of Alain Tanner: *Jonah Who Will be 25 in the Year 2000."* The editors of these journals have my appreciation for permission to include the material.

For the various film stills and frame enlargements I would like to express my appreciation to João Luiz Vieira (for the frame enlargements) and to the following individuals and organizations: The French Film Office, Carlos Clarens and Phototeque, Universal MCA, New Yorker Films, Embrafilme, New Line Cinema, Consolidated Poster Service, United Artists Classics, Gray City Inc., Cinemabilia, and Women Make Movies.

I would like to single out the following for special thanks: Bertrand Augst for his generous pedagogy, an inspiration to many, and Robert Alter for his encouraging attitude and concrete help. The manuscript also benefited from close readings by David Davidson and Ella Shohat. I would also like to thank the editors of *Jump Cut*, John Hess, Chuck Kleinhans, and Julia Lesage, for their supportive criticism in connection with work originally published in that journal. My thanks also go to Christian Metz, with whom I studied in 1973–1974, and who made characteristically generous comments about *Reflexivity* when he read it in 1991. I would also like to express appreciation to the following individuals for their support over the years: Karen Beckstein, Ed Branigan, Bob Burgoyne, Catherine Benamou, Julianne Burton, Ed Buscombe, Manthia Diawara, Sandy Flitterman-Lewis, Randal Johnson, Caren Kaplan, E. Ann Kaplan, Ernest Larson, Elizabeth Lyons, Richard Macksey, Annette Michelson, James Naremore, Sherry Milner, Dana Polan, Richard Porton, Randal Johnson, Bill and Elena Simon, Joao Luiz Vieira, Kathleen Woodward, and Ismail Xavier. Finally, I would like to thank all the students, both at U.C. Berkeley and at New York University, who have contributed immensely to my understanding of both film and reflexivity.

Preface to the Morningside Edition

Reflexivity in Film and Literature: From Don Quixote to Jean-Luc Godard deals with what might be termed the "other tradition" in literature and cinema: the tradition of reflexivity as embodied in novels, plays and films which interrogate literary and filmic conventions, which break with art as enchantment and point to their own factitiousness as textual constructs. Although it culls examples from diverse countries and historical periods, it obviously makes no claim to exhaustiveness. Rather, it treats the modern literary tradition—from Rabelais and Cervantes to Balzac, Jarry, and Brecht, as a vast intertextual background to certain demystificatory and deconstructive strategies in the cinema. Returning frequently to *Don Quixote* as a seminal instance of reflexivity, this essay might have been called, after Ortega y Gasset, a "meditation on the *Quixote*," or better, a mediation on the quixotic, and the Cervantic, as they have been expressed in the theatre, in prose fiction, and especially in film.

Reflexivity subverts the assumption that art can be a transparent medium of communication, a window on the world, a mirror promenading down a highway. If reflexive art has a mirror, it is conjoined, as Borges suggests, with an encyclopedia. The texts discussed here interrupt the flow of narrative in order to foreground the specific means of literary and filmic production. To this end, they deploy myriad strategies—narrative discontinuities, authorial intrusions, essayistic digressions, stylistic virtuosities. They share a playful, parodic, and disruptive relation to established norms and conventions. They demystify fictions, and our naive faith in fictions, and make of this demystification a source for new fictions.

Reflexive strategies, while equally available to literature and film, have distinct materials to work with in the two media. Literature is a purely verbal medium, while the "unattainable text" of cinema forms a multitrack sensorial composite. Without losing sight of the specificity of each medium, our text will attempt to place literature and film, and literary criticism and film criticism, into fruitful and fecund interaction. Both media share a common nature as discourse, *écriture;* both are textual and intertextual; both can foreground their constructed nature; and both can solicit the active collaboration of their reader/spectator.

Reflexivity in Film and Literature does not generally emphasize the avant-garde, already the subject of excellent work by Annette Michelson, Alan Weiss, David James, P. Adams Sitney and many others, nor does it deal in depth with consecrated historical avant-garde movements such as futurism, surrealism, or expressionism. It focusses, rather, on those texts which operate on the borders between the mainstream and the vanguard and between narrative and anti-narrative, which flirt with narrative and taunt it, deconstructing narrative rather than rejecting it entirely. A double movement of celebratory fabulation and demystificatory critique is inscribed in virtually all of the texts, as well as in my discourse about them.

The core of *Reflexivity* was written as a doctoral dissertation in the Comparative Literature Department at the University of California, Berkeley. Begun in the early seventies, it was completed in Berkeley and Paris during the years 1974–1976. Prior to initial publication in 1984, the manuscript underwent a double process of deletion and accretion, deletion because some of the material had appeared in another book, *Brazilian Cinema*, and accretion as I added new theoretical reflexions and textual analyses. The discussions of *Rear Window, Tom Jones, Lolita, The French Lieutenant's Woman, Exterminating Angel, That Obscure Object of Desire, Stardust Memories, Jonah Who Will be 25 in the Year 2000, Every Man for Himself, 8 1/2, Targets, Beware of a Holy Whore, Day for Night, In Search of Famine, Man of Marble, Veronika Voss, The State of Things,* and *Passion,* for example, did not feature in the original thesis version. The literary analyses, except those which reference the work of Gerard Genette, were written in the early seventies. Thus the attentive reader will note a higher coefficient of theoretical "old fashionedness" in those passages. Rather than dress them up in trendy postmodernist clothes, I have chosen to leave them intact in order to fulfill their original purpose of providing an intertextual backdrop for what is essentially a book about modernist reflexivity in film.

The title of the manuscript was also changed in 1984 from *The Interrupted Spectacle: The Literature and Cinema of Demystification* to the more straightforward but in some ways misleading *Reflexivity in Film and Literature.* In retrospect, it seems clear to me that *Reflexivity* constitutes at least two books. On the one hand, it offers a synchronic study of the relatively restricted phenomenon of reflexive devices, while on the other it treats the broader subject of an evolving subversive "other tradition" in both literature and film which consists of those texts that reject naturalism in favor of reflexive, hyper-fabulatory or carnivalesque strategies, a tradition theorized from a specifically Bakhtinian perspective in my subsequent book *Subversive Pleasures: Bakhtin, Cultural Criticism and Film.*

I have resisted the temptation to rewrite a book essentially written almost two decades ago, just as I have refused to indulge in the masochistic exercise of pointing out all the passages that I would now modify in the light of current trends and subsequent research. I would like, however, to provide some preliminary materials and briefly evoke what I would have liked to have done were there "world enough and time." Perhaps because the original manuscript focussed less on "reflexivity" than on "demystification," it never provided a definition of reflexivity, or an explanation of its origins. Thus it is worth pointing out that the concept of "reflexivity," which is derived etymologically from the Latin *reflexio/reflectere* ("bend back on") and was first borrowed from philosophy and psychology, where it referred to the mind's capacity to be both subject and object to itself within the cognitive process. We find reflexivity, in this philosophical/psychological sense, in some of the most celebrated dicta of philosophy such as Socrates's grammatically and philosophically reflexive "Know Thyself" and in Descartes's *cogito ergo sum*, where the skeptical observation of consciousness, consciousness watching itself consciousing, becomes a key to epistemology. In "On Understanding," (1690), John Locke defines reflexion as the knowledge that the mind has of its own operations and the character of those operations. Another source stream of reflexive thinking lies in literature and reflexion on literature. In his "On Naive and Sentimental Poetry," (1795), Friedrich Schiller, distinguished between naive, spontaneous poetry and an "ironic" poetry in which the poet's consciousness of what he or she is doing forms part of the poem's technique.

Reflexivity is of course not limited to what is often mistakenly labelled the "western" tradition. (1) Reflexivity exists wherever language-using human beings "talk about talk," i.e. wherever they reflect on consciousness, language, art and communication. For Henry Louis Gates, the Yoruba trickster figure Eshu-Elegbara is a figure for the parodic and deconstructive "signifying" of African and Afro-diasporic art. Reflexivity is not limited to erudite, literary, or academic traditions; it is equally discernible in the lyrics of samba, rap, calypso, and the commercial products of mass-mediated culture. Multivocal, the term "reflexivity" has a grammatical meaning when it refers to reflexive verbs as verbs that reflect back on themselves such as the tabloid press finds itself in an embarassing situation. It also has a linguistic sense, in that language can be used to reflect on language via a "metalanguage" such as linquistics as a way for language to "speak about language." In artistic terms, reflexivity refers to the metaphorical capacity of cultural productions to "look at" themselves, as if they were capable of self-regard. It is this "self-regard" that leads to the occasional condemnation of reflexivity as "narcissistic" and "self-indulgent."

Throughout this text, I have very broadly defined reflexivity as the process by which texts, both literary and filmic, foreground their own production, their authorship, their intertextual influences, their reception, or their enunciation. This last, I should point out, is the subject of an extremely precise and useful book by Christian Metz, *L'Enonciation Impersonnelle, ou le Site du Film* [Paris:

Klinksieck, 1991]. The French semiotician argues that the theoretical search for the equivalent in the cinema of the "deictics" of verbal language has been misguided since theorists should have simply been looking for the phenomenon of reflexivity. In his book, which one devoutly hopes will be translated into English, Metz provides admirably theorized analyses of a broad arsenal of reflexive devices such as direct visual address to the camera, verbal direct address, reflexive intertitles, the frame-within-the-frame, the film-within-the-film, subjective imagery, and the display of the apparatus, in ways largely congruent, although with a greater linguistic emphasis, with my own analyses.

The penchant for reflexivity must be seen as symptomatic of the methodological self-scrutiny typical of contemporary thought, its tendency to examine its own terms and procedures. Thus we find reflexivity forming part of diverse fields and universes of discourse—in linguistics's concern with "enunciation" and "metalanguage;" in psychoanalysis's method of relying on verbally-transmitted self-reflexions, in cybernetics' use of the reflexive concept of "feedback," in the Heisenberg Principle's assertion that acts of scientific observation necessarily modify the phenomena observed, in contemporary anthropology's concern with "self-anthropology" and anthropological *écriture,* and in the historian's concern with "metahistory" and "modes of emplotment." A philosophy of reflexivity, for Paul Ricoeur:

> considers the most radical philosophical problems to be those which concern the possibility of self-understanding as the subject of the operation of knowing, willing, evaluating, etc. Reflexion is the act or turning back upon itself by which a subject grasps in a moment of intellectual clarity and moral responsibility, the unifying principle of the operations among which it is dispersed and forgets itself as a subject. (2)

The broad notion of reflexivity has generated a swirling galaxy of satellite terms pointing to specific dimensions of reflexivity. The terms associated with reflexivity belong to morphological families with prefixes or roots deriving from the "auto" family, the "meta" family, the "reflect" family, the "self" family, and the "textuality" family. (3) Thus in art and literature, we find a proliferation of critical terms designating reflexive practices: "self-conscious fiction" (Robert Alter) for those novelists (e.g. Cervantes, Fielding, Machado de Assis) who call attention to the novel's status as artifact; "metafiction" (Patricia Waugh, Linda Hutcheon) for fiction about fiction that comments on its own narrative or linguistic identity, and "narcissistic narrative" as "the figural adjective designating this textual self-awareness." "Anti-illusionism," in this context, refers to novels or films which take a conscious stance against the verist tradition by foregrounding improbabilities of plot, character or language. "Self-referentiality" designates the ways in which texts can refer or point to themselves. And "mise-en-abyme refers to the infinite regress of mirror reflections to denote the literary, painterly, or filmic process by which a passage, a section, or sequence plays out in miniature the processes of the text as a whole.

Reflexivity also forms a key term in both modernism and postmodernism. For artistic modernism, those movements in the arts (both in Europe and outside of Europe) which emerged in the late 19th century, flourished in the first decades of the 20th century, and became institutionalized as "high modernism" after World War II, the term "reflexivity" evokes a non-representational art characterized by abstraction and fragmentation. Whether through the aggressive implausabilities of Jarryesque theatre, the subjective discontinuities of Joycean stream-of-consciousness, or the atonal dissonances of Schoenbergian serialism, it is art which deforms and "dehumanizes" representation. Modernist artists draw attention to the materials with which they work or to the creative processes which engender their texts. (4) Reflexivity within modernism evokes the artistic self-consciousness of Cubism, whereby the artist calls attention, in Ortega y Gassett's famous metaphor, not to what is seen through the window but rather to the window itself. Modernist artists challenge the taken-for-granted solidity of the world. Modernism, however, has a right-wing (Eliot, Pound, the Futurists) and a left-wing (the surrealists, the constructivists), and although modernism grows out of "high art," as Patrick Brantlinger and James Naremore point out, it is also deconstructive of certain high art values. (5) Indeed, Michael Newman posits two artistic modernisms, one derived from Kant and stressing the absolute autonomy of art, the other deriving from Hegel and stressing the dissolution of art into life and praxis. (6)

Although reflexivity has formed part of philosophy since its inception, reflexive questions have become absolutely central in a period which systematically valorizes the category of language. In our language-haunted century, language has come to constitute a fundamental paradigm, a virtual key to the mind, to artistic and social practice, and indeed to human existence in its entirety. Thinkers as diverse as Saussure, Peirce, Wittgenstein, Cassirer, Heidegger, Levy-Strauss, Bakhtin, Derrida, and even Merleau-Ponty share a recognition of the crucial, constitutive role of language in human life and thought. A corollary of this "linguistic turn" has been an awareness that concepts and representations can not be transparent; they are inevitably caught up in discourse, power, intertextuality, dissemination, and *differance*.

Reflexivity, as the negation of ideas of transparency and verism, is in this sense crucial to both post-structuralism ad post-modernism, both of which share a sense of problematized referentiality. Although the term "postmodernism" itself, as many analysts have pointed out, has been "stretched" to the breaking point, showing a protean capacity to change meaning in different national and disciplinary contexts, all its meanings carry an element of reflexivity. In the work of Jean Baudrillard, reflexivity takes the form of a view of the contemporary world as entailing a new economy of the sign, and a consequently altered attitude toward representation. This new era is characterized by what Baudrillard calls "semiurgy", the process by which the production and proliferation of mass-mediated signs has replaced the production of objects as the motor of social life and as a means of social control. In "The Precession of Simulacra," Baudrillard charts a trajectory within representation that moves from transparency to simulation; a first stage in which the sign "reflects" a basic reality; a second stage in which the sign "masks" or "distorts" reality; a third stage in which the sign masks the absence of reality; and a fourth stage in which the sign becomes pure simulation bearing no relation whatsoever to reality. The disappearance of the referent and even of the signified leaves in its wake nothing but an endless pageant of empty signifiers.

Within the context of post-modernism, reflexivity evokes the quotation-like aspects of pastiche art, the hyper-real world of media politics, and the incessant self-consciousness of contemporary television programming; in short it represents the referentless world of the simulacrum, where all of life is always already caught up in mass-mediated representation. It evokes a world where the various media apparati (TV monitors, VCRs, camcorders, etc), are a taken-for-granted presence. It evokes the mediacratic environment of *Max Headroom* and the scattered television screens of Nam June Paik. I should warn the reader that *Reflexivity* does not develop any in-depth discussion of post-modernism, a word invoked here only in a rather idiosyncratic sense to refer to the work of Brecht as "going beyond" the aporias of modernism and the avant-garde. (7) On the other hand, my use of the term "postmodernism" to apply to Brecht is at least implicitly reconcilable with what Hal Foster calls "resistance post-modernism," and it is in accord with those critics of Baudrillard who accuse him of "sign fetishism" and "semiological idealism."(8) The descriptive fact that we currently inhabit an unreal world of mass-media manipulation and simulation politics does not mean that all alternatives are forever banned.

More than an argument, *Reflexivity in Film and Literature* presents a kind of cubist contemplation of the object reflexivity from a diversity of angles and perspectives. We will concentrate on works with a high coefficient of reflexivity, but our approach will not be Manichean. No textual dogmatism will simplistically pit "good" reflexive texts against "bad" illusionistic texts. Instead of a binaristic division between reflexive/non-reflexive, we will find a nuanced spectrum or continuum of reflexivity. We will encounter texts that are both reflexive and reactionary (many television commercials, certain TV talk shows), texts that are reflexive and realist (*Numero Deux*), and texts that are anti-illusionist but only sporadically reflexive (*Macunaima*).

Reflexivity comes with no pre-attached political valuence; it can be grounded in art-for-art's sake aestheticism, in media-specific formalism, or in dialectical materialism. It can be individualistic or collective, narcissistic or inter-subjective. It can be a sign of bohemian flippancy or of politically-motivated sincerity. By a simplificatory fiction, I have disengaged three perennial modes of reflexive art: *ludic,* for example, the playful self-referentiality of a Borges novella, a Keaton two-reeler or a TV sitcom; *aggressive,* the modernist dehumanization typical of Jarry's *Ubu Roi* or Bunuel's *L'Age d'Or;* and *didactic,* and the Brechtian materialist fictions of Godard, Berger, Tanner. I make no grand theoretical claims for the three modalities; their usefulness is rhetorical rather than scientific. They are by no means mutually exclusive nor can they be simplistically attached to a given period, artist, or even text. Although certain historical periods and movements might favor the flourishing of a specific mode (the modernist avant-garde is especially prone to aggressivity, postmodernism is often ludic), all three modes are also as perennial as the human impulses that lie behind them. Many texts simultaneously deploy all three modes, the question is one of proportion, tendency, thrust.

Each major section of *Reflexivity in Film and Literature: From Don Quixote to Jean-Luc Godard* explores reflexivity from a distinct vantage point. The "Introduction" elaborates the historical background and conceptual tools essential to our enterprise. After sketching out the Renaissance background of modern reflexivity, it isolates three artistic moments: 1) the moment of the self-conscious novel in the Cervantes-Fielding-Sterne tradition; 2) the moment of modernism and the avant-garde; and 3) the moment of postmodernism, specifically its politicized version in Brechtian theatre and the Brecht-influenced films of Godard, Tanner, and others. It then explores key conceptions—realism, modernism, reflexivity—and tropes orienting contemporary film discourse—film writing, film discourse, textuality, and intertextuality—and attempts to demonstrate their relevance to filmic and literary reflexivity.

Chapter 1, "Allegories of Spectatorship," explores theories and films which foreground the complicity of the reader/spectator in creating artistic illusion, the examples ranging from *Don Quixote* to *Les Carabiniers,* from *Sherlock Jr.* to *Rear Window* and *That Obscure Object of Desire.* Chapter 2, "The Process of Production," takes as its subject those works which treat either the literary or cinematic milieu or the concrete technical and aesthetic processes of fiction-making, whether in a novel like *Lost Illusions,* or films like Vidor's *Show People,* Vertov's *The Man with a Movie Camera,* Sturges' *Sullivan's Travels,* Wilder's *Sunset Boulevard,* Godard's *Contempt,* Truffaut's *Day for Night,* Fassbinder's *Veronika Voss,* Coni Campos' *Cinema Thieves,* and Wenders' *The State of Things.* Chapter 3, "The Genre of Self-Consciousness," compares the narrative and rhetorical strategies of what Robert Alter calls the "self-conscious genre" in the novel—*Don Quixote, Tom Jones, Tristram Shandy, Dom Casmurro, Lolita, French Lieutenant's Woman*—to the filmic adaptations or prolongations of that tradition. Chapter 4, "The Carnival of Modernism," pinpoints a specific anti-illusionist tradition within modernism, the carnivalesque avant-garde—ultimately traceable to Menippean satire and Rabelias—of *Ubu Roi, L'Age d'Or, Exterminating Angel, The Riflemen,* and *Macunaima.* The final chapter, "The Pleasures of Subversion," contemplates the lessons of Brecht for a cinema which combines aesthetic celebration and political critique, as exemplified by such films as *Numéro Deux, Jonah Who Will be 25 in the Year 2000,* and *Every Man for Himself.*

Methodologically, *Subversive Pleasures* draws inspiration from a wide spectrum of thinkers and schools. It is designed to function as metacriticism, a reflexion on the act of criticism in a way that mirrors the meta-fictional and meta-cinematic works it analyzes. Apart from the many critics who have usefully treated reflexivity in film—Bruce Kawin, Noel Burch, Martin Walsh, Don Frederickson, Alfred Appel Jr.—this text is deeply indebted to the tradition of literary criticism—to Erich Auerbach's conception of the progressive democratization of western literature, to Robet Alter on "partial magic" and the "self-conscious genre," to Walter Benjamin's notion of "aura" and his view of Brechtian theatre as the "art of interruptions" to Roland Barthes on "écriture" and the "text of pleasure," to Frederick Jameson on "competing class discourses" and the "utopian" dimension of culture, and to Bakhtin's idea of the "dialogic" and "the carnivalesque." At times, these conceptions will become ideational personages that pop up at regular intervals, rather like characters in a Balzac novel. In film-theoretical terms, meanwhile, I draw on the basic descriptive categories of contemporary film theory and criticism, and especially on the theory of identification and the cinematic "apparatus" inflected by contemporary psychoanalytic theory and developed by Christian Metz, Jean-Louis Baudry, and others.

Had there been "world enough and time," I would have liked to have discussed many more films, including some which I saw only after the 1985 publication of the book. The chapter on "Allegories of Spectatorship" might easily have included *Peeping Tom, Videodrome, Body Double* and *The Purple Rose of Cairo.* The chapter on "the Process of Production" might have featured *The Stunt Man, Barton Fink, Postcards from the Edge, Intervista,* and many others. I also would have liked to discuss a number of films which play with documentary form, such as *Zelig* which is discussed in *Subversive Pleasures* and *Tribulation 99,* Craig Bladwin's hilarious collage of tongue-in-cheek paranoid right wing voice-over with found footage from monster and science fiction films. I would have liked to have included John Grayson's *Urinal,* with its outlandish staging of an impossible Toronto encounter between Eisenstein, Langston Hughes, Frida Kahlo and Yukio Mishima who are summoned to research the state of washroom sex and homphobia in Ontario, Canada.

I particularly reget not having been aware of William Greaves' extraordinary *SymbioPsychoTaxiPlasm—Take One.* Filmed in 1967 but never commercially released, the film is only now being appreciated as the prophetic text that it is. Indeed, the film virtually calls for a rewriting of the history of filmic reflexivity. In this reflexive film, the filmmaker-in-the-film becomes the catalyst whose very refusal to direct instigates a revolt (devoutly desired by the director) on the part of actors and crew. Using the filming of "Over the Cliff" in Central Park—a film that seems to consist of endless reshooting of the same scene of marital breakup, using a succession of five couples in the roles—as a decoy, the director provokes the crew and cast to film themselves arguing about his manipulative refusal to direct. With Miles Davis's *In a Silent Way* on the sound track, the film is built, like jazz itself, on signifying "mistakes": the film runs out, the camera jams, and the actors become restless and irritable. The film analogizes jazz's relation to the European mainstream by performing a filmic critique of dominant cinema conventions and subtly evoking, in a tour de force of improvisation, multiple resistances against diverse authoritarianisms and oppressions.

Finally, Julie Dash's *Illusions* perfectly exemplifies the "double critique" of which I speak in *Reflexivity*, i.e., the double critique made by texts which criticize fictions—in this case the mystificatory illusions fostered by Hollywood filmmaking in order to critique the dominant society which generates such self-serving fictions. In this context, I would have liked to counterpoint an analysis of *Illusions* with my discussion of *Singin' in the Rain*. Both films reflexively focus on the cinematic technique of postsynchronization, and both deal with the issue of appropriation. While the former film exposes the intraethnic appropriation whereby silent movie queen Lina Lamont (Jean Hagen) appropriates the silky dubbed voice of Kathy Selden (Debbie Reynolds), *Illusions* focuses on the same issue—dubbing—but for very different, more politicized ends. Set in a Hollywood studio in 1942, the film features two "invisible" blacks: Mignon Dupree, invisible as an African American studio executive "passing for white," and Esther Jeeter, as the invisible singer hired to dub the singing parts for white film star Leila Grant. In one segment, Esther Jeeter performs the vocals for a screen role denied her by Hollywood's institutional racism. Black talent and energy are sublimated into an idealized white image. However by reconnecting the black voice with the black image, the film makes black talent "visible" and therefore "audible," while designating the operation of the erasure and revealing the white star's debt to black talent.

Were I writing *Reflexivity* today, I would also devote more attention to the films of Raul Ruiz, with their fusion of the theorized reflexivity of the modernist avant-garde with the baroquely polyphonic "marvelous realism" of Latin American literature. I also would have liked to incorporate some of the feminist attempts to construct a filmic "Oedipus Interruptus," in Teresa de Lauretis' apt phrase, whether through the witty deconstruction of musical comedy as in Chantal Akerman's *The Golden Eighties* (1983), the polyphonic orchestration of discourses as in Yvonne Rainer's *The Man Who Envied Women* (1985), the anti-naturalistic in-quotes "realism" of Marleen Gooris' *The Question of Silence* (1984), the carnivalesque overturning of patriarchal myths of Barbara Hammer's *Superdyke* (1975), or the media-spoofing militancy of Lizzie Bor-

Figure A. *Symbiopsychotaxiplasm: Take One* (1967)

den's *Born in Flames* (1983). In the transgressive transvaluations of such films, one divines the possibility of "highjacking" the magic of dominant cinema and deconstructing/reassembling it for different purposes, projecting the possibility of the filmic realization of what Laura Mulvey has called a "new language of desire."

A politicized cinema, and a politicized criticism, need not suffer from Woody Allen's "anhedonia," the inability to have a good time. My aim is to speak of the pleasurability of the text as well as of its politics, of desire as well as demystification. Although the contestatory impulse behind this textual "pleasuring" will only gradually come to the fore, the pleasuring itself, hopefully, will be present from the outset.

Figure B.   *Illusions* (1982)

Notes to the Morningside Preface

1. I say "incorrectly" because scholars like Martin Bernal have exposed the Afro-Asiatic roots of classical Greek civilization and the colonialist racism which insisted on fabricating a racially "pure" and "western" Greece.

2. See Paul Ricoeur, "On Interpretation," in A. Montefoire, ed. *Philosophy in France Today* (Cambridge: Cambridge University Press, 1983).

3. For an extended discussion of the terminology of reflexivity, see Luiz Antonio Coelho, *Towards a Taxonomy of Reflexive Structures for American Television*, Ph.D. dissertation written for the Media Ecology Department at New York University (1989).

4. Eugene Lunn identifies "aesthetic self-consciousness" or "self-reflexiveness" as one of the crucial features of modernism. See Eugene Lunn, *Marxism and Modernism: An Historical Study of Lukacs, Brecht, Benjamin and Adorno* (Berkeley: University of California Press, 1982).

5. See James Naremore and Patrick Brantlinger, eds. *Modernity and Mass Culture* (Bloomington: Indiana University Press, 1991).

6. See Michael Newman, "Postmodernism," in Lisa Appiganesi, ed., *Postmodernism: ICA Documents* (London: Free Association Books, 1989).

7. See Elizabeth Wright, *Postmodern Brecht* (London: Routledge, 1989).

8. See Douglas Kellner, *Jean Baudrillard: From Marxism to Postmodernism and Beyond* (Stanford: Stanford University Press, 1989) and Christopher Norris, *What's Wrong with Postmodernism* (Baltimore: Johns Hopkins, 1990). See as well Robert Stam et. al. *New Vocabularies in Film Semiotics: Structuralism, Poststructuralism and Beyond* (London: Routledge, 1992).

Introduction

All art has been nourished by the perennial tension between illusionism and reflexivity. All artistic representation can pass itself off as "reality" or straightforwardly admit its status as representation. Illusionism pretends to be something more than mere artistic production; it presents its characters as real people, its sequence of words or images as real time, and its representations as substantiated fact. Reflexivity, on the other hand, points to its own mask and invites the public to examine its design and texture. Reflexive works break with art as enchantment and call attention to their own factitiousness as textual constructs. This tension between the two tendencies characterizes all art, even the most "primitive." The practitioners of the sacred rites of archaic culture, Huizinga argues in *Homo Ludens,* simultaneously believe in and doubt the reality of their ritual representations. Since they themselves have staged the ceremonies, carved and decorated the masks, and learned to mimic the lion's roar, they cannot but know that the lions are counterfeit. As fabulating animals, we human beings enjoy pretending fictions are true even while knowing them to be false. The charms of spectacle transform us into wide-eyed children, astonished by lions we know to be illusory. Just as the members of tribal cultures relish being frightened by the lion's mask, we enjoy being temporarily traumatized by films of terror. (Is it that terror, that delicious provisional trauma, that constitutes the implicit promise of MGM's leonine logo?)

Western literature has long habituated us to fictions which point to their own fictitiousness. The stories-within-stories of the comic epic *Don Quixote,* for example, find their epic antecedents in the heroic songs which dot the larger heroic song which is *The Odyssey.* The carnivalesque anti-illusionism of a Rabelais traces back to the Menippean satire of Lucian, Petronius, and Apuleius. The parodistic critique of fiction found in Cervantes is already present in Aristophanes, Euripides, Horace and Ovid. Chaucer, for his part, intervenes in his own tales and destroys the illusion generated by the narrative. In *Canterbury Tales,* Chaucer the poet has the Host break off Chaucer the pilgrim's dreary Tale of Sir Thopas, itself a parodistic exercise in chivalric doggerel, with an exasperated "Namoore of this, for Goddes dignitee." Thus the arch-contriver of all the tales, the ultimate host and sponsor of the entire pilgrimage, appears in his own tale in the guise of a ludicruosly inept surrogate, whose tale is interrupted and censured by still another of the contriver's creatures.

Modern Reflexivity: Shakespeare, Cervantes, Brecht

Although all art has thrived on the tension between reflexivity and illusionism, between *trompe-l'oeil* and *clin d'oeil,* the tension becomes especially pronounced and sharpened with the Renaissance. Reflexivity takes center stage; artistic self-consciousness becomes endemic, and, more importantly, bears a changed meaning. Foucault, not surprisingly, traces the modern episteme to the Cervantic critique of representation and to Don Quixote himself as a purely textual entity, a thin graphic equestrian embodiment of writing itself wandering through a problematic world.[1] *Don Quixote* betrays a precociously modernist anxiety, wonderfully illuminated by Marthe Robert, concerning the very possibility of narrative. How can the artist—in the absence of the gods, the muses, or any communal tradition—validate the narrative? How can a modern writer forge a new *Odyssey* in a world where epic values have lost their currency? The epic order, once intimately linked to a social and mythological ethos, no longer exists, and the artist is thrown back on meager personal resources. In the face of this historical and ontological challenge to the credentials of narrative, Don Quixote maintains the doctrinaire position that all texts—those concerning Moses and Jesus and those concerning Amadis de Gaulle—are authentic.[2]

Proleptically modernist writers like Cervantes and Shakespeare register, with seismographic sensitivity, the shockwaves that rocked the feudal order and its epistemic underpinnings. The new science of Galileo, Kepler, and Copernicus cast into disarray the divinely sanctioned social hierarchies as well as the metaphysical certitudes of the Thomist synthesis of Scriptures and Greco-Roman thought. A ballad singer in *Galileo,* Brecht's theatrical reflection on the contradictions of the Renaissance, put it this way:

> When the Almighty made the universe
> He made the earth and then he made the sun.
> Then round the earth he bade the sun to turn—
> That's in the Bible, Genesis, Chapter One,
> And from that time all beings here below
> Were in obedient circles meant to go.[3]

But the millenium of faith gave way to the millenium of doubt, and neither serfs nor stars continued their obedient course. Galileo's new vision of the globe and

Shakespeare's experiments in the Globe Theatre reflected cosmic and social transformations. The "discovery" of the new world inspired the skeptical musings of Montaigne in "Des Cannibales" with its heightened awareness of the relativity of human culture and morality. Descartes' methodological skepticism exposed the problematic nature of ontology. All the established hierarchies came under attack with the rise of the bourgeois class. The period of our discussion coincides roughly with the rise of bourgeois Europe to positions of mastery in the world and as a class within Europe. And many of the demystificatory texts examined here constitute attacks, progressively more radical, on the mystifications and idealizations of that class.

Renaissance art highlights, paradoxically, both the possibilities and the limitations of mimesis. The same era that perfected the technique of perspective and *trompe l'oeil* illusionism also gave us the paintings-within-paintings of Velázquez and the mannerist distortions of El Greco. The insistent specularity of the former's *Las Meninas,* as Foucault demonstrates in the opening chapter of *Les Mots et les Choses,* embodies the dialectic of transparent representation and reflexive auto-representation, for in it "representation undertakes to represent itself."[4] The same Elizabethan theatre, meanwhile, that violated classical decorum by infusing tragedy with the words and rhythms of everyday speech was also centrally preoccupied with the problem of representation. The very *Hamlet* that provides the classic definition of the aims of mimetic art—"to hold the mirror up to nature"—foregrounds its own artifice through the play-within-the-play. The same character Hamlet who recommends naturalistic acting to the players constantly underlines the theatricality of the play of which he is the protagonist by alluding to the theatre and its conventions, comparing the consequential gestures of everyday life to "the actions that a man might play." "Prompted" to revenge, he murders Claudius and entreats the "audience" to "applaud" what he has acted. Even a lesser dramatist like Thomas Kyd bears witness to this concern with theatricality and the possibilities of representation. Throughout *The Spanish Tragedy,* Hieronimo searches for an adequate means of representing his grief for his lost son. He interrogates the painter: "Canst paint me a tear, or a wound/a groan, or a sigh?... canst paint me a doleful cry?" He has the painter recreate the entire scene of the murder, to better grasp the effigy of his suffering. That he finally resorts to exhibiting the bloodied filial corpse can be taken, on one level, as a brutal object lesson in the insufficiencies of mere representation.

Shakespeare's theatre thrives on this dialectical struggle between realistic imitation and self-conscious artifice. The play of *The Taming of the Shrew* is performed for the entertainment of Christopher Sly, who remains on stage and confuses what he sees with his own dreams, rather like Buster Keaton mentally somnambulating into the movie-theatre screen in *Sherlock, Jr.* But Shakespeare does not merely include plays-within-plays, he shows them in the very process of their elaboration. The palpable gross play of Peter Quince, Bottom and Company rehearsing "The Most Lamentable Comedy and Cruel Death of Pyramus and Thisby" in *Midsummer Night's Dream* mocks the very pretension of realism in the theatre. The title of the bracketed play already offends decorum by mingling tragedy and comedy. Worried that a lion costume might frighten the ladies, Snout recommends a prologue to assure the audience that the lion is no *real* lion. Bottom further suggests that the actor should expose half his face and "tell them plainly he is Snug the joiner." Struggling with the problem of bringing "moonlight into a chamber," the actors ultimately opt for the dramaturgical equivalent of location shooting by having literal moonbeams shine through a casement window. The "chinked wall" elicits a more Brechtian solution—covering a man with plaster to "signify" wall. The "Most Lamentable Comedy" demystifies realism twice over; first by its patent absurdities ("Now I am dead," groans Pyramus) and self-flaunting artifice, and secondly by showing a play in the very process of its engendering.

Shakespeare, accounting for the signifying power of theatre, invokes the analogy of mathematics. After apologizing for the crude materials of his stage, he compares the words of his play to "figures" and "ciphers:"

> O pardon, since a crooked figure may
> Attest in little place a million;
> And let us ciphers to this great accompt
> On your imaginary forces work.

The rich ambiguity of "imaginary forces," simultaneously evoking amassed troops in an imagined Agincourt and the force of imagination which enables the spectator to envision them, pinpoints the active role of the spectator, who must awaken the dormant signifiers and make them speak. More important, Shakespeare finds in mathematics a kind of signification which outstrips literal word-for-thing representation. In the sign-system of mathematics a crooked figure can signify a million, just as in the theatre a bit of loam can "signify" a wall. The referents of mathematical language, moreover, do not exist in nature. Square roots and the concept of infinity are not empirically available; they exist only in a closed, highly coded system called mathematics. Dramatic art, by analogy, need not literally reconstitute the world; it need merely signify it.

Both the call for the active spectator—who must behold the play, the Chorus tells us, in the "quick forge and working-house of thought"—and the emphasis on literature as sign inevitably recall Brecht's "epic" theatre, and it is no accident that Brecht saw Shakespeare as a precursor and his work as a storehouse of alienation effects. Brecht praised Shakespeare's habit of transparently basing his work on already existing plays, conserving entire fragments in a montage of heterogenous elements. For Shakespeare, according to Brecht, a play was not so much a finished work as something in process. In *The Messingkauf Dialogues* Brecht cites with approval a Shakespearean note to his actors advising them to change their lines if they did not "work" with the public.[5] More generally, Brecht respected the immanence of Shakespeare's meanings, the historical time-bound nature of his subjects, and the self-denouncing artifice of his technique.

Epic theatre, Walter Benjamin informs us, proceeds by interruptions. Shakespeare's plays, similarly, are not only interrupted by plays-within-plays, but the plays-within-plays are themselves interrupted. The mousetrap play in *Hamlet* is stopped midway, and Bottom's production in *Midsummer Night's Dream* is deprived of its epilogue. The masque in *The Tempest* is halted by its presumed author, Prospero, who brusquely dismisses his spirits: "Well done! Avoid, no more."

> Our revels now are ended. These our actors
> As I foretold you, were all spirits, and
> Are melted into air, into thin air.
> And, like the baseless fabric of this vision,
> The cloud-capped towers, the gorgeous palaces,
> The solemn temples, the great globe itself—
> Yea, all which it inherit—shall dissolve
> And, like this insubstantial pageant faded,
> Leave not a rack behind.

The passage, as countless commentators have pointed out, calls attention to the artifice of theatre. Actors, in their temporary incarnations as characters, are but spirits; the towers and palaces are but woven figures on a background tapestry; and the great globe is nothing more than the enclosing edifice of the Globe Theatre in Elizabethan London. But more to our purpose is the fact that the play world, after being laboriously constructed, is quickly shattered—"Our revels now are ended." *The Tempest,* in this sense, exemplifies a crucial procedure of reflexive art. It indulges in play and then pulls us out of the play world. It casts a spell and then as quickly disenchants.

This "art of interruptions" also characterizes *Don Quixote.* The narrative freeze frame which "stops" the literary image of Don Quixote and the Biscayan, with sword upraised, is, in this sense, emblematic of Cervantes' general procedure. It reminds us of Walter Benjamin's comparison of Brecht's epic theatre and the experience of looking at a film on an editing table. The gestures of epic theatre become "quotable" by being interrupted, for the more we interrupt someone in process of action the more gestures we obtain. Another comparison of Benjamin's simultaneously reminds us of freeze frames and of the Greuze paintings, capturing congealed moments of familial pathos, which so impressed Diderot. Benjamin compares the alienation effect of epic theatre to the sudden freezing of a domestic quarrel when a stranger enters the room. The stranger is confronted with a set of conditions—troubled faces, an open window, a devastated interior. The interruption has made the conditions strange.

From Comic Epic to Epic Theatre

The "fits and starts" of both comic epic and epic theatre bring us back once again to the original meaning of "epic." Many commentators on Homer have remarked on the "retarding element" in the Greek epic. Auerbach lingers brilliantly on the 70 verses of the *Odyssey* which intervene between Euraclea's surprised recognition of Odysseus' scar and the moment that she lets his foot drop in the basin. Her gesture is frozen while the poet recounts the story of the origin of the scar. Goethe and Schiller, Auerbach goes on to say, regarded this "retarding procedure" as proper to epic, as opposed to tragic, procedure. It is no accident that both Cervantes and Brecht define their aims in counterdistinction to tragic. Cervantes calls his novel a *comic* epic, and Brecht describes his theatre as "anti-tragic" and "non-Aristotelian." The interruption of action, Benjamin points out, "is one of the principal concerns of epic theatre." Cervantes interrupts the action through interpolated tales, through parodistic exercises, and through incursions of literary criticism. Like Master Pedro's assistant, Cervantes wanders from the straight line of his story and goes off on "curves and tangents." Brecht, for his part, interrupts the action by songs, by the intrusion of other media, by frozen *tableaux* and by direct address to the audience. The result, with both Brecht and Cervantes, is the same—the substitution of distanced reflection for suspenseful and empathetic involvement.

Our investigation of reflexivity highlights the shared procedures of the comic epic of Rabelais, Cervantes, and Fielding and the epic theatre of Brecht. The common characterization of their work as "epic" is not a coincidence arising merely from the historical evolution of the meaning of the term, but rather suggests a fundamental feature of their art. All of these writers refer back to the original Greek conception of epic as a specific kind of narrative structure. Epic composition, Cervantes has his canon remark, can be treated in prose as well as verse. Henry Fielding, defending his definition of *Joseph Andrews* as a "comic epic poem in prose," cites Aristotle to the effect that a comic version of epic existed, but subsequently disappeared, in Homeric antiquity. In Brecht's usage, similarly, "epic" refers, as it did in German critical discourse generally, to Aristotle's view of epic as a narrative form unconstricted by the theatrical unities of time, space, and action. The structure of *Don Quixote,* as innumerable commentators have pointed out, is episodic—its incidents could easily have been reshuffled into a different sequence. Whereas tragedy requires a beginning, a middle, and an end, in both epic and comic epic events are simply laid end to end. *Don Quixote* is made up of episodes with their own narrative validity, just as Brecht's plays are composed of autonomous scenes without necessary causal links to other scenes. In an epic work, Brecht suggested, one can cut up the work into individual pieces which remain fully capable of life.

Implicit in this episodic, nonorganic kind of structuring is a pronounced lack of interest in psychology as such. A number of critics have pointed out this antipathy on the part of epic to the internal and psychological. Epic, Goethe remarked, shows human beings as they act outwardly, in their battles and travels, while tragedy sees them from the inside. Homeric heroes, Auerbach tells us in *Mimesis,* do not know problematic psychological situations. Achilles and Odysseus, existing in the ever-present foreground of Homeric narrative, show no ethical development; their character is decreed from the beginning. Don Quixote's psychology, similarly, is reducible to an *idée fixe;* we are less interested in the movements of his soul than in his ideas and their problematic application to the real world. And for the epic theatre of Brecht, individual psychology is an appendage of social process. "In modern society," Brecht claimed with calculated overstatement, "the motions of the individual psyche are utterly uninteresting."[6] Brecht saw cinema, in fact, as a potential means of shattering the introspective psychology of the bourgeois novel by focusing on external action. The films of Keaton and Chaplin were prototypes of the epic form he wanted for the theatre, consisting of set characters performing with stylized gestures in flimsily connected episodes.

The writers and filmmakers whose texts we shall examine, from Cervantes to Brecht, Buñuel, and Godard, wield a power they only intermittently exploit—the power of casting a narrative or dramatic spell. Fully capable of charming their audience, they choose, for a variety of reasons, to subvert and undermine their tale. Their central narrative strategy is one of discontinuity. While illusionist art strives for an impression of spatio-temporal coherence, anti-illusionistic art calls attention to the gaps and holes and seams in the narrative tissue. To the suave continuities of illusionism, it opposes the rude shocks of rupture and discontinuity. Although the modalities of this discontinuity vary from era to era, from genre to genre, and from medium to medium, the discontinuity itself is omnipresent.

Modernism and the Impossible Narrative

With the advent of modernism, discontinuity becomes programmatic and rather aggressive. Interruption pre-empts spectacle; in fact, it *becomes* the spectacle. The modernist avant-garde subverts "good sense" and "reason" in a veritable explosion of otherness, incorporating madness, chance, discontinuity, and difference.[7] In the theatre, Alfred Jarry virtually invented the avant-garde in texts that are dramatically, generically, psychologically, and even rhetorically discontinuous. With him and the avant-garde generally, discontinuity becomes a weapon of provocation and offense to the bourgeois public. The surrealists, in Jarry's wake, allow the discontinuities of the psyche—dreams are spatially and temporally discontinuous—to disrupt and fecundate art.

While the nineteenth-century mimetic novel and the "realistic" drama presupposed a kind of good-natured complicity between artist and public, modernism implies a more aggressive stance. Whether the artist despises his bourgeois public from above as a nostalgic aristocrat or Baudelairean dandy, or execrates it from below as an intellectual who has deserted his class, the goal becomes to "épater le bourgeois," to provoke the public in order to see, as Jarry put it, "by its bear-like grunts where it is."[8] Condemning the bourgeoisie without embracing any other class, the artist becomes a social exile obsessed with difference and uniqueness. The modernist artist, knowing how to charm in the traditional way, refuses to exploit this power. Nothing so infuriates anti-modernist critics as the awareness that Picasso could have painted "normal" portraits, that Joyce could have delighted us with late Victorian prose, and that Beckett and Godard could have moved us in the conventional way if they only so desired.

In the novel, the problematics of narration come to be associated in modernist art with an anti-essentialist phenomenological view of the world. Sartre's *La Nausée* demonstrates the impossibility of what its protagonist calls *aventure*. The linear stories of nineteenth-century realistic novels, for Roquentin, are pure fabrication, the product of the play of human fabulation on the heteroclite materials of existence. Art exploits the consoling potentialities of form, as the human imagination forces coherence on the existential void by telling stories, ultimately meaningless, which compose delusively neat teleological wholes with beginnings, middles, and ends. Life, after all, does not tell stories. The alchemy of fiction tranforms the trivial occurrences of life into literary adventure, but the resultant stories are in no sense "true." Roland Barthes has even suggested that all narratives, by identifying a temporal sequence of signifiers with a sequence of imagined events, constitute variations on the logical fallacy which the scholastics called *post hoc ergo propter hoc*. Confusing mere consecution with real consequence, narratives impose laws of cause and effect on a world characterized by mere recurrence. Thus the modernist "dehumanization" of art implies an emphatic rejection of the desirability—or even the possibility—of realistic narrative. In what amounts to a radicalization of the Cervantic critique of fictions, the modernists go so far as to suggest that *all* stories are lies.

Not only are all stories lies, furthermore, but all human beings are liars, for they are all story-tellers. *La Nausée* represents, perhaps, the most explicitly paradigmatic fictional working-out of this modernist theme:

> This is what fools people: a man is always a teller of tales, he lives surrounded by his stories and the stories of others, he sees everything that happens to him through them; and he tries to live his own life as if he were telling a story.[9]

Thus modernism places all human beings, not just one aging and impoverished *hidalgo,* in the quixotic predicament. Countless modernist antiheroes see life as simply "bad literature" or "bad cinema." We are all secretly agreed, claims Dostoyevsky's Underground Man, that real life is a chore, and that things are better in literature. Godard's Marianne in *Pierrot le Fou* echoes him: "What makes me sad," she laments, "is that we can't live in life the way we can in novels." Life, she goes on to explain, lacks the order, harmony, and logic encountered in works of fiction.

La Nausée is a metalinguistic demonstration of the impossibility of *histoire*—in both senses of that word as "history" and "story." Sartre's protagonist-historian, Roquentin, argues that if stories are lies, *history* is a complete fabrication, "a work of pure imagination." (Here he anticipates those, like Lévi-Strauss, Michel Foucault, and Hayden White, who have stressed the fictive character of historical reconstructions). If he cannot discern coherence in his own life, Roquentin asks, how can he possibly find coherence in the life of a historical figure who died centuries before? While the nineteenth century developed the historical consciousness to an unprecedented degree, the modernists cast suspicion on the whole enterprise. "History is irrational," says Underground Man. "History is impossible," says Roquentin, and abandons the entire project in despair. For the modernists, all historians, and all human beings, are "unreliable narrators."

With post-modernism, and more specifically with Brecht, discontinuity forms part of a politicized esthetic in which discontinuity breaks the charm of spectacle in order to awaken the spectator's critical intelligence. While much of modernism went down the dead-end street of the "literature of silence," Brecht pointed a quite different path out of the modernist morass, a path that both assumed and dialectically leaped beyond modernism. His progess was up from the underground of modernist provocation into an esthetic of political involvement and self-reflective responsibility. If the self-conscious novel was primarily ludic in its relation to the reader, and modernism primarily aggressive, Brecht's theatre is ludic, aggressive, *and* didactic. Its didacticism, at its best, is subtle, dialectical, aimed less at communicating political messages than at teaching the spectator *how to learn.* Brecht's anti-illusionism is meant as a critique of a narcotic, mystifying, politically demobilizing art which offers the public its own fantasies about how things are rather than a radical critique of those fantasies. Our interest here will not be in Brecht's plays as such but rather in the repercussion his ideas have had on cinematic theory and practice, and especially on the films of Godard, Tanner, and others.

The Cinema, Modernism, Realism

The cinema, despite its superficial modernity and technological razzle-dazzle, has generally fostered a retrograde illusionistic aesthetic. Notwithstanding early experimentation—the magical effects of Méliès, the comic implausibilities of Keaton, the soft-focus artiness of the first French avant-garde, the pro-filmic mannerism of the German expressionists, the "creative geography" of the Soviet montage school, the *faux raccords* of a Deren, Anger, or Resnais—the classical fiction film has maintained, on the whole, an aesthetic corresponding to that of the nineteenth-century mimetic novel. The cinema also took on the novel's social function as a school for life, an initiatory source of models for behavior. In its dominant mode, it became a receptacle for the mimetic aspirations abandoned by the more advanced practitioners of the other arts. Film inherited the illusionistic ideal that impressionism had relinquished in painting, that Jarry as well as the symbolists had attacked in the theatre, and that Proust, Joyce and Woolf had undermined in the novel. Critics were not lacking, furthermore, to consecrate the veristic option with theories. Siegfried Kracauer spoke of the medium's "declared preference for nature in the raw" and its "natural vocation for realism." Bazin, for his part, postulated a kind of triumphal progress of realism not unlike a telescoped cinematic version of Auerbach's *Mimesis*. Bazin's annointed tradition begins with Lumière, continues with Flaherty and Murnau, is strengthened by Welles and Wyler, and reaches provisional fulfillment with Italian neorealism. At the same time, the technological histories of the medium performed a teleological recasting of film history, "blessing" the march toward a fuller mimesis with a kind of retroactive inevitability. In this version, the history of film is marked by the milestone "firsts" of genial pioneers, and every technological advance— microphone booms, incandescent lights, deep-focus cinematography, fast film emulsions—becomes a newly acquired weapon in the ever-expanding arsenal of verisimilitude.

A number of film theorists have made the camera's presumed "intrinsic" realism the cornerstone of an illusionistic aesthetic. The mechanical means of photographic reproduction, for these theorists, assures the essential objectivity of film. The fact that the photographer, unlike the painter or poet, cannot work in the absence of a model, would guarantee an ontological bond between the photographic representation and what it represents. Since photochemical processes involve an indexical link between the photoraphic analogon and its referent, photography is presumed to bear unimpeachable witness to "things as they are." Panofsky, Kracauer, and, to some extent, Bazin, all emphasize film as an "art of reality." Even Christian Metz, in his early work, contrasted the linguistic sign, seen as arbitrary and unmotivated, with the photographic image, seen as analogous and motivated.

Such a position is historically and theoretically problematic. Historically, photography replaced other methods of representation less because of its high mimetic fidelity than because of the speed and simplicity of its operations. Photography showed from the beginning a delight in transforming as well as imitating reality. As early as the 1840s, daguerreotypists renounced life-likeness for soft-focus and painterly effects, thus initiating the perennial inflection of photography by pictorial conventions. Although mimetic hardliners might see such "distortions" as a perverse violation of the nature of the medium, they can also be seen as anticipating cinema's vocation of expanding the signifying power of film rather than remaining a slave to appearances as conventionally perceived. A moment's reflection on the actual processes of photography lays to rest the theoretical claim that the camera literally registers an unmediated "reality." A photographer constructs a photograph through a series of choices: angle, lens, film stock, filters. Once taken, photographs are developed and can be cropped, retouched, and distorted. Several negatives can be superimposed on a single print, brush strokes can be added thanks to gum-bichromate, and unwanted detail can be excised with bromoil. The pro-filmic "reality," in sum, is transformed by these multiple operations into photographic discourse.

If some theorists, such as Bazin and Kracauer, defended the notion of the intrinsic realism of the camera, other later theorists argued that the camera was necessarily complicit with bourgeois ideology. For Marcelin Pleynet, Jean-Louis Baudry, and Jean-Louis Comolli, bourgeois ideology is built into the apparatus itself, not because the camera reproduces the world of ordinary perception, but because it does so according to the code of Renaissance perspective, a system of representation installed at a certain moment of history by a specific class. Baudry, in "Ideological Effects of the Basic Apparatus," emphasizes the false neutrality of a camera which merely consecrates conventions of pictorial representation inherited from Renaissance humanism.[10] The painters of the Quattrocento, observing that the perceived size of objects in nature varies proportionally with the square of the distance from the eye, simply incorporated this law, which characterizes the retina, into their paintings. Thus were planted the seeds of illusionism in painting, resulting in the impression of depth and ultimately leading to impressive *trompe-l'oeil* effects. The camera merely incorporates this *perspectiva artificialis* into its reproductive apparatus and thus expresses, according to Baudry, the "centered space" of the "transcendental subject" posited by Renaissance humanism. While painters may violate the code of perspective, filmmakers cannot, because that code is built into the very instrument with which they work. Even the distorted perspectives of fish-eye or telephoto lenses remain perspectival; they are distorted only in relation to "normal" perspective. Rather than simply record reality, these theorists argue, the camera conveys the world already filtered through a bourgeois ideology which makes the individual subject the focus and origin of meaning. The code of perspective, furthermore, produces the illusion of its own absence; it "innocently" denies its status as representation and passes off the image as if it were actually the world.

While appreciating the importance of such critiques—indeed my own text is marked by their influence—we must be alert to the danger of a monolithic conception of "dominant ideology" or "dominant cinema." We cannot view cultural products undialectically, as if they were exempt from contradiction, the fruit of a unified and self-aware bourgeoisie capable of viewing subsequent centuries with total clairvoyance, constructing its codes of representation with the single goal of defending its class interests. The structuralist inflection of Marxism, by privileging the logical and formal aspects of ideological representations, seen as the expression of a general system, at times lends itself to such an ahistorical and monolithic conception. The historically dated code of perspective becomes itself a kind of transcendental essence rendering the cinema forever permeable to idealist metaphysics.

In the 1970s, as we shall see subsequently (chap. 1), film theory, inflected by Althusser's notion of ideology and by Lacan's conception of the mirror stage, the imaginary, and the symbolic, shifts the grounds of discussion of "realism" away from the question of mimesis toward the question of the "apparatus" and the place of the "desiring spectator" within it. If the spectator's mind is the scene of a psychic process whose origins lie in unconscious formations, the real question is not one of mimesis or realism, but of "investments." It is Don Quixote's desire and "will to believe" that turns windmills into giants and prostitutes into ladies, and it is the cinematic spectator's desire that turns flickering two-dimensional images into perceived "reality."

For theorists such as Jean-Louis Baudry, Christian Metz and Jean-Louis Comolli, the question of illusionism is inseparable from the question of spectatorial identification.[11] These theorists develop a discourse of positionality and thus relocate the question of realism. Baudry, for example, postulates an unconscious substratum in spectatorial identification, in the sense that cinema, as a simulation apparatus, not only represents the real but also stimulates intense "subject-effects." The shadowy images on the screen, the darkness of the movie theatre, the passive immobility of the spectator, the womb-like sealing off of ambient noises and quotidian pressures, all foster an artificial state of regression not unlike that engendered by dream. The cinema, for Baudry, constitutes the approximate material realization of an unconscious goal perhaps inherent in the human psyche: the regressive desire to return to an earlier state of psychic development, a state of relative narcissism in which desire could be "satisfied" through a simulated reality defined as enveloping and in which the separation between one's body and the exterior world, between ego and non-ego, is not clearly defined.

It is not our purpose here to either defend or disprove these theories. In one sense, the achievements of these film thinkers seem irreversible; there can, at this point in the history of reflexion on the cinema, be no nostalgic return to innocence concerning the central importance of the cinematic apparatus, and we will see the analytic usefulness of these concepts in the first chapter. We can however raise some theoretical questions about the position as formulated. One wonders about Baudry's quasi-idealist positing of a transhistorical wish inherent in the psyche, and about a monolithic model of the cinema which fails to allow for either modifying the apparatus, or for "aberrant readings," or for filmic texts which alert the spectator to these very processes. At times the theoretical texts of this school fall into a kind of puritanism in their unnuanced and guilty condemnation of a manipulative apparatus as if it were part of a conspiratorial effort to delude. The despair of subverting this apparatus, one might add, is not without correlation to a certain decline and defeatism on the left in the period in which the theories were being formulated.

The Political Valence of Reflexivity

While Anglo-American cultural criticism has often seen reflexivity as the dead end of modernism, a point at which an exhausted art has little left to do except contemplate its own instruments, the left-wing of film theory, especially that influenced by Althusser, came to regard reflexivity as a *political* obligation. For this tradition—whose theoretical problems we shall examine in a moment—"realism" is reactionary by definition. By trying to reproduce "reality," realism inevitably expresses only the ideology implicit in conventional bourgeois notions of reality. This intellectual current was heavily influenced by the Althusserian concept of ideology, by which human societies secrete ideology as a kind of atmosphere indispensible to their historical respiration and life. The dominant style of dramatic realism, given the omnipresence of ideology, cannot challenge the received wisdom of the public, since spectators will see nothing but their own flickering ideologies in the naturalistic images on the screen. No matter how progressive its intentions, in this view, the subliminal ideology of realism is bourgeois. Rather than give the public a cold invigorating shower of demystification, realism gives it a bath in the tepid water of its own ideology. But Althusser's view of ideology, while in some ways useful and suggestive, has the disadvantage, when applied in certain theoretical texts of *Cinétique* and *Cahiers du Cinéma,* of being formulated so broadly as to be virtually identical to perception itself. Since the realist image can only represent the vague untheorized world of perception—the locus of the illusions of consciousness—it is presumed to be reactionary by nature. Thus the formula of idealist theoreticians, for whom the image is ontologically linked to the real, is neatly turned on its head by the suggestion that the image can *only* reproduce the vagaries of ideology.

In terms of the filmic texts themselves, Althusser-influenced film theory at times became overly dogmatic on the subject of "realist" films. The major thrust of the Althusserian movement in cultural studies was the critique of realism, and the tendency was simply to equate "realist" with "bourgeois" and "reflexive" with "revolutionary." The terms "Hollywood" and "dominant cinema" became code words for all that was retrograde and passivity-inducing. Bourgeois ideology was seen as a kind of ventriloquist, as if the film industry were only a puppet sitting on the capitalist's knee. The identification of "deconstructive" and "revolutionary," meanwhile, led in the pages of *Cinétique* to the rejection of virtually all past and present cinema as "idealist;" only certain films by Vertov, the collaborative work of Godard-Gorin, and a few independent French productions like *Mediterranée* and *Octobre à Madrid* passed the test as truly materialist.

But both of these equations call for close examination. Are realist texts necessarily reactionary? The answer depends very much on which realism we are speaking about, for realism has historically been defined in disparate ways. Instead of a monolithic realism, we find a proliferation of "realisms." A neologism coined by certain nineteenth-century artists and critics, the term originally signified an oppositional attitude toward romantic and neoclassical models in fiction and painting. Yet the concept did not spring from a conceptual vacuum; it represents a late flowering of the occidental mimetic tradition so brilliantly surveyed by Auerbach. A number of twentieth-century movements incorporated "realism" or closely related variations of the word into their self-definition: surrealism, socialist realism, poetic realism, neorealism. Without involving ourselves in the intellectual morass usually triggered by attempts at a rigorous definition of the term, we might posit several broad tendencies within its many definitions. Some definitions, for example, have to do with the aspiration or project of an author or school, seen as a corrective to dominant canons or to antecedent literary or cinematic decorum. At times this "corrective" takes on a moral or social cast, as when Auerbach connects realism in the novel to "the serious treatment of everyday reality" and "the rise of more extensive and socially inferior human groups to the position of subject matter for problematic-existential representation . . ."[12] This critique then can be stylistic—as in the new wave attack on the artificiality of the "tradition of quality"—or social—neorealism aiming to show post-war Italy its true face—or both at once—Cinema Novo revolutionizing both the social thematics and cinematic procedures of antecedent Brazilian cinema. Other definitions of realism have more to do with verisimilitude, the correspondence of a fiction to deeply ingrained and widely disseminated cultural models of "believable" plotting and "coherent" characterization. This definition can also imply a text's degree of conformity to generic codes; a filmic car on a dark night on rain-soaked streets heading toward a private-eye protagonist can "realistically" be expected to run that protagonist down, no matter how statistically infrequent such incidents might be in real life. Another related definition might involve readerly or spectatorial belief, a realism of subjective response, something which often has more to do with the fine tuning of illusionistic technique than with mimetic accuracy. A purely formalist definition, finally, would emphasize the conventional nature of all fictional codes, and would posit realism simply as a body of stylistic devices, a set of conventions that, at a given moment in history, manages to generate a strong feeling of authenticity.

It would be a mistake to regard reflexivity and realism as necessarily antithetical terms. Many of the texts we shall analyze combine a measure of realism with reflexive technique. They illuminate the everyday realities of the social conjunctures from which they emerge, while also reminding their readers or spectators of the artificiality of their mimesis. *The Man with a Movie Camera* documents the realities of filmmaking and of Soviet life in the late twenties, but also constantly foregrounds its status as artifact. *Two or Three Things I Know About Her* reflexively highlights its own nature as filmic construct, but it also speaks to the contemporary realities of prostitution and urban renewal. Realism and reflexivity are not strictly opposed polarities but rather interpenetrating tendencies quite capable of coexistence within the same text. It would be more accurate to speak of a "coefficient" of reflexivity or mimesis, while recognizing that it is not a question of a fixed proportion. Godard-Miéville's *Numéro Deux*, for example, displays a simultaneously high coefficient of both realism and reflexivity. Illusionism, meanwhile, has never been monolithically dominant even in the mainstream fiction film. Illusionism and anti-illusionism have been locked in dialectical struggle since the beginning, with the degree of reflexivity varying from era to era, genre to genre, from film to film, and even from sequence to sequence within specific films. Even the most paradigmatically mimetic texts—as Barthes' reading of *Sarrasine* and *Cahiers'* of *Young Mr. Lincoln* demonstrate—are marked by gaps and fissures in their illusionism. Few classical films perfectly fit the abstract category of transparence often taken to be the norm in dominant cinema. Nor can one simply assign a positive or negative political value to realism, or even illusionism, *as such*. Marx's debt to Balzac, as we shall see in our discussion of *Lost Illusions,* suggests that realism is not inherently reactionary. While realism initially emerged as part of the bourgeois critique of feudal and aristocratic conventions, it has also been used as an instrument of social criticism by the working class, by women, and by emerging third world nations. Pontecorvo's *Battle of Algiers,* for example, is a realist, even illusionist, film, yet it would be a mistake to dismiss it, as some leftist critics did, as a Hollywood exercise in political melodrama. Such rigidity runs the danger of being politically counter-productive, as the Left deprives itself of a powerful instrument of anticolonialist persuasion.

The other equation—reflexive equals progressive—is similarly problematic when applied too rigidly. Texts may foreground the work of their signifiers or obscure it; the contrast cannot always be read as a political one. The reflexivity of *La Ronde* or *Singin' in the Rain* has little to do with leftist politics. The reflexivity of a certain avant-garde is eminently co-optable and easily reappropriated by the hegemonic culture. Even the deconstructed texts defended by *Tel Quel* or *Cinétique* end up, at times, by playing innocuously with purely formal categories such as representation, closure, or the illusion of presence. Or, to take an example from the realm of popular culture, commercial television is often reflexive and self-referential, yet that reflexivity is, to say the least, ambiguous. Talk shows not only display cameras and video switchers as part of their credits but also incessantly turn to talk about television itself. Johnny Carson, rather like Mark Twain in *How Not to Tell a Story,* mocks his own monologue as self-consuming artifact, while the video cameras show the producer just off stage. Many of the distancing features characterized as reflexive in Godard films would seem to typify television as well: the designation of the apparatus (cameras, monitors, switchers); the commercial "interruptions" of the narrative flow; the juxtaposition of heterogenous slices of discourse; the mixing of documentary and fictive modes.

Yet we know that if television is reflexive, its reflexivity is of a peculiarly ambiguous and often debased kind. Rather than trigger "alienation effects," commercial television often simply alienates. The commercial interruptions that place programs on hold, for example, are not pauses for reflection but breaks for manipulation, intended not to make us think but to make us feel and buy. The self-referentiality of commercials that parody themselves or other commercials, similarly, are calculated to mystify rather than disenchant. The self-referential humor signals to the spectator that the commercial is not to be taken seriously, and this relaxed state of expectation renders the viewer more permeable to its message. The self-referentiality, far from demystifying the product or exposing hidden codes, conceals the deadly seriousness of the commercial—the fact that it is after the spectator's money.

The theory and practice of Bertolt Brecht provides a touchstone for distinguishing authentic from debased reflexivity. While authentic reflexivity elicits an active thinking spectator rather than a passive consumer of entertainment, most television is as narcotic and culinary as the bourgeois theatre that Brecht denounced. Brecht's goal was not to satisfy audience expectations but to transform them, whereas the central impulse of commercial television—notwithstanding the often creative and critical contribution of its artists—is to transform only two things: the audience's viewing habits and its buying habits. Brecht's goal was not to *be* popular in box-office terms but to *become* popular, that is, to create a new public for a new kind of theatre linked to new modes of social life, whereas commercial television's goal, at least from the point of view of its managers, is to be popular in the crudely quantitative terms of "ratings."[13]

Brecht also points the way beyond the false dichotomy of realism and reflexivity, for he, more than anyone, demonstrated the compatability of reflexivity as an esthetic strategy and realism as an aspiration. His critique of realism centered on the ossified conventions of the nineteenth-century novel and naturalist theatre, but not on the goal of truthful representation. Brecht distinguished between realism as "laying bare society's causal network"—a goal realizable through a modernist aesthetic—and realism as "well-tried rules" and "eternal aesthetic laws."[14] His quarrel, in short, was not with realism per se but with a historically determinate set of conventions.

Film/Writing/Text/Intertext

In the wake of literary criticism and philosophy, contemporary film discourse has been oriented by the constellation of concepts revolving around "writing" and "textuality." The graphological trope of film writing—from Astruc's caméra-stylo" through Bazinian auteurism to Metz' discussion of "cinema and *écriture*"—has dominated film theory and criticism, especially in France, since the fifties. Interest is progressively displaced from mimesis to textuality, from the picture or fiction depicted to the act of writing itself. Since the concept of writing is performative, rather than one of mere transcription, it implicitly undermines the mimetic view which regards the work as a mirrorlike reflection of preexisting reality.

The directors of the French new wave were especially fond of this scriptural metaphor. Many of them began as writer-critics who found it quite natural to see writing articles and making films as simply two forms of expressive *écriture*. Godard claimed that he was already making films when he was writing criticism and that he continued to do criticism by making films. This preoccupation with *écriture* is translated, in new wave films, by a proliferation of writing imagery. From Truffaut's *Les Mistons* (1958) through Godard's *2 ou 3 choses que je sais d'elle* (1967) we encounter people writing: on walls *(Jules et Jim)*, on cars *(Masculin, Féminin)*, in diaries *(Pierrot le Fou)*, on advertisements *(Le Gai Savoir)*, and in notebooks *(2 ou 3 choses)*. *400 Blows*, the film that more than any other "announced" the new wave, already

Figure 1. *La Chinoise* (1967)

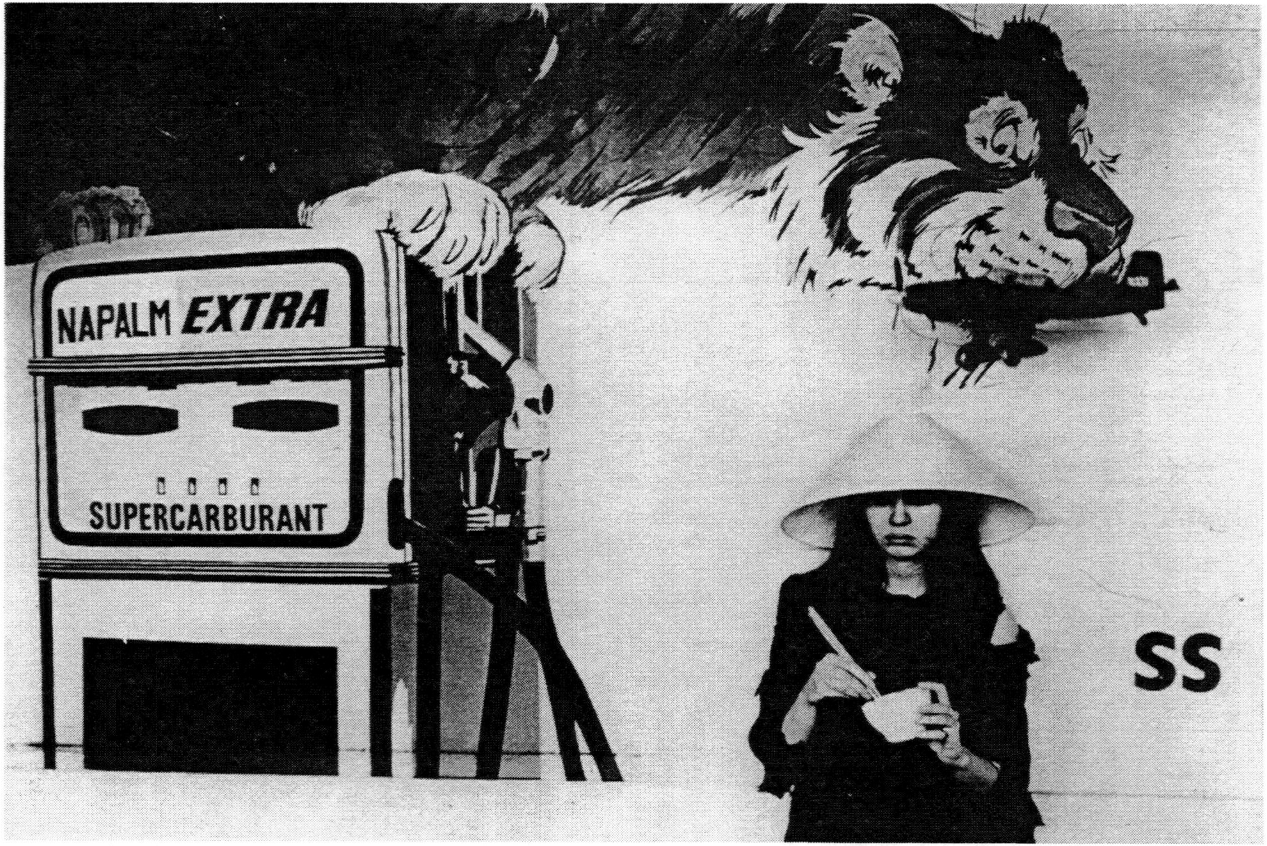

prefigures this obsession. The credit sequence—a series of tracking shots culminating with the director's name superimposed on the image of the cinémathèque—renders homage to the film library where Truffaut's "reading" inspired and informed his subsequent "writing." The first postcredit shot shows a pupil writing. Antoine swears vengeance on his teacher by writing a poem on the wall, and is punished by having to conjugate a sentence, in writing. French composition, his mother tells him, is invaluable, since "one always has to write letters." Antoine, as if to illustrate her claim, mimics her penpersonship in a note of excuse. He subsequently steals a typewriter so that the principal will not recognize his handwriting. In short, *400 Blows* orchestrates variations on the theme of *écriture,* in a way that makes little sense except as part of a structural metaphor subtending Truffaut's vision of filmmaking. Antoine, Truffaut's youthful surrogate in an admittedly autobiographical film, "tries on" diverse writing styles in an attempt to become his own man. He complains that his mother's writing is "hard to imitate." His affectionate pastiche of Balzac elicits accusations of plagiarism.

Writing, for Truffaut, is inextricably linked to power. Miswriting elicits the condemnation of authority figures. The supposedly self-indicting sentence dictated to Antoine by his teacher reads: "I deface the classroom walls and I mistreat French prosody." Antoine's step-father corrects the spelling on his charge's "Why-I-Left-Home" note. The analogy to new wave attitudes toward the cinema should by now be obvious. The accusation of plagiarism anticipates the frequent charge against new wave filmmakers that their best ideas were borrowed, that their films were merely collages of citations and cinematic in-jokes. The mistreatment of French prosody corresponds to the new wave disrespect for the academic conventions of continuity editing. This writerly revolt is not without its oedipal overtones, its "anxiety of influence." *400 Blows* combines a hostile portrait of Truffaut's real-life father—presented as step-father, i.e., false father—who once had him *sent* to prison, with an affectionate dedication to a clear substitute father, André Bazin, who once had Truffaut *released* from prison. When Truffaut was arrested for desertion, Bazin claimed to be his father, and after his release from prison, Truffaut went to live with the Bazins, thus bringing the familial metaphor to concrete and literal realization.[15] In his cinematic family romance, Truffaut portrays himself as a revolted *"bâtard,"* in Marthe Robert's terminology, a parentless child in search of a true symbolic father who is in fact named in the film's dedication.

The new wave, speaking more generally, regarded the writer-critic Bazin as its true symbolic father, just as it regarded the established filmmakers of the "tradition of quality" as false fathers. *400 Blows* foregrounds the problems of writing in the face of parental interdictions which define a new style as illegal or incorrect. In this sense, it is a thinly veiled plea for freedom from industrial and stylistic constraints, a cry of revolt against what the new wave directors so symptomatically called "le cinéma de papa." Adulthood entails forging one's own rules in defiance of "le nom de père." *400 Blows,* in this sense, literalizes the notion of the oedipal scenario.

If the filmmaker is a writer, the film, by implication, is a text. In *Language and Cinema,* Metz reminds us that "text," etymologically, means "tissue," and that the filmmaker "weaves" cinematic and extra-cinematic codes into a textual system. In the contemporaneous essay "From Work to Text" (1971), Barthes theorizes the text according to seven propositions: 1) that the text is experienced as the *activity* of language production; 2) that the text exceeds all genres and conventional hierarchies; 3) that the text practices the infinite deferment of the signified through a radically disruptive play of signifiers; 4) that the text constructs itself out of a multitude of intertextual citations, references, echoes, and cultural languages; 5) that the authorial inscription of the text is ludic rather than privileged and paternal; 6) that the text is actualized by the collaboration of the reader; and 7) that the text is bound to utopia and to pleasure. (Our entire enterprise in *this* text might be seen as a gloss on these seven propositions.)

The term "intertextuality" was first introduced as Julia Kristeva's translation of Mikhail Bakhtin's conception of the "dialogic," that is, the simultaneous presence, within a literary work, of two or more intersecting texts which mutually relativize one another. Bakhtin traces the dialogic back to the Socratic dialogues, with their staging of the contest of two competing discourses. He opposes the dialogic and "polyphonic" texts of Rabelais and Dostoyevsky to the "monologic" and "theological" texts which unproblematically assert a single truth. The concept of intertextuality suggests, at the same time, that every text forms an intersection of textual surfaces where other texts may be read. "The literary word," according to Bakhtin, "is aware of the presence of another literary word alongside it." Every text is what Kristeva calls a "mosaic of citations" which absorbs and transforms other texts. All texts are tissues of anonymous formulae, variations on those formulae, conscious and unconscious quotations, conflations and inversions of other texts. (Gore Vidal refers to this textual process in his novel *Duluth* by having a character tap out romantic novels on a word-processor, with a memory-bank of 10,000 other novels, taking a courtroom scene from Daphne du Maurier and a comical character from Edgar Rice or William Burroughs.) In the broadest sense, intertextuality refers to the vast reservoir of combinatory possibilities provided by the discursive practices of a culture, the entire matrix of signifying systems within which a single work is situated, and which reach the text not only through recognizable influences but also through a subtle process of dissemination. It is perhaps to this broad sense of intertextuality that Borges refers in his fiction *Tlon Uqbar Orbis Tertius:* "We established that all texts are the work of a single author who is atemporal and anonymous."[16]

Authorial intertextuality finds its counterpart in the competent response of the reader or spectator. No text is read independently of the reader's experience of other texts. This intertextual knowledge, for Umberto Eco, encompasses all the semiotic systems with which the reader or spectator is familiar: "Every character (or situation) of a novel is immediately endowed with properties that the text does not directly manifest and that the reader has been 'programmed' to borrow from the treasury of intertextuality."[17] In the case of film, it is as if both filmmaker and spectator were members of a vast audio-visual library. The Marx Brothers assume spectatorial competence in the codes of classical American romantic comedy by having Groucho constantly aggress the same Margaret Dumont that he is presumably courting. Spectatorial competence in the western allows Mel Brooks to systematically deconstruct its codes in *Blazing Saddles*. Competence in the musical allows Godard to "play off" its codes in *Une Femme est une Femme* by featuring dancers who cannot really dance, but who dance nonetheless.

Although all films are intertextual, to paraphrase Orwell, some are more intertextual than others. New wave directors, for a number of reasons, were especially disposed to highlight the intertext of their films. As cinéphiles proud of their inordinate appetite for film, as assiduous frequenters of the cinémathèque, they formed the first filmmaking generation to have the entire history of film available for plunder and homage. Often they made films against the tradition, especially by flouting the generic conventions of antecedent cinema. In a cinematic version of the Sartrean "existence precedes essence," the new wave subverted the metaphysical premises of genres as self-perpetuating essential categories. By pitting antipathetic codes against one another in a single text, the new wave provoked a collision of conventions in a veritable war of conflicting rhetorics, thus actuating a complex spectatorial response. While illusionism strives for generic and rhetorical homogeneity, anti-illusionism favors the cohabitation of languages in what Barthes called the "sanctioned Babel of the text of pleasure."

A film which calls attention to the literary as well as the cinematic intertext is Godard's *Contempt* (1963). The film, whose diegesis revolves around the attempt to make a film adaptation of *The Odyssey*, inserts itself into the broad history of the arts over the centuries. A generic conflation—a tragicomic documentary antiepic—it asserts the irrelevance of the classical ethos in the contemporary world. Godard, explicit about this theme, called *Contempt* the "story of castaways of the western world, survivors of the shipwreck of modernity."[18] Within the occidental tradition, "Greece" has often signified an ideal homogenous totality, the locus of an impossible nostalgia. The loss of this idealized Greece, according to Lukács, defines the situation in which the novel emerges out of the epic as the "expression of transcendental homelessness."[19] *Contempt* stages this sense of loss, virtually illustrating Hegel's reflections on epic as a world out of tune with "our present-day machinery and factories together with the products they turn out. . . ."[20]

This antiepic quality pervades both the world of the film and the world of the film-within-the-film. The characters in the film, like those of Joyce's *Ulysses,* are ironic shadows of their epic prototypes. Paul Javal, an anti-Ulysses, does not fight heroically for his wife; he rather appears to encourage infidelity for his own ends, while Camille, hardly a Penelope, is but dubiously faithful. The film-within-the-film, meanwhile, in a world where "epic" has come to mean "costly" and "spectacular," fails to bring the Homeric ethos to life. The director within the film (Fritz Lang) strives for Olympian grandeur but the rushes of the film betray his purposes. Minerva, Zeus, and Poseidon are gaudily colored statues, and Ulysses struggles awkwardly onto the rocky shores of a putative Ithaca. The tired nymphs do not sing each to each, and Nausicaa is a graceless model lip-synching a hopelessly vulgar song. One shot—showing the actor playing Ulysses swaying from side to side to give the impression he is in a boat rocked by high seas—especially encapsulates this epic letdown. Filmic illusion is shown to depend on the synecdochic isolation of objects from their contexts. What better way to demystify cinema, and indirectly epic, than by showing an epic hero, not in the glorified isolation of the close shot, but in long shot, surrounded by the cumbersome machinery of verisimilitude: dollies, lights, cameras, and recording equipment?

Lang has difficulty conveying the grandeur of the gods because of distance in time—the modern ethos has no place for Greek divinities—and differences in medium. In the realm of art, as in the realm of langauge, "traduire, c'est trahir." Francesca's hurried translations of Lang's poetic quotations illustrate the point; the translations invariably miss a nuance or exclude an ambiguity. *Contempt* in this sense, can be seen as a meditation on the problematic nature of all translation and adaptation. At the same time, the film shows, art renews itself through this process of creative mistranslation. Every artist is inserted within a tradition, constantly betrayed and constantly renewed, which is both broadly cultural and specific to a medium. Godard reminds us of cinema's infancy by citing Lumière's misguided dictum that the "cinema is an invention without a future." Paul at one point suggests that adaptation should bypass modern techniques and resurrect the methods of Griffith and Chaplin. We are reminded that Lumière and Griffith and Chaplin are in a sense the Homers of their medium, but that in cinema as in literature there is no unchanged Ithaca to which to return.

Transtextuality

Elaborating and refining on the discussion of "intertextuality," Gerard Genette in *Palimpsestes* introduces the term "transtextuality" to refer to "all that which puts one text in relation, whether manifest or secret, with other texts."[21] Genette posits five types of transtextual relations, enumerated in order of increasing abstraction and inclusiveness. "Intertextuality," for Genette, is simply the first of these diverse types of transtextuality. He defines intertextuality, more restrictively than Kristeva, as the relation of effective co-presence of two texts in the form of quotation, plagiarism, and allusion. Although Genette cites literary examples of this phenomenon, one might easily imagine filmic instances of the same procedures. Quotation can take the form of the insertion of classic clips into new films. Peter Bogdanovich quotes Hawks' *The Criminal Code* in *Targets;* Godard quotes Resnais' *Night and Fog* in *A Married Woman;* Vincent Minelli quotes his own *The Bad and the Beautiful* within *Two Weeks in Another Town.* Films like Resnais' *Mon Oncle d'Amerique* and *Dead Men Don't Wear Plaid* make the citation of classic sequences a central structuring principle. Allusion can take the form of a verbal or visual evocation of another film, hopefully as an expressive means of commenting on the fictional world of the alluding film. Godard in *Contempt* alludes, through a title on a cinema marquee, to Rossellini's *Voyage in Italy,* a film by one of Godard's favorite directors which recounts, like *Contempt* itself, the slow undoing of a couple. Bertolucci alludes to his own *Last Tango* in *Luna* by having the father discover the very piece of gum that Marlon Brando, in the earlier film, attached to the wrought-iron grillwork of a balcony. Even an actor can constitute an allusion—the Boris Karloff character in *Targets* (Byron Orlok) embodies old-style Hollywoodean horror, the essential dignity of which Bogdanovich contrasts with anonymous contemporary murder. Even a cinematic technique can constitute an allusion: the iris-in to the informer in *Breathless,* the masking à la Griffith in *Jules and Jim,* allude by their archaic nature to earlier periods of film history.

Genette's second type of transtextuality is "paratextuality," that is, the relation within the totality of a literary work, between the text proper and its "paratext"—titles, prefaces, postfaces, epigraphs, illustrations, and even book jackets and signed autographs. The paratext is constituted by all the accessory messages and commentaries which come to surround the text and which at times become virtually indistinguishable from it. The notion leads, as Genette admits, to a mine of unanswerable questions. Do the original chapter titles evoking *The Odyssey,* included in the subscribers' prepublication of Joyce's *Ulysses* but withdrawn in the final version, form part of the text of that novel? These suppressed titles, remembered by the critics, come to orient reading of *Ulysses.* The question, then, is one of closure, of the lines of demarcation between text and "hors-texte."

Here again it is intriguing to speculate concerning the relevance of such a category to film analysis. Do widely quoted prefatory remarks by a director at a film's first screening form part of a film's paratext? Does the "Cannibalistic

Preface" added by Joaquin Pedro de Andrade as an introduction to the film for the Venice Film Festival (and included in the American but not the Brazilian prints of the film) form part of that film? What about widely reported remarks by a director about a film, such as Godard's celebrated characterization of *Numéro Deux* as a "remake of *Breathless*?" How should we regard the original variant versions of films, about which there is often much fanfare in the press, which resonate, as it were, around the edges of a text, as in the case of Erich Von Stroheim's original 42-reel version of *Greed*, or the longer versions of Bertolucci's *1900* or Scorcese's *New York, New York?* What about authorized scripts or screenplays that show variance from the film as released? All these questions, operating on the margins of the official text, might be said to deal with a film's "paratext."

Genette's third type of transtextuality is "metatextuality" or the *critical* relation between one text and another, whether the commented text is explicitly cited or silently evoked. Genette cites the relation between Hegel's *Phenomenology of Mind* and the text that it constantly evokes without explicitly mentioning: Diderot's *Le Neveu de Rameau.* Transferring our attention to the cinema, we might see many of the avant-garde films of the New American Cinema as metatextual critiques of classical Hollywood Cinema. Michael Snow's *Wavelength,* for example, both alludes to and refuses the conventional "suspense" of Hollywood thrillers, as if he were stretching a single Hitchcock dolly-shot into a 45-minute zoom. The multiple refusals of Hollis Frampton's *(nostalgia)*—of plot development, of movement in the shot, of closure—suggest a mocking critique of conventional narrative films. Much of Godard's work, finally, can be seen as a metatextual gloss on conventional filming practices. In practice, it should be pointed out, it is difficult to distinguish Genette's "metatextuality" from his fifth category of "hypertextuality," (the relation between a text and an anterior text which it transforms or modifies).

Genette's fourth category, "architextuality," refers to the generic taxonomies suggested, or refused, by the titles or infratitles of a text. Architextuality has to do with a text's willingness, or reluctance, to characterize itself generically as poem, essay, novel. In literature, Genette points out, critics often refuse a text's self-designation, arguing, for example, that a certain "tragedy" by Corneille is not "really" a tragedy. A text's refusal to designate itself, or to designate itself homogenously, meanwhile, often leads to discussion among the critics concerning the text's "real" generic mix. Fielding's characterization of *Joseph Andrews* as a "comic epic poem in prose" or Godard's description of *Contempt* as a "tragedy in long-shot" are designed to encourage the critics/readers/spectators toward more complex responses.

Some film titles align a text with literary antecedents: *Sullivan's Travels* evokes *Gulliver's Travels* and, by extension, the satiric mode. The title of

Woody Allen's *Midsummer Night's Sex Comedy* begins by alluding to Shakespeare and ends with a comic fall into prurience, all the while echoing Bergman's *Smiles of a Summer Night.* Coppola's *Apocalypse Now* offers a disenchanted seventies variation on the optimistic sixties' *Paradise Now.* Other titles signal a sequel, a generic repetition of a hypotextual source: *Return of... Son of... Rocky III.* The multilingual title of Rocha's *Der Leone Have Sept Cabeças* (drawn from the languages of Africa's major colonizers) signals an attempt to make a truly "tri-continental" and anticolonialist film. The graphic and linguistic unconventionality of the titles of many avant-garde films—Paul Sharits' T.O.U.C.H.I.N.G., Michael Snow's ←→—announce a similar unconventionality in cinematic technique. Although a film need not designate itself as, first and foremost, a film, certain reflexive filmmakers have chosen to accentuate the obvious in their titles: Mel Brooks' *Silent Movie,* Bruce Conner's *A Movie,* Godard's *Un Film Comme Les Autres.* The extended "subtitles" (in the literary sense) of certain films—*Doctor Strangelove: Or How I Learned to Stop Worrying and Love the Bomb; A Married Woman; Fragments of a Film Made in 1964*—finally, suggest a kind of rapprochement with novelistic practices.

Genette's most suggestive category, to my mind, is his fifth type of transtextuality, which is "hypertextuality." The term refers to the relation between one text, which Genette calls the "hypertext," to an anterior text, or "hypotext," which the former transforms, modifies, elaborates, or extends. In literature, the *Aeneid*'s hypotexts include *The Odyssey* and *The Iliad,* and Joyce's *Ulysses* includes *The Odyssey* and *Hamlet.* Both *The Aeneid* and *Ulysses* are hypertextual reelaborations of a single hypotext—*The Odyssey.* Virgil recounts the adventures of Aeneas in a manner generically and stylistically inspired by Homeric epic. Joyce transposes the central mythos of the *Odyssey* into twentieth-century Dublin. Both operate transformation, although of distinct kinds, on a pre-existing text. All literary texts may be said to be hypertextual in the sense that they evoke other texts, but not all are hypertextual in the same manner or to the same degree. Fielding's *Shamela* insistently undercuts, incident by incident, the moralism of Richardson's *Pamela.* (The phonemic substitution in the title, in this sense, plays out in miniature the work of hypertextual variation). Rousseau's *Confessions,* on the other hand, re-elaborate Saint Augustine's only in a more diffuse and generic sense.

Genette's term is rich in potential application to the cinema, and especially to those films which derive from pre-existing texts in a way more precise and specific than that accounted for by the term "intertextuality." Filmic adaptations of celebrated novels, for example, are hypertexts derived from a pre-existing hypotext which has been transformed by operations of selection, amplification, concretization, actualization, and so forth. The diverse filmic adaptations of *Madame Bovary* (Renoir, Minnelli) or of *La Femme et le Pantin* (Duvivier, von Sternberg, Bunuel) can be seen as variant hypertextual "readings" inspired by an identical hypotext. Indeed, the diverse prior adaptations can come to form part of the hypotext available to a filmmaker coming late in the series.

The notion of hypertextuality is useful in that it calls attention to all the transformative operations that one text can operate on another text. Travesty, for example, devalorizes and trivializes a "noble" text. Buster Keaton mocks the lofty platitudes of *Intolerance* in his own *The Three Ages*. Mel Brooks rewrites the Hitchcockian text, with a different style and elocution, in *High Anxiety*. Many Brazilian films, as João Luiz Vieira points out, parodically re-elaborate Hollywoodean hypotexts whose production values they both resent and admire.[22] Carlos Manga's *Nem Sansão nem Dalila* (Neither Samson nor Delila, 1954) takes off from Cecil B. De Mille to satirize Brazilian politics, but also to mock the incapacity of a poor third world cinema to turn out expensive Biblical spectaculars. Other Brazilian films slightly twist the titles of a putative hypotext to exploit the fame of a film which is not in fact parodied. *The Mechanical Banana* (1973)—a variation on the "Mechanical Orange" as *Clockwork Orange* was called in Brazil—took commercial advantage of the furor created by the Brazilian censorship of the Kubrick film.

Other hypertextual films simply update earlier works while accentuating certain features of the original. The Morrisey/Warhol collaboration *Heat* (1972) transposes the plot of *Sunset Boulevard* into the Hollywood of the seventies, all filtered through a gay-camp sensibility. Elsewhere the transposition is not of a single film but of an entire genre. Lawrence Kasdan's *Body Heat* (1981), as Noel Carroll points out, evokes the corpus of 1940s film noir in terms of plot, character, and style. The knowledge of film noir thus becomes a privileged hermeneutic grid for the cine-literate spectator of that film.[23] A more expansive conception of hypertextuality might include many of the films generated by the Hollywoodean *combinatoire:* remakes like *Invasion of the Body Snatchers* (1978) and *The Postman Always Rings Twice* (1981); sequels like *Psycho II* (1983); revisionist westerns like *Little Big Man* (1970); generic pastiches and reworkings such as Scorcese's *New York, New York* (1977); and parodies like Mel Brooks' *Blazing Saddles* (1974). Most of these films assume spectatorial competence in diverse generic codes; they are calculated deviations meant to be appreciated by connoisseurs.

The title of *Play It Again, Sam* (1972), directed by Herbert Ross, as Genette points out, functions as a kind of contract of cinematic hypertextuality for those film-lovers who recognize (or misrecognize) the most celebrated phrase associated with Michael Curtiz' *Casablanca*. The film, too, "plays it again," i.e., it plays again, in its fashion, the "song" which is *Casablanca*. Allan Felix's relation to Humphrey Bogart's persona resembles Don Quixote's to

Amadis de Gaulle. He dreams of emulating a fictive model with whom he has viturally nothing in common. At the end, he repeats the exact situation— "returning" a woman whose love he has won, in this case through his own awkwardness, to her husband—and the words (more-or-less) of Lacy-Bogart in the earlier film. The same text and situation become travesty merely through the substitution of actors, and the ironic distance that separates him from his prototype.

1

Allegories of Spectatorship

Readers of *Don Quixote* will doubtless recall the episode in which the protagonist, in an outburst of chivalric madness, brings Master Pedro's puppet show to an abrupt halt by venting his fury on the hapless puppets which he presumes to be real Moors attacking a real Maiden, while Master Pedro protests that the objects of the Don's wrath, far from being Moors, are nothing but pasteboard figures. And viewers of Jean-Luc Godard's *Les Carabiniers* (The Riflemen, 1963) will doubtless remember a similar incident in which the obtuse Michelange, confounding the screen image of a woman with flesh-and-blood reality, tries to caress the shadowy apparition before him but succeeds only in pulling down the screen.

Both the passage from *Don Quixote* and the sequence from *Les Carabiniers* offer allegories of spectatorship in which an artistic representation is brought to a halt by the naive intervention of a personage who confounds reality with spectacle. The novelist and the cinéaste here unmask the contingent precariousness of the illusion generated by the play-world of their art. Cervantes, through his proxy protagonist, breaks off the purely verbal puppet-shot which is *Don Quixote* itself, suspending the narrative and reminding us of its papier-mâché factitiousness. Godard's suspended film-within-the-film, similarly, exposes cinematic spectacle as "juste une image," not reality but merely patterns of light projected on a two-dimensional screen.

Master Pedro's puppet show provides an unwitting model of anti-illusionistic theatre, an anticipatory storehouse of Brechtian "alienation effects." Cervantes begins his account with a quotation from the *Aeneid*—"Here Tyrians and Trojans, all were silent"—which evokes Aeneas telling the Troy story to Dido and the assembled listeners. The allusion reminds us of the perennial fascination of tales and the excited anticipation, the "growing silent" which invariably precedes the beginning of spectacle, whether it be puppet show, play, or film. The narrative structure of the episode, as Robert Alter has pointed out, is paradigmatic of the narrative structure of *Don Quixote* as a whole—a multiple regress of imitations calling attention to their own status as imitations.[1] Master Pedro's assistant narrates the action while Master Pedro

Figure 2.   *Les Carabiniers* (1963)

manipulates the puppets. He cites the origins of his purportedly "true" story, in imitation of Cervantes himself with his facetious concern about the sources of *Don Quixote*. The assistant acknowledges the poverty of the means of representation ("Turn your eyes, gentlemen, to that tower, which you must imagine to be one of the towers of the alcazar of Saragossa...") much in the manner of Brechtian theatre, with its minimal sets and exposed construction. The assistant presents the characters ("...that character who appears over there...is the Emperor Charlemagne...") and calls attention to certain incidents and gestures ("Take notice, gentlemen, how the emperor..." "See, too, that stately Moor...") much like certain of Brecht's characters, such as Wong in *The Good Woman of Setzuan,* who serve the same function.

The sequence from *Les Carabiniers* similarly provides a Brechtian object-lesson on the nature of the cinematic experience. Its allegory shows a "primitive" spectator going to a "primitive" film. A written title, presumably from Michelange, initiates the sequence: "Tonight I went for the first time to the cinématographe." The calligraphy recalls the celebrated handwriting of Jean Cocteau, while the word "cinématographe" recalls that filmmaker's *Essais sur le Cinématographe* as well as the early days of the cinema when the word was still in vogue. The films cited in the sequence refer to some of the earliest films and to some of the most "primitive" genres. The first alludes to Lumière's *L'Arrivée d'un Train* (1895) and is shot from the same angle as the Lumière film. Michelange's frightened reaction recapitulates that of the first spectators in the Grand Café. The second film, showing a man, a woman, and a baby at table, irreverently mimics another Lumière film—*Le Goûter de Bébé* (1895). While the man reads from an anachronistic Superboy comic, the baby refuses his soup, finally splashing it against the wall, at which point the man, in a comic inversion, starts to throw cream pies at the child. The film-within-the-film is intercut with reaction shots of Michelange, responding with childish glee to the horseplay on the screen. The last film—*Le Bain de la Femme du Monde*—is also interspersed with shots of Michelange smiling with fiendishly retarded lasciviousness. By showing Michelange reacting to mock prototypes of three of the earliest film genres—documentary, slapstick, and pornography—Godard reminds us that spectators have had to learn, historically, to *read* films.

We ourselves, the sequence suggests, have remained magical and primitive in our attitude toward the filmic image. Unlike three-dimensional life, a material continuum where we can touch what we see, the filmic image offers only an imaginary "lure" without the possibility of a "reality-check." When the actress in "The Bath of a Woman of the World" moves off-screen, Michelange vainly pursues his scopophilic object outside the frame. When she enters the bathtub, he tries to peek over the side of the tub, assuming that in the cinema as in everyday life an object blocking our view of another object merely hides the second object *behind* it. And when he begins to caress the image of the woman, he discovers the "betrayal" implicit in the promise offered by the filmic image, the sterile plenitude of its empirical proximity.

Certain technical "errors" in the sequence reveal the unnaturalness of conventional cinematic decorum. The sounds of warfare which accompany the shots of the streets outside the cinema—despite the lack of visible signs of military activity—abruptly cease when Michelange enters the theatre. Thus Godard inverts the conventional pattern whereby a cut to the inside of a movie theatre would normally bring new sounds presumably emanating from the screen, the battle noises, for example, from a war film. The sequence disturbs as well by the anachronistic sound in a silent film (the train whistle in the Lumière Ciotat citation) and by the cream pies which materialize *ex nihilo* in the *Dejeuner de Bébé* sequence. When Michelange pulls down the screen, the image remains, as does the sound of the projector, yet the music stops—doubtless Godard's way of mocking our naive assumption that the screen image somehow "generates" the sounds associated with it.

The cinema sequence in *Les Carabiniers* cites an earlier film—E.S. Porter's *Uncle Josh at the Moving Picture Show* (1902)—which initiates a venerable tradition in which the humor derives from a hayseed's naiveté in his first encounter with the filmic medium. Uncle Josh sees a number of film shorts. The first, *Parisian Dancer,* inspires him to jump from his box seat in order to dance with what he takes to be a real woman. The second, *The Black Diamond Express,* an Edison imitation of Lumière's *L'Arrivée d'un Train en Gare* (1895), inspires him to cower in fear, like Michelange, and like the first spectators at Lumière's Grand Café. The third film, *The Country Couple,* is a staged comedy showing a flirtation between a country woman and a farmer. When the farmer "takes advantage" of the woman, Uncle Josh rolls up his sleeves and angrily rushes toward the projected image, felling the screen and revealing the rear projector and the projectionist.[2] Whatever we may think of them, Don Quixote, Uncle Josh, and Michelange are our doubles insofar as their naive faith in spectacle resembles our own spectatorial investment in illusionistic fictions. But there is something paradoxical about Don Quixote's intervention in the puppet play. On the one hand, he naively confounds spectacle and reality to the point of physically intervening in the spectacle. In this sense, he would seem to embody the undistanced acritical spectator who so horrified Brecht. On the other hand, he represents a distorted version of the ideal Brechtian spectator. He has sufficient critical distance to indicate flaws in the play's verisimilitude—he complains that mosques do not use bells—but more important, he speaks up and acts. He does not remain passive and immobilized like the anonymous and silently respectful spectators of most fiction films; *he* is not a mere voyeur. The same might be said of Michelange. In one sense, he is our grotesque double; like him, we fantasize imaged characters as real ones, we, too, participate vicariously in exploitative films. We are both

Figure 3.   *Uncle Josh at the Moving Picture Show* (1902)

his superiors and his inferiors. While hardly so naive as to take image literally for reality, we are also not so courageous as to physically attempt the realization of our fantasies—we caress them only in the sanctuary of our own minds. In that sense, we are doubled not by Michelange but rather by his strangely impassive neighbors, that dispersed group of expressionless zombies staring blankly at the screen. It would be too easy to make emblematic figures such as Don Quixote and Michelange the scapegoats of our own credulity, the displaced symbols of our own unrecognized faith in fictions. In that case, they would serve the same function as those cinematic dreamers (such as Walter Mitty or the hero of René Clair's *Belles des Nuits*) who attract and discharge, like lightning rods, our own skepticism about fictions, with the ultimate result that we believe even more. If we are honest, we will acknowledge Don Quixote and Michelange as our *frères* and *semblables,* while granting them the supplementary virtue of courage to act on their belief.[3]

The Complicity of the Spectator

Common to *Don Quixote, Uncle Josh,* and *Les Carabiniers* is an emphasis on the active role of the spectator, on his or her necessary contribution to filmic illusion. In the prologues of *Henry V,* Shakespeare touches on the same theme by having the chorus repeatedly lament the physical impoverishment of the theatrical medium. Although he would have preferred a kingdom for a stage, princes to act, and monarchs to behold, the dramatist must in fact make do with unworthy scaffolds and unraised spirits: "Can this cockpit hold/the vasty fields of France? Or may we cram/within this wooden O the very casques/that did affright the air at Agincourt?" Given these material constraints, the dramatist pleads with the spectator to "piece out our imperfections with your thoughts." He calls on them to "eke out our performance with your mind" and "mind true things by what their mockeries be."

All the representational arts would have us mind "true things by what their mockeries be." Without this "minding," representational art is powerless. Master Pedro tells the audience of his puppet show: "Turn your eyes, gentlemen, to that tower, which *you must imagine to be* one of the towers of the alcazar of Saragossa" [italics mine]. It is the reader or spectator, in short, who transforms cardboard miniatures into imposing towers, who turns verbal representations into a novel or filmic images into a "story." The precise nature of the "minding" or "eking out" varies with the medium—a statue, for example, has three-dimensionality but lacks movement; cinema has movement but lacks three-dimensionality—but some sort of "eking out" is always present. The readers of *War and Peace* somehow persuade themselves that the temporality of reading letters on a page corresponds to a sequence of events in nineteenth-century Russia. The spectator of a film, meanwhile, must "eke out" a third dimension, "mind" away the enclosing frame, and "piece out" or mentally erase the technical imperfections which flaw the image. The spectator, in short, must fill out the minimal analogy which links the filmic image to the "what's out there" of our everyday experience.

This notion of "eking out" runs like a thread throughout film and media theory from the beginning to the present day. For Rudolf Arnheim film becomes art to the extent that it is forced to compensate for the mimetic poverty of the image. It could even be argued that spectator involvement increases in inverse proportion to the representational adequacy of the medium. The impression of reality is stronger in films than in the theatre precisely because the phantom-like figures on the screen are too weak to resist our temptation to invest them with our own fantasies and projections. Jean-Louis Comolli speculates that the extreme eagerness of the first spectators to recognize in the images of the first films—devoid of color, depth, nuance—the literal double of life itself, derived precisely from the sense of a lack to be filled. Is there not, Comolli wonders, "in the very principle of representation, a force of disavowal which gives free reign to an analogical illusion that is yet only weakly manifested by the iconic signifiers themselves?"[4] For Marshall McLuhan, finally, the low-definition images formed by television scan-lines—images which are ultimately "not even there"—make television a "hot" medium in which viewer involvement is all the more intense.

Anti-illusionistic art reminds us of our necessary complicity in artistic illusion. All fiction places us in the realm of half-belief, of "je sais, mais quand même," where we believe even while we doubt. No one, presumably, accepts the naive illusions of *trompe l'oeil.* Don Quixote and Michelange notwithstanding, the *impression* of reality does not generally become the *illusion* of reality. No sane person tries to picnic in landscape paintings or converse with statues, and not even the most ardent cinephile literally confuses Elizabeth Taylor with an Egyptian queen. No spectator at a play, Samuel Johnson pointed out, really forgets that he is seated in a theatre. Yet fiction requires the kind of complicity that Don Quixote suggests to Sancho Panza when Sancho presumes to overreach him in the description of an adventure: "Sancho, if you want me to believe what you saw in the sky, I wish you to accept my account of what I saw in the cave of Montesinos. I say no more." It is precisely this pact of reciprocal deception that the anti-illusionist refuses to obscure.

For the eminently Cervantic contemporary writer Jorge Luis Borges, the reader of a text deserves as much credit as its writer. Not only does the world exist only in order to be transmuted into a book, but books exist only in order to be read, reread, and imagined. His exemplary fable on this point is *Pierre Menard, Author of the Quixote.* Menard's attempt to rewrite the *Quixote,* word for word, leads to the narrator's discovery that the two versions are verbally identical yet that their meaning has changed. Borges' narrator credits Menard with enriching "the halting and rudimentary act of reading." Gerard Genette, in his gloss on the story, attributes to Borges the insight that a "book is not a ready-made meaning, a revelation we have to suffer; it is a reserve of forms that are waiting to have some meaning; it is the immanence of a revelation that is not yet produced, and that everyone of us has to produce for himself."[5]

Alain Resnais and Robbe-Grillet's *Last Year at Marienbad* (1961), in this sense, can be seen as a sardonic gloss on the spectator's complicity in the filmic illusion. The title itself calls attention to the twin coordinates of filmic fiction: time (last year) and space (Marienbad). But by positing spatial and temporal impossibilities—single images incorporating different times of the day, characters who disappear (during a continuous shot) only to reappear in improbable places, statues that jump in inexplicable quantum leaps around the filmic space—*Marienbad* triggers mutually contradictory "reality effects" in the mind of the bewildered spectator. The film's tale of seduction, on one level, allegorizes the relationship between film and spectator in the conventional fiction film. X tries to persuade A that something happened, elsewhere, a year before. Like a film director, he orchestrates details intended to convince. A's room, significantly, becomes progressively more furnished, as if the seducer/director were literally adding strategic details. The spectator, then, is the object of a seduction, whose cooperation and complicity is required, who must go with the seducer, for the film to work. Thus *Marienbad* offers a stylized, exemplary, and perversely unsettling demonstration of the processes of all fiction films.

Realism and the Desiring Spectator

In the puppet show episode, Cervantes ridicules Don Quixote's penchant for taking the representational fictions of art as fit objects for passionate love or hatred, for taking them, in a word, as objects of identification. Recent film criticism and theory has focused on the "erotics" of filmic identification. Especially in the 1970s, the discussion of filmic "realism" came to be inflected by psychoanalytic notions of scopophilia and voyeurism and by Lacan's conception of the mirror stage, the imaginary and the symbolic. The focus of interest was no longer on the relation between filmic image and "reality" but rather on the apparatus itself, not only in the sense of the instrumental base of camera, projector, and screen, but also in the sense of the spectator as the desiring subject on which the cinematic institution depends as its object and accomplice. The focus shifts to what Geoffrey Nowell-Smith calls the "intersubjective textual relation," the relationship between the film and the spectator.

In "The Imaginary Signifier," Metz argues that the doubly imaginary nature of the cinematic signifier—imaginary in what it represents and imaginary by the nature of its signifier—heightens rather than diminishes the possibilities of identification. The signifier itself, even before coming to form part of a fictive imagined world, is marked by the duality of presence/absence typical of the imaginary. The impression of reality is stronger in film than in theatre because the phantom-like figures on the screen are too weak to resist our penchant to invest them with our phantasies and projections. Thus the interest shifts, for these theorists and critics, from "What does the text mean?" and "Are its representations true?" to "What do we want from the text?" and "What is our investment?" If the spectator is the site of a psychic process of largely unconscious origin, questions of accuracy and verisimilitude are less relevant than questions of spectatorial desire and the "will to believe."

Many film theorists have explored the perennial analogy of film and dream. Christian Metz, building on the work of Hugo Munsterberg, Suzanne Langer, and others, systematically explores both the analogies and disanalogies in "The Fiction Film and its Spectator." Metz argues that the "impression of reality" achieved by films derives from a cinematic situation that encourages feelings of narcissistic withdrawal and dreamy self-indulgence, a regression into primary process conditioned by circumstances similar to those which underlie the illusion of reality in dream. The conventional fiction film invokes a lowering of wakefulness that positions the spectator's state somewhat closer to that of sleep and dreaming than to other waking states. This lowering of wakefulness implies a withdrawal of concern from the external world and a heightened receptivity to phantasied wish-fulfillment, a receptiveness which in the actual dream state gives rise to a sensation of equivalence between phantasy and perception. In the cinema, we do not literally experience our phantasies as perceptions, since we are dealing with an actual perceptual object—the film itself. Dream is a purely internal psychic process, while film involves real perception, potentially common to other viewers, of actual images recorded on film. The dream, as Metz points out, is doubly illusion; the dreamer believes more, and what he or she "perceives" is less real. The continuing perceptual stimulation of the cinema prevents unconscious wishes from taking a completely "regressive" path, therefore, and what is "illusion" of reality in dream is merely an "impression" of reality in film.

Other parallels between the conditions of film viewing and those of dreams, however, help explain the quasi-hallucinatory degree of the impression of reality that films do occasionally achieve. Both Metz and Baudry compare the spectator's situation to what Jacques Lacan calls the "mirror stage," that is, a stage in the child's development where hyperactive perception coincides with a low level of motor activity. Thus a kind of double whammy operates in the cinema; extremely strong visual and auditory stimuli inundate us at a moment when all other conditions predispose us toward their passive reception. The spectator's solitude, since group affiliations and communications tend to be cut off for the duration of the film, favors narcissistic self-absorption. Then, the film, like a dream, tells a story—a story rendered in images and therefore particularly attractive to the logic of primary process which "figures itself forth in images." Finally, certain specifically cinematic techniques, such as superimposition and the lap-dissolve, "mime" the condensation and displacement through which the primary-process logic of dreams effects its phantasied objects.

Film and Dream: *Sherlock Jr.*

In *Sherlock Jr.* (1924), Buster Keaton plays a neighborhood projectionist who aspires to be a detective. As he falls asleep in the projection booth, his dream-double fantasizes the characters of the film he is projecting—"Hearts and Pearls"—into his real-life girlfriend and playboy enemy. Imagining the heroine's honor threatened, the somnambulent Buster rushes down the aisle, scrambles over the orchestra pit and, after several failed attempts, manages to penetrate the screen world, where he is transformed into the redoubtable son of Sherlock Holmes.

Although framed as a comedy, *Sherlock Jr.* constitutes a profound meditation on the film/dream analogy. It offers a fictive demonstration, first of

Figure 4.   *Sherlock Jr.* (1924)

all, that films, like dreams according to the Freudian hypothesis, are designed
to fulfill wishes. On the most superficial level, Buster's film-dream satisfies his
desire for the girl. But there are also other nonerotic compensations. The real-
life janitor is transformed, in screen-life, into a detective, the legitimate son of
the master detective. The servile and easily intimidated real-life Buster becomes
a suavely imposing master-mind; hardened criminals shrink in fear at the very
sound of his name. The real-life victim of injustice becomes the heroic righter of
wrongs. All the characters, furthermore, move a step higher on the social
ladder; the small-town girlfriend becomes a sophisticated flapper, the penniless
rival a high-society playboy. Even objects participate in this dream of upward
mobility, as watches become pearls within a process of systematic idealization.

    With intuitive brilliance, Keaton makes his hero a projectionist, who not
only projects films but also projects himself into films. The familiar erotic
motivations prompt his entrance into the screen world; like Don Quixote, he
fantasizes rescuing imagined damsels in distress. He clambers over the piano
and leaps into the screen, but the villain throws him out into the orchestra pit.
Then he creeps up from the side, as if in hopes of a discreet lateral infiltration.
Buster's clumsy but finally successful attempts at penetration comically
literalize, I think, the processes whereby spectators identify with the diegesis
and characters of a classic fiction film. The credits and opening sequences keep
us at a certain distance, resisting our entry. But gradually, through the

reciprocal play of filmic seduction and spectatorial introjection, we project ourselves into idealized personages and situations which represent heightened versions of ourselves and our lives.

Once inside the screen world, Buster discovers the treacherous nature of what Suzanne Langer calls film's "inconstant space." The film's unpredictable cutting sends him tumbling over a park bench, sits him in the middle of city traffic, and places him on the edge of a rocky precipice. Betrayed by a splice, he dives from a reef in mid-ocean and lands headfirst in a snowbank. Metz points out in "The Imaginary Signifier" that before we can identify with characters we must first identify with the camera's act of seeing. This "primary identification" makes possible "secondary identification" with characters, just as the primordial identification with self makes possible subsequent identification with others. Primary identification in the cinema usually operates surreptitiously. The camera, like an invisible flying carpet, takes us everywhere. The spectator becomes the all-perceiving subject whose imagination constitutes the film as signifier. *Sherlock Jr.* turns the tables on this spectatorial self by putting Buster, our delegate in the fiction, literally in the places where the camera went. Buster physically accompanies the camera into deserts and icy wastes, rather than mentally identifying with it from a sheltered place in a movie theatre. Keaton collapses the transcendental and empirical subject. Whereas the transcendental subject customarily follows the camera within the sanctuary of his or her mind, here the character is made empirically subject to the space of the image and the time of the editing.

Sherlock Jr. concludes with a graphic object lesson in the educative power and initiatory function of cinematic models, as Buster, peeking through the projection booth window, woos his girlfriend by mimicking the debonair charmer on the screen. He hesitates, however, when he sees the hero suddenly surrounded with children. On a diegetic level, Buster is perhaps wondering if he is ready for marriage and family. On a self-referential level, however, he calls attention to the magic of editing. The copulative powers of the splice turn a couple into a family, and Buster, in this sense, scratches his head in admiration for such a "miracle."

Fiction and Voyeurism

It is the desire to rescue *papier-mâché* maidens from fictional distresses that triggers Don Quixote's intervention in Mater Pedro's puppet show. Many of the self-conscious novelists who come in the wake of Cervantes try to make their readers critically aware of the pitfalls of taking an erotic stance toward their fictions. Both Fielding and Sterne mock readers who look to art for vicarious libidinal satisfaction. Fielding lampoons what he regards as the high-minded prurience of Richardson's *Pamela* in his own *Shamela* and *Joseph*

Figure 5.   *Sherlock Jr.* (1924)

Andrews. And Laurence Sterne, as Robert Alter points out, delights in catching the reader by the scruff of the neck just as he is stooping to peep through some bedroom keyhole. Diderot's *Jacques le Fataliste* incessantly promises, but never delivers, the truth about "les amours de Jacques," while Nabokov's *Lolita* leaves a long trail of broken erotic promises.

Brecht, to transfer our attention to another medium, was deeply aware of the voyeuristic premises underlying the "fourth wall convention." This convention, stipulating that actors treat the open stage as a fourth wall without betraying any awareness of being observed, places the spectator in a voyeuristic position. Brecht has the Actor in *The Messingkauf Dialogues* make the point:

> The audience sees quite intimate episodes without itself being seen. It's just like somebody looking through a keyhole and seeing a scene involving people who've no idea they are not alone. Actually, of course, we arrange it all so that everyone gets a good view. Only we conceal the fact that it's been arranged.[6]

The convention of naturalistic theatre—later "inherited" by the cinema—that actors should not address themselves to the audience assumed that the spectators would become uncomfortable if they were challenged in their position as Peeping Toms. Brecht's theatre, on the other hand, does everything in its power to short-circuit voyeuristic involvement by making the audience critically aware of itself as audience and of the play as artifice. Everything in Brechtian theatre conspires to keep alive our critical intelligence and distance us from the spectacle. The schematic decors, the visible light sources, and the explicit announcement of stage directions remind us that we are in a theatre. The songs, the mixing of genres, and the tension between earthy, proverbial diction on the one hand, and poetic, stylized diction on the other, meanwhile, call attention to the medium of language. The alienated acting, the precisely exaggerated gestures, and the socially emblematic personages, finally, remind us not to empathize but to observe.

Brecht's non-Aristotelian theatre refuses not only pity and fear but also erotic involvement generally. In Brechtian theatre, there is no suspense about outcome, no identification with idealized personages, and no climax. Whereas tragedy builds up to a catharsis which purges the tensions created by the play, epic theatre creates only fleeting moments of empathy which are quickly dispelled. The Aristotelian theory of tragedy, with its climaxes and discharging of accumulated tension, has certain orgasmic overtones. Walter Benjamin compares the *peripeteia* to the crest of a wave which, breaking, sweeps the audience along with it and rolls forward to the end. (Robert Scholes, in *Fabulation and Metafiction,* somewhat hastily posits the orgasmic model as the archetype of all fiction, with its fundamental rhythm of tension and resolution, tumescence and detumescence.) But epic theatre avoids empathy and is uninterested in climax or even in delaying climax. Instead of identifying with alluring personages, the audience is encouraged to regard its own daily circumstances in a new light. Spectatorial tumescence, for Brecht, does not favor insight or reflection.

Cinema inherited the voyeuristic aspects of realism in the novel and naturalism in the theatre. But the cinema, as the privileged medium of the eye, has always been especially susceptible to voyeuristic abuse. Its appropriate aspect ratio, it has been suggested, would be that of a keyhole. An ineluctable logic leads from Vitascope's *The Kiss* (1896) to the latest pornographic productions. The cinema is founded upon the pleasure of looking and it has especially exploited, as feminist critics point out, the spectacle of the female body. But the progressive unveiling of the female body in a kind of interminable striptease parallels the more general process by which the dominant cinema capitalizes on scopophilia by providing more and more to see: color, cinemascope, split-screen. The cinema has been progressively unveiling its thrills in an ever-renewed and commercially motivated search for new variations on the old *frissons.* Whether in the form of the explicitly pornographic or the perversely spectacular, the film industry has endlessly fabricated new objects of constumption to satisfy the cupidity of one of the primary erotic organs—the eye.

Libidinal satisfactions are not incidental but central to what makes the

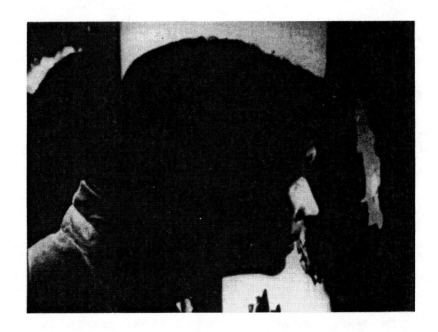

Figure 6.   *Psycho* (1960)

cinema industry work. Existing close to the operative psychic center of the collective conscience, cinema touches subterranean zones of the self. It was not by accident that Edgar Morin subtitled his book on the cinema: *L'homme imaginaire*. Filmgoers, as Metz points out, are not forced into the theatres at gunpoint—they choose to go. The industry's goal is to give the spectators the spontaneous desire to see films. The industry produces not only films but also its own ideal consumers. Cinema in this sense forms part of a social continuum characterized by the sexualization of consumerism and the consumerization of sexuality. The same society which eroticizes everything from cigarettes to airplane flights and practices subliminal seduction as a routine marketing technique inevitably eroticizes cinema as well; not by fostering liberating sexual play among the populace—that *would* be subversive—but by exploiting human dissatisfaction and appealing to the voyeuristic in order to turn a profit.

A Paradigmatic Instance: Hitchcock's *Rear Window*

A brilliant filmic essay on the cinema and on the nature of the cinematic experience, Alfred Hitchcock's *Rear Window* performs the metalinguistic dismantling of the structures of voyeurism and identification operative in dominant cinema generally and in Hitchcock's own films particularly, even while exploiting those very structures.[7] Jean Douchet, writing in *Cahiers du Cinéma* in 1960, was among the first to point out this reflexive dimension in the film. Douchet compared the protagonist, played by Jimmy Stewart, to a projector, the building across from his window to the screen, and added that the Stewart character is a spectator who makes himself his own cinema.[8] Most critics have accepted Douchet's equation of the protagonist with director/spectator without examining the theoretical and textual implications of that equation. My purpose here will be to examine *Rear Window* as a multitrack inquiry concerning the cinematic apparatus, the positioning of the spectator within that apparatus, and the sexual, moral, and even political implications of that positioning.

Set in an apartment complex in Greenwich Village, *Rear Window* spans four days in the life of photojournalist L.B. Jeffries (Jimmy Stewart), emphasizing his interactions with visiting nurse Stella (Thelma Ritter), his girlfriend Lisa (Grace Kelly) and his detective friend Doyle (Wendell Corey), along with various neighbors, particularly Lars Thorwald (Raymond Burr). Temporarily immobilized, Jeffries spends his time spying on his neighbors. Stella massages him and lectures him for preferring to watch the titillating acrobatics of "Miss Torso" rather than marry the mature and beautiful Lisa. That same night, Lisa argues with Jeff about marriage, and after her exit we hear a scream which we later learn signalled the demise of Mrs. Thorwald. Jeff alternately dozes and watches Thorwald, who repeatedly ventures out into the rain with a large suitcase. The last of his departures, this time accompanied by a woman, finds Jeff asleep.

The next day, Jeff begins spying on Thorwald in earnest, first with binoculars and then with a telephoto lens. On sketchy evidence, Jeff concludes that Thorwald has murdered his wife. Despite her initial skepticism, Lisa soon becomes a partner in the investigation. Doyle's assurances that Thorwald is innocent momentarily slows their investigation, but the murder of a dog rekindles their suspicions. The following day they begin to pressure Thorwald. Jeff lures him away from the apartment complex to allow Lisa and Stella to forage for clues. Lisa surreptitiously enters Thorwald's apartment where she finds a vital clue—Mrs. Thorwald's wedding ring. Thorwald returns before Lisa can effect her escape, and she is saved only by police arrest. Stella departs to post bail, leaving Jeff exposed to Thorwald who has now spotted Jeff as his antagonist. A confrontation ends with Jeff's falling out of the rear window and Thorwald's arrest. An epilogue intimates that Jeff and Lisa have reached tentative accommodation concerning their relationship.

The apartment complex setting of *Rear Window* forms an artistic as well as social microcosm. The Greenwich Village locale metonymically evokes "artistic milieu" and the residents take pictures, compose music, and perform roles. Not only do the architectonic stylization and painterly artifice of the set betray what is transparently a studio product, but also the inhabitants reproduce the division of labor typical of Hollywood studio production. Virtually all the members of this *cinematographicum mundi* are artists, or actors, or are engaged in an entertainment-related profession. The composer and Miss Torso are involved in the performing arts, the sculptress in a plastic art. Thorwald sells costume jewelry, with its connotations of glamor and artifice, while Miss Lonelyhearts and the newlyweds participate in the theatricality of everyday life, acting out charades for Jeff's benefit and ours, the groom carrying his bride over the threshold and Miss Lonelyhearts staging a dinner for an imaginary male companion. Within this interplay of art and experience, every human gesture becomes potentially transmutable into a kind of entertainment.

Rear Window foregrounds the generic intertext of this entertainment by presenting the world across the courtyard as a series of framed genre pantomimes. Jeffries begins by watching what amounts to an early silent "tableau" film, stylistically characterized by long shot and static camera. The performing inhabitants of the various apartment/frames, meanwhile, seem to have strayed directly from various genres of the classic Hollywood film: earnest fifties social realist film (Miss Lonelyhearts); murder mystery (Thorwald); musical biopicture (the composer); and musical comedy (Miss Torso). As magister ludi of these cinematic games, Jeffries clearly functions as substitute director/auteur, whose activities partially analogize, and often literally mimic,

Figure 7. *Rear Window* (1954)

those of the director. Jeffries the photojournalist, like Hitchcock, is both artist and technician, professional and visionary. Lisa's succinct resumé of his activities—"going from one place to another taking pictures"—applies equally to Hitchcock. Within the fiction, moreover, Jeffries enjoys partial directorial control over his "film," since binoculars and a telephoto lens facilitate a multiplicity of set-ups and perspectives. His narrative and actantial function, finally, consists in persuading a number of characters, let us call them spectators, to look where he has looked. Like a director, he channels and guides their glance, framing their vision and imposing his interpretation.

Surrogate for the director, Jeffries functions on a deeper level as a relay for the spectator. Indeed, Jeffries and the apartment complex taken together may be taken to prefigure the cinematic apparatus itself, including both the instrumental base and the spectator as the desiring subject on which the cinematic institution depends. That institution, Metz tells us, demands an immobile secret viewer who absorbs everything through the eyes. The wheelchair-ridden Jeffries exemplifies this situation of retinal activity and enforced immobility; he is indeed, as Lisa remarks in another context, "traveling but going nowhere." The cinematic apparatus, "prosthesis for our primally dislocated limbs," combines visual hyperperception with minimal physical mobility. Binoculars and a telephoto lens grant Jeffries the illusory god-like power of the "all-perceiving spectator." Hitchcock thus suggests a congruency between the situation of the protagonist, who experiences his reality within the fiction as though he were watching a film, and our own situation as spectators watching the protagonist watch his film.

In his state of inhibited motoricity and exacerbated perception, Jeffries embodies the living death of the dream-like spectatorial experience. The first time we see Jeffries, significantly, he is asleep, as if everything we are about to see were in some sense his dream. Indeed, the vacillations in his attention almost seem designed to evoke the diverse points on the continuum of sleep and wakefulness anatomized by Metz in "The Fiction Film and its Spectator." At times, Jeffries is sound asleep and presumably dreaming; at others, he dozes intermittently. At still other times, he finds himself in a state of animated attention, dreamlike in its intensity, reminiscent of that provoked in the spectator by Hitchcock's own films, of which *Rear Window* is a particularly spellbinding example.

Rear Window: The Critique of Voyeurism

The mechanism of gratification in the cinema, according to Metz, "rests on our knowing that the object being looked at does not know it is being looked at."[9] *Rear Window* constantly underscores, by analogy, the voyeuristic abuse to which the cinema is so often susceptible.[10] The film proliferates in explicit

Figure 8.   *Rear Window* (1954)

references to voyeurism, to "Peeping Toms" and "window shoppers" and it is hardly accidental that Stella refers to Jeffries' telephoto lens as "a portable keyhole." Jeffries himself is a quintessential exemplum of "a race of Peeping Toms." His profession of photojournalism assumes, and exploits, a kind of voyeurism, and his leisure activities mirror his professional pursuits. At home, he indulges in what Metz calls "unauthorized voyeurism." Overseeing the world from a sheltered position, he indulges his scopic drive, the "desire to take other people as objects, subjecting them to a controlling and curious gaze."[11] He is the warden, as it were, in a private panopticon. Seated in his central tower, he observes the wards ("small captive shadows in the cells of the periphery") in an imaginary prison. Foucault's description of the cells of the panopticon—"so many small cages, so many small theatres, in which each actor is alone, perfectly individualized and constantly visible"—in some ways aptly describes the scene exposed to Jeffries' glance.[12]

Caught in a play between regression and progression, the cinematic spectator receives images from without—and in this sense the movement is progressive and directed toward external reality—yet due to inhibited mobility and the process of identification with both camera and character, the psychic energy normally devoted to activity is channeled into other routes of discharge. It is no surprise, therefore, that the "complement" of Jeffries' voyeurism is a certain passivity. At the beginning of the film, he consistently opts for inactivity and for the inertia of what he himself calls the "status quo." But although he avoids relationships with friends and lovers and neighbors, he is passionately absorbed in the *spectacle* of his neighbors' lives. His involvement with people exists in inverse proportion to their distance from him; such is his code of perspective. Jeffries prefers his thrills vicarious; he would rather watch Miss Torso than touch the flesh-and-blood woman next to him, which is why Lisa contemplates turning herself into a distant and exotic spectacle by "moving into the apartment across the way and doing the dance of the seven veils." The tension between the regressive and progressive paths even takes the form of a physical tussle concerning the direction in which Jeffries' wheelchair will face: will it face out the window toward Miss Torso and, metaphorically, the cinema, or will if face toward the apartment, Lisa, and "reality?"

Jeffries is our specular reflection, our double. We do not merely watch him performing actions; we perform the identical action—looking. But at the same time that Hitchcock leads us to participate vicariously in Jeffries' voyeurism, he also frustrates and refuses to satisfy it. An early shot epitomizes this refusal. Two women on a rooftop, presumably Greenwich Village "bohemians," discard their clothes to sunbathe. A helicopter approaches and hovers overhead. The implication: those aboard the helicopter are spying on the women. The helicopter provides a perfect "vehicle" for the spectatorial desire to enjoy a fantasy omniscience, to go everywhere and see everything, and especially for the socially constructed (and largely male) desire to see women in states of undress. The helicopter evokes the technological resources available to the cinema and enlistable in the service of the scopic drive. Yet Hitchcock withholds the "pay-off" of these resources by denying us the point-of-view shot from the helicopter. We never see the women, we only become aware of our desire to see them. The desire is not fulfilled but only designated and exposed.

Jeffries' voyeurism goes hand in hand with an absorbing fear of mature sexuality. Indeed, the film begins by hinting at a serious case of psychosexual pathology. The first image of Jeffries, aspeep with hand on thigh, is quietly masturbatory, as if he were an invalid abusing himself in the dark. Both the broken leg and the smashed camera can be seen, in the context of the film as a whole, as intimations of a fear of castration or impotence. A radio commercial allusion to men with "that run-down listless feeling" is followed by a series of comments by both Stella and Lisa that might be taken to refer to some kind of sexual inadequacy: "You're not too active..." "How's your leg?..." "Is anything else bothering you?" Stella calls Jeffries "reasonably healthy" but worries about a "hormone deficiency" since even bathing beauties haven't "raised his temperature." She berates him for speaking in euphemistic abstractions ("our relationship is maturing") rather than acting like a sexed human being. Her notion of the normal operations of Eros consists of lust ("You get excited") sanctified by an institution ("You get married.") She defends a kind of *amour fou*—"like two taxi cabs crashing"—blessed by the state.

As an object-lesson for Stella's domesticated version of surrealism, Hitchcock has the newlywed couple enter their apartment. The commentative music of "That's Amore!" underscores the paradigmatic nature of their appearance. The couple, eager to consummate their relationship, demonstrate in pantomime the model relationship of which Jeffries has so far shown himself incapable. They play out the typical final episode of a classical Hollywood film, generally oriented, as Bellour points out, toward the "constitution of the couple." Jeffries, symptomatically, is bored by this spectacle of consummation, much preferring either exhibitionism (Miss Torso) or the morbid concatenation of marriage and violence (the murder of Mrs. Thorwald). Although Lisa is more than willing to go to bed, Jeff prefers to fall asleep with his binoculars. Voyeurism, passivity, and implied impotence are shown to form a melancholy constellation of mutually reinforcing neuroses.

The Shattering of Distance

The central trajectory of *Rear Window* consists in the progressive shattering of Jeffries' illusion of voyeuristic separation from life and the concomitant rendering possible of mature sexuality with Lisa. This shattering progresses by several stages. At the beginning of the film, Jeffries retains the privileged position of the movie-goer; he observes without being observed. This sheltered position gives him a factitious sense of superiority; he feels superior, for example, to his double in solitide, Miss Lonelyhearts. But this illusion of distance and superiority soon comes under attack. Lisa tries to keep Jeff from being a mere spectator by turning on the lights and wheeling his chair away from the window. The danger also looms that Thorwald will discover that he is being watched. When Thorwald comes to the window and looks around the courtyard, Jeff wheels backward in a kind of panic.

The next stage in this shattering of illusory distance occurs when Lisa enters Thorwald's apartment. She leaves her seat in the theatre, as it were, and enters the screen, the space of the spectacle. When Lisa is threatened by Thorwald's imminent return, Jeff reacts like the "naive" spectator lurking within even the most sophisticated; he addresses advice to the unhearing screen: "Lisa, what are you doing? . . . Get out of there." His reactions mirror our own; he articulates our responses as feeling spectators. But this moment is highly overdetermined and polyvalent. Is his emotional involvement proof of newly discovered love for her? Or can he only identify with a Lisa transmogrified into spectacle, framed within the rectangular windows of Thorwald's apartment? What *is* clear is his powerlessness. The "blessing" of passive distance has become a curse. The apartment, formerly his sanctuary, and the apartment complex, his panopticon, have now become his trap.

The progressive breakdown of Jeff's voyeuristic passivity is further marked by two particularly chilling moments. In the first, he is touched indirectly, by Thorwald's look, and in the second, he is touched directly, by Thorwald's hands. The first moment, in which Thorwald looks at Jeff and thus at us, violates the dominant convention, in the classical fiction film, stipulating that the film remain radically ignorant of its spectator and that the actor never acknowledge the camera and hence the audience. This moment of the returned glance, of the *voyeur vu,* is always imbued with anxiety in Hitchcock's work— one thinks of Melanie caught in Mitch's binoculars as she espies him from Bodega Bay—because it is the moment of a kind of power shift. Thorwald, because of his guilty act, had something to conceal; now Jeff, because of his guilty look, is forced to conceal. Jeff's remark to Stella about Thorwald's "guilty look" is made to rebound, ironically and retroactively, against Jeff himself. His first reaction, typically, is to turn off the lights, i.e., to return himself to a privileged cinema-like situation. Like the spectator, he is afraid of the reciprocal glance of discovery.

Thorwald's invasion of Jeffries' apartment brings the scopic inversions of the film to their paroxysm. In a narrative chiasmus—the rhetorical figure which operates by the simultaneous repetition and inversion of the relationship between two words in the course of a sentence—Jeffries and Thorwald come to

Figure 9. *Rear Window* (1954)

exchange places. Jeffries, delegate for the cinema's all-perceiving observer, had visually "broken into" and "entered" Thorwald's apartment; now Thorwald returns the favor. The spectacle, formerly kept at a safe distance by the no-man's land of the courtyard—figuratively the space between spectator and screen—comes to invade the spectator. Thorwald becomes the ambulatory embodiment of filmic displeasure; King Kong is unchained and attacking the audience. Jeff defends himself by setting off flashbulbs, hiding his eyes with each flash. He treats Thorwald as if he were part of a film to be watched in the dark. If the film becomes too frightening, turning on the lights will make it disappear. Failing that, the childlike spectator can hide the eyes; what is no longer seen is no longer there. From another perspective, Jeff tries to blind Thorwald, to deprive him of the look that confers power. But Thorwald demands reaction as a human being rather than as a character in a film. Thorwald breaks down the very condition of Jeffries' voyeurism as the Peeping Tom receives the symbolic equivalent of the hot pokers of which Stella had spoken, but with the punishment displaced from the eyes to the second broken leg which Jeff suffers in his (redemptive) fall.

Voyeurism and Point-of-View

The critique of voyeurism in *Rear Window* is elaborated not only through narrative structure and thematic motifs but also through the manipulation of the precise code most relevant to that critique—the code of point-of-view. This manipulation is far more rigorous and subtle than most critics have acknowledged. For many critics, *Rear Window* is almost completely restricted to Jeffries' point-of-view.[13] But this is simplistic. To begin with the obvious, Jeffries does not see himself *as voyeur*. "If you could see yourself," Lisa tells him, "...with binoculars!...It's a disease!" In the sequences that take place within the apartment, secondly, Lisa, Stella and Doyle are all granted some point-of-view shots, and many shots, as we shall see, embody the point-of-view of *no* character. Some of the most striking subjective shots, finally, are associated not with Jeffries but with Thorwald. Repeated shots render Thorwald's blanched-out vision of Jeffries armed with flashbulbs and trying to blind him. These dazzling shots mark Thorwald's "takeover" of the point-of-view, and in this sense form an integral part of the film's structure of inversions and reversals.

The credit sequence already "announces" the rift between Jeffries' point-of-view and that of the authorial instance. The credit sequence, in which titles are superimposed on a shot of the rear windows of Jeffries' apartment, shows three bamboo matchstick blinds successively roll up, with no sign of human intervention. The apparently self-generating movement of the blinds, combined with the self-designating "Directed by Alfred Hitchcock," anticipates and "triggers" the subsequent slow pan around the courtyard, a shot pointedly unauthorized by any character within the fiction. Hitchcock further underscores its unauthorized nature by revealing Jeffries only at the end of the shot, sound asleep and turned *away* from the window. The camera then leaves the sleeping Jeffries again and makes another self-flaunting tour of the courtyard, this time pausing to inspect specific apartment windows. The twice-asserted autonomy of this initial pair of counterclockwise pans anticipates a structuring series of similar pans, none of which is from Jeffries' point-of-view. In the first two, he is asleep, in the third he is being massaged by Stella, and in the fourth he is being kissed by Lisa. A final pan, during the epilogue, again finds him asleep. Thus Hitchcock repeatedly calls attention to the enunciation, conventionally suppressed in classical films, by emphasizing the gestural autonomy of the camera and its independence from any particular vision.

Voyeurism and Neighborliness

Through Jeffries, Hitchcock indicts not only voyeurism—or more accurately, he reminds us that he himself, his characters, and the spectators share this penchant—but also the social isolation that makes voyeurism, and voyeuristic cinema, the normal condition. Stated differently, the indictment of voyeurism is intimately linked to the film's valorization of neighborliness. At one point, the woman grief-stricken over the murder of her dog excoriates all the neighbors for their selfishness: "You don't know the meaning of the word neighbors." Her question "Which one of you did it?" is "answered" by an extreme long shot which includes all the buildings and observers around the courtyard. Thus the film implies a certain collective responsibility and the critique of a social world constituted by isolated monads.

At times *Rear Window* touches on what might be called the political dimension of voyeurism. If the narrative ultimately confirms Jeffries' suspicions of Thorwald, it also sensitizes us to the danger of political abuse of the power conferred by the look. Like Coppola's *The Conversation* (1974) two decades later, *Rear Window* is also an essay on the nature of that strange form of spectatorship called surveillance. Both films are structured around the come-uppance of the voyeur, or, in the case of Harry Caul, of the "auditeur," although the "cure," in his case, is somewhat less effective. If *The Conversation* clairvoyantly "predicted" the abuses of Watergate and Abscam, *Rear Window* in some ways echoes the historical ambiance of McCarthyite anticommunism. McCarthyism, after all, is the antithesis of neighborliness; it treats every neighbor as potential other, alien, spy. It fractures the social community for purposes of control. Jeffries is an anonymous accuser whose suspicions happen to be correct, but the object of his hostile gaze might easily have been as innocent as Father Logan in *I Confess* or Christopher Emmanuel Balestrero in *The Wrong Man,* to cite two other fifties Hitchcock films with anti-McCarthyite resonances.

Rear Window also explores the sexual politics of looking. Voyeurism in the film is largely defined as a masculine activity, even though the object of that voyeurism, through a kind of displacement, is rendered as male. The cinema, by analogy, is defined as the product of the male auteur/spectator/voyeur who at best merely enlists some women as accomplices in his voyeuristic activities. (Only Jeff, generally, is allowed to look through the phallic telephoto lens.) But while Lisa and Stella, at least in the beginning, look directly at Jeffries, he looks away toward women and men transmuted into spectacle. And when the women turn their eyes toward the spectacle, they see differently, showing enhanced capacities for empathy and comprehension, especially in relation to other women. Lisa understands instantly that Miss Torso is not in love with the man she kisses on the balcony, and knows, without ever having met her, what Mrs. Thorwald would or would not have done. The female spectator in the text, in sum, demonstrates a sensibility quite distinct from that of the male.

Rear Window provides a dramatic object-lesson in the processes of spectatorship. "Tell me what you see and what you think it means," Lisa tells Jeffries, and her words evoke the constant process of vision and interpretation, inference, and intellection involved in the "reading" of any fiction film. "I just want to find out what's the matter with the salesman's wife," says Jeffries, thus articulating one of our wishes concerning the film. Jeffries, Lisa, Stella, and Doyle collaborate in producing the meaning of the spectacle before them, much as we collaborate in producing the signification of *Rear Window.* They pressure the "film," as well, with their desire for a story. In fact, some of them would prefer a murder story; they, like us would be disappointed to discover that Mrs. Thorwald was actually alive and well.

With its insistent inscription of scenarios of voyeurism, *Rear Window* poses the question that so preoccupies contemporary film theory and analysis: the question of the place of the desiring subject within the cinematic apparatus. This theory and analysis shifts interests, as we have said, from the question of "What does the text mean?" to "What do we want from the text?" Indeed, the special achievement of *Rear Window* is to reveal the two questions as identical. "What is it you want from me?... Tell me what you want!" Thorwald says to Jeffries, and his question, ostensibly addressed to the protagonist, might as well have been addressed to us. What indeed do we want from this film or from film in general? To this question, *Rear Window* offers a complex and multileveled response. The spectators in the film—Jeffries, certainly, but also Lisa, Stella, and Doyle—want first of all to *see,* to peek into the private corners of the lives of others. The technical instruments at Jeffries' disposal come "in answer," as it were, to this primordial desire. Beyond that, these spectators want to identify with human figures with the spectacle. When Lisa enters into what had been defined as the space of the spectacle—Thorwald's apartment—Jeffries' "investment" becomes clear. Most of all, these spectators want to experience certain "subject effects." They want to find themselves in a heightened state of pleasurable absorption and identification. Jeffries the spectator begins as listless and apathetic, but he gradually "comes alive" through what he sees. He savors the experience of "coming alive," even though that experience at times entails pain and anxiety. Furthermore, he shares the experience with others within a kind of ephemeral *communitas* of spectators. His metamorphosis from distant observer into excited vicarious participant "allegorizes" the transformation engendered in us by the narrative procedures and identificatory mechanisms of Hitchcock's cinema, and even that engendered by *Rear Window* itself.

While it is true that *Rear Window* short-circuits voyeuristic involvement by making the audience aware of itself as audience and of the film as artifice, it is also true that our relation to the spectacle remains voyeuristic in the sense that we identify strongly with characters in a fiction and identify even more to the extent that we, like the protagonist, are voyeurs. The distancing of *Rear Window* is not, finally, Brechtian. For Brechtian theatre, there is no suspense, no pathos, no catharsis, while *Rear Window* builds to a catharsis that purges the tensions generated by the diegesis. We, like the protagonist, are presumably "cured." *Rear Window* is both indictment and defense of dominant cinema. Just as scopophilia can incline toward normality (a healthy curiosity) as well as abnormality (a morbid voyeurism), so the cinema can be life-enhancing or destructive. *Rear Window*, at once a cautionary tale and an ode to the cinema, presents both possibilities with equal force and extraordinary lucidity.

Godard's Erotic Sabotage

Whereas *Rear Window* exploits identificatory strategies in its critique of voyeurism, Godard's films wed a similar critique with a more consistently distanced and reflexive style. Godard consistently foregrounds the apparatus and the desiring spectator's position within it, in films which are aware of the voyeuristic dimension of the cinema but which mobilize that dimension, often comically, to "wake up" the spectator in a way which more accurately deserves the label "Brechtian." Sex is never prurient in Godard; in fact, sexual titillation is just one more conventional expectation that Godard refuses to satisfy. Despite the sexual audacity of many of his films, and despite the candor with which he treats subjects like prostitution, Godard's work generally demonstrates a *pudeur* which derives not from a puritanical distrust of sexuality but rather from a sensitivity to the generally exploitative nature of such images within dominant cinema. In his early films, therefore, he invariably underplays the eroticism of the image. Michel and Patricia in *Breathless* grope, comically, *under* the covers. Ferdinand and Marianne's roadside lovemaking in *Pierrot le Fou* is discreetly metaphorized by a blinking red signal light. The bare-breasted women in the party sequence of that film are treated with such directorial nonchalance that their nakedness hardly seems worthy of our attention. And in *The Riflemen,* the humor of Michelange's grappling with the image keeps us so busy we scarcely have time to pay attention to the woman in the bathtub.

Godard constantly changes tactics in his ongoing sabotage of eroticism. In *Weekend,* Corinne, dressed in a bra, recounts a triangular orgy—perhaps a parody of those found in the work of Georges Bataille—which culminates with her defecating in a bowl of milk at the moment of orgasm, while someone breaks an egg between her spread buttocks. Godard defuses the erotic potential of the sequence in a number of ways: first, by the comic absurdity and improbable logistics of the recounted episode; second, by her neutral and dispassionate tone of voice; third, by backlighting her body so that we see only its outline; and last, by drowning out her confessions with street noises and intermittent music. Godard's technique here recalls the strategy that Stanley Fish has shown to be characteristic of Milton's *Paradise Lost.* Milton verbally entices the reader to "sin," and then confronts him or her with this "sinfulness." He has the male reader peep with the prowling Satan at the naked Eve, and then brings him up short with the awareness of his readiness to imaginatively participate in Satan's leers. Godard, similarly, offers images which create erotic expectations, and then frustrates or subverts them. Like Milton, he chides the reader/spectator's prurience. At one point in *Weekend,* Corinne takes a bath. We do not see her breasts, but we do see the breasts of a woman in a Renaissance portrait above the bathtub. You have been led to expect some breasts, Godard seems to be telling us, so I will provide you with some breasts, but not those you were expecting. In *British Sounds,* the potential eroticism of the image of a nude woman walking up and down stairs is exorcised by an off-screen voice reading classic feminist texts. In *Tout Va Bien,* Susan shows Jacques a photograph of a penis being fondled by a woman's hand. The image fills the screen for what seems an unnaturally long time, while Susan says: "Admit that this image satisfies you less than it did three years ago." On one level, she is referring to the declining satisfactions of their marriage; on another level, she is asserting the law of diminishing returns in the exploitation of sexual images in the cinema.

Unlike Milton, Godard does not speak in moralistic or religious categories. He does not undercut sexual images *because* they are sexual; Madame Celine's monologue in *A Married Woman* is but one of many verbal odes to sexuality in his work. Godard's real target is not sexuality per se but rather sexual imagery as the locus of exploitation in the cinema in particular

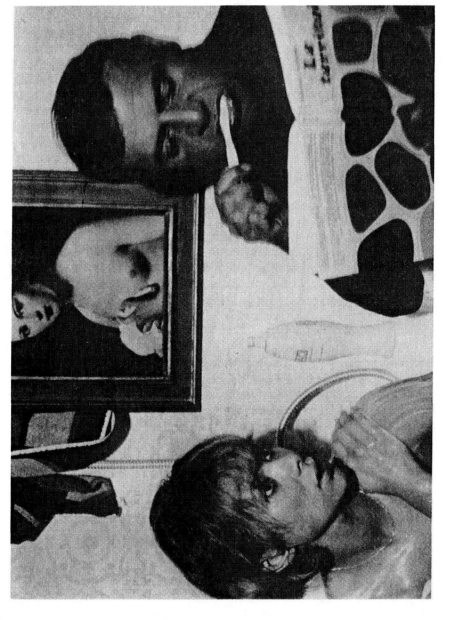

Figure 10.   *Weekend* (1967)

and in the media in general. He exposes the ways a manipulative society uses sex as part of its arsenal for purposes of social control. He unmasks the media's exploitation of sexuality as a daily aggression on its hapless spectators. Charlotte in *Une Femme Mariée* obsessively compares her bust to that of the ideal figures from the women's magazines. She anxiously ponders the questions that advertising and the media throw at her: "Is your bust...?" "How far can a woman go...?" Charlotte anticipates Mademoiselle Dix-Neuf Ans in *Masculin, Féminin,* whom Godard labels "a consumer product," as well as the inhabitants of Alphaville. The fascism of Alphaville—where the entire polity has been transformed into a streamlined and antiseptic bordello—is sexual as well as political.

Indeed, in the Alphaville of a repressively tolerant society, cinema often serves a function analogous to that of houses of prostitution and massage parlors. It becomes one of those potentially subversive zones—those authorized ghettos where certain excesses are permitted—that liberal society tolerates in order to control. The cinema of vicarious thrills allows us to make love to the stars for a price; it doles out minimal libidinal satisfactions even while protecting us from their consequences. The perennial juggling of pornography and prudery stimulates the id while reinforcing the superego. Dominant cinema, like dominant politics, perpetually cheats its public of the utopia it perpetually promises. Godard's hostility is not directed at sexuality but rather at the alienated forms of representation. The point, to paraphrase the envoi of *Tout Va Bien,* is for each of us to become our own *sexual* historians.

A close look at the opening sequence of *Contempt* (1963) tells us a good deal about Godard's distanciating procedures. The film is prefaced by a quotation from André Bazin: "The cinema gives us a world in accordance with our desires." A red cloth screen, on which the word "Contempt" is written, then folds and collapses. The sheet anticipates other Godardian sheets— Michelange pulling down the sheet/screen in *Les Carabiniers,* the white cloth/sheet background for the titles of *A Married Woman,* subsequently revealed as the diegetic sheet on which two lovers make stylized epidermic contact—and condenses a series of associations. The sheet/screen evokes the mental "dream screen" which, according to Bertram Lewin, precedes the dreamer's entry into the dream. The sheet thus evokes cinema's promise of a world "in accord with our desires," in short the world both of sleep and sexuality, of the desire to dream and the dream of desire. It is this world that the title sequence promises and then symbolically folds and collapses.

The first shot after the title opens in deep-focus onto an Italian studio-town—subsequently revealed as Cinecittà—as a small knot of human figures and a camera progress toward us from the depths of the space. As the visible pro-filmic camera approaches, the invisible pre-filmic camera pans slightly to center it, then tilts up respectfully, while the visible camera tilts down, directly fixing the spectator with its rectangular lens. The shot warrants a number of observations. The only completely honest film, Godard once said, would show a camera filming itself in a mirror. Although *Le Mépris* never achieves such an exacting standard of reflexivity, it approximates it by having the pro-filmic camera eye, which in conventional cinema slyly and surreptitiously equates itself with the vision of the spectator, focus on the spectators themselves. It is as if the apparatus itself were nodding at us, in a cinematographic equivalent of Brechtian direct address to the audience. Apart from the camera, we see camera tracks—in a film traversed by tracking shots—along with light meters, electrical equipment, booms. But more important than this pro-filmic display of the cinematic machinery is the fact that we are made aware of the *look* of the camera. Instead of identifying unconsciously, through a process analogous to primary identification in psychoanalysis, with the camera through which we see, here we are reminded that films are constituted by looks: the look of the camera, the spectator's recapitulation of that look, the looks between characters in the fiction, the looks which carry us from shot to shot.

This opening camera-eye is also a camera-gun aimed at spectatorial voyeurism. Fiction films usually shelter us from the glance of the actors; we look at people on screen who do not look at us. But here Raoul Coutard and his camera return our glance. The voyeur has been *vu*. This aggressive designation of our voyeuristic position is reinforced in the subsequent shots of Piccoli and Bardot. The Bazin quotation—"the cinema gives us a world in accordance with our desires"—has already pointed a verbal finger at our desire. The nude shots of Bardot—which Godard was pressured by the producers to include—presumably come to fulfill that same (largely male) desire. In fact, Godard gave in to the producers, but in ways that undercut their intentions, for the three-shot sequence is a typical Godardian exercise in defused titillation. Red, white and blue filters remind us of specifically cinematographic mediations and transfigure the image of Bardot's body into pure chromatic plasticity. The film renders her beauty as statuesque, and comparable in eroticism to the perfectly respectable classical sculptures seen recurrently throughout the film. The two motionless lovers mingle shopping-list trivialities with oddly dispassionate declarations of love. Piccoli makes a verbal inventory of Bardot's body—at this point we know them only as Piccoli and Bardot since we do not yet know their fictive names: "I love your feet... I love your legs... I love your thighs." This Ezequiel's bones approach to female nakedness sends a mocking message to both producer and spectator: "All right, if it's nudity you want, here it is—in words!"

Equally important is the positioning of these shots within the text. Godard gives in to the producers' wishes but subverts their intentions; he vanquishes by submitting. He quickly dispenses the requested shots as if acquitting himself of a disagreeable duty. In classical films, furthermore, love scenes usually come as a culmination to an inexorable crescendo of teased desire, an explosion after a long repressed chase. The final kiss of a Bacall-Bogart film noir "resolves," in a musical rather than literal sense, an erotic tension carefully stimulated throughout the film. The "love scene" in *Le Mépris,* in constrast, occurs in advance of any real spectatorial involvement. Since the processes of secondary identification by which we emotionally invest ourselves in the fiction have not yet taken place, the sequence is syntagmatically displaced, as if narrative orgasm were made to precede foreplay.

A Married Woman and *Masculine, Feminine*

The subject of *A Married Woman* would seem to be made to order for the avid spectator-as-voyeur. The love scenes, the introspective voice-overs, the intimist framing might easily collaborate to create a diegetic world which the spectator might imagine as private and which he or she is surreptitiously observing. Yet Godard uses all this conventional machinery against its usual purposes. The film begins, like *Le Mépris,* with a sheet/screen, a reminder of cinema's affinity with the oneiric and the imaginary. There follows a series of shots of parts of two lover's bodies. The framing is calculated in such a way that the images do not suggest erotic spectacles: the effect is one of dismemberment. Some of the shots constitute sight-gags: two legs, one male one female, neighbor symmetrically as if they belonged to the same person. The shots, in their stillness, resemble photographs that fade in and out. The fades, conventionally used to indicate the passage of time, are here used to isolate the shots and avoid conventional movement continuity. In syntagmatic terms, we are given what Metz would call a bracket syntagma, a typical sample of an activity: not a couple making love, but the idea of a couple making love. There is no teleology, no increased intensity leading to climax. The acting is as if in the third person, remote and understated. We lip-read the words "Je t'aime"—usually the most emotionally charged sentence in classic films—as they repeat it without apparent emotion. The declaration, furthermore, comes at the beginning of the film and not as a romantic closure or fulfillment.

The opening sequence typifies the Brechtianism of the film's procedures. We are confronted with an abstract romantic triangle, an equilateral triangle in which we do not side with either of the rivals for Charlotte's affections. Pierre and Robert strike us as interchangeable units: both professionals associated with airports, they are granted the same amount of time in Charlotte's company; they participate in identical rituals. Everything in the film—the understated acting, the juxtaposition of staged scenes with cinéma vérité interviews; the verbal references to films; the foregrounding both of photography and the gestures of the camera—undercuts our erotic involvement with the characters. Charlotte explains to her husband that she would like to know "all the people in the street," and glances to the right, then the left, and then straight at the audience. Her expressed desire to close the space separating herself from her observer designates the "withdrawal" of the cinematic situation, the withdrawal on which the spectator's scopophilia usually feeds.

Godard's subversion of a certain kind of pleasure is, at times, itself intensely pleasurable. A kind of aesthetic jubilation transports us from the privatized space of individual fantasy to a broader social space in which we see our own desires as comic. Self-directed laughter remains laughter. Godard illuminates the comic underside of the "intersubjective textual relation" by showing us spectators watching films. The "porn-film sequence" in *Masculine, Feminine,* for example, shows us a movie theatre whose air is heavy with eroticism, where usherettes kiss apparent strangers and homosexuals tryst in the mens' room. The film itself—often said to parody Bergman's *The Silence* because it is Swedish and involves impersonal sexual encounters in an unidentified land—is prefaced by an ironic intertitle in ersatz Scandinavian: "4X Ein Sensitiv und Rapid Film." The reflexive self-characterization recalls that of many Godard films—"Fragments of a Film Made in 1964," "A Film in Black and White"—and involves superimposed puns and ironies, the "4X" referring simultaneously to 4X film stock, X as in X-rated, and X as in a 4-star system of evaluating films, and the "sensitiv" and "rapid" referring both to the sensibility and quick pace of the film and to the sensitivity of the film stock. The film-within-a-film mirrors *Masculine, Feminine* as a whole; both concern relations between the sexes, although the porn film offers a particularly reductionist version in which communication is limited to the semiotics of grunts and the proxemics of lust, the absurdity of which is heightened by a distorting mirror which turns the male figure, especially, into a kind of monster. Paul and Madeleine and their friends, while aware of the film's gross stupidity, are unable to leave, thus demonstrating the manner in which exploitative films make spectators the passive accomplices of their seductive aggressions. "We control our thoughts," says Paul's interior monologue, "but not our emotions, which are everything." Feelings lag behind knowledge, and we are left trying to reconcile what we feel with what we know, for the appeal of such films, like that of advertising, is direct and difficult to resist. Paul's poetic monologue speaks of the role of the desiring spectator within the apparatus, of the emotional demands we make of films: "Marilyn Monroe had aged terribly. It made us sad. It wasn't the film we had dreamed of . . . the total film we carried within ourselves . . . that we wanted to make . . . or more secretly . . . that we wanted to live." Paul's melancholy off-screen words coincide with the close-up image of the woman in the porn film. Her face moves down-screen, presumably in the direction of the man's penis. The implied off-screen fellatio, an act of unilateral and impersonal homage to the phallus, metaphorizes the porn film's flattering relation to the male spectator; he remains deliciously passive while being serviced by a competent and contented woman in a nonreciprocated onanism à deux. The juxtaposition of Paul's lament with the pornographic images, meanwhile, suggests a kind of logical/mathematical proportion: a quick blow-job among strangers is to our dreams of real love as pornography is to true cinema.

Feminist Pornography: *Numéro Deux* and *Every Man for Himself*

Numéro Deux (1975), co-authored by Godard and Anne-Marie Miéville, creates what at first glance might seem a contradiction in terms—a political, nonexploitative, porn film. The film politicizes and "feminizes" an apparently irrecuperable genre. The film has the conventional appearance of porn; it displays all the stock shots of x-rated films. Images of fellatio, rear-entry intercourse, and masturbation literally proliferate on the screen. Yet despite this profusion of visual erotica, the film is uncompromising in its refusal to pander to scopophilic lust. Godard-Miéville achieve this remarkable feat not by making the sexual acts repulsive, as pornography often inadvertently does, but rather by politicizing and socializing them. The image of a woman masturbating, for example, is not served up for male delectation but rather to make a feminist point—that women's bodies are their own. The image does not bury us in the white thighs of infinite desire; the woman is filmed head first, and we are reminded that the head is where a good deal of sexual activity takes place. Sandrine masturbates to her memories—"It's like the cinema," she points out—and we are reminded that a woman's thoughts are also her own. The sexual activity, in any case, is subsumed under the more general question of sexual politics. In another image—of an old man masturbating—sexuality is politicized in a different way. The man, an ex-Communist party militant, masturbates, rather ineffectively, to the memories of his activist youth, and his action aptly metaphorizes the nostalgic and largely impotent politics of the French Communist Party.

Numéro Deux demystifies sexuality, and thus subverts the pornographic genre from within. Avoiding the twin extremes of the idealized, sweatless, and odorless sexuality of the haloed pre-porn days and the lobtomized animality of porn, *Numéro Deux* shows sex as a universal, everyday activity. Sexuality, rather than being the private preserve of nubile young adults, is revealed as a general inheritance. Children are shown to be sexually curious, and the elderly sexually active. The children's question—"Do all little girls have holes?"—remind us that what has become so surrounded with a halo of tantalizing interdiction is in some respects quite simple. Whereas children are denied access to x-rated films, *Numéro Deux* invites them into the image itself. At the same time, the film explores the complex repercussions of adult sexuality on children. One remarkable shot superimposes the solarized video close-up of the daughter's face on a long shot of her parents making love, in a strikingly original cinematic version of a Freudian "primal scene."[14] The elderly, for their part, are shown to be sexual creatures like everyone else, only older. A sequence entitled "Venus s'impose" shows an aged woman (the grandmother) going about her routines in the nude, while the sound track enumerates the youth-giving effects of various cosmetics. The sequence mocks our desire for nudity, and the media exploitation of sexuality, but it never mocks the woman. We are reminded that young nude bodies become naked old bodies, that our loving souls are fastened, as Yeats put it, to a dying animal, and that this, too, a mature vision of sexuality must take into account.

If *Numéro Deux's* sensitive approach to the sexuality of the elderly recalls Simone de Beauvoir's *La Vieillesse,* its concern with female liberation evokes *Le Deuxième Sexe.* The film suggests, in startlingly innovative ways, the manner in which sexist power relations taint communication between women and men. Home for her is a factory; for him it is a refuge. She produces at a loss; he profits. The inadequacy of their sexual relationship cannot be separated from the sexual politics of their everyday life. This fact is suggested visually in a number of ways. The image of Sandrine giving head to Pierre is juxtaposed within the *Jeanne Dielman*-like image of the grandmother peeling vegetables. Two forms of service or two forms of servitude? At another point Godard-Miéville use a video synthesizer to overlap images; he goes to work in color, while she stays at home in black-and-white.

Like *Numéro Deux, Sauve Qui Peut/(la Vie)* (Every Man for Himself, 1980) practices an erotic brinksmanship which carries sexually explicit imagery to a point just this side of exploitation. The essential question for the filmmakers is not the images themselves but their mediation. Although *Sauve Qui Peut* proliferates in verbal allusions and visual representations which might be regarded as "pornographic," the erotic potential of the material is consistently defused. It might be argued, of course that defusing the erotic potential of sexual images ceases, after a time, to pay intellectual dividends. How often do filmmakers have to designate the voyeuristic situation of the spectator without the exercise becoming redundant or counter-productive? The answer seems to be that in a situation dominated either by the puritans who would repress bodily pleasure or the pseudo-hedonists who "liberate" only masculine pleasure, while we wait for the utopia of a reciprocal, egalitarian, and decentered sexuality in which sexual images are controlled by both sexes, the kind of Brechtian eroticism practised by *Sauve Qui Peut* still serves a purpose.[15]

The strategies deployed in this Brechtian short-circuiting of voyeurism are multiple. 1) Huppert's transparent boredom and expressionless acting function as a potent antiaphrodisiac. At the same time, she conveys dignity in the face of even the most outrageous proposals. Her surface passivity is undercut by an ironic quality, a stubborn refusal to be impressed. Her resolute blankness becomes a form of resistance. 2) Although women frequently disrobe in the film, the disrobing is merely the sign of a power relation. The women are ordered to strip; the gesture is one of mechanical submission rather than a coy dialectic of concealing and revealing. 3) As often in Godard—one need only recall Madame Celine's soliloquy in *Une Femme Mariée* or the recounted orgy in *Weekend*—the sexual material is displaced onto the verbal register. Or Godard plays on the interchange between the verbal and visual. Mr. Personne's request to see Isabelle's "belle forêt" is answered by a shot of the "beautiful forest" lining Lac Leman. This childlike literalization of a metaphor mocks the spectator's voyeurism.

Rather than pander to desire, *Sauve Qui Peut* concretizes scenarios of desire in distanced, often ridiculous forms hardly designed to flatter the spectator. Rather than vicariously participate in the scenario, we observe it as a comic object; we are too busy laughing to become aroused. The most hilarious example of this erotic grotesquerie involves a listless four-person orgy. Godard stages the sexual fantasies of a contemporary businessman. We are shown a technocrat's wet dream—the Taylorization of sexual production. Sex is programmed and disciplined by the science of management. The boss monopolizes the information, plans the work and sets the procedures. Like a filmmaker, he assigns precise movement and attitudes to the "actors" (his assistant, secretary, and a prostitute). The image taken care of, he concentrates on the sound track. Each participant is assigned a diphthong ("ai," "ei")—presumably the signifier of rampaging lust—to be repeated at regular intervals. The orgy participants, like assembly-line workers, are reduced to well-defined jerks, twists, moans, and quivers. The cineaste-patron literally oversees a hierarchy of domination. The sightlines are arranged by him and work to his benefit. Yet ultimately he cannot enjoy his power. Isabelle reads his face and finds "dark pride, terminal despair, arrogance, and fear." All this, it should go without saying, is highly antierotic. There are no writhing bodies but only the empty multiplication of sexual signifiers in a kind of caricatural formula of an orgy, an orgy rendered as sign.

Obscure Objects of Desire

We encounter a paradigmatic instance of the playful mockery of the desiring spectator in a film whose title sums up what is at stake: *That Obscure Object of Desire*. Buñuel's film demonstrates a kind of Zeno's paradox of passion: the space between two potential lovers—and between the spectator and the screen—is infinitely divisible. No matter how physically close Mathieu gets to

Figure 11.   *Sauve Qui Peut/ (la Vie)* (1980)

Conchita—in her house, in his bed, naked in bed—she remains as spiritually remote as a medieval damsel locked in the castles of courtly love. *Obscure Object* visually renders this inaccessibility by placing Conchita behind bars, fences, grillwork. Mathieu is framed as the prisoner of desire, in a chromatic version of the incarceral obsession of film noir. His vision is barred as he is subjected to cruelly seductive revelations of Conchita's flesh. He watches through glass doors as she dances for tourists and observes her through a locked gate as another man is presumably about to enjoy her. The bars metaphorize the treadmill of desire—since all desire depends on the infinite pursuit of its absent object—always tantalizing, always unfulfilled, perpetually on the brink in a protracted coitus interruptus.[16]

Obscure Object frustrates our epistemophilia as well as our scopophilia. By obscuring the very identity of the characters through the use of two actresses in the same role, Buñuel calls attention to the phantasmatic nature of cinematic spectacle. A key support of illusionistic narrative—our naive faith in the three-dimensional solidity of stable, identifiable characters—is thrown aside. But this two-actress personage also points up Mathieu's blindness: he literally fails to see the woman he claims to love. She is a phantom, a narrative function, an abstract incarnation of male desire. She is a creation of Mathieu's pathology. Playing out a widely disseminated cultural double bind, Mathieu cannot attain what he desires without destroying his desire. The love of virgins, like Humbert Humbert's love for nymphets, is ephemeral and foredoomed by definition.

But more important than Mathieu's desire per se is Buñuel's comic foiling of *our* spectatorial desire. *Obscure Object* is a protracted joke on the spectator, a narrative striptease that refuses to strip. It refuses to let us see what we want to see or know what we want to know. The title's abstract promise of eroticism draws us to the theatre, but the film never delivers on the promise. Like Mathieu, we are cruelly locked out of the spectacle, subjected to a regress of spectatorial frustration. Instead of stimulating desire, Buñuel holds the mirror to our own psychic fix on films themselves. He analyzes the most mystified moment in our culture—the moment of anticipated sexual fulfillment—and scrutinizes, as if under a microscope, our phantasmatic relation to the spectacle, exposing desire as a cultural and cinematic construct.

The obscure object of desire in Joaquim Pedro de Andrade's *Tropical Fruit* (Brazil, 1980) takes the form of a watermelon. The protagonist of the film, that is to say, literally loves watermelons. A parody of the *pornochanchadas* (vapid soft-core porn films popular in Brazil), *Tropical Fruit* demystifies the genre by according to the watermelon the function usually accorded the woman in such films. The protagonist seduces the watermelon as if it were a frightened virgin, deflowers it ritualistically, and ultimately subjects it to sado-masochistic perversities. A series of shots achieves what has remained inaccessible in more conventional non-vegetative pornography—

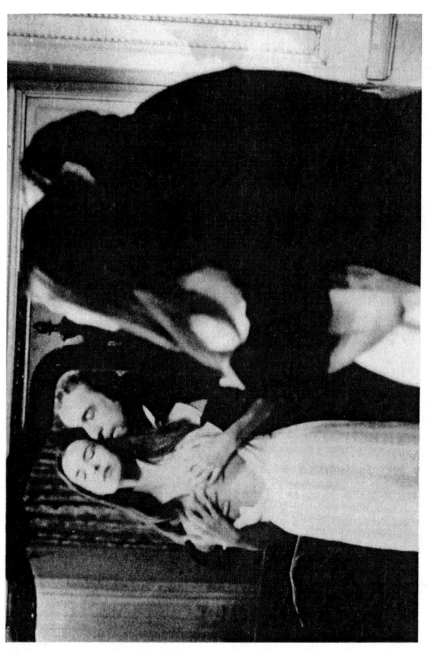

Figure 12.   *That Obscure Object of Desire* (1977)

Figure 13. *That Obscure Object of Desire* (1977)

shots from inside the pink wetness of the watermelon itself. Thus the film mocks the male spectator's desire to see—and only see—everything! It exposes pornography's Pyrrhic victory. After conquering the contours of the female body, the pudenda, and the vulva, the phallic camera takes the last fortress in a fantastic voyage to the very center. But as Pascal Bruckner and Alain Finkielkraut point out, the victory is in every sense a hollow one, revealing only the totalitarianism of masculine pleasure and the sterile plenitude of voyeurism: "the miniscule Eden peopled by impoverished masculine dreams."[17]

Tropical Fruit also switches the terms of secondary identification of the pornochanchada. The woman—usually the coy sex object—is here the spectator's delegate who asks the protagonist precisely those questions we would have liked to ask. The protagonist, for his part, is hardly an ideal figure for male projection. While pornochanchada protagonists are generally playboys living in luxurious apartments, the protagonist of *Tropical Fruit* is physically unattractive and professionally incompetent. Hardly the macho sexual athlete of the pornochanchadas, he suffers from premature ejaculation even with his watermelons. In sum, *Tropical Fruit* answers the male voyeur's implicit request for a female sex object by offering an ironically reified object of desire, a vegetative exemplar of pure alterity. The Brazilian military government, sensing the insult to machismo in a film without nudity or heterosexual or homosexual lovemaking, banned it for three years, while tolerating the much more explicit pornochanchadas which *Tropical Fruit* so acerbically mocked.

We have focussed in this chapter on fictions which foreground the "intersubjective textual relation"—the relation between reader and novel, spectator and play, filmgoer and film. These fictions remind the reader or spectator of his or her complicity in the fiction, their active role in creating it in collaboration with the fictioner. In the case of films, they focus on the cinematic apparatus and the desiring spectator's place within that apparatus. Since the cinematic enterprise has been historically marked by voyeurism both as theme and impulse, they criticise the voyeuristic stance promoted by a certain kind of cinema, largely to flatter and titillate the male spectator. All the texts here discussed strive to promote critical self-awareness in the spectator. Whether they do this through Brechtian comedy (Godard) or near-tragedy (Hitchcock), they all offer an allegorisis of spectatorship in which we can all, to a greater or lesser degree, recognize ourselves. Such is the special nature of their reflexivity.

2

The Process of Production

At one point in *Don Quixote*, Cervantes has his protagonist walk into a Barcelona printing shop where he observes the processes of proofreading, typesetting, and revision and is lectured on the economics of the publishing industry. Cervantes thus focuses attention on the concrete procedures by which all books, including his own, were produced. Just as a novel can take the production of books as its subject, so a film can focus on the processes of filmmaking. Our purpose in this chapter will be to examine a novel—Balzac's *Lost Illusions*—which explores the literary institution in the broadest sense, along with a series of films which take as their subject either the cinematic institution or the concrete technical or aesthetic operations involved in filmmaking. Such novels and films necessarily entail a certain measure of reflexivity in that they foreground, in however indirect or idealized fashion, the institutional practices involved in their own production. They may treat this subject more or less critically, more or less reflexively, but they do have the virtue of reminding the reader or spectator that literary or filmic texts are products, created by individuals or groups and mediated by complex commercial and cultural apparati.

The literary and cinematic institutions, homologous in some respects, are otherwise quite distinct. Not all branches of art are subject to the laws of a specific system of production—for example, capitalist—to the same extent or in the same way. The economic conditioning affecting literature operates even more powerfully in the cinema, whose very nature involves it in industrial production. A novel can be written on napkins in a prison; commercial considerations enter with force only at the stage of publication and distribution. With film on the other hand, economic considerations—large or small budget, color or black-and-white, expensive stars or unknown actors— dictate priorities and preclude possibilities from the very outset. The actual production of the film sets in motion a complex economic mechanism, from the mechanical apparatus of cameras, laboratories, and editing equipment to the commercial apparatus of distribution and exhibition.

Figure 14. *Passion* (1982)

Art and the Culture Industry: Balzac's *Lost Illusions*

Although Honoré de Balzac was a nonarchist in politics and an archmimeticist in art, his *Lost Illusions* exposes the political and economic mechanisms of nineteenth-century capitalism with the same penetrating vigor that it discovers the machinations which operate in the world of art.[1] He reveals in embryonic form the development of what Brecht, a century later, would call the cultural "apparati" and what Enzenberger would call the "consciousness industry." Although Balzac was writing in another century, much of his analysis remains as pertinent today as it was a hundred years ago; it applies, by extension, to both the contemporary cinema as well as the other mass-media.

Lost Illusions, Georg Lukács has said, is the *Don Quixote* of bourgeois illusions. The comparison, although Lukács never elaborates it, is endlessly suggestive. Both texts constitute antiromances, fictions which are at the same time critiques of fiction. While Cervantes ridicules chivalric romance by contrasting its fictions with the realities of seventeenth-century Spain, the central dialectic of Balzac's novel pits human fictions—whether in the form of literature in particular or imaginative idealization in general—against a social reality which belies those fictions. Both novels treat characters whose ideals and fantasies have been shaped by literary texts and who then encounter a world not in conformity with such fantasies. The very title of Balzac's novel recalls the formula which Cervantes provided for the novel: a narrative trajectory of progressive disillusionment engendered by brutal encounters with reality. A no-longer feudal Spain destroys the chivalric imaginings of Cervantes' *hidalgo*, and the developing capitalist world puts an end to the romantic attitudes and Napoleonic ambitions of David Séchard and Lucien de Rubempré.

If *Don Quixote* demystifies romance, *Lost Illusions* demystifies nineteenth-century romanticism by putting it to an exacting "reality test." The twin protagonists of *Lost Illusions*—David Séchard and Lucien de Rubempré—are quintessential romantics, formed by the reading of Schiller, Lord Byron, Walter Scott, and Lamartine. Their attitudes are romantic; they see themselves as sensitive souls defiled by their provincial surroundings. They display the self-delusions of bourgeois artists who live in contradiction and mauvaise foi. Such an artist, Jean-Paul Sartre writes in *What is Literature*, chooses to ignore the reality of his public: "He speaks gladly of his solitude, and ...claims that one writes for oneself alone or for God; he makes literature a metaphysical occupation, a prayer, an examination of consciousness, everything except a communication."[2] Balzac anticipates Sartre by ironically placing similar romantic misconceptions in the infatuated mind of Madame de Bargeton: "According to her, men of genius had neither brothers or sisters nor fathers and mothers; the great works they were destined to construct forced them to appear selfish and sacrifice everything to their greatness . . . Genius was accountable only to itself; it alone knew what ends were to be attained and it alone could justify the means"(p. 66).[3] Thus Balzac casts ridicule on the suspect solitude and Werther-like posturings of the romantic artist who sees himself as supremely autonomous, without connection to the world or to the public, the creator of masterpieces to which he alone detains the key.

Although Balzac does not consciously belong to a reflexive tradition— Robert Alter is quite right to see *Lost Illusions* as a primarily mimetic novel which examines the literary world largely as milieu—the novel can at least be said to reflexively reveal the conditions of its own production. Its protagonists, the poet and the printer, taken together represent the complementary aspects of literary production—creation and mechanical reproduction. *Lost Illusions* inlcudes a novel within the novel (Lucien's *L'Archer de Charles IX*), and thus resembles novels about the writing of novels, like Gide's *Faux-Monnayeurs* or Huxley's *Point-Counterpoint*, although Balzac, as Robert Alter points out, never takes us *inside* the fictitious novel as Gide and Huxley do. More important, however, Balzac shows us the processes of literary creation, the selection process whereby certain practices of language become texts. As Lucien and D'Arthes labor over the revisions of Lucien's novel, writing is shown to be an arduous and time-consuming process rather than the magical result of spontaneous artistic generation or the product of a nebulous "inspiration."

Balzac examines literature in a materially concrete context, highlighting the whole gamut of conceivable influences on the processes of literary production: the origins of the material of which books are made—paper; the technological procedures of their reproduction—printing; and the commercial transactions that affect their publication and distribution. The very first sentence consists of a notation on the technology of printing, and the final paragraph mentions the printing office which Cerizet is forced to sell. At one point, Balzac offers a capsule history of printing ("When the immortals Faust, Coster, and Gutenberg had invented the Book") and he explains the transformation of the means of production from manufacture with wooden presses to industrialized production with Stanhope presses. Balzac's insistence on the technology of printing becomes especially significant when we remember Walter Benjamin's insight that the novel is distinguished from the story and the epic by its essential dependence on the book. What differentiates the novel from other forms of prose literature, Benjamin points out, is that it neither comes from oral tradition nor goes into it: "The dissemination of the novel becomes possible only with the invention of printing."[4] The novel, then, is the only major literary genre to emerge after Gutenberg, whose invention made books available on a large scale and thus led to a situation of mass literacy in which large numbers of people were being influenced by books. In its close alliance with an invention, in fact, it parallels the fiction film, made possible by the mechanical reproduction of the filmic image, which in conjunction with the establishment of networks of distribution led to a situation in which large masses of people came to be influenced, and quixotized, as it were, by fiction films.

By relating the history of paper, hardly out of place, Balzac insists, in a work "whose material existence is due as much to paper as to the printing press," *Lost Illusions* insists on the awkward contingency of literary texts, their humiliating dependence on the paper on which they are printed. Balzac insists on the physical perishability of books. As sound products disappear, he points out, " Neither the shirts nor the books will last . . . "(p. 119). One senses real outrage in Balzac's remark: "What a shame for our epoch to make books that will not last!" (pp. 121-22). The juxtaposition of shirts with books, meanwhile, suggests that literature has become just another salable commodity. Indeed, the central subject of *Lost Illusions* is the degradation of literature, and its transformation, in bourgeois society, into a commodity. In Balzac's novel, the problems of art and what Marx called "spiritual production" resonate to the contradictions within the capitalist system of production generally. Lucien, attempting to sell his novel, is rudely confronted with the situation created by the capitalization of literature. Surprised by the commercial jargon of the publishers, for whom books "were like cotton bonnets to haberdashers, a commodity to be bought cheap and sold dear," Lucien is struck by "the brutally material aspect that literature could assume" (p. 219). This "brutally material aspect" suggests that the perennial "problem of the book" here takes on an economic dimension—the problem of the book as merchandise in nineteenth-century capitalist France.

Balzac explores in *Lost Illusions* the same theme that Godard later elaborates in *Contempt*; the commercial degradation of art. Balzac's imagery underscores the theme, comparing publications to "card tricks," publishers to gamblers ("staking other people's funds on the green cloth of speculation") and prospectors ("looking for Walter Scott, as later one might search for asphalt in shingly terrrain").[5] But the central metaphor for the social degradation of art, for Balzac as later for Godard, is prostitution. The character Lousteau compares the hierarchy of literary reputations to the hierarchy of prostitution: the lowest kind of literature is "the needy whore shivering on street corners"; second-rate literature is the "kept woman straight from the brothels of journalism"; and successful literature is the "flashy insolent courtesan" who "pays her taxes and entertains eminent people" (pp. 273-74). The press, for Balzac, is a grand bordello and journalists are "prostitutes of the pen." The prostitutes accompanying writers like Lucien and Lousteau stand in a kind of indexical relation to their clients; they are more symptom than cause of the journalists' corruption. As literature becomes a salable commodity, the writers begin to treat themselves as commodities that sell, package, and advertise themselves.

At times, *Lost Illusions* reads like a disillusioned screenwriter's Hollywood novel. The literary world, Lucien discovers, is the scene of perpetual Darwinian struggle, corrupted from top to bottom by money: "the only power that this world kneels down to" (pp. 197-98). Books are seen as "capital to be invested" and their artistic merit, Dauriat points out, often *lessens* their chance for publication: "The better a book is, the less likely it is to be sold." Literary criticism, meanwhile, has become an appendage of what would now be called the "cultural industry," and is governed, according to Balzac, by a "strict alliance between criticism and the press." Favorable or unfavorable reviews, when not dictated by the political allegiances of the journal in question, depend on the amount of the bribe paid by the author or publisher. In the theatre, producers view each production as a financial gamble, a "coup de cartes." Since the public wants to be "crammed full of emotions," the theatre simply supplies the market for cheap thrills. For the artist, talent must be accompanied by a certain "genius for intrigue." Actresses, to succeed, display their prowess on the nineteenth-century equivalent of the casting couch, or simply bribe the journalists who write the theatre reviews. Even in art, Lucien comes to realize, success can be "fabricated."

Balzac never allows us to indulge the illusion that Lucien's problem as a writer is merely a personal and psychological one. To underscore the paradigmatic nature of Lucien's disenchantment, he offers parallel instances of the same process in the careers of other poets. The cynical Lousteau begins, like Lucien, with his "heart full of illusions, spurred by the love of art" only to discover the "facts of the métier, the difficulty of getting into print, and the reality of poverty." Enthusiasm, he tells Lucien, had hid "the mechanism of the world!" It was necessary to "get caught up in the works, run foul of the shafts, get covered with grease and hear the rattle of chains and flywheels." (p. 270) Both Lucien and Lousteau exemplify a common Balzacian pattern. Young idealists, progressing through the initiatory fires of "Enrichissez-vous" Restoration France, discover that the values with which they grew up—love, family, religion—have no currency in the sphere of social circulation. Since generosity and idealism lead only to impotence and victimization, they come under relentless pressure to prostitute themselves. Their personal qualities— good looks, enthusiasm, talent—become a kind of capital. Their sentiments become calculations, and love an investment. Balzac, rather than spotlight the lonely struggle of a suppressed "genius," offers the critical dissection of an unexceptional individual trapped in the "mécanisme" of a general malaise.

Lost Illusions constitutes a thoroughgoing critic of both literature and society. The two critiques, in fact, imply and reinforce each other. They are homologous; a critique in one area invariably triggers reverberations in the other:

> By inviting all its children to the same banquet, Society arouses their ambitions in the very morning of life, robbing youth of its graces and vitiating most of its generous sentiments by contaminating them with calculation. Poetry would have it otherwise, but Fact too often belies the fiction one would prefer to believe... (p. 67).

Here we have the dialectic of *Lost Illusions*—between ideology on the one hand and social reality on the other. Ideology, after all, is nothing more than "the fiction one would prefer to believe," the system of representations that the dominating class uses to justify its power and which the dominated need, or think they need, to rationalize their powerlessness. In the Balzacian dialectic, poetry is contradicted by fact, and the fictions in which one would like to believe are juxtaposed with the dismal realities of nineteenth-century France.

Hollywood on Hollywood: The Silent Period

Just as Balzac took the world of literature as his subject in *Lost Illusions*, so countless Hollywood films treat Hollywood itself as milieu, and focus, accurately or inaccurately, critically or uncritically, on the processes of film production. Without attempting an exhaustive summary of a topic already treated by Patrick Donald Anderson, Bruce Kawin, Alfred Appel, Gerald Mast, Robert Eberwein, Rudy Behlmer and Tony Thomas, among others, we might usefully survey a tradition of films which are "reflexive" in one or more of the following senses: 1) they explore the filmmaking milieu; 2) they expose the actual processes of film production, whether directly or by analogy; and 3) they flaunt their artifice through calling attention to filmic technique. A number of questions will orient our discussion: Do these films idealize or demystify the cinema as an institution? What phase of the production process—preproduction, production, postproduction, reception—do they concentrate on? To what extent do they display an anti-illusionistic aesthetic? Are they truly reflexive or do they merely exploit the filmmaking milieu as a decor in which to set a conventional comedy or dramatic realist film? Finally, how do the films comment on the reality of genre within the studio system and which genres exhibit a greater or lesser degree of reflexivity?

Since the very beginning of the cinema, numerous films have focussed on the filmmaking milieu or the processes of filmmaking. In a variation on the mistaking-screen-illusion-for-reality motif, an early French film—*Les Inconvénients du Cinématographe*—shows a Parisian who, witnessing the filming of a staged theft, decides to defend the "victim," much to the irritation of the filmmakers. In Mack Sennett's *Kid Auto Races at Venice* (1913), Charlie

Chaplin inadvertently interferes with the production of a documentary by repeatedly standing in front of the lens, thus enraging the director who tries to boot him out of camera range. In both *His New Job* (1915) and *Behind the Screen* (1916), Chaplin wreaks havoc in a movie studio. Sennett's *How Motion Pictures are Made* (1914) combines a tour of the Thomas Ince studios with typical Keystone buffoonery. Contemporary critics, interestingly, worried that such films might irreparably tarnish the glamor and aura of Hollywood. The *Motion Picture News* warned that *The Goat* (1918), a film about a stunt-man, by disclosing "picture-making as it actually is...will lessen the pleasure a spectator derives from watching a picture, as it will destroy some of the illusion due to the mystery surrounding picture production."[6] The reviewer in *Motion Picture Magazine* echoed such concerns: "Why take away the glamor even momentarily?"[7] Thus Hollywood critics, journalistic appendage of the industry, tried to protect the aura and magic of Hollywood by shielding its Achilles heel—the trade secrets of its illusionism.

Like the novel, the cinema often elaborated the theme of the quixotic confusion of art and real life, image and reality. In the wake of *Uncle Josh*, the father of an actress in *A Vitagraph Romance* (1912) sees his daughter in a dangerous on-screen situation, races to the Vitagraph studio where she works, only to find her alive and well. The father suffers from an intermediate degree of delusion, since he knows his daughter is not on the screen; his delusion consists in believing that she is actually in danger *elsewhere*. Mack Sennett's delusion in *Mabel's Dramatic Career* (1913) is more serious. In a sequence anticipating Bogdanovich's *Targets* (1968)—where a sniper fires at the looming image of Byron Orlok (Boris Karloff) rather than at the "real-life" Orlok coming to apprehend him—Sennett fires at the screen villains threatening his girlfriend (Mabel Normand).

As cinema becomes a mass-medium actually influencing popular aspirations and behavior, it began to satirize those who patterned themselves on filmic models. In *Movin' Pitchers* (1913), children watching the filming of a studio Western envision themselves as participants in the film. In the first version of *Merton of the Movies* (1924), the protagonist's fantasies of stardom in westerns are realized by a silent film-within-the film which then dissolves to the banal realities of life as a small-town grocery clerk. The second version of *Merton* (1932) opens with shots we take to be part of the "real" film, but which are retroactively revealed to be a film screened in the theatre where Merton works as an usher.

Buster Keaton, the poet-laureate of reflexivity in the silent cinema, explored the production processes of film in *The Cameraman* (1928), much as he had dealt with the reception of film in *Sherlock Jr.* In *The Cameraman*, Keaton plays a journalist who buys a movie camera in order to submit some freelance footage to Hearst officials. When a violent free-for-all breaks out at a

Chinatown festival, Buster exacerbates the violence to enliven his material. He lobs exploding bulbs into the midst of the crowd, and puts a knife in the hand of a weary combatant about to abandon the fight. The film exposes documentary "truth" as the product of artifice, anticipating Godard's *boutade* that all films are fiction films. *The Cameraman* also foreshadows Wexler's *Medium Cool*, where media journalists are more concerned with getting exploitable footage than with helping people in pain. The film also capitalizes on cinematic "errors," for Buster's rushes form a compendium of the technical blunders possible to the medium. Keaton even implicitly mocks the idea of mechanical reproduction as guarantor of realism. Bazin's claim that in cinema we enjoy the absence rather than the presence of human intervention finds hilarious confirmation in a sequence where a monkey does the filming. In a *reductio ad absurdam* of the notion that human mediation is dispensable, the simian footage far excels that of the incompetent Buster with its inadvertent double exposures and split frames.

King Vidor's *Show People* (1928) parodies the cliché of the small-time-rags-to-Hollywood-riches genre. Marion Davies, who herself had gone from chorus girl to star, plays Peggy Pepper, a movie-mad Georgia girl who goes to Hollywood in hopes of a career as a serious actress. The "creative geography" of an early sequence has Peggy and her father drive past the Paramount, Fox, First National, and MGM studio lots, all on Hollywood Boulevard, a bit of topographical reshuffling which shows that not even "behind-the-scenes" films about Hollywood need be veracious. The agent at Central Casting misinterprets Peggy's campy imitations of film stars as parodic and offers her a job. She subsequently moves from Comet Studios (a transparent stand-in for Keystone), where she plays a patsy to slapstick comic Billy Boone, to serious stardom at "High Arts Studio." In conformity with the prevailing Francophilia, she changes her name to Patricia Peppoire. She snubs the down-to-earth Billy for an ersatz French leading man, André, who looks and acts like John Gilbert, and calls himself "Le Comte d'Avignon." When Peggy discovers the factitiousness of André's royalty, she returns, considerably humbler, to the unpretentious Billy.

Show People irreverently unveils the actual processes of filmmaking. We see make-up men preparing actors, cameras cranking, directors shouting instructions. At the end of the film, we see Vidor himself directing a World War I epic not unlike his own *The Big Parade*. The film also satirizes the pampered stars of Hollywood and their narcissistic displays of temperament. More importantly, Vidor pits genre against genre, slapstick against costume drama, giving each a precise social connotation. In ways that recall Auerbach's analysis of the political implications of the separation of styles, Vidor portrays comedy as the genre of the unpretentious people, and costume drama as the genre of the elite, of royalty, where prerevolutionary France connotes all that is elegant and aristocratic. In this battle of the high and low mimetic modes, Vidor's allegiance lies clearly with the former.

Film and Productive Labor: The Man with a Movie Camera

A year later, in the Soviet Union, Dziga Vertov made a film which showed art both *as* production and *in relation to* production: *The Man with a Movie Camera* (1929). To appreciate Vertov's achievement we must remember that although all texts are the results of productive labor, not all texts render this work visible to the same degree. In illusionistic spectacle, the traces of work tend to disappear in the magical seamless objects of art. Much as *trompe-l'oeil* painters efface their own work by removing visible brush strokes from the canvas, the illusionistic filmmaker hides the marks of the process of production. Unlike many Hollywood films, even those set in the filmmaking milieu, Vertov's film foregrounds its *own* process of production. The traces of its production cling to the film, as Walter Benjamin said in another context, the way the handprints of the potter cling to the clay vessel.[8]

The multiple themes of *The Man with a Movie Camera*—the life of a person from birth to death, a day in the life of the city, the realization and projection of a film—are in fact subordinated to the film's central subject: the laying bare of the mechanisms of film within the social context of a continuum of productive forces. Applying to cinema the arguments of the Russian formalist-sociologists—who argued that literature was a form of production and that literary producers should engage with their material no differently from a worker in a factory—*The Man with a Movie Camera* shows cinema as one branch of industrial production. Annette Michelson points out that the film systematically juxtaposes virtually every aspect of cinematographic activity with work as it is conventionally conceived.[9] Editing is compared to sewing; cleaning film is compared to cleaning streets. The film industry is likened to the textile industry, which Marx regarded as of paradigmatic importance in the development of capitalism. Cinema, it is implied, will eventually transform socialist society just as the spinning jenny transformed capitalist society. The two forms of production are shown as allied by the similarity of their rhythms and the analogy of their movements. Turning spools of thread are juxtaposed by the editing with the turning reels of a film projector. The hydroelectric plant which provides the energy for the textile industry is revealed as also empowering the vehicles on which the cameraman relies. In every way, film is shown as forming part of the collective life of societal production.

The obligation of the Kinok, for Vertov, was to decipher mystifications, whether found on the screen or in real life. Vertov especially detested the mystification of the "artistic drama," a cinematic form whose purpose, as he

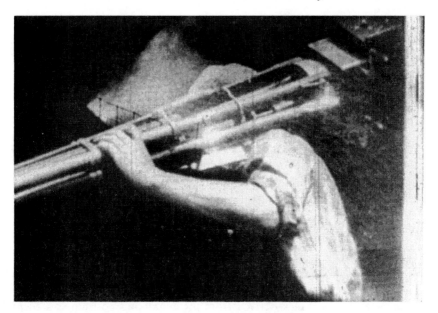

Figure 15.   *The Man with a Movie Camera* (1929)

saw it, was to intoxicate the spectator and insinuate certain reactionary notions into the subconscious. Vertov denounced such films as the new opium of the people, and called for the overthrow of the "immortal kings and queens of the screen" and the reinstatement of "ordinary mortals filmed in life during their habitual occupations." His denunciations tend to have recourse to three kinds of metaphor which will be frequent in the discourse of filmic anti-illusionists: magic ("the cinema of enchantment"): drugs ("ciné-nicotine," "the electric opium of the movie theatres"); and religion ("the high-priests of cinema"). These metaphors, however, were specifically grounded in the historical realities of the moment, for Vertov's struggle against alienated cinema parallels the struggle of the Soviet revolution, in its heroic pre-Stalinist phase, against the triple alienations of magical superstitions among the peasantry, drug addiction and alcoholism among the lumpenproletariat, and the pervasive influence of the Russian Orthodox Church.

The Man with a Movie Camera is a film about film language, whose self-professed task is to "present the cinematic means rather than dissimulate them as is customarily the case" and to "disseminate knowledge concerning the grammar of cinematic techniques."[10] In an act of self-representation, the film presents the movement of its own *écriture*, fulfilling Vertov's ambition of making a "film which produces a film." Rather than pretend to mirror reality, the film shows cinematic art to be a complex signifying practice. Numerous analysts, notably Annette Michelson, Stephen Crofts, and Olivia Rose, have inventoried Vertov's reflexive strategies: the constant foregrounding of the apparatus of camera, projector, and screen; the "diegetic" presence of the roving cinematographer; the recurrent visual puns on lens/eye and shutter/eyelid; the exposure of the trickery involved in filmmaking; the highlighting of the artificiality of filmic movement; the reminders of the screen as surface; the intrusion of animation and slow-motion techniques in the course of conventionally filmed sequences; the subversion of illusion through techniques of fragmentation and temporal and spatial distortion; and the constant appeal to the spectator's intellect. Rarely, in short, has the assault on illusionism been carried out as imaginatively and as uncompromisingly as in *The Man with a Movie Camera.*

Hollywood Reflexivity: The Sound Film

Despite the warnings of visionaries such as Eisenstein and Alexandrov, the advent of sound pushed cinema generally in the direction of realism. But even here there were exceptions, and the exceptions tended to be comic. Much of the poignancy of Harpo Marx derived from his anomolous position as a silent clown wandering in the world of sound comedy, forced to resort to the iconicity of props and mime rather than the symbolism of spoken language, ordering a Scotch, for example, by dancing the Highland Fling. The Marx Brothers also inherited from vaudeville (and indirectly from Elizabethan theatre) their penchant for direct address to the spectator: Groucho invites the audience to go out for a smoke during the piano solo in *Horse Feathers.* The Bob Hope-Bing Crosby "Road" pictures, similarly, reflexively mock their own conventions, as they wink at the camera or muse aloud about how they become involved in such horrendous pictures. In *Road to Utopia* (1945) a shot of the pair looking off-screen segues to a subjective shot of the Paramount logo—the mountain which serves as the studio trademark.

An eccentric Hollywood subgenre—the stuntman film—also merits parenthetical attention. From Ince's *Lucky Devils* (1932) to Rush's *The Stunt Man* (1980) the cinema has exploited the stuntman both in fact and in fiction. The ironic title of *Lucky Devils*, written by former stuntman Bob Rose, refers to a tightknit group of stuntmen who sadly witness the death by accident of one after another of their members. The human casualties of illusionism, they die in staged fires and choreographed crashes. The actors who play the stuntmen, paradoxically, are themselves substituted by stuntmen, in a typical Hollywood redoubling whereby an ounce of demystification is transformed into a pound of mystification. The stunts themselves are tricked up with tacky miniatures and awkward back-projection; the film which exposes trickery itself exploits illusionistic gimmickry. The plots of stuntman films allowed for the incorporation of previous stock footage, and William K. Everson points out that the antepenultimate rapids sequence is partially lifted from Clarence Brown's *Trail of 98*. During the filming of the Brown film in Alaska, a safety device failed, drowning three stuntmen. Is it possible, one wonders, that Ralph Ince included the footage in posthumous homage to these authentic martyrs of versimilitude?

A truly exhaustive discussion of films about film, even restricted to Hollywood, would include murder mysteries with studio backgrounds (*The Preview Murder Mystery*), westerns about the making of westerns (*Movin' Pitchers*), sentimental romances set in Hollywood (*It Happened in Hollywood*), star biographies (*Valentino*), adventure films revolving around filmmaking (*King Kong*), musicals set in the movie capital (*The Goldwyn Follies*), melodramas concerning fictional stars (*A Star is Born*), and adaptations of Hollywood novels (*The Day of the Locust*). Most of these films, however, are not anti-illusionist, and many, far from demystifying the film industry or exposing its mechanisms, idealize it as a wonderland of dreams fulfilled or diabolize it as an enticingly sinful Babylon. Preston Sturges' *Sullivan's Travels* (1941) forms, in this sense, a notable if ambiguous exception. The legitimate heir of the best in silent and sound comedy, of the self-conscious novel, and even, through a childhood spent in Europe, of Dada and surrealism, Sturges offers in *Sullivan's Travels* a sardonic excercise in playful reflexivity. Set in the depression, the film is dedicated "to the memory of those who made us laugh: the motley mountebanks, the clowns, the buffoons, in all times and in all nations, whose efforts have lightened our burden a little."

The protagonist of *Sullivan's Travels* is a comedy and musical director, in some ways reminiscent of Sturges himself, who ventures into the world of poverty to make a "Socially Significant Movie"—*Oh Brother Where Art Thou?* His producers ridicule the idea, insisting that he turn out more of the escapist pablum that has made them wealthy. Proto-auteurist Sullivan complains that the producers regard him as a "minor employee," and finally gets his way. He and his girlfriend (Veronica Lake), closely tailed by a ludicrously overequipped land yacht, hitch freight trains and sleep in flophouses as part of what is essentially a touristic excursion into social misery. Anchored by wealth, they float, in a forties version of radical chic, on the surface of deprivation. After this satiric beginning, however, the film suddenly changes generic and emotional gears. Through a bizarre series of accidents, Sullivan becomes truly wretched, an inmate in a brutal southern prison. At one point he is touched by the affectionate hilarity with which his fellow inmates greet a Mickey Mouse cartoon. Released from prison, he opts for comedy rather than social consciousness, convinced that he does not know enough about poverty to make *Oh Brother, Where Art Thou?* "There's a lot to be said for making people laugh," he says, echoing the film's dedication. "That's all some people have."

Sullivan's Travels forms a generic palimpsest. The Swiftian resonances of the title evoke picaresque satire, in which a voyage becomes the pretext for the critique of diverse milieux and institutions: Hollywood, provincial America, the courts, and prisons. The film's metacinematic weave of genres incorporates the following threads: 1) the Hollywood-film-about-Hollywood; 2) Sennett-style slapstick (the race between land yacht and hot rodder); 2) screwball comedy (the combative romance between Joel McCrea and Veronica Lake); 3) depression documentaries à la Pare Lorentz and "social consciousness" movies like *Grapes of Wrath* (the sequences involving hoboes); 4) chain-gang movies like Mervyn Leroy's *I am a Fugitive from a Chain Gang*; 5) all-black musicals like Vidor's *Hallelujah* (the singing of "Let My People Go" in the black church); and 6) the animated cartoon. In the cockeyed caravan of Sturges' narrative, the anarchic prepubic energy of Keystone chases collides with the sly innuendo of boudoir comedy, and animated cartoons neighbor with chain-gang sequences in a volatile generic mix, moving from comedy to near tragedy and back again with picaresque rapidity. Spectatorial competence is challenged and exhilarated by the dialectical clash of antipathetic codes.

Sullivan's Travels opens with the first of three films-within-the-film. After the dedication to "clowns and mountebanks," the sentimentality of which is underscored by sacharine symphonic music, the film abruptly opens on a desparate struggle between two men on the top of a hurtling train. The two fall off the train, the film ends, and we realize that we have been watching the end of Sturges' previous film. The second film-within-the-film, evoked only through the soundtrack and the shots of Sullivan and company in the movie theatre, is a tearjerker whose mawkishenss is undercut by the burping, wheezing, whistle-blowing, and popcorn-eating audience. The third film is the Mickey Mouse cartoon which elicits such a hearty response from the prisoners. The stylistic diversity of the three films makes us conscious, once again, of genre, while the constant interplay of screen image and spectator makes us aware of ourselves as audience.

Sullivan's Travels is in some ways a deeply critical film. It mercilessly satirizes the Hollywood ethos, the studio system, the success myth, and the American system of justice. It ridicules Hollywood's attempt to capitalize on poverty from a safe and exploitative distance. Unlike Sturges, the jobless (then called "hoboes") had no land yachts to accompany them or doctors to succor them whenever they caught a cold. Sturges also lampoons press-agent hype and the single-minded commercialism of producers. The troop of advance men accompanying Sullivan see his encounters with the impoverished as part of a promotion gimmick. By making the world weep over the plight of the oppressed, Sturges suggests, rich producers hope to get even richer, leaving those who are sentimentally called "the poor" just as deeply enmired in their poverty. He is equally aware of the limitations of American justice. As long as

Sullivan is regarded as a "hobo," he is treated miserably; recognized as a Hollywood director, he wins instant respect. "They don't put directors into prisons like this," he points out, but established power, as long as it sees him as just one more unemployed John Doe, treats him with cavalier inhumanity. Poor people receive one brand of justice, the rich and famous another. Despite *Sullivan's Travels'* apparent endorsement of the protagonist's rejection of "message pictures," the film itself has a high share of messages. The suffering of the chain-gang is portrayed authentically, even if we do experience it through the eyes of a privileged protagonist, and the exposure of class-based justice is clear and effective.

It is Sullivan himself, ironically, who jettisons *Oh Brother Where Art Thou?* precisely at the moment his producers are finally convinced that the film will yield them a fortune. Sullivan ultimately embraces an ideal of purely escapist entertainment, encapsulated by the final prismatic montage of laughing faces, melded into community by animated entertainment, their suffering and status as prisoners momentarily forgotten. Thus the film retreats from the implications of its own satire, drowning mordant critique in a jello of cheap and financially interested sentiment. *Sullivan's Travels* posits, even while it undermines, a false but widely disseminated dichotomy: between serious message pictures (what Veronica Lake disparagingly calls "deep dish movies") on the one hand, and mindless entertainment on the other, a dichotomy, in short between *O Brother Where Art Thou?* and *Hay Hay in the Hay Loft!* The film ridicules the former alternative by the clichés with which the ideal is formulated ("educational tool," "better humanity") and even by the title itself, whose Victorian "O!" and archaically Biblical "Art Thou" condemn it at the preproduction stage. But the dichotomy of sanctimonius Griersonianism and lobotomized pablum is, of course, absurd. The central impulse of Brechtian theatre was to forge an art at once broadly comic *and* intensely political. The notion that art cannot teach, Brecht pointed out, insults both pleasure and learning, implying that pleasure has nothing to teach us and that learning cannot be pleasurable. The Brechtian ideal of joyful learning transcends the dilemma superficially posed by *Sullivan's Travels*. But in the end, Sturges himself subverts the very dichotomy he superficially endorses, for *Sullivan's Travels* is itself instructive *and* pleasurable, entertaining *and* provocative, serious *and* comic.

Sunset Boulevard

The Hollywood-film-about-Hollywood at times serves as a barometer of the state of the industry. Billy Wilder's *Sunset Boulevard* (1950) coming a decade after *Sullivan's Travels*, explores the superimposed crises—economic, technological, esthetic—besetting Hollywood. The postwar period had been marked by serious economic decline. A peak year, 1946, yielded 378 features and a weekly attendance of 90 million people. By 1949, attendance was down to 60 million and only 22 features were in production, resulting in a precipitous decline in studio employment. It is hardly astonishing, therefore, that *Sunset Boulevard*'s protagonist is a scriptwriter down on his luck, or that Hollywood revellers ("writers without jobs, composers without publishers") sing "Buttons and Bows":

> Hollywood for us ain't been so good
> Got no swimming pool
> Very few clothes
> All we earn are buttons and bows.

Other, less direct allusions to the crisis proliferate through the film. Joe Gillis insists that his script can be filmed on location for under a million, an emphasis not surprising in budget-conscious postwar Hollywood. Norma Desmond, in this sense, represents the pampered extravagance of the past. A walking, gesticulating anachronism, she personifies nostalgia for an irretrievable opulence. Wilder systematically pits the new Hollywood of Betty and Arty against the old Hollywood of Norma Desmond and Max von Mayerling, while the amphibian Joe Gillis wanders between the two. He writes one script, oriented toward life and romance, with Betty, and another, haunted by death (*Salomé*) with Norma. Joe and Norma write in a mansion; Joe and Betty write in a cramped cubicle, formerly part of Norma Desmond's dressing room. Norma's $28,000 car sports a 1932 (shortly after sound) license plate, while Joe's has one of "those cheap new things made of chromium and spit." Norma's New Year's party has a full orchestra, gourmet dishes, and champagne; Artie's has communal drinking (bring your own) and music by the partygoers themselves. This newer, in some ways duller world, Wilder seems to be telling us, is considerably healthier than the bigger-than-life decadence of the old Hollywood.

Postwar Hollywood also had to confront the technological challenge of television. Although licensed for commercial use in 1941, it was only in the postwar period that television became the standard electronic furniture of American homes. Hollywood attacked television through advertising ("Don't be a living room captive!") and within its own films, either through systematic exclusion—Jack Warner forbade the appearance of television sets in Warner Brothers films — or through satire (*Will Success Spoil Rock Hunter?*) and calumny (a character in *Dreamboat* calls television the "idiot's delight"). *Sunset Boulevard*, it might be argued, speaks to the television crisis by referring to an earlier technological crisis—the coming of sound. Joe tells Norma that "the audience went away" at a time when Hollywood's audience was literally abandoning it in favor of TV. "I didn't get small," Norma protests, "it's the

Figure 16. *Sunset Boulevard* (1950)

pictures that got small!" Although she is referring to sound pictures, she might as well be alluding to the small screens of television. It is as if Hollywood's postwar anxiety were being displaced onto another crisis that had proved surmountable. Even bad dreams, Freud points out, can reassure. By referring to the needless anxieties of the past, *Sunset Boulevard* indirectly suggests that the film industry would once again survive its present difficulties. It might even be argued that just as aging director Billy Wilder projects his own fears of getting old onto the character of Norma Desmond, so *Sunset Boulevard* projects Hollywood's collective dread of obsolescence onto the antiquated style embodied by Wilder's vampiric personage.

The postwar crisis was also esthetic. The old formulas weren't working, assembly-line production was in decline, and Italian neorealism was making the old studio style seem artificial and passé. *Sunset Boulevard* satirizes the formula writing endemic in Hollywood. Joe describes Norma's script for *Salomé* as a "hodgepodge of melodramatic plots." But Joe's own baseball script is so predictable that the producer guesses its ending immediately. The producer proposes they hybridize formulae in a musical comedy revolving around a women's softball team. The creative potentiality of the dream factory's industrial *combinatoire*, the film suggests, has become temporarily exhausted. Studio creativity has been reduced to the debased intertextuality of file cabinets of plot and formulae.

While on one level Wilder the demanding scriptwriter is mocking the hackneyed writing too frequent in Hollywood, on another he is highlighting the processes by which *all* texts are moulded. Production circumstances as well as history inflect the text. Rain in Arizona forces Artie and crew to rewrite their film for rain. Joe's script about Oakies in the Dust Bowl—a transparent reference to *Grapes of Wrath*—is highjacked by World War II and emerges as a film about a torpedo boat. The war, in other words, forced the social consciousness films of the late thirties to make way for the war films of the forties. The commercial success or failure of other films also inflects the text. Since "psychopaths are selling like hotcakes," Joe proposes a film entitled *Dark Window*—an obvious reference to the popularity of film noir with its nocturnal titles and psychopath protagonists. Every film, in sum, is inescapably shaped both by historical context and filmic intertext.

Sunset Boulevard also inserts itself into the context of postwar critical debate. The film, for example, constantly underlines the role of the scriptwriter. Joe complains that scriptwriters are not sufficiently appreciated: "Audiences forget that films are written; they think the actors make it up as they go along." The adulation goes to those who mouth the words rather than to those who put the words in their mouths. (Holden's naturalistic acting, ironically, makes us forget that *his* words were scripted as well.) This emphasis on the scriptwriter comes in the wake of extensive critical debate in Hollywood concerning the relative importance of the diverse collaborators on a film. Anticipating the auteurist discussions of *Cahiers du Cinéma*, the journal *Screen Writer* in 1947 devoted an entire issue to the question of whether. screenwriters could become film authors. The highly literate and informed Wilder was doubtless aware of these debates, and *Sunset Boulevard* offers his response to some of the questions raised.

Although *Sunset Boulevard* is in many ways an illusionistic film that happens to take Hollywood as its profilmic milieu, there are notable gaps and fissures in its illusionism. The most striking is the film's posthumous narrator presumably telling his tale as he lies floating on the surface of Norma Desmond's pool. While the "first-person" voice-over narrative normally lends itself to anticipation thanks to its avowedly retrospective character, Wilder cheats by making the narration *post mortem*. Although the posthumous narrator is to be found in literature—Machado de Assis' *Posthumous Memories of Bras Cubas* has its defunct narrator censure the banality of the eulogies proffered at his own funeral—and although a number of films use *dying* narrators—for example, Rocha's *Land in Anguish*, Jabor's *All Nudity Will Be Punished*, and Wilder's own *Double Indemnity*—rarely have films been so audacious as to posit a *dead* narrator like Joe Gillis in his acquatic bier. The circular structure of the film further underscores the implausibility of the device. The narrative discourse begins *in ultimas res*, so that the proleptic weight of predestination hangs over the entire enterprise. Gillis' off-screen voice—is a voice "off" when the character is dead?—mocks its former owner in the third person: "Poor dope, he always wanted a pool... and in the end he got one." Hollywood pools are synecdochic, the part standing for the whole of affluence and the good life, and four pool-featuring sequences chart Joe's trajectory toward death. Gillis begins and ends in the pool, as if his "story" had spent the length of the film catching up with his "plot."

The device of the posthumous narrator is especially appropriate to a film which mixes fact and fiction by incorporating characters of diverse ontological status, ranging from actors playing themselves (Buster Keaton, Cecil B. De Mille) to celebrities playing characters partially resembling themselves (Gloria Swanson as Norma Desmond, Erich von Stroheim as Max von Mayerling), to actors playing characters with no clear relation to themselves (William Holden, Jack Webb). The Norma Desmond character typifies this fact-fiction amalgam. Like Norma, Gloria Swanson did in fact work with Sennett and Cecil B. De Mille (and with Stroheim on *Queen Kelly*), and as a silent star was famous for wild romances and extravagant spending. Unlike Norma Desmond, however, she did make a successful transition to sound, winning an academy award for *The Trespasser*. She excoriates sound, ironically, in a fine sound performance superimposed on an exaggeration of the coded gesticulations of the silent cinema. The device is appropriate, finally, in a film about Hollywood, which is at once a spot on the map and a state of mind, in a film which melds fantasy and realism, which simultaneously elicits belief and fosters skepticism. At one point, Betty and Joe walk down a studio street—"all hollow, all phony, all done with mirrors." All of which could be said, of course, of *Sunset Boulevard* itself.

The Musical and Self-Flaunting Artifice

There were at least two generic exceptions to the broad reign of dramatic realism as the dominant aesthetic in the Hollywood fiction film—the musical comedy and the animated cartoon. Since two of the constitutive elements of the musical—music and dance—share a relatively minor interest in conventional mimesis, it might be argued that the musical inclines more readily to self-conscious artifice than other genres. Although music affects us intensely, it makes little direct reference to "reality." Despite rare instances of a "programmatic" nature, music is not intrinsically representational. It forms, rather, what Suzanne Langer would call a "tonal analogue" to mental and emotional life. Dance, similarly, performs a stylized abstraction of everyday movement. Since music and dance are central to the musical, audiences are more disposed to accept outlandish sets, implausible plots, and stereotypical characters. By their generic nature, musicals orchestrate everyday life into choreographed fantasy. Humbert Humbert in *Lolita* defines musicals as "an essentially grief-proof sphere of existence wherefrom death and truth were banned." No audience literally believes that New York gangs actually pirouette down slum streets or that invisibly vast symphonic orchestras accompany lone small-town strollers. The impossibly grandiose production numbers of a Busby Berkeley, with their gaudy extravagances and kaleidoscopic visual effects, owe scant allegiance to verisimilitude. The lovelier-than-life grace of Fred Astaire, the fairy-tale characterizations of *The Wizard of Oz*, the redundantly phallic bananas of *The Gang's All Here*, the painterly charm of *An American in Paris*, Carmen Miranda's tutti-frutti hats and loveably tasteless self-parodies all have this in common—they create an idealized utopia of autonomous make-believe.

Many musical comedies display what Jane Feuer, in her excellent study of the musical, calls "conservative reflexivity."[11] From the beginning the musical has exploited the alienation devices which we normally associate with Brecht and the leftist avant-garde: direct address to the camera/audience; the foregrounding of the processes of artistic production; the inscription of the audience within the film itself; transparently non-diegetic musical orchestration; the disjunction between aural and image scale; and the intertextual quotation of other films. But this reflexivity, as Feuer points out, is ultimately recuperative, an example of "innovation as conservation." Direct address, rather than a calculated violation of conventional cinematic grammar as in Godard, becomes merely an homage to the intimacy of live entertainment, a means of packaging third-person "history" as reciprocal "discourse." The foregrounding of artistic process, similarly, usually ends up by "cheating" in effacing the musical's origins in labor (dance, choreography) and technology (filming).

Two Kelly-Donen musicals—*Singin' in the Rain* (1952) and *It's Always Fair Weather* (1955)—illustrate both the possibilities and limitations of reflexivity in the musical. The former film exploits the ambiance of what are obviously the MGM studios in a study of the transitional era that took Hollywood from silent to sound film, exploring the responses of three emblematic characters to this technological rite of passage. Silent movie queen Lina Lamont (Jean Hagen) becomes one of sound's casualties, done in by a kind of media euthanasia when she is exposed in her vocal mediocrity and Brooklyn patois. Kathy Selden (Debbie Reynolds) begins as a voice double, a kind of aural stuntperson, and rises through talent to a stardom that the silent cinema might not have offered. Matinee idol Don Lockwood, finally, charms his way through the transition with Darwinian adaptability.

Singin' in the Rain plays on the tension, common in musicals, between "high" elite art and popular "low" art: conservatory and honky-tonk, dramatic academy and vaudeville. Kathy Selden initially scorns the "vulgarity" of the movies. The voice of both theatrical superiority and cinematic reflexivity, she dismisses Lockwood as "nothing but a shadow on film." Her high-art snobbery is debunked, however, when she is seduced by Lockwood and his medium, the seduction taking place, appropriately, on a sound-stage. Lockwood leads Kathy onto an empty stage, preparing it as if for a film. He animates the fog and wind machines and paints an electronic sunset as background for a love ballad ("You were meant for me"). Love is presented as a studio construct.

Singin' in the Rain inventories the technical "bugs" of the sound cinema in its first stammering phase: awkward synchronization, microphones hidden in bushes and bodices, the inadvertent recording of thumping hearts and jiggling pearls. The film also evokes Professor de Forest and his synchronized demonstration films by showing a nasal-voiced scientist slowly mouthing an audio-visual tautology: "You are watching a talking picture. It is a picture of me, and I am talking. Note how my lips and the sound issuing from them are synchronized in perfect unison." The witnesses of the demonstration, lacking the hindsight available to the makers of *Singin' in the Rain*, dismiss the invention as a vulgar toy without a future, while the film "estranges" the very devices by which the picture we are seeing was made.

Singin' in the Rain revels in its own intertextuality at what Kelly himself called a "conglomeration of bits of movie lore." The film's point of departure— Arthur Freed's desire to incorporate his best songs from earlier MGM musicals—makes it an anthology of self-quotations. The only two new songs

Figure 17.   *Singin' in the Rain* (1952)

are explicitly intertextual: "Make 'Em Laugh" is a song-and-dance tribute to slapstick, and "Moses" spoofs the postsound elocutionist craze. In *Singin' in the Rain*, films are enclosed within films enclosed within films, forming a veritible Chinese box of regressive duplicating effects. The costume drama *The Dueling Cavalier* is transformed into the Broadway musical *Dancing Cavalier* by having the protagonist-dancer *dream* the already-filmed costume drama while resting between performances. The film ends with a clinching self-citation: Selden and Lockwood embracing before a billboard advertising *Singin' in the Rain*.

Its painterly sets, lavish colors, exuberant dancing, and intertextual homages make *Singin' in the Rain* a summa of playful Hollywood self-flaunting artifice. The film exposes some of the machinations of illusionistic trickery to engender illusion anew. The film has the "real" voice of Debbie Reynolds, for example, replace the "false" one of Jean Hagen. In fact, however, Hagen dubbed her own voice precisely on those scenes where Kathy Selden is supposedly dubbing hers onto Lina's. Thus the film has it both ways; the reflexive devices designate film as illusion, while the film itself casts an illusory spell. It portrays a world where singers in the rain do not catch colds, a world characterized, as Richard Dyer suggests concerning musicals generally, by magical energy, inexhaustible abundance, and utopian community, in a film whose transparent artifice designates that very world as factitious.[12]

Like *Sunset Boulevard* before it, *Singin' in the Rain* "displaces" contemporary crises—the crises in the musical genre, the challenge of television—onto earlier crises already surpassed and other rapids safely negotiated, thus nourishing the illusion that the studio system itself was not in crisis. *It's Always Fair Weather*, in contrast, directly reflects both crises, resulting in an "anti-musical" which goes against the optimistic grain of the genre. The real subject of the musical, as many critics have pointed out, is entertainment, and often, as Thomas Elsaesser puts it, "the world of the musical becomes a kind of ideal image of the [film] medium itself."[13] While not set in Hollywood like *Singin' in the Rain*, *It's Always Fair Weather* addresses the subject of cinema's rival medium—television—while it deconstructs the musical genre. The film's premise has three World War II friends reunite 10 years after their discharge only to discover that they have virtually nothing in common. An animated tryptych, using split-screen and freeze-frames, initially charts their parallel trajectories from soldier to civilian: Doug (Dan Dailey) has shed his artistic ambitions to become a gray-flannel executive and designer of television commercials. Angie (Michael Kidd) has accumulated children as part of the postwar Baby Boom, while Ted (Gene Kelly) has accumulated, and de-accumulated both women and money as a gambler and fight promoter. *It's Always Fair Weather* does offer some of the traditional satisfactions of the genre: the transfiguration of the quotidian (the dance of the garbage lids), the utopian transformation of work into play (the Stillman's Gym sequence), and happy endings for its three major characters. At the same time, a morbid backbeat pounds throughout the film. The title, with its meterological echo of *Singin' in the Rain*, becomes an ironic allusion to the shallow optimism of the fifties. Rather than the ritual affirmation of shared values, the film offers the mise-en-scène of social loneliness. Donen/Kelly repeatedly exploit the wide-screen format to simultaneously mingle, and separate, the three major characters. The disastrous reunion-dinner sequence uses interior monologue and masking effects to reveal the hostility of each of the men toward the other two, virtually literalizing the notion of the "lonely crowd." The "Once I Had a Dream" sequence, meanwhile, shows the threesome, together on the screen but alone in the diegesis, doing a privatized dance whose gestures signify disgust and disillusionment.

In *It's Always Fair Weather*, the characters seldom dance to express joy. In at least two sequences, they dance because they are drunk. The first dance occurs after Ted has received a "Dear John" letter and drinks to drown his sorrow. Doug's "situation-wise" dance, similarly, is fueled by eight martinis. On the verge of a breakdown, unable to maintain a coherent conversation—back projection emphasizes his sense of separation from his colleagues—he dances in a kind of improvisatory rage. Along with the traditional affirmation of spontaneity and self-expression, we find here a revolt against corporate uniformity. The dance is satirical, a revolt against normality rather than a transfiguration of it.

It's Always Fair Weather also alludes directly to cinema's emerging rival—television. Like Kazan-Schulberg's *A Face in the Crowd* (1957), the film highlights the consequences of live transmission. During a "This-is-Your-Life" style program, the gangsters chasing Kelly break in and start a brawl. Knowing the television cameras are running, Kelly extracts a confession from the gangster. The film therefore associates television with a positive function—sending criminals to jail (doubtless an allusion to the televised Kefauver hearings on organized crime)—along with a negative aesthetic which mingles the cloying phoniness of the show's host (Dolores Gray) with high art pretensions and exploitative vulgarity. In any case, the three friends only regain their wartime sense of camaraderie in a new war against the common enemy chosen by countless fifties films—the mob.

Reflexivity and Animation

The animated cartoon also opted for fantasy despite a general climate favoring realism. In order to satisfy the expectations of the genre, the animation artist has not only the freedom but even the duty to be antirealistic. In the surreal world of animation, characters are endowed with magical resiliency and gravity-defying powers. Figures flattened into pancakes by bulldozers simply shake themselves back into life. Since the genre is premised on the absurd—no one really believes that Bugs Bunny represents an actual species of anglophonic rabbit—the temptation to illusionism is diminished. Even if multiplane cameras permit the simulation of tracking and dolly shots, furthermore, animation still tends toward antimimesis since it consists of the frame-by-frame *construction*, rather than the *imitation* of movement. Bodies can be bifurcated and just as easily reunited. An athlete's race across a football field can be rendered by a streak of paint, a fleeing cat reduced to a tail and a vertiginous blur.

A series of mutually reinforcing prejudices—against comedy, against the reflexive mode, against the "childish" fables and fairy tales that constitute their source material—have generally relegated cartoons to the bottom rung of the generic ladder. For anti-illusionists, on the other hand, cartoons offer alternative models of representation and continuity. In the two-dimensional world of film, it might be said, some genres are more two-dimensional than others. Since the drawings from which cartoons are made *begin* as two-dimensional, unlike the profilmic "reality" usually registered by a camera incorporating the code of perspective, the impression of depth depends entirely on tricks of design. Kristin Thompson points out that the cel animation technique—which consists of separating portions of a drawing onto different layers to eliminate the necessity for redrawing the entire composition for each frame—encourages certain formal disruptions by allowing for an overlay of two perspectival systems (independent of the lens) within a single image.[14]

Cartoons frequently exploit the kind of self-referential gags considered anathema in "straight" cinema. Krazy Kat habitually announced his arrival by saying: "Envy me, mice, I'm going into pictures." In Chuck Jones' *What's Opera, Doc?*, we see the drawn pencils and erasers of the animator placing Porky Pig within a parodistically Wagnerian landscape. At the tragic conclusion, Bugs Bunny mocks the naiveté of his audience: "So what did you expect in an opera, a happy ending?" Tex Avery, for his part, often parodies Disney. *Crazy Squirrel* begins by evoking a serenely Disneyesque animal world presided over by a squirrel hero subsequently thrown out by a "crazy" squirrel whose sadomasochistic cartoons arguably make a satiric comment on the filmmaking milieu. Stromboli's Marionette Theatre in Disney's *Pinocchio* (1940), according to William Paul, presents analogies to Hollywood's production hierarchies. Gepetto, the dedicated artist (read filmmaker) contrasts with Stromboli, the corrupt producer, in ways that translate Disney's own distrust of Hollywood moguls.

Chuck Jones' *Duck Amuck* (1953), meanwhile, provides a paradigmatic instance of the reflexive cartoon. The film consists of a running battle between an eraser-and-pencil-wielding artist and his creation, Daffy Duck. The artist subjects Daffy to swift and arbitrary changes in scenery, creating a space as wildly discontinuous as the simultaneously arctic and tropical "hybrid" decor of Jarry's *Ubu Roi.* The beleaguered duck hardly knows whether to shiver or swelter, sing Hawaiian love songs or "Dashing Through the Snow." At one point, the artist erases the duck's feet to prevent escape; when Daffy protests, the creator paints his mouth shut. Deprived of scenery, Daffy protests: "Buster, it may come as a complete surprise to you to find that this is an animated cartoon, and that in animated cartoons they have scenery. . . . " At the finale, the camera tracks back to reveal the animation board and the animator—Bugs Bunny—itself being painted by what is presumably the hand of the ultimate animator—Chuck Jones.

The subject of *Duck Amuck* is the nature of animation technique itself. By extension, the film constitutes a frame-by-frame celebration of the cinematic apparatus itself, an essay by demonstration on the nature of illusion not only in animation but in film generally. The first sequence—an unbroken right-to-left tracking shot discovering a series of sets and designs—focuses attention on the cinematic frame. Daffy jumps in and out of the frame in a desparate attempt to keep up with the camera and with the costume changes required by the shifting scenery. When the frame lines, subsequently, appear to collapse on Daffy, he tries to prop them up. When that tactic fails, he shreds the encroaching black areas and demands that the picture begin, only to be cut off by an iris-in to black superimposed with the words "The End." At another point, the image wanders vertically from its proper frame, splitting the screen and leaving two images of Daffy. The newly schizoid duck regards his double in the other frame—and begins to fight with it. Another instance highlights the difference between off-screen space in animation and off-screen space in live-action films. As Daffy is playing a musketeer before a castle background, a brush enters the frame and paints in a farmyard. Daffy then exits screen-left and returns with the appropriate hoe and overalls. But his exit is absurd, since cartoon characters, unlike live actors, cannot possibly change costume or fetch props off-screen: their very existence is defined as on-screen and intra-frame.

Duck Amuck highlights the innumerable technical and aesthetic decisions involved in filmmaking. When a minuscule Daffy pleads with distant voice for a close-up, the animator gives him only a tiny rectangle to isolate the duck's face in the corner of the frame. When Daffy insists on a *real* close-up, the animator zooms in violently to an extreme close-up of two infuriated eyeballs. Jones also calls attention to the fact of sound synchronization. When no sound emerges from a strummed guitar, Daffy raises a sign requesting "Sound Please!" He strums again, and machine-gun fire explodes on the soundtrack. Daffy tries to protest, and a rooster's crow issues from his lips. *Duck Amuck* even anticipates *Persona* by incorporating projection mishaps into the film itself; Jones simulates a situation in which the film catches in the projector gate.

At the end of the film, totally exasperated and his voice failing, Daffy, rather like a Bergman character gesticulating against the silent heavens, pleads to his tormentor: "Who is reponsible for this? I demand that you show yourself!" Thus, *Duck Amuck*, while underscoring the awkward material contingency of film—depending as it does on functioning projectors and resilient film stock— also stresses the humiliating servitude of the created character, subject to every whim of the omnipotent designer's brush.[15]

Auteurism and Its Discontents

The decline of the Hollywood studio system, shown already in *Sunset Boulevard* and continuing throughout the fifties and sixties, coincided with the rise of auteurist film theory and of public awareness of European filmmakers like Godard and Fellini. Although the idea of the film author was a fairly traditional one in the cinema, implicit in the very concept of cinema as the "seventh art," it was only in the postwar period that the auteurist metaphor became a key structuring concept subtending film theory and criticism and, at times, filmmaking practice. In France, auteurism was closely allied with the attack by the new wave directors on the rigid production hierarchies and conventional narrative procedures of the established system. In defending the rights of the director vis-à-vis the producer, the new wave directors attempted to dynamite out a place for themselves.

One American film which reflects this changing conjuncture is Vincent Minnelli's *Two Weeks in Another Town* (1962). The period of transition from the studio system saw the rise of international co-productions—films shot in Europe on slightly lower budgets, featuring veteran American actors and directors. By 1962, many American film technicians, actors and directors sought work in Italy, to the point that Rome came to be known as Hollywood-by-the-Tiber. *Two Weeks in Another Town* concerns the making of such a co-production. Thomas Elsaesser sees most of Minelli's films as thinly disguised auteurist parables, whether in the musicals, with their magic triumphs of vision over reality, or in the dramatic comedies, where tragedy takes the form of constraints on an emotional or artistic temperament, or in the melodramas, many of which feature artist-protagonists: the painters of *Lust for Life* and *The Cobweb*, the musician of *Tea and Sympathy*, the novelist in *Some Came Running*[16]. Minnelli's films, in this sense, "stage" the artist's struggle against constraints and thus simultaneously prepare for and illustrate in advance the auteurist argument that studio directors like Minnelli are in fact auteurs exhibiting a strong thematic and stylistic personality consistent over time.

Although based on Irwin Shaw's novel, *Two Weeks in Another Town* undoubtedly reflects Minnelli's feelings about his career and his craft. The director figure is split into two protagonists: the prestigious but aging Maurice

Kruger (Edward G. Robinson) and the younger but emotionally unstable actor-turned-director Jack Andrus (Kirk Douglas). Minnelli refers to his own career and his own director-actor relationship with Kirk Douglas by positing Andrus and Kruger as a team that had made many films together. Kruger, working on an international co-production at Cinecittà, offers a small role to the recuperating Andrus. When the filming goes badly, Kruger invites Andrus to take over the dubbing, and after a heart attack, he implores him to take over the direction. By this slow substitution, Minnelli allegorizes, as it were, the death of the old system and the birth of a new one.[17]

Jean-Luc Godard's *Contempt* (1963) fits squarely into the tradition of films about filmmaking and even of Hollywood films about Hollywood. It shares with *Two Weeks in Another Town* its auteurist subtext as well as its Italian setting. Indeed, in his *Introduction à une Véritable Histoire du Cinéma*—a sequential discussion of his own films paired with the films that inspired him—Godard links *Contempt* to two antecedent self-referential films: *The Man with a Movie Camera* and *Two Weeks in Another Town*. As an international co-production (French, Italian, and American) in an era of co-productions, when American money was being invested in European film production, *Contempt* also reflects on this internationalization of European cinema, painting a world in which the camaraderie of a Renoir production and even Hollywood-style studio collaboration has given way to the ephemeral, artificial, and polyglot reality of multinational cinema.

Contempt's twin diegesis concerns love and filmmaking and their interrelations—"the unmaking of a couple and the making of a film," in Marie Claire Ropars' succinct phrase. The American producer Jeremiah Prokosch (Jack Palance) invites scriptwriter Paul Laval (Michel Piccoli) to collaborate on a film version of *The Odyssey*. Prokosch expresses dissatisfaction with his director, Fritz Lang (Lang himself). Paul's wife Camille (Brigitte Bardot), meanwhile, tells Paul that she despises him, for reasons that remain obscure but which presumably derive from Paul's apparent readiness to pander her to Prokosch in order to advance his own career. In Capri for the filming, she allows Paul to see her kissing Prokosch. Camille and Prokosch die in an automobile accident, but Lang continues filming *The Odyssey*.

Contempt adapts Alberto Moravia's novel *Il Disprezzo*. Although less cavalier than other Godard adaptations, the reworking involves significant changes, particularly in terms of focalization and point-of-view. The novel is narrated in the first person by screenwriter Ricardo Molteni (Paul in the film) whose wife has died in an automobile accident. Thus the entire novel is a reminiscence, by a narrator of often dubious reliability, attempting to make retroactive sense out of the decline of their relationship. The film version is neither narrated in the first person, nor is it a reminiscence, nor is it told from any particular point-of-view, beyond, perhaps, that of the cinema itself, incarnated by the camera which frames us in the first shot. In short, Godard has, typically, depersonalized and depsychologized his source material.

Godard also slightly shuffles Moravia's characters in relation to their expressed opinions. The configuration of characters—producer (Battista in the novel, Prokosch in the film), writer (Ricardo, Paul), woman (Emilia, Camille), and director (Rheingold, Lang), is homologous but their opinions are redistributed. In the film, it is the director (Lang) who defends the unproblematic heroism of the Homeric world (and not the writer as in the novel), while the writer (Paul) emphasizes the interior drama of Ulysses, onto whom he projects his own present-day marital difficulties. The producers in both film and novel envision the film version of *The Odyssey* as spectacular— "Homer put monsters and prodigies into the *Odyssey* and I want you to put monsters and prodigies into the film"—but Godard melds the traits of Battista in the novel with features of the actual producers of *Contempt*: Carlo Ponti and Joseph Levine, both of whom were associated with the spaghetti epics mocked in the film. Joseph Levine is reported to have demanded the nude shots of Brigitte Bardot, and Godard eventually gave in to the pressure, but in ways, as we have seen, that undercut the producers' intentions.

The casting of Jack Palance, an actor typically identified with film noir gangsters, tells us something about Godard's view of the cultural role of producers. His encounters with Hollywood producers, Godard once said, were his apprenticeship in oppression; they taught him, at 35, what it must feel like to be black in Mississippi. On another level, Godard's sparring with his financial backers recalls Sterne's facetious dedication in *Tristram Shandy*: "Offered to the highest bidder." "I will prostitute myself," Godard seems to be saying, but not without denouncing the sordid processes in which we are taking part. If producers are pimps, directors are prostitutes, and the real subject of *Contempt* is artistic prostitution. Camille despises Paul, perhaps, not so much because he is willing to prostitute her but because he is willing to prostitute himself.

Contempt constitutes an auteurist cry of resentment against producers generally and against Carlo Ponti and Joseph Levine in particular. Jeremiah Prokosch, whose name combines the initial letters of Levine's first name and Ponti's last name, is portrayed as a kind of savage god. In fact, he claims a special relationship with the divinities: "I like the gods," he tells Lang, "because I know how they feel." Prokosch is the thundering Jupiter of the cinematic Olympus, wielding lightning power through the electrifying force of megabucks. If Lang conveys the dignity and prestige of the cinema, Prokosch evokes the self-importance of its industrial managers. Just as Paul Laval represents a debased shadow of Ulysses, Jeremiah Prokosch, more profiteer than prophet, represents a grotesque parody of his Biblical namesake. His voice, his stride, and his flatulent sports car suggest vast stores of unwarranted arrogance. His body language signifies and communicates domination, and his discourse inclines to the imperative. His semiliteracy goes hand in hand with an elitist scorn for the public he presumably serves: "This is fine for you and me, Fritz, but do you think the public will understand?" A twentieth-century Polonius, he quotes maxims from his *vade mecum* (a little red book of vacuous proverbs): "The wise man does not impress others with his own superiority." Prokosch, in sum, plays the barbarian to Lang's Greek.

Lang, on the other hand, incarnates the dignity of the cinema which is the only true hero in *Contempt*. Observing the scene with Olympian serenity, Lang exudes courtesy and grandeur, the nature of his monocular gaze evoking the superior look of an impassive camera eye. Godard turns the director in the Moravia novel, named Rheingold and described as "not in the same class as the Pabsts and the Langs," into Lang himself, and embroiders the film with references to the Lang career and persona. Lang aptly personifies the history of the cinema, having actively helped shape it from the silent period in Germany through sound innovation in *M* and later in Hollywood. Lang is an "epic" director in both the Greek and Brechtian senses of that word. One of his early silent films—*Die Nibelungen*—treated the Germanic equivalent of Homeric song. His rigorous antinaturalism and disinterest in characterological depth recall Brecht, and indeed Lang collaborated with Brecht in Hollywood on *Hangmen Also Die* and refers at one point to our "poor B.B." *Contempt*, in fact, offers the distanced eroticism of B.B. (Brigitte Bardot) as seen by B.B. (Bertolt Brecht).

Godard does not limit his critique to the personality of one producer; he focuses rather on the structure of relations between the producers and the artists and technicians who actually make the film. It is this insight into the material and organizational infrastructure of cinema that prevents *Le Mépris* from being merely an outburst of auteurist pique at uncomprehending producers. Prokosch represents the industrial "owners" of cinematic culture; he sees art as a consumer product to be bought and sold. The artist is obliged to sell his own talent as if it were a commodity. Lang quotes Brecht, his friend and colleague who also had his share of problems with Hollywood producers:

> Each morning to earn my bread
> I go to the market of lies
> And hopefully take my place
> Alongside the vendors.

This frank recognition that the artist in capitalist society has to be a merchant in the market of lies deepens the critique in *Contempt*. Although the analysis of cinema's economic infrastructure remains superficial in comparison with Godard's later work, *Contempt* does show the director as subject to the aesthetic whims and financial manipulations of producers. Godard even brings

Figure 18.   *Contempt* (1963)

out certain Fascist overtones in Prokosch's heavy-handed manipulation of the cinema. Lang, as Paul points out, fled Nazi Germany immediately after Goebbels asked him to head the Reich's film industry. Prokosch interrupts Paul to say: "It isn't 1933 any more, it's 1963." The precise dating of the text is typical of Godard, who never pretends that his films are timeless or outside history. But the juxtaposition of the two dates suggests that Prokosch, in Godard's view, reincarnates fascism in a subtler form. Godard reinforces the suggestion elsewhere in the film. Prokosch, Lang claims, "isn't a producer but a dictator." Cinecittà, where the *Odyssey* is being filmed, was founded by the Italian Fascists in 1937. When Paul mentions the word "culture," Prokosch responds: "Whenever I hear the word culture, I get out my checkbook," a variation on Goebbels' notorious and too-well-executed *diktat*: "Whenever I hear the word culture, I get out my revolver." Prokosch, then, embodies the fascism of money and its contempt for all values other than monetary ones. Goebbels' fascism literally murders culture; Prokosch's buys it off. The former works through racist totalitarianism, the latter through tyrannical economic pressure on art.

    Le Mépris incorporates the Brechtian principle that art should reveal the principles of its own construction. The film documents all the stages of film production: scripting, location hunting, casting, rehearsals, rushes, and so on. Filmic texts are shown to be the end-result of innumerable practical and aesthetic choices, shaped by diverse collaborators before being frozen into a definitive sequence of images and sounds. The filmmakers debate alternative strategies of adaptation: Paul proposes a psychoanalytic reading closely reflecting his personal domestic crisis, while Lang hopes to transmit a sense of Homeric grandeur and Prokosch prefers a nicely packaged "artistic" spectacular. *Contempt* itself, we are reminded, resulted from the very processes we are observing. By showing the process of constitution of the text, Godard shows it to be a made thing, a laboriously constructed artifact which is not "natural" and therefore need not be "naturalistic."

Fellini and *8 1/2*

The same year as *Contempt*, Fellini released his *8 1/2*. Borrowing the *mise-en-abŷme* strategy deployed by Gide in *Paludes* (which features a novelist writing *Paludes*), *Faux-Monnayeurs*, and *Les-Caves du Vatican*, Fellini offers us a film which Metz calls "doubly doubled," with a "double mirror construction": "It is not only a film about the cinema, it is a film about a film that is presumably about the cinema; it is not only a film about a director, but a film about a director who is reflecting himself onto his film."[18] Rather than explore in depth a film already anatomized by others in great detail, we will limit ourselves here to sketching out the singular qualities of its multi-leveled

Figure 19.   *Contempt* (1963)

reflexivity.[19] A retrospective summa of Fellini's work, *8 1/2* is reflexive, first of all, as a film about filmmaking. But the film is also reflexive in less obvious ways. Fellini allegorizes the cinema, for example, by proposing surrogate artists whose work bears analogies to filmmaking—the function of the magician, for example, is to stage spectacles, transmit thoughts, put people in communication—and by generally highlighting the theatricality present in privileged moments of collective existence. At the same time, Fellini provokes audience awareness of its own experience of film through abrupt redefinitions of orientation and mode. The film offers, finally, a metacritical account of the cinema through Guido's conversations with Daumier/Carini. Through these conversations, Fellini not only dialogues with past and future commentators on his films, but also conveys the dialogic process of directorial inner speech, the incessant internal debate of exuberant creator and nagging critic.

Fellini's film about filmmaking especially concentrates on the preproduction phase. The only moment where we see Guido actually directing—the moment near the end of the film when he picks up a megaphone and gives orders to players and crew—is a highly ambiguous one because it forms part of the very sequence in which Guido presumably decides to *abandon* his film. What we do witness generally is the agony of preproduction choice-making: consultations with the screen-writer, financial haggling with the producer, the casting of major and minor roles, the projection of screen tests. Guido's relation with his producer, while more amicable than Lang's with Prokosch, is nevertheless fraught with tension. (Impatient, the producer announces a press conference as a way of forcing Guido to begin the film). *8 1/2* also privileges, as does Fellini's own filmic practice, the painstaking search for the right physiognomies. The screentests show different actresses incarnating the part of the mistress, and we become aware that each choice would not only modify the character's relation to the "real-life" Carla but would also subtly alter the feeling of the film.

The most striking feature of *8 1/2* in comparison to the other films-about-filmmaking we have discussed is the absolute centrality of Guido as the source of the sounds and images we experience. There is virtually no sequence in the film which Guido, whether as man or boy, indeed at times as *both* man and boy, does not dominate. The film oscillates constantly between interiorized and exteriorized sequences, but Guido is crucial to both. At times Guido is visible in the image, and at times he is equated with the camera which is addressed, questioned, waved to, harassed. At times this oscillation between Guido-seeing and Guido-seen is so abrupt and ambiguous that we cannot be certain of the precise diegetic status of the filmic event. When the ethereal Claudia turns down Guido's bed, are we witnessing a fantasy or a proleptic concretization of a sequence in the film-to-be? What do we make of Guido's "subjunctive" suicide, or of the twin dénouements of the film? It becomes virtually impossible to distinguish between the film, the film-within-the-film, the imagined film, and the general flux of Guido's mental activity.

The auteurist subjectivism of *8 1/2* renders Guido's inner speech audible and visible. In this sense the film features, as Kaja Silverman has suggested, "its own author as the text's transcendental signified."[20] What saves the film from total solipsism is the fact that the film-about-film narrative becomes the springboard for a meditation on the psychic processes of memory, desire, and creation. Thus *8 1/2* is personal but not private; the associative processes of Guido's mind are not without analogies to our own. Guido's mind is a heterotopia, a mental carnival in which we hear the echoes of a multiplicity of socially constituted voices: the father, the mother, the wife, the lover, the critic, the Church. He *is* this multiplicity of voices: "I am this confusion." If in one sense the film concretizes the internal discourse of a protagonist who *happens to be* a filmmaker, in another it asserts a special affinity between cinema and the inner speech of voluntary and involuntary memory, of vision and the oneiric. It is, finally, no accident that Guido is a cinéaste, a man given to strong mental imagery, or that the very film which foregrounds subjectivity is also the film that multiplies reflexive devices and calls attention to the work of a signifier deeply imbued with the imaginary.

In the wake of *Contempt* and *8 1/2*, the sixties, the seventies, and the eighties witness a mitotic proliferation of reflexive films, many of them "descendants" of these two landmark films. More broadly, the diverse international "new waves"—Brazilian cinema novo, new German cinema, and the new Hollywood of Bogdanovich, Scorcese, and Coppola—build on the self-referential intertextuality of the French new wave as well as on the growing corpus of films-about-filmmaking. While an exhaustive account of reflexivity in the last few decades is beyond the scope of our study, we can, perhaps, survey some key films in this fecund tradition, if only to indicate the lines of interest they might present for a future in-depth analysis.

The New Hollywood: Peter Bogdanovich and *Targets*

As an early representative of what might be called the "American New Wave," (with Malibu standing in for the Left Bank), Peter Bogdanovich melds the influence of the French movement with the closer-to-home impact of Roger Corman's American International Pictures where Bogdanovich got his filmmaking start. Many features of his *Targets* (1969)—its low-budget sensationalism, its improvisational feeling, its mobile camera style—are typical of Corman productions. At the same time, Bogdanovich sprinkles his films with references to his adored directors: verbal mentions of Preminger and Antonioni; direct quotation of Hawks' *The Criminal Code*; a postmortem clean-up modeled on Hitchcock's *Psycho*: a vertical track up scaffolding reminiscent of *Citizen Kane*. "All the best pictures have been made," Sammy (Bogdanovich) complains to Orlok (Boris Karloff), thus recognizing the potentially paralyzing weight of the intertext. *Targets*, in fact, is quite literally woven from prior texts, in the sense that it combines, following Corman's suggestion, 18 minutes of outtakes from another Corman picture, *The Terror*, with 20 minutes of new material featuring Karloff, plus 40 minutes of new material determined by Bogdanovich, through the narrative device of interviewing two stories, one concerning Karloff, the other concerning an anonymous assassin, having them intersect by coincidence and literally interface in the climactic sequence.

Targets addresses the situation of filmmakers in Hollywood almost two decades after *Sunset Boulevard*. The moguls are now gone, and the studio system is in its final agony as a new generation of whiz-kids like Sammy propose attractive "packages" based on bankable stars like Orlok. A revisionist horror film set in a filmmaking milieu, *Targets* contrasts two brands of horror—the gothic creaky-door horror of the old Karloff films and the anonymous horror of clean-cut suburbanite mass-murderers.[21] "My kind of horror's not horror any more," Orlok tells Sammy, noting that the daily headlines have made old movie-horror seem quite innocuous. The final drive-in sequence, however, brings the two kinds of horror together by having the assassin spray sniper fire over an audience watching an Orlok retrospective.

"Real" horror thus literally destroys movie horror by killing the projectionist and the spectator, and trying to kill the actor. The horror film terror becomes real horror, the joke being, of course, that it remains movie horror, in the form of a fiction film by Peter Bogdanovich.

Targets proliferates in Hitchcock-style doubling imagery: Orlok watching himself in *The Criminal Code*; Orlok frightened by his own mirror image; Orlok facing down Bobby Thompson just as he had faced down the prisoner in the Hawks film; Bobby hesitating between the real-life Orlok and the looming image on the screen. (Even the imaged reels winding down in the diegetic projection room double those winding down in the theatres where *Targets* is screened). The two social worlds portrayed in the film—the world of Hollywood filmmakers and the world of bland suburbanites—are also doubled by their salient contrasts. The filmmakers are cultivated, equipped with English accents and Oxford degrees (or at least considerable film viewing at the Museum of Modern Art), while the suburbanites are presented as vacuous yahoos with execrable taste. Orlok and Bobby are constantly contrasted, the former in his black limousine, the latter in his white Mustang. Orlok drinks whiskey in warm sheltering interiors; Bobby drinks beer and Pepsi in antiseptic tract houses. More interestingly, the two characters are rendered by markedly different filmic styles. Orlok is generally filmed in the classical studio style, while Bobby is filmed in a more voguish new wave style, characterized by location shooting, long takes, minimal dialogue, and freely roaming hand-held camera. The technique itself highlights Orlok's anachronistic quality: his complaint that he has become a relic is aurally contexted by the directly-recorded sound of a Los Angeles freeway. The rush of traffic virtually drowns out his words; without studio filming and commentative music, Orlok seems quite harmless.

New German Reflexivity: *Beware of a Holy Whore*

No survey of reflexive filmmaking could possibly fail to mention the work of the new German cinema, although such a topic would doubtless merit a book-length study in itself. In the wake of the 1962 Oberhausen manifesto and the subsequent foundation of a distribution collective (*Filmverlag der Autoren*), new German cinema emerged in the seventies as a vibrant and sophisticated movement. The attitude of the filmmakers toward their intertext—memories of the grand Germanic film past, the "abyss" of Nazism, the love-hate relation to the dominant American film of the postwar period—was shot through with ambivalence. Here was rich soil for a historicized reflection on filmmaking, and new German cinema has indeed furnished a number of films either concerned with filmmaking (*Beware of a Holy Whore, Veronika Voss, The State of Things*), or with writer-protagonists whose activities metaphorize the process

Figure 20. *Targets* (1969)

of filmic écriture (the journalist in *Circle of Deceit*, Wilhelm in *The Wrong Move*); or with characters who watch or reflect on films (Bloch watching American films in *The Goalie's Anxiety at the Penalty Kick*, Bruno watching the porn loop in *Kings of the Road*, Marianne and Julianne watching footage of the concentration camps). We will restrict ourselves here to a brief and selective examination of films that explicitly treat the cinematic milieu and the filmmaking process.

Fassbinder's *Beware of a Holy Whore*, one of six films made by the director in 1970, shares with *Contempt* its Mediterranean settings, its multilingual ambiance, and its subtending metaphor of prostitution. The oxymoronic "Holy Whore" of the title points to the cinema's double potentiality for spiritual purity as well as commercial degradation. As the film begins, a German film crew and actors are waiting in a "Spanish" hotel—various cultural indices (license plates, advertisements, language) tell us we are actually on the Italian Riviera—for the arrival of the principals: the director (Lou Castel), the star (Eddie Constantine), the government money, and the film stock. As they wait, the production manager, played by Fassbinder himself (much as Godard cast himself as assistant director in *Contempt*), browbeats the crew and the waiters. When the rather manic director, Jeff, arrives, he treats the production manager as badly as the production manager had treated everyone else. He deploys every strategy—harangue, mockery, flirtation, threats—to whip his collaborators into order and obedience, but they subtly sabotage his work and even beat him up. Playing the long waiting game which is filmmaking, they dance to Elvis Presley and Ray Charles, get drunk on Cuba Libres, and make casually embittered love. The human relationships slowly disintegrate in an atmosphere of morbidly comic psychodrama, while the cinematic style mirrors the breakdown as the slow circular pans of the beginning of the film give way to arbitrarily splintered fragments of images and sounds. Despite the human and cinematic breakdown, however, the film-within-the-film finally does get underway.

Instead of the slow unraveling of a couple as in *Contempt*, Fassbinder gives us a mobile constellation of ephemeral liaisons—heterosexual, homosexual, bisexual—which break apart almost as quickly as they form. While the producer is the tyrant in *Contempt*, here it is the director who is dictatorial. While Godard pits the auteurist Lang against the capitalist Prokosch, Fassbinder is more interested in exposing the contradictions that rend a supposedly progressive group penetrated by the bourgeois attitudes they excoriate in their art. "You say your film is against power," someone tells the director, "yet it is supported by the state." *Beware of a Holy Whore* investigates the possible tensions between the conscious politics of a text—in this case the presumably antifascist attitudes of *Patria o Muerte* ("a film against state-sanctioned violence")—and the *realpolitik* of the production process.

Fassbinder anatomizes the political and psychoanalytic dynamics of collaboration, of "trying to live and work as a group." *Beware of a Holy Whore*, in this sense, offers a slightly fictionalized account of Fassbinder's own experiences with collaboration, including 1) the break-up of the Anti-Teater group, originally conceived as a collective without hierarchy or fixed division of labor, but which ended up operating along patriarchal lines; 2) the reportedly traumatic filming of *Whity* just a few months before, and 3) Fassbinder's disillusionment with the *Filmverlag der Autoren*, also created as a collective but which soon became a kind of dumping ground for those films which the *autoren* were unable to distribute elsewhere. At the same time, as Fassbinder himself has pointed out, *Beware of a Holy Whore* observes *itself* being made. The mimesis, in this case, is not between film and "reality" but between a film and its own process of production.

The most original contribution of *Beware of a Holy Whore*, perhaps, is to focus on what Félix Guattari calls "the micro-politics of facsism" as it operates within film production—the intricate play of domination and dependency, manipulation and complicity, exploitation and sadomasochism. In the wake if what he saw as the failure of utopian experiments, Fassbinder concentrates on the other violence, that which is not "sanctioned by the state but which is nevertheless real." This violence inhabits the social monad and can permeate even progressive groups. Fassbinder underlines the complicity of the "oppressed" in their oppression. Jeff's collaborators, as Ruth McCormick points out, seem eager to cast him as father-psychoanalyst-oppressor-lover within their private scenarios. In this sense, Jeff acts out the fears and desires of his co-workers, forcing Ricky's homosexuality out of the closet, playing the sadist to Irm's masochist. The director, the patriarch, bullies and exploits, but not without the tacit encouragement of his "victims."

Truffaut and *Day for Night*

The atmosphere of Truffaut's *La Nuit Américaine* (Day for Night, 1973) is the antithesis of that of *Beware of a Holy Whore*. Here the tone is cheerful, the problems are soluble, the film is made and will presumably give pleasure. *Day for Night* explicitly and implicitly compares filmmaking to happy events— picnics, parties, summer camp—connoting joyful collaboration. Truffaut's emphasis is on the actual shooting of a film and on all the bizarre or amusing events that occur or might occur during a production. The film being shot, in this case, is *Meet Pamela*, a Hollywood-style melodrama about a woman, Julie (Jacqueline Bisset) who falls in love with Alexandre (Jean-Pierre Aumont), the father of her fiancé Alphonse (Jean-Pierre Léaud). The temporal perameters of the film are circumscribed by the seven weeks it takes to shoot *Meet Pamela*, but since *Meet Pamela* is deliberately presented as terribly conventional, the real interest is displaced onto the material contingencies and emotional vicissitudes involved in filmmaking.[22]

An affectionate summa of over 15 years of filmmaking, *Day for Night* is full of self-quotation. The character Alphonse, with his "tough childhood," is obviously Antoine of *400 Blows* grown up and become an actor. The male friendship of Alexandre and Christian, celebrated by barely perceptible freeze-frames, recalls that of *Jules and Jim*, and Ferrand drives around the studio square the way Catherine drives outside Jim's apartment in that film. Ferrand's reference to his work as a "flop" in England is an obvious reference to the commercial and critical failure of *Fahrenheit 451*, shot in England just a few years before. But Truffaut's real concern is less with self-analysis than with composing an ode to the pleasures of the film craft. *Day for Night* constitutes a kind of production manual designed to initiate the spectator into a number of specific cinematic procedures. These procedures include: 1) *scripting*: Ferrand's collaboration with Joelle (reportedly mirroring Truffaut's own with Suzanne Schiffman); 2) *art direction, decor*: facades, illusory spatial relations, a bungalow constructed for the camera alone; 3) *camera work*: the opening "sequence," performed transparently by a tracking shot and then retroactively "explained" by crane shot, thus revealing the intricate choreographing of camera movement and movement within the shot; 4) *lighting*: trick candles fitted with light bulbs designed to give the impression that the candles are casting the light; 5) *editing*: repeated shots of the editing machine stress its central role; 6) *continuity*: Bernard cutting cigarettes in half for Alexandre to maintain continuity while Severine repeatedly flubs her lines; 7) *commentative music*: the credit sequence shows the soundstrip, while we hear the conductor directing a rehearsal, with the resultant inversion as we see what we usually hear (the music) and hear what we usually do not hear (the conductor's instructions to the musicians).

Day for Night shows considerable sensitivity to the challenges confronting actors and actresses. This theme is first sounded by the film's dedication to Dorothy and Lillian Gish, and is maintained throughout. Truffaut shows us actors as vulnerable crisis-ridden human beings operating under extreme pressure; while a technician in emotional crisis can still "go through the motions," an actor must concentrate totally. Severine speaks her lines badly not only because she is drunk but also because her son is dying of leukemia. She is, furthermore, unaccustomed to the demands of direct sound recording, which necessitates memorizing her lines. With Federico in Italy, she explains, she would simply pronounce numbers, in full confidence that the dialogue could be added in postsynchronization.

Day for Night repeatedly poses the question of the relative importance of cinema versus life. For Ferrand, the cinema is more important. For Alphonse, the cinephile, life, paradoxically, is more important. An ordinary language

Figure 21.   *Day for Night* (1973)

philosopher would dismiss the question as unanswerable and unverifiable (how does one sufficiently separate out film from life and life from film to judge their relative merit?) but *Day for Night* attempts to explore the multiform interactions between the two. Film borrows from life: Ferrand pilfer's Julie's real-life lines for the dialogue of *Meet Pamela*. Film anticipates life: the filmic car accident in *Meet Pamela* foreshadows the "real" disaster that kills Alexandre and Christian. Film resembles life: in both *Meet Pamela* and *Day for Night*, Alphonse loses the woman, and in both stories there are clear oedipal overtones. Film also resembles life in another sense. The technicians shown making *Meet Pamela* are played by the very technicians who collaborated on *Day for Night*; cameraman Walter Bal plays cameraman Walter, editor Yann Dedet plays editor Yann, and so forth. On the other hand, film contrasts with life. The audacious romantic woman of *Meet Pamela* is shy "off-screen," (i.e., in the on-screen of *Day for Night*); and the continental lover of Hollywood and *Meet Pamela* is, in fact, discreetly homosexual.

If *Contempt* offers a political anatomy of Hollywood, and *Beware of a Holy Whore* morbid self-criticism by Fassbinder, *Day for Night* offers an indulgent hypo-critical idealization of the filmmaking process, portrayed as a happy whirl of harmonious activities, in which virtually every crisis is painlessly integrated into the final product. There are a few allusions to the financial contingencies of film production—insurance policies, union contracts, and the like—but without the structural critique evoked by *Contempt*. There is vague talk of American money behind the film (like that financing much of Truffaut's later work) but no sign of doubt or resentment. Godard's cry of revolt gives way to Truffaut's good-natured genuflexions. The oppressive barbarian Prokosch yields to the avuncular, sentimental and financially disinterested Bertrand, while the real financiers remain off-screen. Along with its many homages to Hollywood, *Day for Night* reproduces the Hollywood formula of minimal demystification in the service of a greater mystification.

Filmmaking in the Third World

Third-world filmmakers, for their part, rarely have the luxury of making either *Meet Pamela* or *Day for Night*. Two third-world films about filmmaking, one from Brazil and one from India, emphasize the precarious nature of making films in a neocolonial context. The title of Fernando Coni Campos' *Ladrões de Cinema* (Cinema Thieves, 1976) alludes to De Sica's *Ladri di Biciclette* (Bicycle Thieves, 1948), but this time in a reflexive film set in a Brazilian world even poorer than that portrayed by Italian neorealism. The film begins with a group of slum-dwellers, in Indian garb, stealing filmmaking equipment from an American crew documenting Rio's annual carnival. Once back in the favela, the cinema thieves decide not to sell the equipment, as they normally would, but to make a film, with the favelados as actors. A Frenchman named Jean-Claude Rouch (played by film critic Jean-Claude Bernardet) initiates them into the secrets of the craft, and they set out to make their film. They choose a theme—an abortive eighteenth-century revolt against Portuguese colonialism—as well as costumes, performers, music. Gradually the film comes to energize the favelados as they apply to it the same enthusiasm and procedures that they would normally apply to the carnival pageant. The film no longer belongs to the cinema thieves but to the entire community. This boldly ironic film highlights the special conditions of third-world filmmaking: the neocolonial dependence on foreign equipment, the need for guerrilla strategies, the necessity of adopting aesthetic and production strategies rooted in the material realities of neocolonialism. In the third world, the film suggests, filmmaking, while materially impoverished, must be imaginative and communitarian, while absorbing the energy of popular culture, of samba and carnival.

While disadvantaged in relation to their first-world counterparts, third-world filmmakers often constitute an elite in their own countries. Mrinal Sen's film-about-filmmaking, *Aaakaler Sandhane* (In Search of Famine, 1980), explores the multiform contradictions inherent in this situation. *Aaakaler Sandhane* centers on a film crew led by the director (Dhritiman Chatterjee) which goes to a remote village to shoot a film entitled *Aaakaler Sandhane*, a fictive study of the 1943 Bengal famine. Sen especially highlights the social abyss separating the urbanized middle-class filmmakers from the impoverished rural world they attempt to portray. The title itself is ironic, since only artists enjoy the luxury of "searching" for famine. Despite their progressive ideas— they sing leftist songs while en route to the village—they remain incorrigibly bourgeois, tourists on a whirlwind tour of misery. Ardent consumers, they provoke drastic changes in the local economy. The cost of essential commodities rises; "They're not only filming a famine," an old peasant remarks, "they're creating one." The actors and actresses, meanwhile, have internalized the ideals of the star system and Hollywood glamor; one actress complains when her peasant role obliges her to don unfashionable clothes. Sprinkling their conversation with English expressions, the filmmakers are deeply imbued by colonialist culture and exercise a kind of internal colonialism over the oppressed people who are their subjects/objects. One moment especially captures their privileged condescension. Judging by the grain and hue of old photographs, the filmmakers guess at the year of the famine represented. The human tragedy of a holocaust in which millions died is reduced to a gimmick in a parlour game.

But it is not only the filmmakers who are criticized. Famine itself is revealed as a socio-historical rather than "natural" pheomenon, a by-product

Figure 22.   *Man of Marble* (1977)

of the war economy thrust on India by the British. Famine continues to threaten postindependence India, since the conditions generating famine have not fundamentally changed. The local elite is show to have acquired its wealth and privileges by dubious means during the 1943 famine. Cultural colonialism is mocked, meanwhile, by an advertisement for *The Guns of Navarone*— "Starring the greatest beauty in the world, Anthony Quinn, in the lead." Sen also offers a strong critique of patriarchal attitudes. When Devika, the starlet, is discovered to be unsuitable for her role, a search is begun for a replacement. Many of the well-to-do middle class volunteer their daughters, but are shocked to learn that the role is that of a village woman who turns to prostitution for survival during the days of famine. No one condemns a male actor for playing a drunk, someone remarks, but everyone condemns an actress for playing a prostitute. The film ends with what by now has become a reflexive topos: the filmmakers decide not to make the film. But the audience knows the film has been made, and that it is called *In Search of Famine.*

Andrzej Wajda and *Man of Marble*

Andrzej Wajda's *Man of Marble* (1977) explores the social contingencies of filmmaking in a quite different context, that of contemporary Poland. Here the film-about-filmmaking format becomes a springboard for a critique, at once social and cinematic, of a bureaucratic socialist regime. The film follows a neophyte director named Agnieszka (Krystyna Janda) in her attempts to make a diploma reportage about Mateusz Birkut (Jerzy Radziwilowicz), a naively idealistic bricklayer who briefly becomes a "star" of socialist propaganda before he runs afoul of the authorities. Agnieszka and her crew piece together the story of his rise and fall from old newsreels and classified outtakes and by interviewing Birkut's colleagues and acquaintances. A paunchy director of fifties propaganda films explains how he created the Birkut myth by staging a marathon bricklaying competition on the site of a model city. A former spy, now a supervisor of government-sponsored strip shows, recounts how Birkut's fellow workers sabotaged his Stakhanovite demonstrations by handing him a red-hot brick. Through such embedded narratives, clearly reminiscent of the investigative strategies of *Citizen Kane*, the film gradually constructs the truth about Birkut—that he rebelled against party corruption, that he was framed and imprisoned, then released and presumably killed.

The closer Agnieszka gets to the truth about Birkut, the more nervous the authorities become. She begins to encounter the same petty corruption and bureaucratic obstacles that Birkut did. Indeed, the two come to double each other as rebels from two distinct historical periods: he disrupts union meetings and throws a brick through the window of the Security Police; she kicks a supervisor in the shins. He is a worker; she is a cultural worker, a cinematic mason, to recycle a favorite metaphor of the Soviet montage school. Given this implied alliance of two rebels, it is quite logical that the film should end with Agnieszka striding down the corridor of the television building with Birkut's son, and that she will have married him prior to the beginning of Wajda's sequel film *Man of Iron*. But if Birkut ultimately retreats from politics—the last piece of classified footage shows him casting an unmarked ballot in local elections—Agnieszka plunges ever deeper into the fray. She practices a kind of guerilla filmmaking—hopping onto a forbidden statue of the fallen hero to film when her own cameraman lacks the courage, secretly recording an ex-party-spy, and generally shooting first and asking permission later.

If Agnieszka mirrors Birkut, her film-in-the-making mirrors *Man of Marble* itself. Wajda had to surmount the same obstacles to make his film that Agnieszka confronts in her attempt to make "Falling Stars." Wajda waited 13 years for permission to shoot *Man of Marble*, and a final sequence was excised. In Agnieszka's case, the authorities erect subtle and not-so-subtle obstacles to her project, declaring discarded footage "classified," encouraging her to explore alternative subjects, and ultimately depriving her of both camera and film. (Wajda cinematically renders the frustrations of bureaucracy through repeated tracking shots trailing Agnieszka down interminable corridors.) In this compilation film about the making of a compilation film, Agnieszka assembles "Falling Stars" largely from pre-existing footage. *Man of Marble*, similarly, presents a prismatic collage of newsreel, pseudo-newsreel, and outtakes, together with staged material set in two time-periods (the difference marked by the stylistic contrast of tripod versus hand-held shooting). Agnieszka's preferred style is a kind of Americanized *vérité*: "Hand-held camera," she instructs her aged cameraman (who, in a gesture of historical continuity, had earlier worked on Stalinist propaganda films), "no tripod. Wide-angle lens. You know—haven't you seen all the new American films?"

In music and painting, Godard once pointed out, the documentary-fiction dichotomy is regarded as meaningless. No one claims that Stravinsky is fiction and Schonberg is documentary, or that Kandinsky is fiction and Klee documentary. *Man of Marble* illustrates the truth pointed to in Godard's *boutade*, showing that all films are, in a sense, fiction films. Stalinist propaganda films, we learn, pass off idealized fantasies about the workers' state as if they were documentary truth. Wajda includes a 20 minute example of the genre, *Architects of Our Happiness*, featuring a Stakhanovite hero, massive gymnasts, and uplifting music. (Since he had himself worked on such filmic odes to socialist construction, Wajda gives himself a credit line as assistant director.) Birkut's documentary marriage to a gymnast in that film, we learn, was a fabrication in the name of image-enhancement. The *Zelig*-like incorporation of staged footage of Birkut into what looks for all purposes like authentic Stalinist propaganda also has the effect of blurring the distinction

Figure 23.   *Veronika Voss* (1982)

between documentary and fiction. The discarded footage from the propaganda films, meanwhile, makes the point that the real story is often in the outtakes. It is there that we see evidence of worker religiosity (Birkut crossing himself before a bricklaying competition) and revolt (workers throwing food at their foreman). Birkut himself, in reality a kind of East Bloc Candide, is also shown to be a kind of fabrication. He is told to straighten his hair and look pleased to conform to his role as media star, and even the feat of bricklaying prowess which catapulted him to fame is revealed to be a staged event.

Man of Marble operates a double demystification—one political, the other aesthetic. It deconstructs two styles of representation—the patronizing top-down manipulation of Stalinist communism and the idealizing edification of socialist realism. *Man of Marble* performs the mise-en-scène of the contradictions of a new class system, a debased form of socialism in which "solidarity" has become a dirty word. At the same time, the film critiques an aesthetic style of representation, that of socialist realism. This aesthetic, in its Stalinist variant, claims that art should speak to the people in the transparent language of model heroes and prettified reality. It practices the cult of personalities, whether major ones like Stalin or minor ones like Birkut. *Man of Marble* clearly rejects such a style, eschewing hagiography (his heroine for example, is often barely sufferable) in favor of a reflexive strategy which combines a thematic construction with an aesthetic of deconstruction.

Declining Stars: *Fedora* and *Veronika Voss*

Two recent films, Billy Wilder's *Fedora* (1979) and Fassbinder's *Die Sehnsucht der Veronika Voss* (Veronika Voss, 1982) spin variations on the theme of Wilder's earlier *Sunset Boulevard*—the decline of the star. Based on Thomas Tryon's *Crowned Heads*, *Fedora* turns the journalist-protagonist of the novel into the producer-protagonist of the film, in the form of William Holden, fished out of Norma Desmond's swimming pool to relate still another posthumous tale. His fictive name is now Barry Detweiler, and he has been promoted from scriptwriter to independent producer, but he is still self-ironic, still down on his luck, and ready to be ensnared again by a legendary actress living in spooky exclusion.

Fedora highlights its intertext by constant allusion to the history of film. The opening shot of *Fedora* throwing herself in front of a back-projected train à la Anna Karenina cites the classic Hollywood romanesque tradition. Docteur Vando (José Ferrer) evokes both Caligari and Mabuse, a reference to the Germanic cinema in which Wilder finds his roots. Fedora's bath in the outsized swimming pool of *Leda and the Swan*, set in the '40's, and Antonia's waltz with Michael York, set in the '70's, evoke a kind of atemporal grandiose Hollywood style; the images call up an ethos as well as an aesthetic. Like *Sunset Boulevard*,

Fedora mingles real and fictional characters. Henry Fonda and Michael York play themselves, under their own names but in fictional roles, while Fedora herself amalgamates features of Gloria Swanson, Marlene Dietrich, and Greta Garbo. The mixture of reality and fiction elicits the familiar vertigo: where do the real characters leave off and the fictive ones begin?

Billy Wilder shows himself in *Fedora*, once again, to be the ironic poet of the twilight of the stars, the chronicler of the human cost of cinematic obsolescence. *Fedora* has to do with face, with saving face, with the desperate attempt to preserve physical beauty against time's relentless melt and thus prolong the ephemeral streak of stardom. Stars, especially women stars, are not allowed to age gracefully. They are designed, as Wilder himself said, to disappear in the firmament and not fall to earth like wet firecrackers. *Fedora* exposes the ravages of the star system even as it parasitically feeds on that system. It makes fun of our voyeuristic curiosity about the lives of stars—why should it matter to us that Humphrey Bogart, Pablo Picasso, and Maurice Chevalier were among Fedora's lovers?—even while it exploits that very curiosity.

If Wilder is commenting on Hollywood, he is also commenting on his own place within it. In the Tryon novel, the male protagonist is a journalist; in the film he is a producer. Barry Detweiler's difficulties in scraping up funds for a remake of *Anna Karenina* parallel Wilder's own problems in financing *Fedora*. Counting on Fedora's "bankability," Detweiler hopes to persuade "some tax-shelter guys" to finance the project. *Fedora* itself, ironically, was made from tax-shelter money, obliging Wilder to film in studios in Munich and Paris. But if *Fedora* reflects Wilder's resentments against the commercial pressures of the film industry, it also forms part of that which it criticizes. The film acidly records the protracted agony of the star system and the studio style, while it prolongs that agony. The film's style is antiquated, a face-lifted version of classical Hollywood cinema. The attempt to "bury" Hollywood here comes to resemble an exercise in galvanizing a corpse. It is one last dismantling, one last sale of studio scrap. Nothing is more eloquent, in this regard, than the cool TV report of Fedora's death, with its frigid studio decor and shrewdly chosen retrospective images of Fedora's life. Fedora the personage, and *Fedora* the film, seem oddly out of place in the world of network news.

Fassbinder's *Veronika Voss*, like *Sunset Boulevard*, focusses on the entanglements of a young writer, Robert Krohn (Hilmar Thate), and a declining actress, Veronika Voss (Rosel Zech), who is fatally addicted to drugs. But the Fassbinder film sets up an even more complex play of mirror effects: between film-within-the-film and film, between protagonist and prototype, and even between the protagonist and Fassbinder himself. The film opens in a movie theatre as the aging Veronika, a UFA star from the Nazi period, watches herself in a lurid melodrama entitled *Creeping Poison*. With her in the audience are the writer and Fassbinder himself. The sequence being screened shows a drug addict, played by Voss, being manipulated by a woman into ceding her property, and thus mirrors in microcosm the trajectory of *Veronika Voss* as a whole, where the parasitic Dr. Katz (Annemarie Düringer), under the guise of therapeutic concern, tricks Voss into signing away her property in exchange for regular injections of morphine. (The Voss character was based on the life of the German actress Sybille Schmitz, a UFA actress who worked with Carl Dreyer and Max Reinhardt. Schmitz continued her career in the Nazi period and died of a suicidal drug overdose in 1955. One of her most celebrated roles, ironically, was as the victim of a female vampire in Dreyer's 1932 film *Vampyr*.)

Veronika Voss merits an extensive textual analysis, but we will limit ourselves here to its characteristics as a reflexive film set in a filmmaking milieu. The male protagonist of the film, like Joe Gillis in *Sunset Boulevard*, is enticed into the vortex of the life of a fading star. He enlists his woman companion of many years, Henriette (Cornelia Froboess), in an investigation aimed at discovering the secret of her enigmatic behavior. They discover her devotion to Doctor Katz and her relationship with an ex-husband who seems to enjoy his status as witness to the demise of a star. Like Norma Desmond, Veronika Voss is no longer able to practice her profession. She fumbles an insignificant film role, and must resort to glycerine tears to show emotion. And again like Desmond, she revels in the spotlights of her own delusions, fondly imagining that limousines are taking her off to Hollywood.

Veronika Voss, like Norma Desmond, is associated with an irrecuperably luxurious studio style. Her memories of the gloss and glitter of UFA and her ill-fated comeback attempt at Bavaria (another prominent Third Reich studio) link her to the studio system. When Krohn and Voss board the tramway, the tramway exits screen left but the camera remains fixed on a sign—Geiselgeistag—a suburb outside of Munich and home of several Hollywood-style film studios. In fact, *Veronika Voss* proliferates in verbal and visual references to studios and to studio films, especially those directed by Germans or German emigrés in America. The sequence of the star watching herself, as we have seen, is modeled on *Sunset Boulevard*, by the emigré director Billy Wilder. Krohn's offer of an umbrella to the rain-soaked Voss recalls Edward G. Robinson's rescue of Joan Bennett in *Scarlett Street*, by the emigré director Fritz Lang. At one point, Voss stands in front of a stylized studio forest reminiscent of Lang's *Die Nibelungen*. The tramway sequence evokes a similar sequence in a film by another German expatriate, F.W. Murnau. The hounding to suicide by drugs of Veronika Voss recalls the Nazi-like hounding of Ingrid Bergman in *Notorious*, the work of a filmmaker who did his first work as director in Germany under the shadow of UFA. In this sense, *Veronika Voss* constitutes an allusive meditation on the complex reciprocal play of influence between Germany and the United States. Even the over-decorated

Figure 24.   *Veronika Voss* (1982)

mise-en-scène of the film evokes not only specifically German antecedents but also the elaborate studio-based Hollywood cinema in which so many German emigrés gained their fame.

Apart from its filmmaking milieu and intertextual allusions, *Veronika Voss* is a thoroughly reflexive film which constantly calls attention to its own status as an artifact. The hyperbolic virtuosity of the style renders the authorial inscription visible, calling attention to the enunciation. The aesthetic exhibitionism of the film mirrors that of the star protagonist; here cinematic style primps and looks at itself in the mirror. Let us look, for example, at what Fassbinder does with filmic "punctuation," i.e., those demarcating effects which simultaneously separate and connect sequences. *Veronika Voss* displays more than 30 distinct types of optical transitions in a virtuoso demonstration of the potentialities of what might be called a subcode of punctuation. Fassbinder favors those devices materialized by optical effects, and especially the wipe. These wipes represent, first of all, an archaic device associated with the studio style evoked by the film. More importantly, as the most "visible" form of puntuation due to their obvious optical manipulation, they call attention to the signifier. Fassbinder then hyperbolizes this visibility through spectacular effects through which the wipes mimic or anticipate the sequences they precede. A horizontally striated wipe, for example, announces the sequence of conversation between Robert and Voss's ex-husband, where a similarly patterned partition casts horizontal stripes across their faces. Another wipe violently bifurcates the screen and arches upward, anticipating the violence of Robert's breaking into Dr. Katz' office.

Cinema, Veronika tells Robert, is nothing more than light and shadow, and bids him observe the effect of light on her face. Several shots later, she walks up stairs and out-of-frame, followed by her expressionist shadow, as if in illustration of her earlier comment. Throughout, Fassbinder calls attention to the *lichtspiel*—play of light—which is film. He surrounds minor characters with semi-darkness or annihilates them with blinding light, while he illuminates Voss with shifting lights and flickering candles. Here again Fassbinder draws on the resources developed by the Germanic tradition, both in terms of Max Reinhardt's emphasis on actual light sources on stage/in frame and in terms of Joseph von Sternberg's manner of enveloping Dietrich in an air of glittery artifice. As the character disintegrates, finally, the lighting loses its chiaroscuro vibrancy, finally blanching out the protagonist as she approaches suicide: the film which began in the darkness ends in an explosion of white light.

Veronika Voss develops a multi-leveled metaphorical discourse concerning the cinema in which the key trope is that of addiction itself. To Veronika's literal addiction corresponds Robert's figurative addiction to glamor and spectacle. How else explain his fascination with a story which, according to his editors, would be more appropriate for the society columns?

How else account for his self-destructive preference for the spectacle of Veronika to the quotidian affection of Henriette? Fassbinder resuscitates a venerable metaphor within critical discource on film and theatre—recalling Vertov's denunciations of "the electrical opium of the movie theatre's" and Brecht's of "spiritual drug traffic"—i.e., the cinema as opiate. But he historicizes the trope by alluding to the national and international institutional matrix of the narcotic trade. The German State and the Health Ministry, Robert discovers, collaborate with Doctor Katz. Could it be that German cinema, by analogy, also "owes its soul to the company store," to cite the fifties pop song constantly played over Armed Forces Radio? The presence of the American soldier (Gunther Kaufman), seen around Dr. Katz' office and who seems to be involved in the morphine traffic, also contributes to this portrait of manipualtion in postwar Germany. It was partially American pressure, scarcely disinterested, which led to the snuffing out of German cinema in the immediate postwar period and the massive influx of American films, cultural products to which Germans were now "addicted."

Into the Eighties: Godard and Wenders

The eighties have already been extraordinarily fecund in films-about-filmmaking. In *Les Années 80* (The Golden Eighties, 1983), Chantal Akerman deconstructs a Jacques Demy-style musical in a kind of rehearsal film about rehearsals. The film consists of two sharply divided section: an hour-long videotaped collage of rehearsals of songs, movements, and dialogue, presumably destined for the film-to-be; and a 20 minute "sample," shot in 35mm, of what the finished production number, after careful editing, might look like. Alain Tanner's *Dans la Ville Blanche* (In the White City, 1983), similarly, is structured around contrasting filmic modes: the super-8 images—grainy, jiggly, restless, spontaneous—that Bruno Ganz shoots in Portugal for his woman friend in Switzerland, and the surrounding "normal" 35mm material in which the traces of subjectivity and the enunciation have been largely effaced. Tomas Gutierrez Alea also interweaves heterogenous modes within a film-about-filmmaking format in his *Hasta Cierto Punto* (Up to a Certain Point, 1983). The film revolves around a director and screenwriter making a film about machismo among dockworkers, and interweaves videotaped interviews of the dockworkers with the filmed story of a romance between a woman docker and the scriptwriter, all as a springboard for a multifaceted reflexion on relations between sexes, between media, and between intellectuals and the people for whom they presume to speak. Not only is the film-within-the-film about machismo, we gradually discover, but so is the surrounding film about the making of the film-within-the-film, for the filmmakers themselves are no strangers to machismo. Sexism, we learn, is not the monopoly of the working class; it pervades the filmmaking milieu as well.

To conclude this overview of films-about-filmmaking, we will briefly touch on two recent films: Godard's *Passion* (Passion, 1982) and Wim Wenders' *Der Stand der Dinge* (The State of Things, 1982). In *Passion*, Godard's surrogate is Jerzy (Jerzy Radziwilowicz), a Polish filmmaker making a film in which he turns famous paintings into *tableaux vivants*. On the set, he is hounded by financial backers who demand a coherent script and a story. But for Jerzy, as for Godard himself, scripts are bureaucratic straitjackets invented by bookkeepers, and stories are an irrelevance. In his obsession with beauty and "the perfect light," he scrutinizes the slow-motion video image of Hanna Schygulla's face. He realizes the pointlessness of freezing such mysterious flux into the cause-effect logic of conventional narration. *Passion* itself, as a consequence, is structured around centrifugal disruptions. The unveiling of an Ingres-like young beauty is interrupted by the sudden entrance into frame of a television camera. A couple's conversation about their intimate feelings is disrupted by frantic knocking which scrambles their dialogue. Typically, Godard navigates between the aleatory and the definitive, between noise and communication, between chaos and structure, between the narrative system and its incessant anarchization.

Wenders' *The State of Things* also treats the subject of paralysis of filmic *écriture*, the filmmaker's terror of the empty white screen. In the film, the cast and crew of a science-fiction film are marooned on the Portuguese coast. The director, Friedrich (Patrick Bauchau), scans the horizon for a signal from the absent producer, Gordon (Allen Goorwitz), apparently in flight and unwilling or unable to deliver the promised film stock. The film-within-the-film is a fifties-style postholocaust film called *The Survivors*, and is purportedly a remake of Allan Dwan's *The Most Dangerous Man Alive*. The first part of *The State of Things* portrays a situation of inertia—the endless waiting of the makers of *The Survivors*. (This endless waiting does not correspond, reportedly, to the making of *The State of Things*, which was written, cast, and shot in a kind of fevered rush.) In this part of the film, Wenders shows a world in which, as Flaubert said of *Madame Bovary*, "nothing happens," (at least in the conventional sense). The characters take pictures, talk about art, get drunk, and read aloud to one another. The stasis is broken only when Friedrich abruptly resolves to track down Gordon in Los Angeles. Suddenly, we are plunged into a Hollywood roller-coaster of dramatic events. Within this regime of narrative density, we are offered a southern Californian noir cityscape, a smooth lawyer (Roger Corman), a creditor fleeing in a mobile home (Gordon), a few thugs, and a climactic shootout in a deserted parking lot. Friedrich's "gun," in this case, is the super-8 camera with which he films his killers and his own death in a last vertiginous pan. Both Gordon and Friedrich, it turns out, are being slaughtered for the crime of having made *The Survivors* in black-and-white. In return for investing its laundered money, the mafia has received in

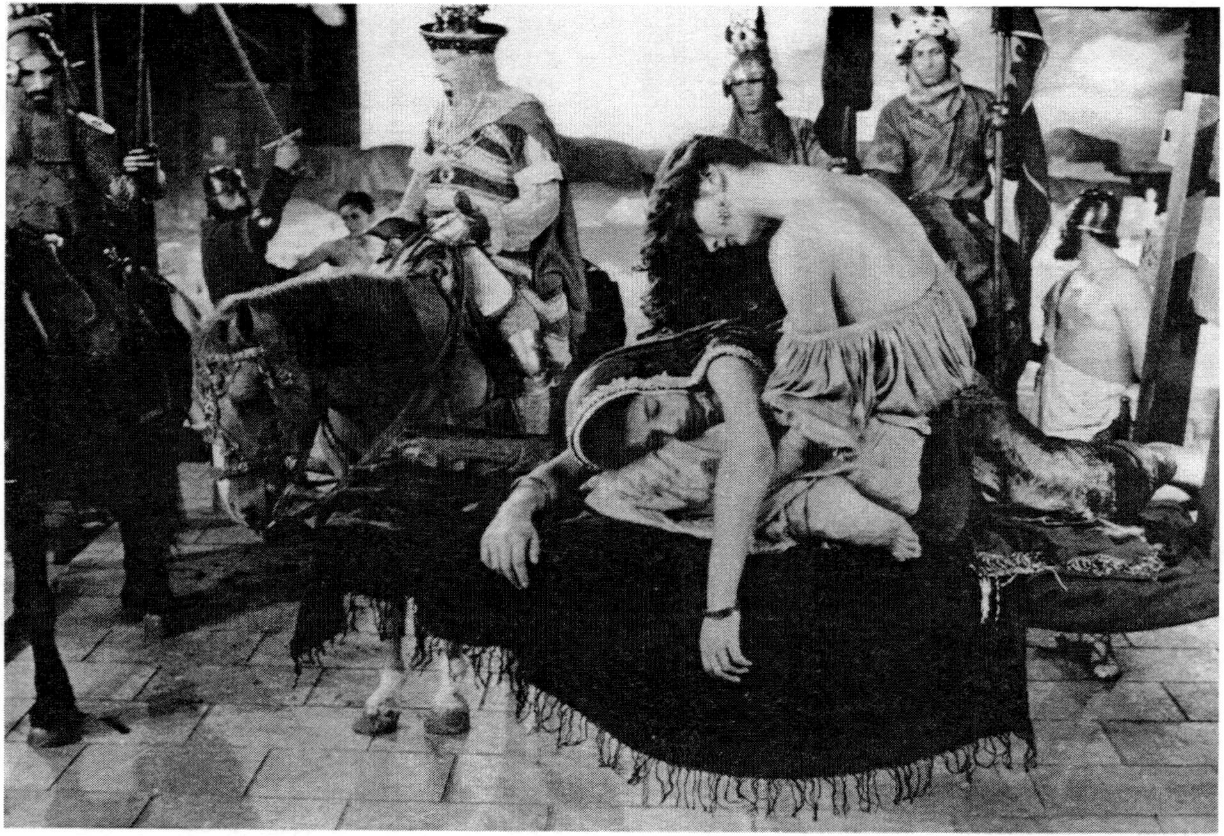

Figure 25. *Passion* (1982)

return an unprofitable black-and-white art film; the gangsters, understandably, feel doublecrossed.

Both *Passion* and *The State of Things* can be seen as a kind of stock-taking concerning the state of film art in the early eighties, and both are requiems for a certain kind of filmmaking. The requiem, in both cases, is for the non-Hollywood film, the film without a script, the low-budget art film which has come to seem anachronistic in the age of blockbusters and technological exhibitionism. (The requiem aspect is underlined, in the Godard film, by a soundtrack featuring requiems by Mozart and Fauré.) Both films are haunted by the question of story. The producers of *Passion* keep asking: "Where is the story?" and "What kind of story is this?" In *The State of Things*, meanwhile, the director tells his drunken crew: "Stories? There are no stories, only life, in the course of time, without the need to turn out stories." In both films, the cinema has clear enemies. By having Jerzy Radziwilowicz, the Birkut of *Man of Marble*, play his filmmaker-within-the-film, Godard shows solidarity with the workers of the cinema (as against its owners), and indirectly compares the enemies of filmmaking to Stalinist bureaucrats. Wenders, for his part, compares the cinema to a mafia operation. Hollywood's dirty money needs laundering; the producers are gangsters or in the pay of gangsters. Both films, however, finally rescue an ephemeral beauty from the hands of despair. *Passion* reflects not only on the conjunction of love and work in the cinema, but also on cinema's relation to two neighboring arts perennially used as metaphors for film itself—painting and music. *The State of Things*, despite Friedrich's negation of the possibility of storytelling, delivers an original and reflexive tale abut filmmaking itself.

As a constitutive element in human life, stories partake of the "natural." It is not natural, however, that only certain types of stories should be told, or that they should be told without calling attention to the means of their telling. What distinguishes most fiction films, Metz points out, is not the absence of the work of the signifier, but rather its presence in the mode of denegation; the signifiers, rather than working for themselves, labor busily at effacing their own traces, immediately opening into the transparence of a story which is in fact produced by these very signifiers but which the film pretends merely to illustrate. Filmmakers have the perennial choice of obscuring or revealing the codes by which they create illusions. They can keep the codes as a closely guarded professional secret or they can initiate the public into their operations. The films-about-filmmaking discussed in this chapter have shown a varying proportion of critical consciousness, but we can affirm that they all demystify the cinema in some measure, in the sense that they all make us aware, to some degree, of the medium, of its codes, and of the work of its signifiers.

3

The Genre of Self-Consciousness

Literary critics speak of a self-conscious genre in the novel, a tradition which has historically been slighted or condemned. "Self-conscious," in this sense, refers to a novelistic decorum corresponding neither to the "documentary strategy" of novelists like Defoe, nor to the solidly bourgeois fictions of the great nineteenth-century realists like Balzac or Flaubert, nor to the interior realism of a Virginia Woolf or a Henry James. In his *Partial Magic: The Novel as Self-Conscious Genre,* Robert Alter disengages an ongoing tradition of self-consciousness going back to Cervantes, continuing with Fielding and Sterne in England and Diderot in France, ambiguously revived by Thackeray, and undergoing a veritable Renaissance in the twentieth-century with writers like Gide, Queneau, Borges, Nabokov, and Fowles. The works of these novelists form "the other great tradition," in which novels systematically flaunt their own condition of artifice, showing the fictional world as an authorial construct set up against a background of literary tradition and convention.

The idea of self-consciousness in novels as well as films initially encountered resistance from a chorus of hostile critics. F.R. Leavis, working from moralistic Arnoldian premises, argued for a rather arbitrarily anointed "Great Tradition" in the novel—a tradition which had no room for the "sport" of a Fielding or Sterne. Behind his dismissal of novels like *Tristram Shandy* and *Tom Jones* one senses a puritanical hostility to the comic mode, as if fiction, by playing with its own conventions, had become suspectly onanistic. Critics like Ian Watt, on the other hand, tracing the novel back to Defoe rather than Cervantes, overemphasized the novel's rootedness in the world of bourgeois fact. Still another critical tradition, fathered by Henry James and disseminated by Percy Lubbock, favored "dramatic" fiction which "shows" rather than "tells." Even Auerbach, while not fundamentally hostile to reflexivity, at times implied that the novel had achieved a kind of definitive mimetic accuracy with the great nineteenth-century realists, while Lukács enshrined the forms of "critical realism."

Film criticism as well has tended to downplay both the tradition and the creative potentialities of reflexivity in the cinema. Until fairly recently, the very

Figure 26. Stan Laurel and Oliver Hardy

phrase "self-conscious" was almost invariably meant in its pejorative sense of "stagey" or "affected." Reflexive techniques, even when tolerated in the frankly comic films of Woody Allen or Mel Brooks, tend to be recuperated as the expression of their "zany" or "neurotic" authorial personae. The anti-illusionistic elements in Godard's work were long considered unfortunate lapses in seriousness or the indulgence of a personal vice rather than the key to his aesthetic. The mainstream of film criticism, both academic and journalistic, continues to be subtended by the assumption that truly serious films must be verisimilar representations concerning plausible characters set in a believable social context. While fashionable in the pages of small-circulation journals, reflexivity remains anathema to popular journalistic critics—including those appearing on television—who continue to excoriate lapses in plausability, characters who cannot be believed in, and techniques that call attention to themselves. Reflexive films, in this sense, form an object of paranoia for mainstream critics, who see reflexive filmmakers as spoilsports who deprive the cinematic game of its illusion (from Latin "in play," from *inlusio, illudere,* or *inludere*). Game-players, Huizing points out in *Homo Ludens,* have always been more indulgent with "cheats" than with "spoilsports."

Reflexive fictions defiantly call attention to their own artifice and operations, refusing a transparent self-effacing language that opens quietly onto the world. When Cervantes interrupts the story of Don Quixote's battle with the Biscayan, in a novelistic equivalent to the freeze-frame, leaving them both with swords upraised, on the grounds that his source went no farther, only to resume his account upon discovering a parchment depicting the very same battle, he is consciously destroying the illusion created by his story. When Fielding halts the flow of his narrative to expatiate on the novelist's craft, he reminds us of the artifice involved in writing a novel. And when Diderot boasts, at the beginning of *Jacques the Fatalist,* that he can marry off the *maître* or cuckold him, just as he pleases, he, too, is a self-conscious narrator, asserting absolute power over his own creation. By seeing themselves not as nature's slaves but as fiction's masters, reflexive artists cast doubt on the central assumption of mimetic art—the notion of an antecedent reality on which the artistic text is supposedly modeled. Their nonreferential discourse is not subject to the laws of sublunary nature; it is subject, ultimately, only to the constraints of language itself.

In their freedom and creativity, anti-illusionistic artists imitate the freedom and creativity of the gods. Like gods at play, reflexive artists see themselves as unbound by life as it is perceived (Reality), by stories as they have been told (Genre), or by a nebulous probability (Verisimilitude). Unlike the self-effacing artist of Stephen Dedalus, who, "like the God of creation, remains within or behind or beyond or above his handiwork, invisible," the self-conscious artist, with a differing sense of supernatural decorum, is fond of making comic epiphanies in the created universe. The god of anti-illusionist art is not an immanent pantheistic deity but an Olympian, making noisy intrusion into fictive events. We are torn away from the events and the characters and made aware of the pen, or brush, or camera that has created them.

The Cameo Appearance: From Cervantes to Woody Allen

These comic epiphanies, in the cinema, often take the form of a cameo appearance by the author. Just as Cervantes himself enters *Don Quixote* as a captive soldier, or Vladimir Nabokov appears anagramized as "Vivian Darkbloom" in *Lolita,* so some directors make walk-on appearances in their own films. Buñuel, the most Cervantic of filmmakers, often "signs" his films with walk-on roles. His brief appearances in *Le Chien Andalou* as the man who razors a woman's eye figures forth not only his role as editor (the man who does the cutting) but also the aggressive thrust of his cinema of cruelty. His brief appearance in *Belle de Jour* as a Spanish tourist pinpoints his situation as a Spaniard making films in France. In *Phantom of Liberty,* he dons a beard and monk's frock and has himself assassinated in a highly condensed expression of his own ambivalence toward Catholicism. And in *That Obscure Object of Desire,* it is Buñuel who asks to be driven to the bank and is promptly blown up by terrorists, a reminder that the film mocks *his* obsessions, *his* class, and *his* privileges. Hitchcock's cameo appearances, meanwhile, form a celebrated personal trademark, and tend to be shrewdly apt and overdetermined with meaning. We see him putting a double bass on a train in *Strangers on a Train,* the very film which places two characters, both "base," on a train. Godard's appearances progress from the informer in *Breathless*—as director, who could be better placed?—through the assistant director to Fritz Lang in *Contempt,* to himself as fully visible director in his studio in *Numéro Deux.* In the seventies, indeed, such signatures become almost *de rigeur:* Coppola directing his actors in *Apocalypse Now,* Scorcese watching Cybill Shepherd in *Taxi Driver.*

Even when not literally visible, directors have often been figuratively present in the form of delegates within the fiction. Preston Sturges casts Joel McCrea as a director not unlike himself in *Sullivan's Travels;* Woody Allen goes farther by himself playing the director Sandy Bates in *Stardust Memories,* a film explicitly indebted to the Sturges film. The putative director Guido Anselmi partially substitutes for Fellini in *8 1/2,* as does "Monsieur Godard" for his authorial namesake in *Every Man for Himself.* At times the substitution is somewhat less direct. The lanternist in Bergman's *The Magician,* the fashion photographer in Antonioni's *Blow-Up,* the newscameraman in Wexler's *Medium Cool*—all stand in, on some level, for their directors. At times the authorial surrogate is transposed into another art or medium. The saxophonist Jimmy Doyle (Robert de Niro) in Scorcese's *New York, New York,* as a be-bop musician ahead of his time in the twilight of swing, also evokes Scorcese himself, impatient with the outmoded conventions of respectable "entertainment." The Rolling Stones, adding note to note to compose "Sympathy for the Devil," collectively analogize the compositional work of Jean-Luc Godard, joining shot to shot in a film called, symptomatically, *One Plus One.*

The Self-Conscious Genre: Summa, Anatomy, Carnival

The self-conscious novel began with *Don Quixote* as a parodic summa, mocking in turn epic, pastoral, romance, comedy, and devotional literature. The self-conscious novel has strong affinities with what Northrop Frye calls the "anatomy," a strand of fiction characterized by digressive strategies and voraciously comic erudition. The great anatomists are those on whom no genre is lost. Exploiting the widest possible range of sources, from Sancho Panza's earthy proverbs to the Don's celestial flights, they take high and low materials and tease them into art, often seducing minor genres into brilliance, as Cervantes did with Renaissance chivalric romance and Godard did with the gangster movie.

Both the novel and the fiction film, summas by their very nature, have the potential of setting in motion a polyphonic play of generic voices. Their essence is to have no essence or master voice, to be open to all cultural forms. Both novel and film have consistently cannibalized other genres and media. The novel began by orchestrating a polyphonic diversity of materials—courtly fictions, travel literature, allegory, jestbooks—into a new narrative form, repeatedly plundering or annexing neighboring arts, creating poetic novels, dramatic novels, cinematic novels, and journalistic novels. What is true of the novel is even more true of cinema, for while the matter of expression of the novel is words, and only words, cinema is a composite language by virtue of its diverse matters of expression—sequential photography, music, phonetic sound, noise—and thus "inherits" all the art forms associated with these matters of expression.

A rich, sensorially composite language characterized by what Metz calls "codic heterogeneity," cinema is open to all kinds of literary and pictorial symbolism, to all collective representations, to all ideologies, to all aesthetics, and to the infinite play of influences within cinema, within the other arts, and within culture generally. Cinema can literally include painting, poetry, and music or it can metaphorically evoke them by imitating their procedures; it can show a Picasso painting, or emulate cubist techniques or visual dislocation, cite a Bach cantata, or create montage equivalents of fugue and counterpoint. Godard's *Passion* not only includes music (Ravel, Mozart, Ferré, Beethoven, Fauré) but is conceived musically, and not only includes animated tableaux based on celebrated paintings (Rembrandt's *Night Watch,* Goya's *The Third of May,* Delacroix's *Turkish Bathers*) but also expresses a painterly concern with light and color. The famous definitions of cinema in terms of other arts—"sculpture in motion" (Vachel Lindsay); "music of light" (Abel Gance); "architecture in movement" (Elie Faure)—merely call attention to the synesthetic multiplicity of signifiers available to the cinema.

Novelists and filmmakers have often been obliged to define and stake out territory for new genres. Cervantes explains that he is not writing a romance in *Don Quixote,* just as Diderot protested in a title: *Ceci n'est pas un Conte.* Fielding in *Joseph Andrews* proposes his own generic synthesis: "the comic epic poem in prose." Anti-illusionists hybridize genres in such a way that the signification of the work partially arises from the creative tension generated by their interaction, tensions which force us to reflect on the nature of genre itself as one of the ways "reality" is mediated through art. Godard, throughout his career, has promiscuously engendered "illegitimate" generic combinations: existential gangster film in *Breathless,* sociological romance in *Masculine, Feminine,* political western in *Wind from the East,* and feminist pornography in *Numéro Deux.* Through a process of artistic alchemy, genres are contested and contaminated by other genres. *Pierrot le Fou,* especially, constantly highlights its character as generic cocktail: "Our story continues," Belmondo's off-screen voice tells us, "full of sound and fury, with a small port as in a Conrad novel, sailing ships as in a Stevenson novel, an old bordello as in a Faulkner novel, and two guys to beat me up as in a Chandler novel." Such an orgy of citation, besides constituting a self-parody, literarizes the narrative, empties it of its diegetic substance and forces us to contemplate the film as a crazy quilt of literary and cinematic pastiches.

Since the stuff of self-conscious art is the tradition itself—to be alluded to, played with, outdone, or exorcized—parody has often been of crucial importance. Implicit in the idea of parody are some self-evident truths about the artistic process. The first is that the artist does not imitate nature but rather other texts. One paints, or writes, or makes films because one has seen paintings, read novels, or attended films. One writes a novel in imitation, whether affectionate (pastiche) or critical (parody), of novelists one has read. Art, in this sense, is not a window on the world but a palimpsest, an intertextual event, in which references to other texts hover between the lines or linger in the margins. One may write, like Fielding, "in the manner of" Cervantes. One writes within a tradition; the medium, the genre, and the sub-genre pre-exist the artist. The intertextual references may be explicit or implicit, conscious or unconscious, direct and local or broad and diffuse. These truths apply with equal self-evidence to films. Filmmakers choose, or are pressured, to make films in a certain genre, or "in the manner of" a certain director, or according to a set of conventions. They can call attention to these influences or choose to

Figure 27. Rembrandt's *Nightwatch* in *Passion* (1982)

obscure them. They can cover their tracks or, like Godard, cite their sources by cinematic "footnotes" in the form of titles, film posters, or the physical presence of the directors themselves (Fritz Lang in *Contempt,* Samuel Fuller in *Pierrot le Fou*).

The Centrality of Parody

Parody, far from being a marginal sub-genre within the history of literature or film, can be seen as an ever-present tendency which renders explicit the intrinsic processes of textuality. Mikhail Bakhtin's revalorization of parody and the carnivalesque suggests not only a rereading of the diverse genres which generated the modern novel, but also controverts what had been the orthodox Marxist view of its development. What had been considered central—the realist tradition studied by Auerbach and Lukács— becomes but one moment in a much more complex dialectic. In a typically carnivalesque gesture, Bakhtin dislocates the center to the periphery and the marginal to the center. What had been considered marginal and eccentric—the parodic sport of Sterne or the overheated polyphonic madness of a Dostoevsky—becomes in Bakhtin the paradigm of a new kind of "dialogic" literature.

Bakhtin's rereading, with Rabelais as point of departure, of the history of modern European literature suggests the possibility, if not of an inversion, at least of a certain recasting of the history of the cinema as well, in which parody would be granted its perennially fecund and paradigmatic importance. The conventional histories of the cinema tend to privilege Griffith rather than Keaton, Pudovkin rather than Vertov, serious dramatic films rather than musical comedies. Susan Sontag compares the novel's Samuel Richardson to the cinema's D.W. Griffith as two innovators of genius who combine supremely vulgar intellects with a "fervid moralizing about sexuality and violence whose energy comes from suppressed voluptuousness."[1] She might have gone on to point out that silent cinema, after its Richardsonian beginnings, soon took a turn toward Fieldingesque parody. Just as Fielding rendered Pamela's behavior ludicrous by transforming Squire B into the lecherous Lady Booby and Joseph Andrews into the assailed virgin, so filmmakers like Mack Sennett and Buster Keaton ridiculed the maudlin love scenes of Griffith films. Many seductive vamp figures from the silent era play the Shamela to Griffith's Pamelas. Even Fielding's reductive comparison of love to a piece of beef finds its literal cinematic counterpart in Keaton's *Go West* (1925), where the ingenue is played by a cow and the lover by Keaton himself. Eisenstein, in *The Old and the New* (1929), provides the cow with a more appropriate mate. After a bovine *coup de foudre,* he has the editing stimulate the image to a metaphorical climax, followed by a shot of the newly delivered cow and her offspring. All of which, had it not taken place in the context of a collective farm, might have constituted an animalistic equivalent to the happy bourgeois endings—usually consisting of an iris-in on a cheerful nuclear family—of so many Griffith films.

Parody constructs itself on the destruction of outmoded literary or cinematic codes. Cervantes' comic epic shows a world impermeable to epic values, where such values can only be comic. Cervantes weaves a novel by needling romance, pitting the *mensonge romantique* (the romantic lie), in René Girard's pithy formula, against the *vérité romanesque* (the novelistic truth). Cervantes' battered *hidalgo* tries to act out the feudal idealizations of chivalric literature in a no-longer feudal Spain. Since there is no textual precedent for monetary payment in his sacred texts, he refuses to pay Sancho for his services. Since Homer never mentions Agamemnon's salary or Nestor's pension, and since romance never mentions the *per diem* of Amadis de Gaulle, Don Quixote dismisses such questions as beneath his dignity.

Parody, one might argue, emerges when artists perceive that they have outgrown artistic conventions. Man parodies the past, Hegel suggested, when he is ready to dissociate himself from it. Literary modes and paradigms, like social orders and philosophical epistemes, become obsolescent and may be superseded. When artistic forms become historically inappropriate, parody lays them to rest. Parody highlights art's historicity, its contingency and transcience. It sweeps away the artistic deadwood, "clearing rubble from brains," as Brecht put it, associated with stultifying social conventions. Parody performs the perennial rehistoricization of the artistic process. As new novelistic and cinematic forms, like rising social classes, struggle for power and respect, they often fight with the weapon of parody.

The Quixotic Theme

Many of the novels central to the European tradition—*The Red and the Black, Lost Illusions, Madame Bovary*—chart a Cervantic trajectory of disenchantment in which the illusions fostered by adolescent reading are systematically undone by experience in the real world and mocked, in literary terms, by parody. Many films, similarly, mock quixotic protagonists who envision their everyday experience through deforming cinematic lenses. Godard, for example, constantly rings the changes on this theme, hardly surprising in a person who once claimed to have learned "everything" from the cinema. Many Godard characters conceive life on the model of fhe filmic text. Paul in *Contempt,* according to Godard, is a character from *Marienbad* who wants to be a hero in *Rio bravo.* Angela in *A Woman is a Woman* emulates the agile grace of the dancing heroines of MGM musicals. Elsewhere, Humphrey Bogart comes to fill the actantial slot of Amadis de Gaulle as textual exemplar. Michel in *Breathless* apes Bogart's hardened nonchalance as he blows smoke into a Bogey poster. Haskell Wexler has his protagonist in *Medium Cool* echo Bogey at a further remove by having him blow smoke into a Belmondo poster. Woody Allen, as Allan Felix in *Play It Again, Sam* also attempts to project the Bogart persona, with ludicrous results. The Brazilian filmmaker Fauzão lends the theme an anticolonialist dimension by having his Bogart-admirer, in *J.S. Brown: The Last Hero* (1979), emulate the American hero to the point of wearing trench coats in the tropics, to the amusement of his compatriots.

The characters in Godard's *Band of Outsiders* (1964)—Parisian hoods imitating Hollywoodean and *série noire* gangsters—are similarly quixotic. Their lives are constantly mediated by the fictions of the pop culture intertext. Like the narrator of John Fowles' *The Magus,* they confuse metaphorically accounts of modes of feeling with literal prescriptions for everyday behavior. They have imaginary shootouts, and Arthur does a gut-clutching mime of the death of Billy-the-Kid. Asked whether she loves him, Odile tells Franz: "I only love the cinema." Even their robberies are planned in conscious imitation of "second-rate thrillers." Their first theft, symptomatically, is not of money but of a text. Franz steals a paperback while watching himself in a mirror, in a gesture that neatly epitomizes Godardian cinema—law-breaking, bookish, self-conscious.

The Cervantic interface of art and life also entails, at times, the promiscuous mingling of characters of diverse ontological status within the same fiction. Robert Alter speaks of the "ontological vertigo" that arises when Don Quixote converses with a character from the spurious continuation of *Don Quixote* by Alonso de Avellanda—"a fictional character from a 'true' fictional chronicle confronting a character from a false one in order to establish beyond doubt his own exclusive authenticity."[2] A similar confrontation between "true" and "false" characters occurs in Godard's *Weekend.* A hippie-guerrilla asks Corinne if she is real or in a film. When Corinne responds that she is in a film, the guerrilla snaps back: "Liar!" *Weekend* also has purely fictitious characters—Corinne Roland—rub elbows with actors representing historical personages (Emily Bronte, St. Juste). Other films have "real people" playing themselves in-character (Roger Leenhardt in *A Married Woman;* Francis Jeanson in *La Chinoise*) converse with fictional characters. In such instances, one wonders does the diegetic universe annex the real or the reverse? "This isn't a novel," Corinne tells Roland in *Weekend,* "it's life. A film is life." One moment in *Pierrot le Fou* points up the problematic ontology of many Godard films. Ferdinand goes to a cinema where *Le Grand Escroc* is playing. As he enters the theatre, Jean Seberg, on-screen in the film-within-the-film, asks: "At what moment had we abandoned the fictitious character to return to the real one . . . if in fact the real one ever existed." The spectator presumably recalls that Jean Seberg played opposite Belmondo in *Breathless* and thus another dimension is introduced. When an actor incarnates many roles, which represents the "fictitious" character and which the "real" one?

Figure 28.   *Breathless* (1959)

The paradox about *Don Quixote,* Harry Levin points out, is that it casts a spell while dispelling an illusion. This doubleness of what Borges calls the "partial magic" of self-conscious art, its simultaneous joy in both mystification and demystification, is reflected both in the process of art's creation and in the process of its consumption. Within the artist a struggle takes place between the will to create an illusion and the conscious decision to destroy that illusion. The lucidity of the illusionist, the puppeteer, or the filmmaker does battle with the desire to create a believable and lifelike image. For the reader or spectator, meanwhile, all the reflexive devices in the world do not necessarily preclude affective participation. The play *Hamlet* self-consciously exposes the processes of playmaking; yet, innumerable spectators have identified with the character Hamlet. Don Quixote is rendered as a purely textual entity, a verbal artifact, yet his imaginary self has served as a pole of identification for readers for centuries.

The Narrative Strategies of Reflexivity

Apart from thematic parallels, self-conscious novels and self-conscious films share fundamental narrative and rhetorical strategies. One strategy they share is, as we have seen, to cast suspicion on the central premise of illusionistic narrative—the premise of an antecedent anecdotal nucleus or substratum from which key blocks have been extracted. Illusionism pretends that stories pre-exist their telling, that the events of the story actually transpired and are therefore researchable, verifiable like the positivist's truth. Henry Fielding mocks this pretense of a historical referent in *Joseph Andrews,* when he tells us that Parson Adams ate "either a rabbit or a fowl, I could never with any tolerable certainty discover which...."[3] Thus Fielding suggests that self-conscious art need not certify itself by association with the capitalized abstractions of Nature, Reality, or History. Cervantes implies the same point by his transparently ludicrous attempts to authenticate his "sources" in *Don Quixote.* Why else would he admit that his major source, Cid Hamete Benengeli, comes from a nation of notorious liars?

Anti-illusionist novelists parody the documentary strategy of writers like Defoe who pretend to be the mere editors of correspondence found in an attic. By claiming to select only "matters of consequence," such novelists imply that their stories antedate their telling. The presumed artistic selection of an antecedent tale constitutes narrative sleight-of-hand; in fact we are given all there is, but the suggestion that there was originally more somehow enhances the ontological status of the story. To speculate, as Fielding often does, about what a given character is thinking, is to foster the illusion that the character enjoys some existence outside of the book, that he or she is more than a mere puppet. The technique recalls, on some levels, the exploitation of off-screen space in the cinema, whereby synecdochic fragments create in our mind the illusory sense of a continuum extending beyond the frame. The rectangular slice of profilmic reality included within the frame is assumed, by the laws of diegetic implication, to extend beyond the four edges of the frame and to the space behind the set and behind the camera. Off-screen looks or gestures, even when in fact directed at nothing more than a chalked line on a wall, are assumed to imply a larger diegetic space, just as the events of a novelistic character's life that *are* recounted are assumed to form a continuum with those that are *not* recounted. Just as the filmmaker "fills" the imaginary space surrounding the screen, so the novelist implies the existence of a narrative substratum below the verbal surface of the text.

Anti-illusionists often perform their narrative legerdemain with such studied clumsiness that we cannot but notice the card up the sleeve or the invisible string. Fielding veils his trickery so thinly that the very whimsicality of the formulation points up the ludicrous inadequacy of the conventional ways of authenticating a story. In *Joseph Andrews,* for example, he speculates about his protagonist's ancestry. Subsequent to a wild-goose chase after the origin of his hero's name, including facetious suppositions about an epitaph, he conjectures that Joseph Andrews probably "had as many ancestors as the best man living, and perhaps, if we look five or six hundred years backwards, might be related to some persons of very great figure at present." But let us suppose, Fielding continues, "that he had no ancestors at all, but had sprung up out of a dunghill."[4] Fielding's irony is superficially directed at an absurd pride in ancestry, but on a deeper level he is making a point about the nature of fiction. Fictional characters, he suggests, are not part of a spatial or temporal or, in this case, geneological continuum. All literary characters, if not sprung out of dunghills, are the product of spontaneous artistic generation, and delivered, to mix metaphors, by the mid-wife of literary convention. They can have, therefore, neither ancestors nor, like Lady Macbeth, children.

Fielding's playful hypothesizing about Joseph Andrews' lineage reminds us that realistic narrative often "cheats" by implying the existence of an anteriority that precedes the beginning of the story and a futurity that follows the ending. In many westerns, for example, vague references to a murdered brother supposedly "motivate" the revenge plot. Thus one story—the revenge—spreads around itself a network of narrative implication suggesting earlier stories—the original murder. *L'Année Dernière à Marienbad* can be taken, on one level, as mocking this spurious anteriority by having its fictitious characters try in vain to establish the "true" antecedent story. In fact, of course, the characters begin to exist, as Robbe-Grillet himself pointed out, with the first page of the novel (or the first shot of the film) and cease to exist with the last page. Other narratives "cheat" by implying a factitious futurity. Countless Hollywood films end with intimations of marriage and the implied futurity of happy conjugal union. The notoriously phallic train-entering-the-tunnel in *North by Northwest*, presumably, foretells years of tumescent sexuality on the parallel tracks of marriage.

Story and Discourse

One of the functions of narrative, Metz points out, is to invent one time scheme in terms of another. All narratives construct themselves out of the interarticulation of a double time sequence, that of the time sequence of plot events—story—and the time of their textual presentation—discourse.[5] The duality of this time scheme—the time of the telling and the time of the told—makes possible the commonplace distortions of narrative. Story time, or the imagined events of the fiction, might cover an entire lifetime, while discourse time is constituted by the time it takes to read the novel, attend the play, or see the film. This double time-scheme corresponds to the Russian formalist distinction of *fabula* (story) and *sjužet* (plot), and to Genette's distinction of *histoire* (story)—the narrative actions taken in themselves without reference to their discursive mediation—and *récit* (narrative)—the oral or written discourse that undertakes to convey an event or series of events.

Narrative artists, whether in literary fiction or film, have the choice of highlighting or obscuring the discordances between these two time-schemes, between discourse and story. De Maupassant formulated the illusionistic ideal in the novel when he suggested that writers must manage "skillful and dissimulated transitions" so as to give the "complete illusion of the real." The mainstream fiction film, especially from the advent of sound through the late 1980s, has tended to model its temporal conventions on the procedures of the realist novel. Metz' "grande syntagmatique de la bande image" attempts to delineate the conventions of spatio-temporal continuity in the classical fiction film. The diverse syntagmas, as he explains them, presuppose a pre-existing reality, a substratum of "story," on which a selection has been operated to produce the filmic discourse. Classical films, like the realist novel, pretend to skip over the dead spaces or *temps morts* through narrative ellipses which are smoothed over by dissolves or fades. They, too, manage "skillful and dissimulated transitions" so as to give the "complete illusion of the real."

Self-conscious novelists often call explicit attention to the shifting relations between the twin time schemes of story and discourse. Henry Fielding in *Tom Jones* posits a kind of sliding proportion between the two, according to the intrinsic interest of the "protextual" events:

Now it is our purpose, in the ensuing pages, to pursue a contrary method. When any extraordinary scene presents itself (as we trust will often be the case), we shall spare no pains nor paper to open it at large to our readers; but if whole years should pass without producing anything worthy [of] his notice, we shall not be afraid of a chasm in our history, but shall hasten on to matters of consequence, and leave such periods of time totally unobserved.

In another passage, Fielding exercises a tasteful, Lubitsch-like, selectivity in his treatment of an amorous scene:

> Not to tire the Reader, by leading him through every Scene of this Courtship, (which, tho', in the Opinion of a certain great Author, it is the pleasantest Scene of Life to the Actor, is, perhaps, as dull and tiresome as any whatever to the Audience) the Captain made his Advances in Form, the Citadel was defended in Form, and at length, in proper Form, surrendered at Discretion.

By pretending to excise scenes in the name of the reader's patience, or by pretending to be lying in wait for the appearance of "extraordinary scenes," (scenes which he is in fact inventing) and by implying the existence of a narrative substratum from which all such scenes are "mined," Fielding both performs and exposes one of the classic confidence tricks of illusionism.

Laurence Sterne, in *Tristram Shandy,* further exposes the tenuous relation between the two time-schemes of story and discourse by portraying himself, as narrator-author, worrying over providing sufficient time for the actions of his fictitious characters:

> It is about an hour and a half's good reading since my uncle Toby rung the bell, when Obadiah was ordered to saddle a horse, and go for Dr. Slop, the man midwife;—so that no one can say, with reason, that I have not allowed Obadiah time enough, poetically speaking, and considering the emergency too, both to go and to come; though, morally and truly speaking, the man, perhaps, has scarce had time to get on his boots.[7]

Sterne portrays the opposition of "true" and "poetic" speaking—an eighteenth-century version of "story" and "discourse"—as a kind of frantic race between two temporal schemes. The narrator of Machado de Assis' *Dom Casmurro,* meanwhile, evokes the process by which a novelist laboriously secretes fictive time: "This page already covers some months, others will cover years, and thus we will finally come to the end." But it is Sterne who gets the most comic mileage out of pointing up the difference between the time it takes to produce the discourse and the story time of the discourse itself:

> I am this month one whole year older than I was this time twelvemonth, and having got, as you perceive, almost into the middle of my fourth volume—and no farther than to my first day's life—'tis demonstrative that I have three hundred and sixty-four days more life than when I first set out; so that instead of advancing, as a common writer, in my work with what I have been doing at it—on the contrary, I am just thrown so many volumes back . . . as at this rate I should just live 364 times faster than I should write.[8]

Behind Sterne's ingenious paradoxes lies a serious point about what has now become the *triple* temporality of narrative—the time of the story, the time of the discourse, and the time of the *production* of the discourse.

In *Narrative Discourse,* Genette speaks of the special difficulties involved in comparing the duration of story time and narrative discourse time in a literary text. Since reading time varies with individual readers and particular circumstances, nothing allows us to determine a "normal" speed of execution. A continuous dialogue scene suggests a rough equality between story and discourse time, but ultimately we can only affirm, as Genette points out, that such a passage reports what was said, either really or fictively, but does not necessarily transcribe the speed of the conversation or register the dead spaces between sentences. Comparisons between the duration of story and discourse time would seem somewhat less problematic in the cinema, where the text unfolds in controlled and measurable time, measurable in minutes or feet of film, unlike the pseudo-time or literary discourse, measurable only in pages. But even in film the question is complicated.

Take, for example, the attempts to create a strict equivalence between story and discourse time. In both novel and film, rigid isochrony is so rare as to almost invariably constitute a kind of tour de force. Robert Alter points out an amusing novelistic example in Joseph Andrews, where the time it takes to read Fielding's account of Lady Booby's horrified reaction to Joseph's protestations of "virtue" approximates the time she spent before responding—two minutes. Such a passage constitutes the novelistic equivalent of the one-shot sequence in the cinema, generally characterized by a strict isochrony between the duration of the shot and the presumed duration of the fictive event.

The occasional attempts, within the fiction film, to establish a strict congruence between story and discourse time—notably in such films as *Rope, High Noon, Cleo from 5 to 7*—constitute anomalies within the tradition, and are often obliged to "cheat" (as in the case of the final half-hour of *Cleo,* for example). Even the case of the one-shot sequence is more complex than at first appears. Apart from the perhaps spurious example of a single continuous shot showing the turning pages of a calendar or the rapid advance of a clock, one might cite a film such as *The Travelling Players,* in which a single continuous shot embraces two historical periods. As a fixed camera frames a provincial square, the costumed players representing one era withdraw and are replaced by costumed players representing another, with no change of shot. Woody Allen achieves a similar effect in *Stardust Memories.* We see young Sandy Bates, in a Superman costume, receiving a gift from Dorrie. He runs off-screen, as the camera stays fixed on Dorrie, only to return as the adult Sandy Bates. A single continuous shot, in other words, has evoked the passage of several decades.

Literary and filmic storytellers enjoy complete freedom to play with the temporal coordinates of their stories; they can vary the proportion between referential time and discursive textual time at will. Genette sums up the possible variations in the novel as ranging from what he calls the "infinite speed of ellipsis" to the slowed motion of descriptive pause. He offers a schematic summary of four alternatives which form part of the conventional decorum of novelistic tempo: *pause,* in which discursive time elapses but story time does not; *scene,* in which discursive and story time are identical; *summary,* in which story time exceeds discursive time; and *ellipsis,* in which story time elapses but discursive time does not. He notes, finally, the possibility of a fifth possible relation, in which discourse time exceeds story time—"a sort of scene in slow-motion"—which he excludes because of its virtual nonexistence within the literary tradition.

The cinema, for its part, enjoys special advantages in this area. It can deploy all the "normal" variations between story and discourse time available to any narrative medium. The relationship can vary from extreme compression—the two hours of *Space Odyssey* spanning millennia of human evolution—to rough equivalence—the two hours of verbal traffic of *My Dinner with André* corresponding to a plausible duration of a dinner conversation—to a kind of dilation whereby discourse time far outstrips story time, as in the oft-cited *Occurrence at Owl Creek Bridge,* which "stretches" a split-second of story-time into a half-hour of filmic discourse. At the same time, film is equipped with slow and accelerated motion, effects which can be only metaphorically emulated in a verbal medium. Film can be slowed down through undercranking and speeded up through overcranking. Time-lapse photography can make a day pass in seconds. Jerky animation effects can be obtained through frame-by-frame shooting. The saccadic slow-motion sequences which dot Godard's *Every Man for Himself* demonstrate the possibility of a polyrhythmic, variable-speed cinema, a possibility largely denied to poetry and the novel.

Although Genette claims that a relation in which narrative discourse time exceeds story time—"a sort of scene in slow motion"—is virtually unknown in literature, Nabokov's Humbert Humbert complains that literature is always slow when compared to the cinema. He laments the prodding deliberateness of prose fiction, with its congenital incapacity to seize moments in their lightning simultaneity. Gleefully relating his wife's providential death by car crash, he deplores having to put "the impact of an instantaneous vision into a sequence of words," whose "physical accumulation on the page impairs the actual flash, the sharp unity of impression."[9]

Although Genette finds authentic "pause" quite rare in the novel, it seems that both novelists and filmmakers can pretend to "freeze" time if they so desire. Cervantes leaves Don Quixote and the Biscayan poised for battle, swords in the air and with ferocious mien, in a combat eternally frozen and eternally in progress, in what amounts to a narrative freeze-frame. The device recalls Hogarth's *The Rake's Progress*, where figures are satirically caught in bizarre and compromising postures, their hands deep in other people's pockets or bodices. René Clair's *Paris Qui Dort* (1923) structures an entire film around such Hogarthian freeze-frames. Its story concerns a mad scientist whose mechanical ray paralyzes whomever it touches, freezing the pickpocket in mid-flight with the just-picked wallet, and petrifying the unfaithful wife in *flagrant délit,* freezing her in almost Dantean fashion in the arms of her lover. Chris Marker's *La Jetée* tells of a man catapulted into a new space-time continuum, trying to retrieve a lost childhood image, the film consisting of a succession of frozen timeless moments.

While Humbert Humbert, who has only words to play with, lusts after the cinema's "fantastic simultaneousness," he might also envy its potential for *non*simultaneousness, its capacity for mingling apparently contradictory times and temporalities. Film can deploy temporalities simply not available to any purely linguistic medium. Each of its tracks—moving image, phonetic sound, noises, music, writing—can potentially develop an autonomous temporality entering into complex relations with the other tracks. A quoted piece of music, respected in its integral continuity, can "accompany" a discontinuous or elliptical sequence. One of the problems in the formulation of Metz' "grande syntagmatique" is precisely its failure to take the temporality of the nonimage tracks into account. The classification of the opening segment of *Adieu Phillipine* as a "bracket syntagma," without clear temporal development, for example, ignores the clear temporal development of the diegetic and often on-screen music which plays throughout the segment. Dialogue continuity, similarly, can play against the continuity of the image track. In *Sullivan's Travels,* Joel MacCrea tells Veronica Lake, as they're being stopped by highway policemen, not to worry because "there's nothing they can do." The next shot shows them locked up in jail, as Veronica Lake asks: "What did you say?" and he answers: "I said there's absolutely nothing they can do!" The spatial discontinuity of the image track, then, is coupled with the apparent continuity of the dialogue, in such a way as to better convey the contradiction between Sullivan's claims and his real situation. Godard, as we shall see in our discussion of *Numéro Deux,* orchestrates the temporalities of the diverse tracks with even greater audaciousness.

Tempo in Film and Novel

Fielding's claim that he treats only "matters of consequence" and passes over trivia implies that the artist exercises control over the tempo of the story. The conventional expectation, in both literature and the cinema, is that discursive time will be proportional to the intrinsic narrative importance of the event being recounted. We expect only key events and only key aspects of those events. Literary narrative, however, has undergone steady redefinition of the notion of what is "key" in a story. Emma Bovary's desperately suffocating "heures des repas" would not have been considered key until Flaubert made them key, as Auerbach so effectively shows in analyzing Flaubert's use of the imperfect. We would scarcely expect Balzac to describe his characters' masturbatory or defecatory fantasies, but we are not surprised when post-Joycean novelists do, for Joyce annexed the territory of psychic trivia as a legitimate subject for literature. Between the Odyssey as recounted in 41 days and 24 books and the Odyssey as told by Joyce in one day and hundreds of pages, literary narrative has suffered myriad sea-changes in its temporal conventions.

In mainstream cinema, on the other hand, the conventions of narrative tempo have remained fairly archaic. The assumption that films should "entertain" has prevented commercial cinema from tampering too audaciously with habitual notions of what constitutes an acceptably marketable tempo. The subversion of these conventions has come mainly from the avant-garde or from filmmakers associated with socially oppressed groups. The strictly observed linear time of Andy Warhol's *Empire*—460 minutes of static shots of the Empire State Building taken overnight and into dawn—equates the referential and the discursive in a radically provocative way. Hollis Frampton, meanwhile, tampers not only with the temporal conventions of filmic discourse but also with the conventions of projection. His planned 36-hour film cycle *Magellan* was intended to be projected over a period of 371 days—a full year plus three-day prologue and epilogue—with a part of the film screened every day, and with longer films slated for special days of the year like equinoxes and solstices. Socially oppressed groups, meanwhile, have felt the need of impressing their films and their audiences with a different sense of lived duration. The slow pace of certain third world films such as Nelson Pereira dos Santos' *Barren Lives* (1963) or Haile Gerima's *Harvest: 3000 Years* (1975) mimetically evoke the lived pace of a peasant milieu. Their unusually slow rhythm comes as a kind of cultural shock to the spectator accustomed to the swift pace and saturation of incident typical of conventional fiction films. Chantal Akerman's *Jeanne Dielman, 23 Quai du Commerce, 1080 Bruxelles,* meanwhile, condenses three days of referential time into three hours and twenty minutes of discursive time in its portrayal of the life of a middle-class Belgian widow. Akerman allows her protagonist the time to complete her habitual actions—each step in the preparation of the morning coffee, each step in the preparation of a dinner, each step of washing the dishes and placing them in drawers and cupboards—in such a way as to force the spectator to reflect on the nature of time as experienced by the Jeanne Dielman's of the world. The relatively strict fidelity to the tempo and lived duration of an oppressed life forms part of the film's meaning.

For the viewer conditioned by commercial fiction films, an event seems complete if its "key" parts are shown within an expected period of time. A dinner sequence, typically, consists of a few establishing shots of the diners sitting down to their meal, some shots and counter shots conveying some intensely meaningful dialogue, and a concluding shot of the diners rising from the table. Louis Malle eschews this cinematic foreshortening in *My Dinner with André* by respecting the plausible "real time" of a dinner shared by friends. On another level, however, his film does not really question the temporal decorum of cinematic fiction. It merely displaces the fictive intensity, usually parcelled out over image, dialogue and sound, onto the dialogue track. What becomes "key" is the conversation, a play of minds and words so preternaturally charming, so unmarred by banality or pause, so reminiscent of the philosophical dialogues of a Voltaire or a Diderot, that we "forgive" the film for its lack of conventional dramatic action and its literal time.

Questions of tempo in both the film and the novel are more subtle than a mere matter of proportion between the importance of the event and the time allotted to its treatment. In the novel, perceived duration intimately depends on such minute questions as syntax—truncated Hemingwayesque or convoluted Jamesian?—density of information, and even euphoniousness. One might say that Fielding's periodic sentences slow down novelistic time for comically aggressive purposes. Stylistic flights and essayistic digressions, similarly, inevitably retard the flow of narrative. One might view the novel as progressing historically toward an ever more subtle temporalization. Whereas description once constituted a kind of halt in the narrative, a moment when the temporal concatenations of the verbal signifiers ceased to refer to a temporal relation, signifying only spatial coexistence, Flaubert, recounting Charles Bovary's first encounter with Emma, managed to temporalize description. His style speeds up mimetically at moments of excitement. It waltzes with Emma and excites itself to metaphorical climax in the carriage at Rouen. Thus the novel seems to tend toward the incorporation of Bergsonian *durée,* to approximate more and more the psychic "feel" of time.

In the cinema, likewise, questions of tempo cannot be reduced to some simplistic proposition between event and treatment. Matters of cinematic tempo are inextricably bound up with questions of style and editing. The tempo varies with the frequency of the shots, the amount of variation in angle and focal length, and the complexity of the soundtrack. The "speed" of even a static shot depends on the density of information conveyed by the shot. A shot of a couple riding in an automobile will seem more rapidly paced if we see passing countryside. The perceived duration of such a sequence depends as well on the soundtrack. Complete silence will seem slow; the purr of an engine will speed things up; and music will charm the spectator into forgetting the passage of time. The point is that cinematographic time is a complete fabrication. Even the apparently literal equivalence of the one-shot sequence can cheat by crowding staged and rehearsed events into an unnaturally short period of time. But more typically, time is manipulated, stretched and condensed in the ordinary processes of editing. Diegetic moments are artificially prolonged through *faux raccords*. The celebrated baby carriage in *Potemkin* teeters on the edge of the step for what seems an eternity, and Eisenstein lengthens the Odessa steps to a point that Odessa residents would scarcely recognize them. Hollywood musicals, similarly, prolong certain moments in a choreographic sequence by collating various takes of the same episode. This kind of manipulation, admittedly, is usually rendered invisible through cutting on movement, adroit variation of camera angle, and the continuity of the music on the soundtrack. Only with self-conscious artists is the manipulation made visible.

Titles and Intertitles

Henry Fielding in *Joseph Andrews* sheds light on what he calls one of the mysteries of the novelistic trade—the practice of dividing works into books and chapters. He likens the spaces between books to an inn or resting place for the reader, and the contents prefixed to the chapters to inscriptions over the gate of the inn. He cites classical precedent to justify his practice and then, in a sudden deflating metaphor, compares dividing books to a butcher jointing his meat. The analogy is revelatory of the artificiality of such divisions, for a steer does not naturally apportion itself into neat pieces of shank and rump. Chapter titles in Fielding are often symptomatic of this unnaturalness. Both he and Cervantes preface a series of chapters with variations on "in which the history is continued," "further continued," "even further continued," and so forth in such a way as to mock the very idea of novelistic consecution. This play with titles calls attention to the joints, to the temporal architecture and plumbing of fiction, instead of using titles as more or less invisible binders in a narrative continuity. Fielding's titles mix spatial notations—"containing five pieces of paper"—with temporal ones—"containing the time of a year"—in such a way as to make us reflect on the complex interaction of spatiality and temporality in the novel.

The cinema of the silent period often exploited the unreality of titles and the temporal conventions behind them. Silent film, deprived of the more complete mimesis afforded by synchronous sound, was in some ways more receptive to anti-illusionism. Keaton often pokes fun at the very gratuitousness of the titles that interrupt silent film narrative. In *The Navigator* (1924), Buster casts an anchor. A title, projected for approximately ten seconds, informs us: "ten seconds later," followed by a shot of the anchor floating to the surface. The only conceivable usefulness of such a title is to explain a temporal ellipse; it becomes absurd in a situation of straight continuity. In *The Paleface* (1922) we see Buster in statuesque embrace with his Indian bride. A title then alerts us to a time shift: "two years later." The shot which follows shows us the couple again, identically dressed, in the same position and in the same setting. They pause for breath, and then resume their embrace. The sequence beautifully highlights the nonequivalence of story time and discourse time, for we know that even lovers, with their special respiratory patterns, cannot hold their breath for two years, any more than Don Quixote could hold his sword in the air while Cervantes looked for supplementary sources.

Christian Metz has suggested that just as the novel required something longer than the word and shorter than the book itself, and thus came up with the chapter, so the fiction film needed a unit longer than the shot and shorter than the film itself and thus came up with the sequence. As if to illustrate the parallel, Godard apes novelistic practice in *Pierrot le Fou* by dividing it into chapters. To point up the unreality of such divisions, Godard has chapter seven *follow* chapter eight. The chapter titles, furthermore, have neither parallelism nor coherence. They mix numbers (chapter 12) with general rubrics ("Désespoir") and plot resumés ("Nous traversons la France"). Others represent literary allusions ("Une Saison en Enfer") while others are remarkable only for their uselessness. The gratuitous consecution of "chapitre suivant" is followed by the even more gratuitous "chapitre suivant sans titre." Godard seems to be heralding the awkwardness, the arbitrariness of divisions in art generally, whether it be the frame in painting, acts and scenes in the theatre, chapters in novels, or sequences in films.

Many Godard films superimpose what Genette calls "normal sequence," in which story and discourse proceed in an isochronous manner, with more "achronic" schemas. *2 or 3 Things I Know about Her* combines a "day-in-the-life" chronology familiar from documentaries with a digressive treatise on urban life and the nature of filmmaking. The title of *Weekend,* meanwhile, calls attention to what we assume to be the story time of the film, an impression reinforced by the succession of disconcertingly literal temporal notations at the beginning of the film—"Saturday, 10 A.M.," "Saturday, 11 A.M.," and so forth. But gradually the film begins to explode literal time, finally alluding to a wide spectrum of historical events. The title "One Tuesday in the 100 Years War" precedes a *L'Age d'Or*-like shot of an earthworm. Other titles make whimsically sophomoric reference to literature—"One Friday Far from Robinson and Mantes la Jolie"; and "Light in August," or to the months in the Republican calendar—"Thermidor," "Pluvoise," and "Vende Miaire"; or to months heavy with historical or cinematic resonance: "September Massacre," "October Language," and "From the French Revolution to UNR Weekends." The cannibalistic finales lead to the ultimate title: "Fin de l'histoire," with its ambiguity in French, suggesting either "end of the story" or an apocalyptic "end of history," followed by "Fin de Cinéma."

The Dialogue of Author/Reader/Spectator

Reflexive artists often foreground the narrating instance, and in so doing call attention to the reader or spectator. They favor the I-You of "discourse" to the He-She-It of "histoire." Rather than narratorless fiction, where no one speaks and "events seem to tell themselves,"[10] reflexive fiction models its discourse on human conversation, from which it borrows its manner of expression. "Discourse" is dialogic by definition; its "I" implies immediately a "You" to whom the utterance is directed. The presence of the reader or spectator is inscribed and signaled in the text, shifting the interest from the diegesis to what Geoffrey Nowell-Smith calls the "intersubjective textual relation," which comes to form a kind of parallel plot. Wayne Booth describes the process as it operates in *Tom Jones:*

> If we read straight through all of the seemingly gratuitous appearances by the narrator, leaving out the story of Tom, we discover a running account of growing intimacy between the narrator and the reader, an account with a kind of plot of its own and a separate dénouement.[11]

Fielding himself underlines the relationship by the metaphor of the voyage, on which the reader and the narrator are traveling companions, the real voyage being not so much the picaresque one of the literary personage but rather the literary one of reader and writer.

Filmmakers as well have created texts in which the ongoing dialogue between the implied author and the spectator is as important as the story itself. Max Ophuls' *La Ronde* (1950) provides a classic example. The "host" of the film (Anton Wolbrook) is clearly an authorial stand-in. At the outset of the film, he introduces himself directly to the audience:

> You are probably wondering what my part in the story is. Author? Compère? A passer-by? I am...well, I could be anyone among you. I am the answer to your wish to know everything.... I see in the round, as it were, and that allows me to be everywhere at the same time...everywhere.

The host's ubiquity and omniscience, it becomes clear, derive from his special relationship to the magical powers of the cinematic apparatus. At diverse points he passes before studio equipment and film-making paraphernalia. We see him manipulating a spotlight and turning the crank of his metaphoric carousel. His speeches stress his power to evoke history, effect changes of season, pander for his characters, alter lighting, and summon music. At one point, we see him in an editing room where he unrolls a strip of film, examines it, and then physically cuts out what we take to be a sexually explicit scene.

The off-screen narrator of Godard's *Band of Outsiders* displays the amiable omniscience of a Cervantes or a Fielding, and makes precisely the kinds of authorial interventions that they might have made. The narrator—the voice is Godard's—provides plot summaries, draws metaphors, points morals, tells tales within the general tale, and promises future episodes. At one point, Godard spoofs a device dating back to the days of Griffith—the practice of furnishing a few lines of narrative synopsis for the benefit of latecomers. The narrator makes a deliberately graceless intrusion about 10 minutes into the film: "Here's a plot summary for you latecomers." The summary, perversely, is inaccurate and misleading, as if Godard were scolding the spectator for even caring about the bare bones of plot.

The narrator also shows off his omniscience by precisely detailing the innermost thoughts of his characters, often in tenderly poetic terms which seem incongruous in a story about petty gangsters. As Arthur dies interminably on screen, the narrator informs us that Arthur's last thought was of Odile, whom he remembered as resembling the legendary bird of the Indians who never stops flying. Only an omniscient narrator could penetrate his hero's thoughts at such a moment, and only a self-conscious one would place such a recherché simile in the mind of an agonizing hoodlum. The narrator makes his final intervention as the two remaining hoodlums, Franz and Odile, make their getaway from France. As a globe of the world revolves before us, the author-narrator tells us that his next picture will be in technicolor and will recount the adventures of Franz and Odile in Brazil. Apart from spoofing serial formula movies, this final promise from the narrator reminds us of the self-conscious novelists, whose very chapter titles often advertised coming features: "In which the reader will be surprised"; "a chapter which will instruct and delight the reader."

We hear Godard's voice again in *2 or 3 Things I Know About Her*, but this time the off-screen commentaries challenge and interrogate the film text. While some are philosophical or political in nature, many concern the specific choices involved in making a film. They imply technical choices having to do with sound recording ("Am I speaking too loud?"), focal length ("Am I looking from too far or too closely?") and so forth. The fact that the commentaries are whispered typifies the film's methods, for whispering obliges the spectator to make a special effort to understand; he or she has to meet the filmmaker halfway. A calculated under-determination obliges the coded spectator to become hyper-critical and alert. The text is intended to be open, collaborative, the public hopefully producing as well as consuming, or better regarding the making and seeing of the film as different moments of the same production.

Figure 29. *Two or Three Things That I Know About Her* (1967)

The Self-Correcting Style

Self-conscious fabulists often seem incapable of telling stories straight, both in the sense of telling them with a straight face and in the sense of telling them linearly, sequentially. Their narratives provide comic demonstrations of Mark Twain's *How Not to Tell a Story*. Godard, for example, systematically undermines suspense, prematurely intimates endings, and progresses by irrelevancies. Machado de Assis, like an inept raconteur who forgets crucial details, interrupts *Dom Casmurro* to correct an oversight: "... Pardon me, but this chapter ought to have been preceded by another, in which I would have told an incident that occurred a few weeks before, two months after Sancha had gone away." Machado contemplates shuffling the order of the chapters, but decides that it would be "too great a nuisance to have to change the page numbers."[12] Sterne's narrative in *Tristram Shandy,* similarly, on which much of Machado's work was explicitly modeled, is constantly stalled, sidetracked, and derailed. His "choicest morsel," concerning Uncle Toby and the widow, is postponed until the ninth volume. And Diderot, in still another text inspired by *Tristram Shandy,* perpetually digresses from the oft-promised "amours de Jacques."

Style in reflexive fiction is often self-correcting; it is writing *"sous rature,"* Machado de Assis, for example, constantly anatomizes his own expression in an obsessive metalinguistic dismantling of his own practice. His critical sense is forever on the alert, ready to censure any lapse into bathos or vulgarity. The narrator-protagonist of *Dom Casmurro* claims at one point that his forced departure for Europe elicited more tears than all those shed since Adam and Eve. Instantly regretting his hyperbole, he acknowledges the exaggeration, but insists "it's good to be emphatic now and then." Whereas metaphors habitually function as transparent conveyors of analogies, Machado often explicates or dissects them. Rather than serve them up as finished products for consumption, he exposes them in their process of elaboration, often proposing metaphors only to dismiss them as less than apt: "No, that comparison won't do." At times, he even enlists the reader's aid in his quest for the right trope: "My idea was really fixed, as fixed as ... I cannot think of anything sufficiently fixed in this world: perhaps the moon, perhaps the pyramids of Egypt, perhaps the late Germanic Diet. Let the reader make whatever comparison best suits him ..."[13] The text, in such instances, ceases to comport itself as a finished corpus, evoking instead some endlessly modifiable work-in-progress. The writing writes and rewrites itself under the reader's eyes, and presumably with the reader's help. Thus Machado renders explicit a fundamental truth about literary creation, that, as Todorov puts it, "every work, every novel, tells through its fabric of events the story of its own creation, its own history."[14]

In the novel *At Swim-Two-Birds* (1939), Flann O'Brien opens by a first-person reflection on narrative openings: "A good book may have three openings entirely dissimilar and interrelated only in the prescience of the author, or for that matter one hundred times as many endings" (p. 9). O'Brien then constructs three parodic "beginnings," none of which is literally a beginning since they follow the narrator's opening remarks. Woody Allen, in *Manhattan*, borrows this literary device by having his narrator-protagonist Isaac (Allen) voice different possible beginnings to the novel he is presumably writing:

> "Chapter One. He admired New York City. He idolized it all out of proportion." Oh, no, make that: "He-he...romanticized it all out of proportion. Now...to him...no matter what the season was, this was still a town that existed in black and white and pulsated to the great tunes of George Gershwin." Ahhh, now let me start this over. "Chapter One. He was too romantic about Manhattan as he was about everything else. He thrived on the hustle...bustle of the crowds and the traffic."

By introducing the author and the question of authorship into the text via a virtuoso collision of possible fictive voices, displaying variable proportions of starstruck romanticism and disenchanted "realism," all coinciding with Gordon Willis' glistening montage of Manhattan imagery, Allen sollicits the spectator-interlocutor's reflections on the modalities of his art.

The Indeterminate Text

Since reflexive texts inscribe the reader/spectator within their own rhetorical space, they often perform their own hermeneutics, counseling their audience on certain pitfalls of reading or interpretation. The interest shifts from "meaning" to the productive interaction of reader and text. Fielding warns the reader not to travel too rapidly through his pages, so as not to miss the "curious productions of nature which will be observed by the slower and more accurate reader." Machado de Assis, echoing Fielding, remonstrates with his readers for their impatience:

> (You are in a hurry to get old, and the book goes slowly; you like straight, solid narrative and a regular and fluent style; but this book and my style are like drunks, they stagger to the right and to the left, they start and they stop, they mutter, they roar, they guffaw, they threaten the sky, they slip and they fall.)[15]

Machado develops a playful, semi-aggressive relationship with his readers. Just as Godard makes fun of his public's expectations, Machado mocks his "obtuse readers." In *Bras Cubas,* he tells his readers that *they* are the worst problem with the book: "The worst defect in this book is you, dear reader." This direct address to the reader recalls many moments in Godard's films. At the beginning of *Breathless*, Michel, driving alone, looks directly at us and says: "Me, I love the sea, I love the country, and I love the city. If you don't love the sea, if you don't love the country, if you don't love the city—then go fuck youself." Ferdinand in *Pierrot le Fou*, driving alone with Marianne, turns and directly addresses the camera: "You see, that's all they think about...amusing themselves." Asked whom he is speaking to, Ferdinand answers: "To the spectators."

Self-conscious novelists often enlist the reader's active collaboration. They see their texts as indeterminate, full of gaps, as schemes that need to be filled out by the realizing acts of the reader's imagination. Sterne halves matters amicably with the reader, keeping the reader's mind as busy as his own. He asks their advice ("What would your worships have me do in this case?") and, as evidence of his faith in their creative powers, leaves two blank pages for the reader, in which to paint the Widow Wadman for himself, "as like your mistress as you can—as unlike your wife as your conscience will let you" (VI, 38). Machado de Assis, similarly, has his narrator Dom Casmurro request the reader's help in locating stylistic errors, asking that readers write him so he can correct the errors in the next edition. The same narrator tells us that he is not disturbed by books with omissions; he simply closes his eyes and evokes everything that was not in the book. He then invites his readers to do likewise: "This is the way I fill in other men's lacunae; in the same way you may fill in mine."[16]

This fondness for textual indeterminacy anticipates, on a modest scale, the strategies of what Umberto Eco calls "open works," i.e., texts which grant considerable autonomy to their readers/spectators/performers, explicitly inviting choice and participation. Eco cites musical pieces by Berio and Stockhausen designed to be delivered unfinished to the performer like the components of a construction kit. Joyce's *Finnegan's Wake*, similarly, proposes, instead of a conventional story, a network of verbal relationships, a polysemic space where labyrynthian paths of possible meanings endlessly intersect, a moving fabric of traces referring back to themselves. Calder's "Mobiles," as they move in the air, continually recreate their own space and dimensions along with the observer's relation to them.[17] Cortazar ends each chapter in *Hopscotch* with the number of another chapter the reader might proceed with.

The Incorporation of Criticism

Literary criticism is intrinsic to the fictional world of the self-conscious novel. In *Don Quixote*, in *Tom Jones*, in *Dom Casmurro* literary criticism does not constitute an alien intrusion but rather a dialectical moment within the process of generation of the text. In the cinema, no one better illustrates the possibilities of the dialectical interplay of creation and critique than Godard, whose entire oeuvre constitutes a sustained inquiry into the nature of cinematic language, an inquiry made explicit in the myriad passages of film criticism that dot his work. Samuel Fuller appears in *Pierrot le Fou* to offer his definition of the cinema as a battleground of hate, action, violence, and death, "in a word, emotion." Fritz Lang, Paul Laval, and Jeremiah Prokosch debate the nuances of cinematic adaptation in *Contempt*. *Le Gai Savoir* constitutes a veritable *Discourse on Cinematographic Method*, while *Every Man for Himself* speculates on the relations between cinema and television. In short, just as Cervantes and Fielding counterpoint their narrative with expositions of literary theory, so Godard makes the critical act an integral part of filmic creation.

In *8 1/2*, Fellini deploys film criticism within the text to amusing ends. He places in the mouth of the insufferable (and highly unphotogenic) critic-collaborator Daumier—whose very name evokes both realism and caricature—all the strictures that critics might address to *8 1/2* itself: that it lacks narrative structure and philosophical premise, that it shows ambivalence toward the Catholic church, that it displays all the vices of the avant-garde and none of its virtues. Fellini's surrogate Guido takes vengeance on Daumier by condemning him, at least in the privacy of his imagination, to death by hanging, while Fellini himself undercuts him as director by 1) including in *8 1/2* all the sequences that Daumier would have excised, and 2) by commanding the camera to abandon Daumier whenever the critic begins his dreary monologues. Thus Fellini foresees and disarms any deconstructions the critics might propose.

Woody Allen deploys a similar proleptic strategy in *Stardust Memories*, a film clearly indebted to *8 1/2*. Both films are about a filmmaker in the process of making a film, and in both cases the filmmaker is in emotional and intellectual crisis. Both films are structured by a constant shuttle between past and present, fantasy and reality, film and films-within-the-film. Allen casts himself as Sandy Bates, a celebrity-director who reluctantly attends a retrospective in his honor, where he has to listen to the fawning praise of his fans and the inane censure of his critics. The film inventories all the conceivable charges that might be leveled at Allen's oeuvre in general and at *Stardust Memories* in particular. The studio executives who screen what is retroactively revealed to be a clip from "Suppression," Bates' latest film, find it "horrible," "a disgrace," and "pretentious." Indeed, most of the charges that were in fact leveled at *Stardust Memories* are pronounced by these studio executives:

Walsh: He's pretentious. His filming style is too fancy. His insights are shallow and morbid. They try to document their private suffering and fob it off as art.

Taylor: What does he have to suffer about? Doesn't the man know he's got the greatest gift that anyone could have? The gift of laughter?

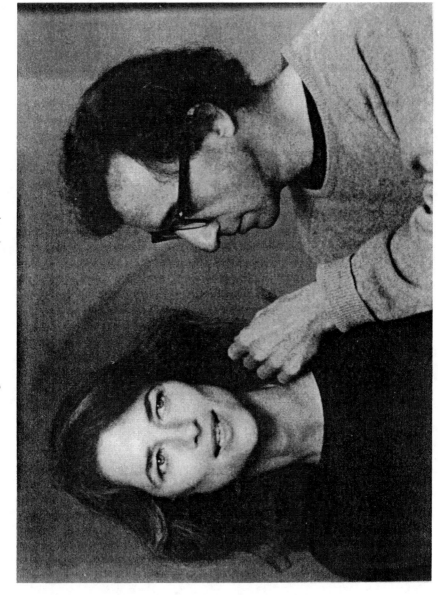

Figure 30. *Stardust Memories* (1980)

Sandy Bates' fans, meanwhile, vacillate between naive adoration—"It's so deep. I mean it's . . . All that stuff about life and . . . how we should, everybody should love each other, I mean, you know, he's telling us heavy, original things"—and vindictive rage—"Cop-out artist!" . . . "Why do all comedians turn out to be sentimental bores?" Even the "naive" spectators, as embodied by an elderly man speaking in Yiddish-accented English have their complaints: "For this he makes a living? I like a melodrama, a musical comedy with a plot."

The critics, apparently lacking all sense of irony, proceeded to make all the mistaken interpretive moves anticipated by the film itself, while dismissing the satire on the critics as a neurotic defense-mechanism. Like Bates' critics, they found *Stardust Memories* derivative, self-indulgent, and unfunny. The theme of derivativeness was evoked even by the titles of many of the journalistic reviews—"Woody Doesn't Rhyme with Federico" (Sarris), "Inferiors: Woody Allen hides behind Fellini" (Schiff), and "Woody's 8 1/2 Wrongs" (Shalit). The charge seems especially ironic in the context of a film which so clearly acknowledges its debts, especially to Fellini and Sturges. The initial sequence, for example, operates on a principle of systematic degradation from its prototype—the initial tunnel sequence from *8 1/2*. In both, the male protagonists are trapped within vehicles in a nightmarish world marked by selective nondiegetic silence, but Woody Allen's owlish face substitutes for Marcello Mastroianni's handsome one, an old train replaces a new car, and a Jersey dump takes the place of the Mediterranean seashore. The charge of derivativeness, in any case, misses the point. Allen has always focused attention on what we have called the intertext, a fact made obvious already in his titles: *Play It Again, Sam* evokes Michael Curtiz and Humphrey Bogart, *A Midsummer Night's Sex Comedy* renders homage to Shakespeare and Bergman. When asked if the mad-scientist routine in one of the films-within-the-film was an homage to Vincent Price, the Tony Roberts character answers: "No, we just stole it outright." Woody Allen does not hide his borrowings; rather, he suggests that such borrowing is universal, a fundamental part of the process of creation.

Apart from the more conventional objections to *Stardust Memories,* there were two which seemed more emotionally charged. The two objections might be summarized very simply as 1) the critics dislike Woody Allen/Sandy Bates; and 2) Woody Allen/Sandy Bates despises the critics and is therefore despicable. The two arguments are of course connected as a kind of emotional non sequitur quite common in everyday social life: he dislikes me therefore I hate him. We see this illogic in its pure, almost childlike form in David Denby's review in *New York:* "Woody's Poison-Pen Letter." (The title of the article assumes that the film constitutes a direct communication between author and spectator/critic.) Denby begins by establishing that Woody Allen/Sandy Bates does not like us:

> If you have ever admired a film of Woody Allen's, you are a creep. And if you've admired all
> of them, you are a sycophantic little bug, a person without class, self-respect, manners or
> style... As for me—a critic—I'm all of these things and worse. We're all creeps, all of us who
> admire Woody Allen.[18]

In the very next paragraph, Denby responds to what he takes as an attack on
himself with massive retaliation:

> *Stardust Memories* is a poisonously bad movie—incoherent, madly self-important, often
> boring—and the strongest emotion in it is disgust for other people.[19]

This response to the film seems anchored in a double fallacy, one rooted in
emotions, the other in misconceived critical categories. The criticism of the film
is based on the equation of Woody Allen/Sandy Bates. Since Sandy Bates is
despicable—itself a debatable point—Woody Allen is also despicable.
Although Bates is not without biographical links to Woody Allen, he is also a
character, even if that character is played by Woody Allen himself. Here a
responsible criticism must distinguish between a number of distinct, albeit
occasionally overlapping, entities: 1) the biographical Woody Allen, about
whom most of us know little beyond the evidence of journalism and films; 2)
the Woody Allen persona, a cumulative construct based on Allen's comic
monologues and diverse film roles; 3) the character Sandy Bates, in some ways
reminiscent of 1) and 2) but also a character depicted as on the verge of a mental
breakdown—the Bates name suggesting perhaps a family resemblance to
another filmic Bates who "let his hostility escape"; and 4) the authorial
instance, not only the Woody Allen insofar as he directs (rather like Proust's
"autre moi" that writes) but also his collaborators and their collective intertext.
This conflation of diverse entities is also foreseen in *Stardust Memories* itself.
Since Sandy Bates has made "funny movies," Daisy expects him to be
personally funny, and is surprised to find him "kind of a depressive." And an
aspiring actor tells Bates' "I love you," and then corrects himself: "I mean I love
your films." Many critics of *Stardust Memories* proved themselves incapable
of making the distinction.

The very violence of the language employed against Allen's film—
"vicious," "mean-spirited," "vain"—suggests that we are dealing with what
Christian Metz calls "bad object" criticism. Building on Melanie Klein's
analysis of the role of objects in the infant's fantasy life—their tendency to
project libidinal or destructive feelings onto certain privileged objects such as
the breast—Metz speaks of the critical tendency to confuse the actual film, with
its complex weaving of multiple codes, with the film such as it has pleased or
displeased. The critics' hysterical language of Manichean denunciation—"bad
film!"—is symptomatic of a neurosis which belongs to the critics more than it
belongs to Woody Allen, who from all appearances *knows* that he is neurotic.

Reflexive films have often been "bad objects" for critics, who resent their sabotaging of the conventional pleasures of illusion and identification. It is surely no accident that Woody Allen's most widely despised film is also his most self-conscious and avant-gardist. The critics complained that "the characters do not come alive" and "the big scenes never take off," apparently failing to notice that the film is consciously built on a principle of systematic interruption familiar from the self-conscious tradition. Sandy Bates' argument with Isobel is interrupted by a publicity-seeking Armenian; his first kiss with Daisy is interrupted by his relatives; even his one-liners are interrupted. At the same time, the film deploys avant-garde strategies familiar from reflexive films—a constant shuttle between past and present, memory and fantasy à la *8 1/2;* the scrambling of spatial and temporal categories à la *Marienbad;* the sustained utilization of jump-cuts à la *Breathless;* and the metacritical discussion of aesthetic questions à la *Contempt.* The same strategies tolerated or even praised in Allen's fiction and essays are condemned in *Stardust Memories.* Foster Hirsch, who condemns *Stardust Memories* as "narrow," "parochial," reflective of "meanspiritedness" and "misanthropy," praises in Allen's *Side Effects* the same techniques he has condemned in *Stardust Memories:* "Woody's narrators are continually interrupting themselves, straying from the subject, meandering off on tangents of a steadily increasing delirium, as parentheses within parentheses slide into a miasma of absurdist irrelevancies."[20] It is only because of the differential expectations applied to literature and the cinema that the disruptive techniques lauded in prose fiction are rejected as hostile and self-indulgent in film. Modernist and reflexive strategies, accepted in literature, remain, at least for the mainstream of journalistic critics, anathema in the cinema.

Reflexive Adaptations: *Tom Jones, Lolita, The French Lieutenant's Woman*

Many of the cinematic adaptations of self-conscious novels, including the more successful ones, often flounder on precisely this point. While they incorporate certain reflexive devices, they do not metalinguistically dissect their own practice or include critical discourse within the text itself. Tony Richardson's filmic adaptation of *Tom Jones,* for example, is frequently cited as a model transposition of the codes of reflexivity from novel to film, in which complicitous winks to the spectator "cinematize" Fielding's direct address to his "dear reader," and accelerated motion and freeze-frames call attention to cinematic mediation. Just as Fielding makes parodic allusion to his literary antecedents, it is claimed, so Richardson alludes to his filmic antecedents through archaic devices (especially wipes) and silent film sequences. Richardson's narrator, however, functions largely as a classical off-screen narrator; in no case does he address questions of literary (or filmic) criticism or theory. The narrator's discourse, and the stylistic devices, are consistently subordinated to the diegesis rather than forming a metatextual commentary on it.

Karel Reisz's version of *The French Lieutenant's Woman* retreats from the reflexivity of the John Fowles source novel in a similar fashion. Instead of Fowles' analytical shuttle between Victorian plot and a metacommentary on the nature of Victorian fiction, Reisz, with the collaboration of Harold Pinter and the apparent approval of Fowles himself, intercuts a Victorian and a modern love story, with the former becoming a kind of film-within-the-film. The flimmaking apparatus is metonymically evoked by a single clapperboard placed in front of the lens in the opening sequence, when we discover that Meryl Streep is playing both Sarah, the French Lieutenant's woman, and Anna, the actress playing Sarah in a film. While Fowles' characters exist in the context of a writer ruminating over his prerogatives, it is appropriate that the transmuted characters of the adaptation should live in the context of the production of a film. But as Fowles himself recognizes in the "Foreword" to the book, "all those long paragraphs of description, historical digression, character analysis and the rest that the vast portmanteau of novel form was especially evolved to contain..." had to be crushed into the "small valise" of the fiction film.[21]

While Reisz' and Pinter's solutions are ingenious, and effective in their own terms, they tend to push the film in the direction of naturalism. Fowles' anachronistic references to Victorian science and political theory are largely discarded. More seriously, there is no equivalent for the authorial persona of Fowles' narrator, costumed in Victorian frock and beard, sharing a train compartment with his protagonist, comparing two eras and constrasting the conventions of Victorian fiction with those of the French New Novel, initiating us into the theoretical codes and technical secrets of his craft. The film has neither a writer reflecting on writing nor a filmmaker reflecting on filmmaking. Instead we are offered a kind of bifurcated romance, two parallel love stories set in distinct referential time-frames, which finally tend to merge in the mind of the spectator. Although the two stories beautifully play off the trendily modern against the romanticized archaic, and although the transitions between them are often brilliant, their interaction merely generates a kind of saving ambiguity, a touch of Pirandellism, rather than a more thoroughgoing subversion of referentiality.

The mainstream fiction film's relative impermeability to reflexivity also explains the partial failure of Stanley Kubrick's adaptation of *Lolita* (1962). While the novel constantly flaunts its own status as linguistic artifact, the film is largely cast in the illusionistic mould, presenting rounded characters in plausible settings through a self-effacing style. While the book is a veritable palimpsest of parodies—of Proust, Poe, Dostoyevsky, Sade—Kubrick opted

Figure 31.   *The French Lieutenant's Woman* (1981)

to downplay style in a text in which style is of the essence. The film is intermittently parodic—the homage to Chaplin's tussle with a bed in *One A.M.*, the allusion to Kubrick's own *Spartacus*, the disorienting direct cut to *The Curse of Frankenstein*—but never so consistently or effectively as the novel. Most of the Nabokovian wit is displaced onto Peter Sellers as Clare Quilty, for Sellers' shape-shifting capacity to mimic personages as diverse as Gabby Hayes and T.S. Eliot makes him an ambulatory intertext, a body of quotations whose very modus operandi is parodic in the best Nabokovian sense.

Nabokov's screenplay, of which Kubrick used but a small portion, is rather more audacious, although Nabokov himself recognizes in its preface that the "author's goal of infinite fidelity" may be a "producer's ruin." The screenplay includes a cameo role for Nabokov himself, a Hitchcockian touch that recalls his guest appearance in his own *Despair*, and which would have constituted the filmic equivalent of his anagrammatic presence in *Lolita* as Vivian Darkbloom. The Nabokov screenplay also expands the role of the pedantic D. John Ray, developing a constant interplay between Ray presenting Humbert's notes and Humbert presenting himself. The screenplay is more prone to interruption and dedramatization. Charlotte's fateful car crash is treated less dramatically, for example, by means of a quick cut to traffic policemen examining diagrams of the accident, a narrative dislocation which visually translates the nonchalantly perverse syntax of Humbert's account of his wife's death.

Lolita is, among other things, a fine work of film and literary criticism. But Kubrick fails to exploit the cinematic references (lovingly inventoried by Alfred Appel, Jr. in *Nabokov's Dark Cinema*) in the novel; the envy of cinema's "fantastic simultaneousness"; the description of Humbert himself as a "handsome hunk of movieland manhood" or Charlotte as a "weak solution of Marlene Dietrich"; the advice proffered to any future filmic translator of his work ("If you want to make a movie of my book, have one of those faces gently melt into my own, while I look"); and the incisive discussions of *Lolita's* generic tastes. Indeed, Nabokov shows himself to be a brilliant genre critic. He artfully details the formulaic visuals of westerns: "the rearing horse, the spectacular stampede, the pistol thrust through the slivered windowpane, the stupendous fistfight, the crashing mountain of dusty old-fashioned furniture, the table used as a weapon, the timely somersault, the pinned hand still groping for the dropped bowie knife...." He describes musicals, meanwhile, as a "grief-proof sphere of existence where from death and truth were banned" and "underworlders" as fostering a "robust atmosphere of incompetent marksmanship."[22]

While Nabokov constantly highlights the verbal factitiousness of his text, Kubrick finds no filmic equivalent for this device. While the novel frequently

Figure 32.   *Lolita* (1962)

violates the reader's expectations, the film rarely does. The novel consistently disorients its reader, especially as to the degree of "sincerity" of the text, while the film almost never does (the sudden cut to the drive-in horror film constituting a rare exception). While the novel systematically develops contradictions between what is being related (for example, Charlotte's death) and the tone and style in which it is being related, the film is, in the main, stylistically homogenous. While the novel conveys eroticism through hilarious indirection, applying sexual language to nonsexual events and vice versa, the film conveys eroticism largely through love scenes (as explicit as censorship would then allow), through point-of-view editing, and through shots of characters' whispering ("Did I do that!" Quilty responds to Charlotte's whispered insinuations). In short, Kubrick substitutes three-dimensional illusionism and stylistic continuity for the recklessly flamboyant virtuoso anti-illusionism of the book. One almost wishes that a later Kubrick, the Kubrick of *Strangelove* and especially of *Clockwork Orange,* might take another try at Nabokov's novel.

The Multiplicity of Styles

Reflexive art constantly reminds us of the multiplicity of styles available to an artist. For Cervantes and Fielding, merely stating the time offers the pretext for stylistic variations. When Henry Fielding suddenly deflates an elaborate epic simile with a vulgar "translation" into everyday English, we are made aware that even the most mundane facts can be recounted in any number of styles. In a sense, anti-illusionist works do not concern their ostensible subjects but are rather stylistic exercises in Queneau's sense. In *Exercises de Style* Queneau offers a kind of transformational grammar of literary possibilities. He composes stylistic variations on a story supposed constant—a trival anecdote about an exchange of insults on a bus and a subsequent coincidental meeting— successively telling the story as a comedy, as a sonnet, as an official letter, and as a telegram; then in negations, questions, exclamations; then in words of Latin origin, Greek origin; then as *hai kai* and free verse. The same story, subjected to generic, rhetorical, and etymological transformations, emerges different in each case. Such literary calisthenics, whimsical as they seem, make an important point about the nature of literary representation—that there can be no reality unmediated by style.

The cumulative effect of Queneau's exercises is to make us realize that stories themselves change as they are filtered through different ways of telling. The technique parallels that of novelists like Nabokov or Robbe-Grillet. In *The Real Life of Sebastian Knight,* Nabokov explains the literary methods of *The Prismatic Bezel,* a fictional novel embedded in the larger text:

... the heroes of the book are what can be loosely called "methods of composition." It is as if a painter said: look, here I'm going to show you not the painting of a landscape, but the painting of different ways of painting a certain landscape, and I trust that their harmonious fusion will disclose the landscape as I intend you to see it.[23]

There is a certain cubist logic in the method that Nabokov describes, the multiplicity of perspectives finally disclosing the complex perceptual truth of the object. Robbe-Grillet goes farther by robbing the entire process of its supposed "object," in a systematic struggle against the hegemony of the referent. The "hero" becomes reducible to different ways of engendering narrative or generating meanings. The film *Trans-Europe Express* exemplifies the process: a novelist-scenarist on a train begins to mentally try out scenarios suitable for filming on a train. His improvisations oddly resemble spy movies which begin to play and are then erased to give way to more "serious" efforts. Thus Robbe-Grillet foregrounds the processes of *écriture*, both filmic and literary; writing writes itself.

I have tried in this chapter to compare the textual processes of the self-conscious novel with those of the self-conscious film, insofar as they are comparable but also in the senses in which they defy comparison due to their material specificity. In the texts here discussed, or at least in the dimension here discussed, the relationship between creator and public, transmitter and receiver, as well as between text and intertext, has tended to be playful, even if that playfulness at times takes on an aggressive tinge. In its ludic dimension, reflexive fictions exploit to the maximum the comic or tragic possibilities of exposing the mechanisms of the text. It relinquishes the claim to realism and transforms art into what Huizinga calls "playfields of the minds." Inside these playfields, Huizinga writes in *Homo Ludens,* "an absolute and peculiar order reigns." The only kind of creation and destruction truly beyond good and evil, Nietzsche suggested, is to be found in the play of the artist and the child. Kant, in his third *Critique,* argues that poetry is the highest of aesthetic forms because it recognizes, in its potential as play, a subversive force for undermining serious business. Play, after all, constitutes a sphere of freedom, a realm of disinterestedness which transcends the restrictive codes of stratified societies or petrified art forms and thus constitutes a principle of liberation.

The dimension of ludic reflexivity described here represents a first and relatively superficial level of demystification, of subversive pleasure. In a purely formal contestation, art points to its own artifice. Such play, to paraphrase Auden, echoes in the valley of its playing; it makes nothing happen. In a society which regards idle hands as the devil's workshop, playful texts flaunt their own impish superfluity. Such texts are potentially, but not necessarily, subversive of an established order, whether capitalist or pseudo-socialist, which fetishizes productive labor. But such reflexivity also runs the danger of falling into a

Kantian trap of scorn for all that is instrumental or politically purposeful. Autonomous verbal or cinematic structures can resound uselessly, forming what Meyer Abrams has called, in a quite different context, "a ceaseless echolalia... bombinating in a void."[24] A socially strategic reflexivity, on the other hand, can lay bare the devices of art while exposing the mechanisms of society. The strategies we have discussed in this chapter have laid bare the device and exposed the conventions in the act of using them, but without aggressively developing the cultural or political dimension of this exposure. It is to those dimensions that we now turn.

4

The Carnival of Modernism

*The art of which we speak is inhuman not only because it
contains no things human, but also because it is an explicit act of
dehumanization.*
Ortega y Gasset, *The Dehumanization of Art*

*It is the transposition of carnival to the language of literature
that we call the carnivalization of literature.*
Mikhail Bakhtin, *Problems of Dostoyevsky's Poetics*

If our focus in the previous chapter was on metalinguistic self-consciousness in
the novel and film, our emphasis in this chapter will be on aggressive anti-
illusionism, as seen in modernist texts which adopt strategies of carnivalesque
fantasy and absurdity by creating an impossible meta-real or "surfiction"
which explodes and transcends conventional narrative categories. In *Problems
of Dostoyevsky's Poetics* (1929), *Rabelais and His World* (1965), and *The
Dialogic Imagination* (1981), the Russian literary theorist Mikhail Bakhtin
traces these carnivalesque strategies back to Rabelais and to the Menippean
satire of Lucian, Petronius, and Apuleius. The carnivalesque represents the
transposition into literature of the spirit of the carnival—that is, popular
festivities in which the people gain brief entry into a sphere of utopian freedom
by turning the world upside down. The carnivalesque is profoundly subversive
of all that is official and oppressive since it abolishes hierarchies, levels social
classes and genres, and creates an alternative second life free from conventional
rules and restrictions. In carnival, imagination and fantasy take power. All that
was marginalized and excluded—the mad, scandalous, and aleatory—comes
to the center in a veritable explosion of otherness. The material bodily
principle, especially of the body's "lower stratum"—hunger, thirst, copulation,
defecation—becomes a positive and corrosive force, and festive laughter enjoys
a symbolic victory over death, over all that is held sacred, over all that
oppresses and restricts. After Rabelais, carnival, at least in Europe, went

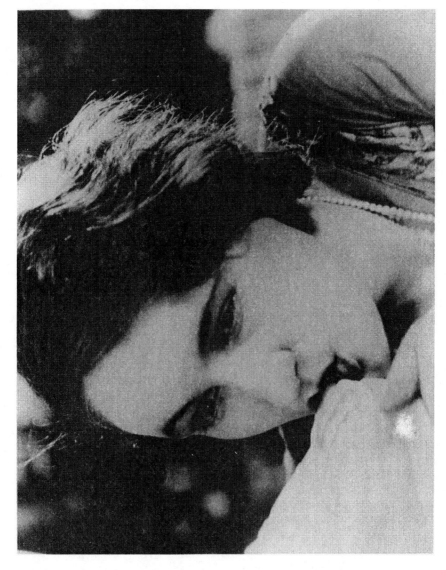

Figure 33. *L'Age d'Or* (1930)

underground, although it remained a strong presence in Shakespeare—as lovingly delineated by C.L. Barber in *Shakespeare's Festive Comedy*—as well as in Cervantes, Diderot, and in what Bakhtin calls the "polyphonic" and "dialogic" novels of Dostoyevsky. In the modernist period, the carnivalesque ceases to be a collective cleansing ritual open to all "the people" to become the monopoly of a marginalized caste. Carnival, in this modified and somewhat hostile form, is present in the outrageousness of Dada, the provocations of surrealism, in the travesty-revolts of Genet's *The Maids* or *The Blacks*, and indeed in the avant-garde generally.

Rabelais remained misunderstood, according to Bakhtin, because of his "nonliterary" nature, that is, because of the nonconformity of his images to the norms and canons predominant in the sixteenth century, and to some extent, even today. It is in this formal aggression that the carnivalesque betrays its profound link to the avant-garde, to marginal and subversive art with its permanent adversary relationship to power and to official culture. The linguistic corollary of carnivalization entails the liberation of language from the norms of decency and etiquette. Carnivalesque language is designed to degrade all that is spiritual and abstract; it transfers the ideal to a brute material level. The cheerful vulgarity of the powerless is used as a weapon against the pretense and hypocrisy of the powerful. Even the rules of grammar are suspended by what Rabelais calls a "gramatica jocosa" in which grammatical categories, cases, and verb forms, are transferred to a material and often erotic or scatological plane.

Although the carnivalesque traces roots far back in European and indeed in world culture, it takes on very specific coloring in modernist texts. Texts such as Jarry's *Ubu Roi* (1896), Buñuel's *L'Age d'Or* (1930), Godard's *Les Carabiniers* (1963), and Joaquim Pedro de Andrade's *Macunaíma* (1969), combine modernist "dehumanization with carnivalesque strategies of parody and dehierarchization."

A Seminal Instance: *Ubu Roi*

Alfred Jarry's *Ubu Roi* (King Ubu) forms a seminal instance of the modernist carnivalesque, combining artistic strategies rooted in Menippean satire and Rabelais with the modernist hostility both to the audience and to conventional *histoire*. The carnivalesque strategies of Jarry's play begin with its title—*Ubu Roi*—an uneuphonious and mocking echo of *Oedipus Rex*. The play itself devours the high literary tradition and regurgitates it for its own ends, hybridizing genres in a defiant cocktail of tragedy and *grand guignol*. The opening expletive—"merdre!" (shittr!)—heralds the play's carnivalesque penchant for the scatological and the "material bodily lower stratum." The frequent feasts, and Ubu's irrepressible gluttony, reflect the defiant orality of

Figure 34.   F.M. Cazal's Portrait of Alfred Jarry (1897)

carnival, an orality which borders, at times, on the cannibalistic. Père Ubu, especially, seems always on the brink of unleashing his anthropophagous tendencies. "I'm going to sharpen my teeth on your shanks," he tells Mère Ubu. *Ubu* explodes the spatio-temporal conventions of the naturalistic theatre through the utopian syncretism of the carnivalesque. In the program notes distributed to the first-night audience, Jarry explained that the action was set in "Poland, that is to say, Nowhere." He elaborated. "Nowhere is everywhere, and first of all in the country where one happens to be. That is why Ubu speaks French." The initial setting, then, is simultaneously nowhere (with its etymological overtones of utopia), everywhere, and France. Then, in a whirlwind tour of Europe which must have startled even those spectators accustomed to the spatial freedom of Shakespeare's histories, the play takes us to Russia, the Ukraine, Lithuania, and Livonia. The final scene brings us, in the space of a brief, presumably continuous dialogue, from the Baltic past Germany, past Hamlet's Elsinore, and into the North Sea. Thus, by transgressing both the Aristotelian unities cultivated by classical tragedy and the fastidious verisimilitude sought by naturalism, Jarry reveals the spatial procedures of theatre for what they are—mere conventions.

Menippean satire, according to Bakhtin, displays freedom from historical limits and a total liberty of philosophical and thematic invention. Defending his practice in *Ubu*, Jarry wrote: "We do not find it honorable to construct historical plays," and his text performs the mise-en-scène of the modernist attack on the very possibility of meaningful history. The antimythos of *Ubu* constitutes a protracted *non sequitur*. Although the play alludes to classical as well as Elizabethan tragedy, Jarry suspends the conventional laws of motivation. Ubu, the reincarnated Macbeth of the play, is as much motivated by the prospect of eating sausage as by any ambition for wealth and power. Whereas Shakespearean tragedy inexorably leads to transfigured moments of anguished lucidity, Jarryesque theatre exploits tragic mechanisms only in order to empty them of all significance. When Ubu's schemes end in catastrophe, he does not declaim a soliloquy on the model of "Tomorrow and tomorrow and tomorrow." Escaping from Poland with his vanquished fellows, Ubu points to Germany and, summing up a wisdom forged in tragedy, declares: "Ah! Gentlemen! Beautiful as it may be, it cannot compare with Poland. For if there were no Poland, there would be no Poles!" Having left the realm of the non sequitur, we enter the kingdom of tautology.

In his attack on naturalism, Jarry drew inspiration from Elizabethan theatre. In *Douze Arguments sur le Théâtre*, he praises the "eternally tragic" theatre of Ben Jonson, Cyril Tourner, Marlowe, and Shakespeare. The epigraph to *Ubu* facetiously suggests that the Shakespearean tragedies were in fact inspired by the exploits of Ubu, and the play itself forms an anthology of Shakespearean references: a central plot modeled on *Macbeth* (with Mère Ubu playing the ambitious Lady Macbeth to the sluggish Ubu), a conspiracy modeled on *Julius Caesar*; and a revenge hero ("How sad it is to find oneself alone at fourteen with a terrible vengeance to pursue!") patterned on *Hamlet*. But apart from plot borrowings and references, Jarry exploited the anti-illusionistic procedures of Elizabethan dramaturgy, and especially its rudimentary proto-Brechtian staging. Since no decor or props can represent the "Polish army marching through the Ukraine," Jarry uses a cardboard horse's head ("as in the old English theatre") for the "equestrian scenes." As in *Julius Caesar*, crowds are epitomized in two or three actors. Jarry calls attention to the disproportion betwen the signifier—a single actor—and the signified—a huge crowd—by having Ubu exclaim, "What a mass of people!" Whereas the dominant French tradition regarded Shakespeare as somewhat of a barbarian—French audiences as late as 1827 were offended by Desdemona's handkerchief—Jarry appreciated the liberating force of his violence, his implausibilities, his plays-within-plays, his bawdy wordplay and general verbal exuberance. It was precisely those features that Voltaire censured in Shakespeare—"without the slightest spark of good taste or the slightest knowledge of the rules"—that Jarry found so exhilarating.

In his own time, furthermore, Jarry was hardly alone in his hostility to illusionism. Mallarmé, who saluted Jarry as a "sober and sure dramatic sculptor," called for an "immaculate" discourse purified of all referentiality. The difference between naturalism and poetry, he said, "is like the difference between a corset and a beautiful throat."[1] Jarry was also indebted to Isidore Ducasse Lautréamont and his *Chants de Maldoror*, where the reader encounters the same parodistic irreverence toward the high literary tradition, the same allusions to Shakespeare, the same orchestration of generic pastiches, and the same aggressive stance toward the public. Jarry's writings on theatre bristle with hostile intentions toward a public which he regarded as "illiterate by definition." It is because the public is an "inert, obtuse and passive" mass, Jarry wrote in "Theatre Questions," that "one must slap it from time to time, in order to know by its bear-like grunts where it is, and where it stands."[2] By presenting the public with its "ignoble double," made up of the false shame and patriotic virtues of a well-fed audience, Jarry provoked the howls of execration which alone could tell him that he had reached his target. With Jarry, we are very far from the amiable "dear reader" of the self-conscious novelists. "Dear reader" has become "hypocrite lecture, mon semblable, mon frère."

If aggression characterizes Jarry's attitude toward his public, abstraction defines his artistic method. Jarry praises what he called the "abstract theatre" of the Elizabethans, and lauds the character Hamlet as a "walking abstraction." This *parti pris* for abstraction—which has its counterpart in what Bakhtin calls the "abstract intellectual nature" of Mennipean comic adventures—permeates and structures every aspect of *King Ubu*. Rather than reconstitute the world in a recognizable bourgeois form, Jarry fabricates a world which is disconcertingly synthetic. Shunning what he called the "superfluous duplication" of *trompe-l'oeil* realism, Jarry constructs a "hybrid" and "abstract" decor. *Trompe-l'oeil* only deludes those who see roughly, that is, those who don't see at all, but it scandalizes those who see nature intelligently and selectively.[3] In keeping with this distinctly modernistic aesthetic, and with the spatial freedom of Menippean satire, the decor of *King Ubu* consisted of a painted backdrop evoking diverse landscapes and contradictory climates. Arthur Symons described the premiere scenery as representing, "by a child's convention," both indoors and outdoors, and the tropical, temperate, and arctic zones all at once. In the dislocated theatrescapes of *King Ubu*, snow fell near palm trees and doors opened on the sky. At the same time, the public was disconcerted by the heterogenous nature of costumes which were as "unchronological and as lacking in local color as possible."[4] Pere Ubu's costume progressively accretes disparate and irreconcilable elements. Mère Ubu begins with a "concierge's outfit" but then becomes an ambulatory monument to social mobility, with each stage in her progress leaving traces on her costume. The revenge-hero Bougrelas is dressed as a "baby in a little skirt and bonnet." Bordure, despite his English accent, sports a Hungarian musician's costume. Even the music originally programmed for *Ubu Roi* had this absurdly synthetic character, consisting of the rarest instruments with the most recondite names—flageolets, blutwurst, sackbuts—and producing the most horrible sounds. Like the decor, the music evokes an impossible summa of times and places.

The carnivalesque, according to Bakhtin, laughs at death and violence. Its blows are only "to laugh," to be taken no more seriously than a clown's feigned fall or a puppet's demise. Ubu is full of comic dismemberments and distanced outrages, of "beheading and twisting of legs," of "twisting of the nose and teeth and extraction of the tongue" but it is all, ultimately, "pour rire." Even the protagonist's imagined death is merely a pretext for comedy: "Aaaah! I'm frightened. Lord God, I'm dead! No, no, I'm not." And later: "Ah! Oh! I'm wounded. I'm shot full of holes, I'm perforated, I'm done for, I'm buried. And now I've got you!" At the same time, *Ubu Roi* reveals in caricatural form the actual mechanisms of society. A polite summary of Ubu's political philosophy would be: eliminate the opposition so as to appropriate all the wealth, and then levy onerous taxes on everyone and everything. To those who object, Ubu answers: "Dans la trappe!"—the Ubuesque equivalent of "Off with their heads!" Thus Jarry unmasks one of the central truths of politics—that power comes out of the barrel of a gun, or, in the case of Ubu, from the "shittry saber" and the "phynancial stick." The economic motive, the concern with "phynance," is omnipresent in *Ubu*. "I'm going to get rich," promises Ubu, "and I won't give up one sou." His exacerbated lust for property is reflected in an unnatural (for the French language) emphasis on possessive adjectives: "I'm going to make MY list of MY goods. Clerk, read MY list of MY goods." The logic of power is simplified, stripped of all idealization, mystification, and pretense of larger purpose.

Ubu's Children: *L'Age d'Or* and the Surrealists

Although the premiere performance of Jarry's play postdated the first Lumière films by only one year, we must wait for the surrealists to find the true first-generation cinematic progeny of *King Ubu*. Impassioned admirers of both the artistic work and personal style of Jarry, the surrealists—who do in some ways offer little more than an erudite and somewhat effete salon version of the carnivalesque—saw film as a privileged instrument in their struggle against outmoded social and artistic conventions. As Jarry denounced the well-made play, Buñuel attacked the "ciné-dramas" "saturated with melodramatic germs, entirely infested with sentimental typhus, mixed with naturalist and romantic bacilli."[5] *L'Age d'Or* (1930) exploded the cinema scene much as *King Ubu* had exploded the theatre scene. In both works, one encounters the same carnivalesque strategies, the same aggressive attitude toward the public, the same tendency toward abstraction, and the same radical subversion of the conventions of illusionism.

Both *Chien Andalou* (1929) and *L'Age d'Or* (1930) mock the conventional temporal decorum of fiction films. After its precisely non-indexical title, *Chien Andalou* opens with a temporal title, the perennial "once upon a time" of fable. After the celebrated slashing of the eyeball, another temporal title intervenes— "Eight Years Later"—followed by a sequence with no apparent relation to the initial sequence. The first few minutes of the film, then, outrageously jumble the accustomed generic categories of narrative time, forcing us to reconcile the temporal precision of chronicle or novel with the nebulous atemporality of fable. We are left pondering the possible meaning of "eight years after once upon a time." Could it be the same as "six years before happily ever after?" In *L'Age d'Or*, similarly, the title "Some Hours Afterward" intervenes between a shot of a dying rat and a shot of an arid landscape. The title is doubly absurd. Such temporal connectives have meaning only when they form part of a coherent story in which what happens "afterward" bears some consequential relation to what transpired "before." In this case, the shot of the desolate landscape has no *narrative* relation to the scorpion sequence. We generally associate narrative time, furthermore, with the human time of characters and plots. The life of scorpions continues instinctively and is unmarked by narrative coherence. The pseudo-documentary presumably treats the characteristic behavior of scorpions, not a narrative incident in which a scorpion Demetrius attacks a rat named Jason. Scorpions and rats are not

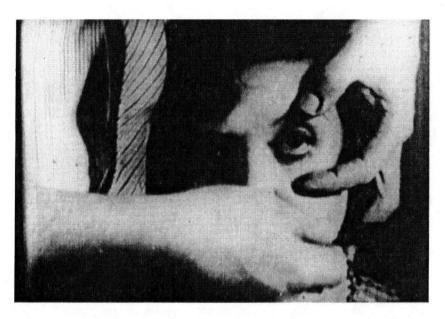

Figure 35.   *Chien Andalou* (1929)

conventionally implied by "some hours afterward." Buñuel's radical, almost Darwinian, equation between animal existence and human life constitutes an aggression because it undermines the privileged status usually accorded the human subject in narrative. *L'Age d'Or* plays with time in an analogous fashion. Buñuel has the Majorcans—a gallery of humorless figures representing the military, ecclesiastical, and political establishment—lay the foundation of the city of Rome. Since they are the end products of what they are founding, the sequence is logically absurd. At another point, the "pseudo-iterative" title "Sometimes on Sunday," with its Flaubertian ring of comfortable predictability, precedes a shot of house façades collapsing under the force of explosions.[6] It is as if a writer were to violate the conventions of grammatical tense and create such syntactic monstrosities as "the marquis having go at night, had will met the morning." Buñuel's deliberate misapplication of temporal conventions, his cinematic equivalent of Rabelais' *gramatica jocosa*, forces us to reflect on the nature of cinematic "tense."

L'Age d'Or, like *Ubu Roi*, proceeds by temporal, spatial, and thematic abstraction. The final sequence, to take just one example, shows the survivors of the Chateau de Selliny staggering out of a castle after a night of orgies. The sequence is introduced by a title:

> At the exact moment when these feathers, torn out by his furious hands, covered the ground below the window, at that moment, as we said, but very far away, the survivors of the Chateau de Selliny were coming out, to go back to Paris.[7]

The title, by protesting too much—"At the exact moment, . . . at that moment as we said . . . but very far away . . . "—debunks the factitious simultaneity. Described by a title whose moralism surpasses Griffith at his worst as "four well-known and utter scoundrels" celebrating "the most brutal of orgies," friends with "no law but their own depravity, they bring with them four depraved women who fire their lust with their tales." The first of these degenerate scoundrels to appear is dressed like a Hebrew of the first century and bears an unmistakable resemblance to the pictorial Jesus. The second is the Duke of Blangis, and the remaining two are costumed as eighteenth-century French aristocrats. The sequence typifies Buñuel's use of temporal abstraction. The two sequences, supposedly taking place "at the same instant," cannot possibly be contemporaneous since one of them is taking place near the chateau of the Marquis de Sade, that is, in the eighteenth century, while the preceding sequence takes place in 1930 in Rome. Christ, of course, lived neither in eighteenth-century France nor twentieth-century Rome. The implied equation of Christ and Sade, futhermore, constitutes a surrealist antinomy as well as a temporal oxymoron.[8]

The view that reduces Buñuel to the quintessential film surrealist is, finally, rather superficial. His roots really go back to Cervantes, and beyond that, to the Middle Ages and the medieval tradition of carnivalesque irreverence. As a child, Buñuel practiced black masses, and as an adolescent, he and Garcia Lorca would shave closely, powder their faces and masquerade as nuns in order to flirt with male passengers on streetcars. Buñuel's attacks on the Church are not merely "surrealist provocations;" his insistent desacralization derives, rather, from a carnivalesque tradition which parasitically feeds on what it attacks. Just as medieval monks indulged in ludic self-mockery, in feasts of fools and grotesque parodies of the liturgy, so Buñuel exploits blasphemy as a habitual aesthetic strategy, a fond method for generating art. Echoes of carnival laughter resound within the walls of Buñuel's festive cloister. The religious travesties so frequent in his films—parodistic liturgies of *Simon of the Desert*, the orgiastic Last Supper sequence of *Viridiana*—form the twentieth-century counterpart of the monkish pranks and *parodia sacra* of the Middle Ages.

Speaking more generally, *L'Age d'Or* carnivalizes etiquette in all its forms. Modot's slap of Lya Lys' mother has the same relation to social decorum that *L'Age d'Or* itself has to religious and political, as well as narrative and cinematic, decorum. Religious decorum is undermined by the systematic association of religion with Death, as well as by the decontexting of Catholic symbols, dignitaries, and artifacts—the monstrance in the limousine, the prelate out the window, the divinity at the orgy. The pompous politician, celebrating the founding of imperial Rome is undercut by a sudden intrusion of the lower bodily principle—two lovers in the mud. The upper class is slapped in the face (Lya Lys' mother) or covered with flies (her father). Narrative decorum, finally, is laid low by a perversely purposeless trajectory that leads us from one non sequitur to another, and finally to a promising love affair which turns into a frustrating *coitus interruptus*.

Ubu's Grandchild: The Modernism of Jean-Luc Godard

Godard did for the "well-made film" what Jarry had done for the "well-made play." He perpetrated aesthetic transgressions which shook the confidence of the reigning system. The work of both was seminally corrosive, functioning as a negative catalyst speeding up a process of artistic disintegration already in operation. Godard, like Jarry, might have insisted that the artist must strike the public from time to time to "know by its bear-like grunts where it is." Godard's well-aimed slaps at his bourgeois public have, during his long career, elicited more than their share of bear-like grunts. Godard's definitions of cinema, especially in the late 1960s, tended to explode with the polemical violence of military and terroristic metaphors—art as a "special gun" and film as a

Figure 36.   *L'Age d'Or* (1930)

"theoretical rifle." In his most aggressive period, Godard saw himself as a cultural terrorist or intellectual guerilla, mounting raids on bourgeois culture. And like Jarry, he attacked the bourgeoisie at the heart of its self-conceit—its class pride in its culture. With both Jarry and Godard, art became, as Walter Benjamin said of the dadaists, "an instrument of ballistics." Rather than make the theatre or the cinema a temple for the celebration of the mysteries of high culture, they make art the scene of scandal.

The modernist desacralization of art is an ambiguous one, for modernists like Jarry and Godard are deeply imbued with the very culture they so vehemently attack. Just as the density of allusions in *King Ubu* betrays a cultivated familiarity with classical antiquity as well as with Rabelais, Racine, Corneille, and Shakespeare, so Godard's films proliferate in intertextual references to all the arts. Crowded with book covers, paintings, posters, and literary echoes, they allude to the entire range of high and low-brow culture. (*Pierrot le Fou*, for example, alludes by word or image to Velázquez, Balzac, Auguste Renoir, Céline, Faulkner, Conrad, Van Gogh, Picasso, Modigliani, Defoe, and Verne as well as to comic books, *série noire* novels and musical comedies.) At times, Godard sadly registers, much like T.S. Eliot but without Eliot's patrician nostalgia, the loss of a meaningful past by highlighting his character's isolation from traditional culture. Michel in *Breathless* responds to Patricia's comment about William Faulkner by saying: "Who's he? Someone you slept with?" Venus and Cleopatre in *Les Carabiniers* complain of a postcard showing a Parthenon in ruins and therefore "worthless." Thus Godard reveals the cultural impoverishment of his characters while he participates in the modernist ritual of desecrating the temples of high art. He laments the contemporary irrelevance of high culture even while he sticks out his tongue at "monuments of unaging intellect."

Godard's modernism must be situated within the context of the artistic avant-garde in general. Godard owes to dada and surrealism, for example, a feature which especially typifies his films in the late sixties—the incorporation of the aleatory into his art. Although indebted to Lautrémont's celebrated image of "the fortuitous encounter of an umbrella and a sewing machine on a dissecting table," and while anticipated by Picasso's *papiers collés*, which incorporated random scraps of newspaper into painting, the surrealists and the dadaists were the first to systematically exploit aleatory techniques in order to generate artistic texts. Tristan Tzara once recommended writing poetry by cutting out newspaper articles, snipping out the individual words, mixing them in a bag, and then selecting them at random. Godard stages Tzara's conception in *2 or 3 Things I Know About Her* by having two characters, aptly named Bouvard and Pecuchet, take down random quotations from diverse stacks of paperbacks on diverse topics and in diverse languages. The result of their paradigmatic—choosing the passage—and syntagmatic—placing them in sequence—operations is a "text" which is simultaneously structured and aleatory, thus providing an analogue for the film as a whole, which exploits what Breton called the "hasard objectif" and what Godard called the "definitive by chance."

Fragmentation, which Ortega y Gasset considered definitive of modernism, marks virtually all of Godard's films. Pasolini, in fact, called Godard a "vulgar Braque" who gratuitously fragments the narrative elements only in order to recompose them afterward. As if to highlight the analogy, Godard often places cubist paintings in precisely those sequences handled in a fragmented way. In *A Married Woman*, Pierre with his head out of frame, stands in front of Picasso's Harlequin, with *its* head out of frame. A Picasso painting also graces the apartment from which Marianne and Ferdinand flee, in a highly fragmented and discontinuous sequence, in *Pierrot le Fou*. The subtitle of *A Married Woman* reads: "Fragments of a Film Made in 1964," and the film itself proceeds by fragments: bits of scenes, segments of interviews, posters, words, words decomposed into smaller words, scraps of overheard conversation. The titular character is herself fragmented, lost within a dense electronic thicket of media-proffered images and sounds. Godard surrounds her with fragments of the ambient culture: snips of classical music, book covers, headlines, billboards, ads. Rather than fragments shored against her ruin, the fragments constitute and signify her ruin.

Godard has compared the improvisational method of his early filmmaking to a kind of "automatic writing." The wordplay in the early films at times recalls the aleatory techniques of the "Surrealist Games." "If I were stupid," says a character in *Made in USA*, "I wouldn't speak French," recalling the surrealist game by which nonsensical affirmations are formed by joining "if" clauses written by one person to "then" clauses written by a second person unaware of the initial clause. A young laborer in the same film delivers sentences reminiscent of the surrealists' "the exquisite corpse will drink the new wine," the surrealist game in which words are combined in syntactically correct but logically impossible ways: "The barman is in the pocket of the pencil's jacket".... "The doors are throwing themselves through the window." Godard's *gramatica jocosa* assaults us by violating our conventional expectation of coherent dialogue, but also imparts a feeling of carnivalesque triumph over the inhibiting confinements of logic and grammar.

Godard's incorporation of the aleatory takes on broader significance in the context of a dominant style which sought to eliminate chance by hermetically sealing out the accidental. The Hollywood studio system aspired, like any efficiently run business, to reduce chance to a minimum. Godard's early films resonate with nostalgic echoes of the silent comics, the filmmakers who worked in an atmosphere of delirious improvisation, at a time when the dominant style was not yet fully institutionalized and control by producers was minimal. His films proliferate in homages to this lost paradise of cinematic freedom. *Pierrot le Fou*, filmed, according to Godard, "exactly as in the days of Mack Sennett," has Marianne borrow a "trick from Laurel and Hardy" to knock out a gas-station attendant. In *Tout Va Bien*, Godard strips away the wall of the factory to show us events on both floors, as Keaton did with the house in *The High Sign*. Godard alludes to Keaton in both films and interviews, and physically mimicked him in Agnes Varda's *Cleo from 5 to 7*, where he does a competent imitation of Keaton's swift but deadpan style of running in a film-within-the-film homage to silent comedy. The traffic-jam sequence in *Weekend* recalls the automotive destruction derby in *Two Tars*. Indeed, the pervasive free-for-all mayhem of that film recalls countless burlesque comedies structured around the notion of proliferating violence. Two social monads fight over some petty incident, the fight spreads, and soon the entire collectivity is throwing pies or destroying automobiles. For slapstick comedy, any object is a potential weapon in Darwinian skirmishes; in *Weekend*, the weapons range from spray paint to tennis balls. The supermarket sequence in *Tout Va Bien*—the permission for which was won by Godard's claim that he planned to film a Sennett-like farce—lends these mini-riots a political dimension by having Maoists encourage customers to take their food for free. But even when the references are less explicit, the comicity of the gestures in many Godard films—Prokosch accosting Paul by hanging on his tie, Roland forcing Corinne to carry him piggyback in *Weekend*, even the grotesque positioning of the "orgiasts" in *Every Man for Himself*—recall the studied inappropriateness of the gestures of silent comedy.

Godard and Avant-Garde Theatre

Godard's distanced, often comic treatment of physical violence is indebted not only to silent film comedy but also to the avant-garde theatre going back to *Ubu*. It ultimately derives, of course, from the venerable tradition of carnivalesque violence which informs both traditions. In Rabelais, in puppet theatre, and *commedia dell'arte*, death is often a comic episode. The unpitying nature of carnivalesque art is organically connected with its clear conventionality. The reader/spectator perceives the staged violence as if it were occurring to puppets. Their sufferings and misfortunes are seen not as the suffering of real people, but in a spirit of carnival and ritual. Murders in *Ubu* are flippant, performed with the nonchalance with which one tosses away a cigarette. Several people die instantly when Père Ubu poisons them with a lavatory brush, but no one reacts with horror, and Ubu's own response is to ask Mère Ubu to pass the cutlets. It was precisely this neutral tone in the face of the most outrageous violence that impressed Godard in Jarry's play. When asked if he would like to adapt *King Ubu* to the screen, Godard responded that he saw

Ubu very much as a gangster with soft hat and raincoat, who says his "merdre" in the tone of "I've missed my train," with the "dialogue very neutral in the Bresson manner."[9]

While critics often cite cinematic antecendents for Godard's anti-illusionistic techniques, they tend to neglect his debt to avant-garde theatre. Apart from the influence of Jarry, Godard's work presents analogies with both surrealist and absurdist theatre. The theatre must return to nature, Apollinaire argued in the preface to *The Breasts of Tiresias*, but not imitate it in the manner of photography. "The People of Zanzibar" figure in *Tiresias* recalls the one-man armies of *Ubu* and anticipate the bizarre and incongruous personages—such as the dwarf and the mad exiled queen of Lebanon in *Pierrot le Fou*—that pop up in Godard's early films. Godard's experimentation with voices, similarly, prolongs the innovations of the avant-garde theatre. From the mechanical "parler Ubu" of Jarry, through the megaphones of *The Breasts of Tiresias* and the phonographs of Cocteau's *The Wedding on the Eiffel Tower*, avant-garde dramatists have tended to distort or alienate the voice, dissociating it from the personality of the character and from the tone of the dramatic moment. Godard's films, in fact, often sustain a kind of "parler Ubu"—a constant, emotionless tone even in the most extravagant circumstances—that can be most unsettling.

Avant-garde theatre, beginning with Jarry and continuing with Artaud, Genet, and Arrabal, has often been a theatre of rare violence. *Ubu Roi* is full of "casual slaughter," mass executions and violations of the human person. Artaud called for a theatre that would confront the spectator with "the truthful precipitates of dreams, in which his taste for crime, his erotic obsessions, his savagery, his chimeras, his utopian sense of life and matter, even his cannibalism, pour out, on a level not counterfeit and illusory, but interior."[10] *Weekend*, Godard's most Artaldian film, would seem to incarnate Artaud's recommendations for a "theatre of cruelty," for the film animates a good deal of crime, eroticism, and ritualized violence. Hippies dance around a woman, splash her in psychedelic colors, and penetrate her with a gigantic fish. In another scene, Roland pours his mother-in-law's blood over a skinned rabbit. We even have cannibalism when the hippies dine on English tourist and Corinne feasts on her dead husband. The ultimate spectacle, of course, is ritualized murder, so Godard has us witness the ritual slaughter of a pig and a goose, in what seems a weirdly twisted version of a religious sacrament.

Godard, disturbed by the popularity of *Weekend*, came to see the dangers inherent in the Artaldian alternative. The more one indulges in spectacle, he admitted subsequently, the more one becomes immersed in what one is trying to destroy. The mere spectacle, as opposed to the analysis, of violence, is infinitely cooptable by the bourgeois entertainment industry. The public, for its part, seems reluctant to admit its pleasure and complicity in the spectacle of

Figure 37. *Weekend* (1967)

violence, a gratification to which it has become increasingly addicted. Guillaume in *La Chinoise* says of his father that he once worked with Artaud, but that he now works with *Le Club Méditerranée*, an organization whose schema resembles that of the concentration camps. Godard indirectly suggests, then, that spectacles of ritualized violence are quite recuperable by bourgeois or even fascist society. That the comparison fails to do justice to the subtlety of Artaud's thought is quite beside the point; the fact remains that although certain themes remind us of Artaud, such themes are treated, increasingly, in a distanced and Brechtian manner. For Artaud, theatre should push our aggressive impulses to their paroxysm; Brecht and Godard would have us reflect on the violence that inhabits ourselves and our world.

The casual muggings and offhand slaughter in Godard's films are designed to highlight what Godard calls, paraphrasing Hannah Arendt, "the banality of the atrocious and the atrociousness of this banality." When Paul sees a woman threatening her husband with a gun as she moves out of a cafe, Paul's only concern is that she shut the door so as not to let in the cold winter air. When the man falls, presumably to his death, the camera retains its laconic distance, refusing to underline the horror of the incident by heightened proximity, selective framing, or any kind of rhetorical emphasis. The ideal film on the concentration camps, for Godard, would observe a similar distance, coolly demonstrating the banality of the torturers and the nature of their daily challenges: "How to get a body measuring two meters into a coffin measuring fifty centimeters? How to load ten tons of arms and legs onto a three ton lorry? . . . The really horrible thing about such scenes would not be their horror but their very ordinary everydayness."[11] This banalization of the atrocious characterizes many Godard films: the random urban violence of *Masculine, Feminine* anticipates the corpse-strewn landscapes of *Weekend* and the moral anesthesia of *Alphaville*, where systematized murder is greeted with polite applause.

Carnival and the Apocalypse: *The Exterminating Angel*

A film that betrays links both to the carnivalesque spirit of silent comedy and to the theatrical avant-garde is Buñuel's *The Exterminating Angel* (1962). Buñuel offers a more politicized version of the themes that obsessed the "theatre of the absurd": entrapment (one thinks of Sartre's proto-absurdist *No Exit*); paralysis (Hamm in his wheelchair, his parents in their dustbin in *Endgame*); proliferating chaos (*Rhinoceros*); and the devaluation of language (*The Bald Soprano*). The film's central premise—the inexplicable entrapment of a pride of socialites—is as calculatedly implausible as those subtending many Beckett or Ionesco plays. The film also shares with absurdist theatre its affinity with burlesque film comedy. Beckett, like Buñuel, adored Buster Keaton, and collaborated with him on his own *Film*. Ionesco cited Groucho, Chico, and Harpo Marx as the three biggest influences on his work, and, in *The Chairs*, he has the old man impersonate the month of February by "scratching his head like Stan Laurel." *The Exterminating Angel*, like *The Chairs*, is structured on the comic formula of a slow descent from normality into anarchy, all performed in Keatonesque deadpan. The bear that wanders into *The Exterminating Angel* descends not only from the bear that frightens Père Ubu in Jarry's play but also from the one that follows Chaplin along an icy precipice in *The Gold Rush*. Cannibalism is evoked in both films, and Buñuel's butler eats paper as if it were a delicacy, just as Chaplin dines on shoe and lace as if it were a gourmet meal.

Buñuel radicalizes these burlesque and avant-garde *topoi* by linking them to the carnivalesque theme of the "world turned upside down." The "Exterminating Angel" executes a mission of social justice, an apocalyptic laying low of the noble and the powerful. In fact, *The Exterminating Angel* should be paired with Buñuel's *Los Olvidados*, for the logic of the former film is to reduce its upper-class protagonists to the miserable condition of the slum-dwellers of the latter. One of the aristocrats alludes to this irony by complaining that they have been forgotten ("olvidados"). Social distinctions are leveled in a spirit of carnivalesque degradation.[12] The subversion of conventional hierarchies begins when the servants abandon the Nobile mansion, the way "rats abandon a sinking ship," an excuse for Buñuel to mock the helplessness of aristocrats when they are forced to take care of their own needs. As the social contract begins to break down, the "castaways of Providence Street" are thrown increasingly into the promiscuous slum conditions of *Los Olvidados*. The mansion becomes an overcrowded mini-slum, without running water, with people sleeping on the floor in forced cohabitation with one another and with animals. The butler chops at the wall with an axe, revealing bare bricks and cement as in lower-class Mexican dwellings. The search for food and firewood leaves the floor dotted with rubble. Stripped of their class advantages, the aristocrats degenerate into distinctly ungenteel behavior. As in a slum, copulation and defecation, expressions of the "lower bodily principle," shed the privilege of privacy. Bourgeois etiquette disintegrates: Letitia picks at her blackheads, the conductor makes unseemly advances, and Raul and Nobile and the others scrap over petty offenses like drunks in a cheap bar. They scramble openly for the drugs that they formerly took in secret, and Raul, like a lumpen vagabond, pokes through the garbage looking for stray cigarette butts. The aristocrats who would normally only consume the results of the slaughter of animals, in the form of *ragoût* or *steak au poivre*, are here forced to witness the slaughter itself. The same aristocrats who have spilled food as an amusing theatrical device are now ravaged by hunger and on the verge, it is suggested, of ritual murder and even cannibalism. In short, as Noblie laments, all that they have hated since childhood—"vulgarity, violence, dirt—have become [their] companions."

Ubu and *Les Carabiniers*

Godard's *Les Carabiniers* (1963) clearly forms part of the modernist carnivalesque and happens to be explicitly indebted to *King Ubu*. Godard underlines this debt by having one of his heroines utter precisely the word that scandalized Jarry's public in 1896—"Merdre!" (Shitr). The epitaph-title with which Godard concludes the film and "buries" his two heroes—Michelangelo and Ulysses—paraphrases the letter to Madame Rachilde with which Jarry, himself near death, "buried" Père Ubu: .

> With this Père Ubu, who has earned his rest, is going to sleep. He believes that the brain, during decomposition, continues to function after death, and that its dreams are our Paradise.[13]

The Godard version substitutes "the two brothers" for "Père Ubu":

> And with that, the two brothers went to sleep for eternity, believing that the brain, during decomposition, functions after death, and that its dreams are our Paradise.

But more important than these explicit homages is the fact that *Les Carabiniers* adopts the carnivalesque strategies of the Jarry play—parody, abstraction, and aggression.

If *King Ubu* is tragic farce, *Les Carabiniers* is absurdist epic. The title of Jarry's play syntactically and lexically evokes classical tragedy and Shakespearean history play, but its protagonist represents the antithesis of the classical hero. *Les Carabiniers* treats the perennial epic subject—war—but its male duo of protagonists present, like Ubu, a precipitate of gluttony, cupidity, and brutality. The narratives of the two texts follow parallel trajectories which obey the carnivalesque pattern of comic crownings and uncrownings. Ubu overthrows the king, exercises arbitrary power, and is overthrown and exiled. Ulysses and Michelangelo go to war for "the king," win chimerical booty in the form of postcards which they take to be deeds to property, and are finally betrayed by the soldiers who enlisted their services. The motives of the protagonists in the two texts are equally ignoble. Ubu wants to get rich, eat sausages, and roll around the streets in a carriage. Ulysses and Michelangelo want to rape women, steal Hawaiian guitars, and leave restaurants without paying their bills. Both constitute debased caricatures of their namesakes, two of the quintessential culture heroes of the western world. Ulysses is decidedly uncrafty, and Michelangelo is far from the Renaissance man. His culture consists in the comic books which provide him with his brutally simplistic *weltanschauung*, while Ulysses emulates the gangster heroes of B-films. Together, they embody the basest instincts and the most petty sadism, while their personal and collective enterprise lacks all dignity and redeeming purpose.

Godard's location of the scene of *Les Carabiniers* as "at once everywhere and nowhere" quite literally echoes Jarry's situating of Ubu "in Poland, that is to say, Nowhere" and in a "Nowhere" that is "everywhere." Both texts constitute inverted utopias, "the world upside down," not only because they create dislocated worlds of abstractly comic horror, but also because they reflect the "nowhere" of an antimimetic art uninterested in reproducing the spatial or geographical configurations of the conventionally perceived world. Michelangelo and Ulysses live with Venus and Cleopatra in a shack located in a featureless *terrain vague* in what appears to be France. They are approached by two riflemen bearing a letter from the King. Flattered by what they take to be a personal royal request for their services, and excited by the prospect of satisfying all their sadistic impulses and consumerist desires, they march eagerly off to war. Their ironic odyssey, like Ubu's quick tour of Europe, takes them to Italy, Silesia, Mexico, Egypt, Russia, and the United States. But instead of location shooting and a cast of thousands, an approach Godard would have regarded as obscenely wasteful and contrary to his aesthetic, the film offers shorthand evocations via handwritten intertitles and still photographs. The spatial displacements, as in *Ubu*, are swift and implausible. A trip to Egypt consists of a shot of Michelangelo taking photographs followed by a shot of the Sphynx. Shortly thereafter, the two heroes salute what the cinematic logic of eyeline matches tells us to be the Statue of Liberty. Just as Shakespeare's Bottom and company "signify" a wall with some lime, and Jarry's actors denote the "Russian and Polish armies crossing the Ukraine," so Godard "signifies" global travels in minimalist fashion.

King Ubu is a verbal carnival in which language celebrates its freedom from the usual hierarchies and dominations. Language becomes opaque, detached both from its referential function and from its human source. Ceasing to be a transparent conveyor of meaning, it begins to generate its own momentum. The play often works by the principle of absurd accumulation, whether of past participles ("I'm wounded," moans Père Ubu, "I'm punctured, I'm perforated, I'm administered, I'm buried. . . .") or substantives (Père Ubu threatens Mère Ubu with "twisting of the nose, tearing out of the hair, penetration of little bits of wood into the ears, extraction of the brain by the heels, laceration of the posterior, partial or perhaps even total suppression of the spinal marrow . . . and finally the grand re-enacted decollation of John the Baptist, the whole taken from the very Holy Scriptures. . . ."). In an epic exchange of insults between Bougrelas, Père Ubu and Mère Ubu, what is said is determined only by the final phoneme of the words: Bougrelas' "sacripant, mécréant, musulman" elicits Ubu's "Polognard, soûlard, bâtard, hussard, tartare." Not to be outdone, Mère Ubu adds: "capon, cochon, félon, histrion, fripon."

The Riflemen also generates absurd lists and accumulations, parodic versions of "epic catalogues." To persuade Ulysses and Michelangelo to go to war, one of the riflemen recites, in a bored monotone, the fruits of war that will be within their grasp: Maseratis, women of the world, jewels, lighters, metro stations, cigar factories, supermarkets. The list is absurdly discontinuous; one might presumably steal jewels and Maseratis, but how does one steal metro stations and supermarkets? The narrative is "framed" by these catalogues, for when the pair return with their booty—a huge stack of postcards—we find the same surrealistic enumeration. Calling for "order and method," Michelangelo divides the postcards into arbitrary and incongruous categories—monuments, means of transport, works of art, women of the world. His classificatory mania has all the trappings of rational analysis with none of the substance; the entities are simply too heteroclite. The concreteness of "large department stores" accords ill with the abstraction of "industry" or the generality of "wonders of nature." The sequence seems to mock the ways in which occidental logic structures and orders its universe. We are reminded of the Borges reference to a certain Chinese encyclopedia which classifies animals as: 1) belonging to the emperor; 2) embalmed; 3) tame; 4) sucking pigs; and so on. The exotic charm of the taxonomy demonstrates, as Michel Foucault points out in his gloss on the story, the limitations of our own. Such absurd enumerations do away, by implication, with the site, the ground upon which it is possible for entities to be juxtaposed. On one level, Godard, in a provocative attack on the ideological hierarchies of the spectator, is equating the most cherished monuments of western culture with the commercialized fetishes of the consumer society. Side by side we find the Parthenon and the Galeries Lafayette, pornographic photographs and Madame Récamier. But on another level, Godard is creating an imagistic heterotopia, juxtaposing entities that come from categories so alien to each other that it is impossible to find a common place of residence for them.

The freedom of invention characteristic of carnivalesque art allows for anachronism as a textual strategy. The very language of *King Ubu*—at times archaic and at times neologistic, ranging from Rabelaisian echoes to contemporary slang—is anachronistic. *Les Carabiniers*, similarly, creates an anachronistic synthesis of diverse historical periods. Evidence of modern-day France—comic books, consumer products, automobiles—commingles with references to royal decrees. Michelangelo goes to the "cinématographe," a term linked to the silent era, yet he sees sound films. The war in the film condenses allusions to many conflicts. The intertitles are copied from authentic letters by

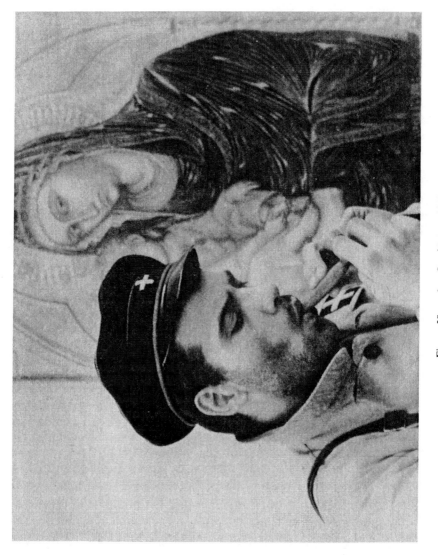

Figure 38.   *Les Carabiniers* (1963)

soldiers circled at Stalingrad, from Napoleon's campaign in Spain, and from circulars distributed by Himmler, and the film visually and verbally evokes the Korean War, the Algerian War, Gettysburg, and the French resistance. Even the uniforms, like carnival costumes, are anachronistic as well as impossibly international, combining a tsarist officer's cap, the jacket of an Italian tramway controller, and the boots of a Yugoslav partisan.

Carnivalesque art is uninterested in psychological verisimilitude or audience identification. Both *King Ubu* and *Les Carabiniers* cut off all sentimental participation in spectacle. Jarry's play renders the most rudimentary empathy, not to mention pity and fear, impossible, by offering figures from *grand guignol*, ideological marionettes lacking in psychological substance. The characters are ambulatory oxymorons, given to sudden and improbable ethical turnabouts. Mère Ubu, who generally displays not so much as a *soupçon* of conscience, abruptly lectures Ubu: "the young Bougrelas will win, because he has justice on his side." Père Ubu, learning that his rival will gain the crown that he himself has coveted and murdered for, acquieces with unexpected nonchalance, adding that "I don't envy him his crown." *Les Carabiniers* is peopled with pasteboard buffoons devoid of psychological density who renders sympathetic identification virtually impossible. Even their self-consciously grandiose names remove them to a realm beyond identification, for contemporary people are rarely named Ulysses or Cleopatra. The film aggressively blocks all entrance points for our projection; unable to even identify the opposing sides in the battle, much less can we identify with specific characters. Such distanciation might have been more tolerable had we been granted spectatorial omniscience in exchange, but *Les Carabiniers* often makes us feel as irrelevant and manipulable as its characters. We are placed in the position of Michelangelo struggling to possess the film.

The protagonists of both *Ubu* and *Les Carabiniers* shock us by the light-hearted candor with which they relate their crimes. "In every direction," Ubu blithely reports, "you can see only burning houses and people bent under the weight of our phynances." In their letters to Venus and Cleopatra, the two protagonists of *Les Carabiniers* coolly boast of mass murder: "We sow death among families, and fulfill our bloody mission." Such passages display, on one level, a typically modernist dissociation between horrible events and their distanced recounting, but on another they reflect a carnivalesque strategy of radical simplification aimed at the unmasking of Power, a strategy which carries out the promise implicit in the Borges quotation which prefaces *Les Carabiniers*: "More and more, I am moving toward simplicity." The discourse of Power, in these texts, is simplified, stripped of all euphemism. Godard's professed goal in *Les Carabiniers* was to make the logic of war so simple a child could understand it, and if war is anything in the film it is a pretext for pillage, a kind of bellicose consumerism. The "Maserati sequence" reveals, on a microcosmic level, this central mechanism. Ulysses lacks the money to buy the Maserati he desires; so he kills and steals to get it. The "postcard sequence" shows the photographic image as a vain attempt to appropriate the world, and the camera, in Susan Sontag's words, as "the ideal arm of consciousness in its acquisitive mood." The logic of property deprives even images of their innocence. Which is why Godard repeatedly stresses the analogy between *prises de guerre* and *prises de vue*, rifles and cameras, murderers, and voyeurs.

Les Carabiniers: The War Film Intertext

Les Carabiniers operates a triple demystification—of war itself, of the war film, and even of the antiwar film. War itself is divested of its glamor and shown to be a confusion and a muddle. Like Fabrice at Waterloo, we as spectators wander bewilderedly through the smoke of a tedious, undramatic, and decentered war. Godard counterpoints sound and image to point up the contradictions between the patriotic glorifications of war and the gray realities they mask. Noble official pronouncements precede confused military scenes which do not match at all. Shouts of "la guerre est finie" coincide with the continuing sound of gunfire on the soundtrack. The conventional ethical hierarchies of war— massive aerial bombardments are antiseptic and humane; disemboweling with a knife is evil and barbaric—are leveled and revealed to be prevarications. Such codes are shown to be as absurd as those of Ubu's coconspirators who, while outraged at the idea of poisoning Venceslas with arsenic, can hail a plan to bifurcate him with a sword as "noble and valiant."

   Les Carabiniers demystifies war by carnivalizing a genre—the war film. Godard systematically denies us the satisfactions of the genre: drama, spectacular battles, vicarious games of strategy. War is trivialized and divested of its glamor, denuded of all heroism or even of compensatory male camaraderie. A majority of high-angle shots show the action against a background of mud; there are no helmets silhouetted boldly against the sky. Most war films concentrate on images of sudden death; *Les Carabiniers* repeatedly shows us rotting corpses, death in its most unpalatable form. Rather than emphasize glorious battles, Godard focuses on the military execution of prisoners, while the more spectacular actions—gougings, hangings, mass executions—take place off-screen or are conveyed by anachronistic or "uncinematic" intertitles. War is primarily evoked through the soundtrack and through archival footage. But while archival footage conventionally undergirds realism, here it destroys it. The stock shots are intrusive and unintegrated into the dramatic structure of the film. A "sylleptic" montage of stock shots mixes World War I tanks with World War II planes, thus forming the visual equivalent of the anachronistic intertitles.[14]

Figure 39. *Les Carabiniers* (1963)

Les Carabiniers demystifies the antiwar film as well. Many antiwar films, after all, indirectly glorify war. *M.A.S.H.*, while satirizing the bureaucratic inefficiency of war, creates such an appealing image of army camaraderie that the spectator is tempted to enlist. Films like *All Quiet on the Western Front* or *La Grande Illusion*, on the other hand, make war the scene of a heroic refusal. Most antiwar films accept the conventions of dramatic realism, but for Godard "realism," with all its costly procedure of reconstituting war on the screen, teaches us nothing *about* war. He rejects, consequently, both realism and the human image. The potential objects of our identification—Michelangelo and Ulysses—display the moral somnambulism of an Eichmann; they are murdering robots, Ubufied Lieutenant Calleys. There is no lachrymose insistence on the suffering of war's victims, no cheap catharsis. Since the film offers us no human alternative for identification, we are denied the suspect pleasures of *la bonne conscience.*

In his introduction to the film, Godard called *Les Carabiniers* a "conte de faits," that is both a fairy tale (*conte de fées*) and a documentary (story of facts). The film, in this sense, superimposes an archly simple fable on an essayistic dissertation on war and fascism. This confounding of generic categories offended many critics, hardly surprising given the close link between generic and social conventions. The separation of styles, as Auerbach shows in *Mimesis*, has tended historically to be tied to the separation of classes, and any generic or discursive "leveling" in the realm of art portends, for the conservative critic, an ominous leveling within society itself. In texts like *Ubu* or *Les Carabiniers*, the censoring faculty simply goes on strike in protest against all cultural rigidity. Just as the surrealists praised "la sauvagerie" as an antidote to a stultifying "civilization," Jarry and Godard give free reign to their taste for nonsense and horseplay. Their puerile and scatological references reflect the childlike irreverence of artists on a raucous holiday from the strictures of official culture.

Carnival and Latin American Culture

Bakhtin's theory of the carnivalesque arose not only out of his literary studies of Rabelais but also out of a vital culture—the Russian—which was in some ways marginal to mainstream European culture. Some Latin American literary critics, not surprisingly, have begun to see the notion of the carnivalesque as the key to the specificity of Latin American cultural production. Since Latin America has been economically, poltically, and culturally marginalized, its best artists have made this marginalization, this parodic consciousness of being on the periphery, this ironic sense of belonging to two cultures—one's own and that of the metropolitan centers of power—absolutely central to their work. Borges, on first glance a most patrician writer, often carnivalizes European literary classics, turning Dante's *Divine Comedy*, for example, into a trivial love story in *El Aleph*. The novels of Manuel Puig constantly remind us of the presence of Hollywood films as a kind of cultural *lingua franca* in countries like Argentina. All Latin America, in a manner, has been "betrayed by Rita Hayworth," in that cultural colonialism has given it a pervasive sense that real life is "elsewhere," not in the provinces of Argentina or Brazil.

But Latin America is "carnivalesque" in still another, more concrete sense. Whereas carnival in Europe is either nonexistent or but a pale echo of the Rabelaisian frenzies of yore, carnival in Latin America—especially in those countries impregnated by the African culture brought by slaves—is a living and vibrant tradition. A profoundly mestizo culture—Amerindian, European, and Afro-American—has given birth to an immensely creative cultural phenomenon. The kind of ecstatic Dionysian festival for which Nietzsche was so nostalgic—in which "singing and dancing crowds, ever increasing in number, were whirled from place to place under [a] Dionysian impulse" exists in full force in certain parts of the Caribbean and in Brazilian cities like Salvador or Recife. It was contact with such festivals that led the Cuban writer Alejo Carpentier to formulate his concept of the "real maravilloso americano" and to contrast Europe's labored attempts to resuscitate the marvelous with the quotidian magic of Latin American life.[15] While most European carnivals have degenerated into the ossified repetition of perennial rituals, Brazilian carnival remains a protean, ever-changing cultural expression, combining ecstatic polyrhythmic percussion and "orgiastic" behavior with the elaborate "folk opera" of the samba schools and the spontaneous street theatre of costumed revelers mingling in free and familiar contact.[16]

Brazilian anthropologist Roberto da Matta describes carnival in terms almost identical to those of Bakhtin, as a time of festive laughter and gay relativity, a collective celebration which abolishes the separation between actors and spectators. He describes carnival as the privileged locus of inversion, in which all the marginalized—the poor, the black, the homosexual—take over the symbolic center. The business quarter, usually dedicated to productive labor, is given over to playfulness. Night changes position with day, as revelers dance all night and sleep during the day. Men dress up as women and women, with somewhat less frequency, as men. Grown-ups drink cachaça out of baby bottles, while socialites dress up as prostitutes and prostitutes dress up as aristocrats. The festival, at least in the tendencies of its symbolic system—I am not suggesting that three days of carnival *actually* overturn social structures reinforced throughout the year—is profoundly democratic and egalitarian. A party to which everyone is invited, carnival ideally offers a world of gestural freedom and unbridled fantasy, in which revelers play out imaginary roles corresponding to their fondest desires.[17]

Art in Brazil has been enriched by the perennial interchange between erudite culture and the popular world of carnival. The novels of Jorge Amado, for example, constantly draw inspiration from the Africanized carnival of Bahia. Carnivalesque imagery has also pervaded Brazilian cinema throughout its history. The Brazilian musical comedies called *chanchadas* of the thirties, forties, and fifties were also called "carnivalesque" films since they were often timed to be released during carnival and meant to promote carnival songs. These films, as João Luiz Vieira points out on his article on "Carnival and Parody in Brazilian Cinema," often parody the American films on which they were partially modeled.[18] In doing so, they make fun not only of the American films but also of their own inability to faithfully reproduce American production values. In short, they make all that is marginal in the Brazilian situation the very center of their discussion. In José Carlos Burle's *Carnaval Atlântida* (1953), the Brazilian director Cecilio B. de Milho (Cecil B. de Corn) abandons his plan to film a serious epic *Helen of Troy*, opting finally for a comic and carnivalesque version on the same theme. "Helen of Troy won't work," says Regina to her father, the producer of the proposed epic, "for the people want to dance and move." In the end, foreign high-art stodginess gives way to native carnivalesque debauchery. These parodies, as Vieira points out, often center on American super-productions, and express mingled resentment and admiration for the technically superior product of the metropolitan center of neocolonial power. *Os Cosmonautas* (The Cosmonauts), for example, speaks of a Brazilian space scientist, working at Cape *Carnival*, whose ambition is to send three Brazilians on the first moonflight. *Costinha Contra o King-Mong* (Costinha Against King Mong) spoofs the Dino de Laurentis super-production by pitting the comic actor Costinha against a crudely fashioned monster on the top of Sugarloaf and Corcovado.

Brazilian Modernism and the Cannibalist Metaphor

A film that reflects the carnivalesque, in the anthropological as well as the literary sense, and a work indebted to Rabelais, to the European avant-garde, and to Brazilian carnivalesque films, is Joaquim Pedro de Andrade's *Macunaíma* (1969) based on the novel of the same name by Mario de Andrade. The book, published in 1928, was one of the seminal achievements of Brazilian modernism, a movement which began around 1913 and gathered momentum until it exploded the Brazilian cultural scene in 1922 with the "Week of Modern Art," a multimedia event featuring poetry, music, and the plastic arts. Mario de Andrade, as one of the prime movers of Brazilian modernism, was widely conversant with the European avant-garde, including the futurists, the dadaists, and the surrealists (some of whom were his friends and whom he "invited" into his book). At the same time, he remained a defiantly Brazilian artist. Like other Brazilian modernists, Mario de Andrade called for the democratization of Brazilian literature through the incorporation of popular forms of speech. In his "Brazilwood Manifesto," fellow modernist Oswald de Andrade called for a "popular language" which represented "The Way We Speak" and "The Way We Are." By embracing the creative "errors" of the people, the modernists sounded a barbaric yawp of protest against a double colonization, first by Europe itself and second by the European-dominated cultural elite within Brazil.

Oswald de Andrade called modernism a "Movimento Antropófago" (a Cannibalist Movement), which advocated the forging of an authentic Brazilian culture through the critical devouring of native and foreign influences. For the modernists, cannibalism was an authentic native tradition as well as a key metaphor for their own cultural independence. "Only cannibalism unites us," Oswald proclaimed, "Tupi or not Tupi—that is the question." Oswald dated his Cannibal Manifesto 374—"the year Bishop Sardinha was swallowed"—in reference to the historical deglutition by Brazilian Indians of their first Portuguese-supplied bishop. The metaphor of cannibalism, then, was a way for Brazilian "redskin" artists to thumb their noses at their own literary "palefaces" and at colonizing overcultivated Europe, while heeding surrealism's call for "la sauvagerie" in art. It was also, as Emir Rodriguez Monegal points out, the carnivalized response to the problem of cultural colonialism. By comically underlining the cannibalistic nature of all processes of cultural assimilation, the modernists not only desacralized European models, they also desacrilized their own cultural activities. [19]

Cannibalism as metaphor has a long history, going at least as far back (if one bypasses its centrality in certain religious rituals) as Montaigne's essay "On Cannibals," based, ironically, on interviews with Brazilian Indians. Civilized Europeans were ultimately more barbarous than cannibals, Montaigne argued, for cannibals ate the flesh of the dead only to appropriate the strength of their enemies, while Europeans tortured and slaughtered in the name of a religion or love. Herman Melville echoed Montaigne by asking: "Which of us is not a cannibal?" With the avant-garde, the metaphor took on renewed vigor. The dadaists entitled one of their organs *Le Cannibal* and Picabia issued a "Cannibal Dada manifesto." As exploited by Brazilian modernists from the twenties through the present, the metaphor showed a positive and a negative pole. The positive pole entailed admiration for Amerindian culture and the proposal of cultural anthropophagy as an anticolonialist artistic strategy, i.e., to devour what is useful in the foreign and excrete what is not. The negative pole of the metaphor makes cannibalism a critical instrument for exposing the exploitative social Darwinism of bourgeois society. The two poles complement each other in the sense that the cannibalism-as-critique contemplates the melancholy distance separating contemporary society from what is imagined as the ideal communitas of the Amerindian.[20] Oswald de Andrade, in his manifestoes, emphasized both poles. Writing under the pseudonym "Marxillaire" (the name combines Marx, Apollinaire, and "maxillary"), he wrote the manifesto "Why I Eat," where he posits the Indian as a cultural model: "The Indian had no police, no repression, no nervous disorders, no shame at being nude, no class struggle, no slavery, no Ruy Barboso, no secret vote..." In his "Cannibalist Manifesto," meanwhile, he called cannibalism "The only law of the world. Masked expression of all individualisms and all collectivisms. Of all religions. Of all peace treaties."[21]

Mario de Andrade and the Carnivalization of Language

Mario de Andrade, an anthropologist as well as poet and novelist, compiled African, Amerindian, and Iberian legends to create *Macunaíma*. He called his text a "rhapsody," (eytomologically: "stitcher") and indeed he does stitch tales together to form a linguistic crazy quilt. *Macunaíma* offers the same abstract, invented language encountered in *King Ubu*. Just as Jarry's play forms a kind of linguistic cocktail composed of blasphemous archaisms (*cornebleu, jambedieu*: "God's horns," "God's legs"), contemporary slang (*fiole* for head), and phony old French ("Adonc le Père Ubu hoscha la poire, dont fut nommé par les Anglois Shakespeare: "Then Father Ubu shook his peare, who was afterwards yclept Shakespeare by the Englishe), so the language of *Macunaíma* forms what Mario de Andrade himself called "a veritable Esperanto." A linguistic "nowhere" taken from all regions of Brazil and ranging from the archaic to the neologistic, it exploits to the maximum the rich potentialities of Brazilian Portuguese, weaving rhymed maxims ("Eat shit but never bet"), gnomic wisdom ("The whole marsh doesn't mourn when one crab dies"), and popular superstitions into a splendid linguistic tapestry. *Macunaíma* taps the linguistic genius of the Brazilian people by fusing its jokes, legends, songs, and nursery rhymes, along with its Indianisms and Africanisms, into a panfolkloric saga. The novel captures the aphoristic cynicism of the people ("Each man for himself and God against everyone!" and "God gives nuts to people without teeth!") and its gift for nonsense ("Our hero closed his eyes so as not to see himself being eaten"). Despite its radically popular origins, however, the novel inevitably remained inaccessible in a country where illiteracy remains rampant. Thus Joaquim Pedro de Andrade performed an enormous service by making the novel "readable" to a vast public. Indeed the film's popular success suggests that *Macunaíma* does touch something in the carnivalesque depths of the Brazilian psyche.

    Macunaíma, like *Ubu*, carnivalizes language by comically exploiting linguistic incongruities. Père Ubu threatens murder, for example, in the polite language of a wedding announcement: "I have the honor of announcing that in

Figure 40.   *Macunaíma* (1969)

order to enrich the kingdom I am going to slay all the nobles and take all their goods." Elsewhere he apostrophizes his grossly named weapons: "Shitry sabre, do your duty, and you, financial stick, lag not behind!" The Ubus frequently break without warning into literary inversions ("que ne vous assom'je"), archaisms ("vous estes"), and epithets ("madame ma femelle ... madame de ma merdre"). Père Ubu even delivers himself of a labored and pleonastic epic simile: "As the poppy and the dandelion are scythed in the flower of their age by the pitiless scythe of the pitiless scyther who scythes pitilessly their pitiful parts—just so little Resnky." *Macunaíma*, similarly, has its presumably illiterate protagonist learn Latin and Greek (in order to collect "dirty words") and compose a letter in the chaste Portuguese of Camões. In the world of *Macunaíma* even monkeys speak Latin. In the film version, *Macunaíma* sees a vagabond, substituting for the monkey, eating his own testicles. The vagabond offers him a bite, *Macunaíma* approves, and the vagabond urges Macunaíma to try eating his own. So Macunaíma takes a stone and crushes his balls. As he howls in pain, the vagabond mumbles *"sic transit"* and walks away.

Macunaíma flaunts the freedom from historical limits and the liberty of philosophical invention typical of Menippean satire. The "scene" of the novel bounds improbably and without transition from the Amazon to the backlands to São Paulo in an impossible zigzag. Mario de Andrade mingles the flora and fauna of the diverse regions in a verbal equivalent of *Ubu's* "hybrid decor." He anachronistically mingles historical periods, facilitating what Bakhtin calls the "dialogue of the dead with the living," so that seventeenth-century characters rub elbows with contemporary ones. Mario de Andrade achieved this freedom of invention not only by drawing on the carnivalesque tradition in literature but also by reaching into the Amerindian preliterate past. The arbitrary hierarchies of occidental prejudice exalt classical Greek mythology as profond and poetic while denigrating Indian myths as "primitive." Mario de Andrade, for his part, used these myths to liberate Brazilian literary language. Animism and totemism inform the imagery of *Macunaíma*. "Fish used to be people just like us," Macunaíma tells his brothers. In the world of *Macunaíma*, characters literally turn into stars, as they do in Indian legends, becoming constellations to be deciphered by those who remain on earth. For *la pensée sauvage*, the night's starred face is indeed inscribed with "huge cloudy symbols of a high romance."

Mario de Andrade explores the antimimetic logic of folktales, which never pretend to be realistic. They tend, rather, to spatial and temporal indeterminacy: "In a certain kingdom ... once upon a time ... in the depths of the virgin forest...." The characters of folktales, as Propp points out, tend to lack psychological depth. They are "functions," instruments of action rather than interior revelation. Mario de Andrade's novel, in a not insignificant coincidence, was published the same year as Vladimir Propp's *Morphology of the Folk Tale*, in which Propp analyzes folktales into 31 "functions" or interchangeable incidents. The Brazilian structuralist critic Haroldo de Campos has, in fact, written a Morphology of *Macunaíma* (*Morfologia do Macunaíma*), in which he applies the Proppian categories to the de Andrade novel.[22] The logic of *Macunaíma*, he argues, is the logic of folktales, not the logic of individual tales but the logic of the processes by which the folk imagination constructs tales. Mario de Andrade exploits folklore as a way of generating stories, not by mechanistically compiling tales, but rather by setting them into vital interaction. Mario de Andrade "breeds" new stories by having characters from one body of legend (say Amerindian) perform actions taken from another body of legends (say African) so that the two traditions cross-fertilize each other. Thus *Macunaíma* anticipates Dundes' observation (in the second edition of Propp's *Morphology*) that Propp's scheme could be used to generate new stories. Novels like Ulysses have accustomed us to the use of classical myth as a kind of infrastructure for modern narrative, but with *Macunaíma* we have something quite different. In *Macunaíma*, folktales become part of a productive *combinatoire* by which the collective codes of *langue* are transformed into literary *parole*.

Macunaíma the book delights in its own artifice, much as Macunaíma the character tells lies for the sheer love of fiction. At the end of the book, Mario de Andrade explains that Macunaíma turned into a star, that his tribe disappeared and that only a green and yellow parrot remained to tell the story:

> And only the parrot in the silence of Uraricoera preserved from forgetfulness these events and the forgotten language. Only the parrot conserved in the silence the words and works of the hero.

This strange parrot, patriotically dressed in the Brazilian national colors, as the embodiment of the spirit of primary epic and the oral tradition, undoubtedly belongs to the metalinguistic species. He is an avian intertext, the custodian of the tribal memory, the archivist of inherited stories. But the illiterate parrot is helpless without someone to take down his tales. Therefore Mario de Andrade explains how the parrot *did* tell his story to one man:

> And that man is me, my dear people, and it is I who stayed to tell you the story ... I raised a howl singing in an impure dialect the words and deeds of Macunaíma, hero of his people. That's all folks.

Thus Mario de Andrade, like Rabelais and Cervantes before him, appears in his own text under his own name, speaking the impure dialect of his tribe. And he and the parrot represent the creative source of *Macunaíma*—the spirit of carnivalesque fiction itself.

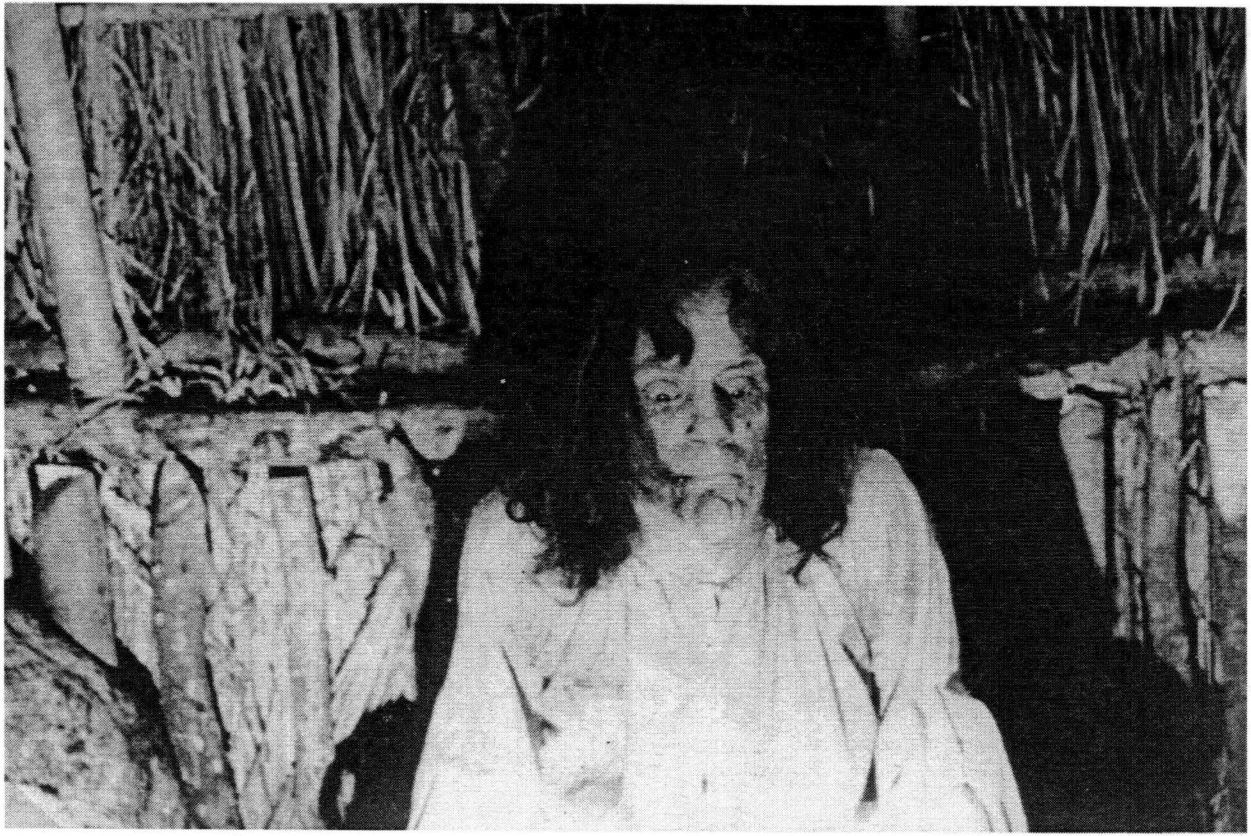

Figure 41. *Macunaíma* (1969)

Macunaíma: From Novel to Film

The first narrated words in both film and novel—"In the depths of the virgin-
forest was born Macunaíma, hero of his people"—signal entry into the
carnivalized world of comic epic. The film shows us an improbably old white
woman (played by a man) stand and grunt until she deposits a wailing 50-year-
old black "baby" on the ground. Thus, with a Rabelaisian flourish,
Macunaíma, "the hero without any character," sets out on his outrageous
career. This initial sequence constitutes a model of modernist abstraction and
carnivalesque inversions. The scene, like *Ubu's* simultaneous arctic and
tropical "hybird decor," represent an amalgam. A white man/woman with an
Indian name gives birth to a black man/child, one of whose brothers is black
and wears an African robe and the other of whom is white and wears a priest's
frock. The hut which serves as maternity ward is half backlander and half
Indian, while the manner of giving birth, in a standing position to take
advantage of gravity, is Amerindian. The birth itself, at once prodigious and
grotesque, encapsulates the imagery of carnival: the old, near death, giving
birth to the new. At the same time, the institution of the family is
desentimentalized and comically degraded. Instead of the usual exclamations
of "How cute!" the family reacts to the hero's birth with "How ugly!" and "He
stinks!" The film further underlines the surreal nature of this family by having
the same actor (Paulo José) play both the original "mother" of Macunaíma and
Macunaíma himself (in his later white incarnation), while another actor
(Grande Otelo) plays both the first and the second black Macunaíma. Thus the
white Macunaíma gives birth to the black Macunaíma who transforms himself
into the white Macunaíma who marries Ci the guerilla and fathers the original
black Macunaíma.[23]

Macunaíma's oxymoronic protagonist is a composite character, a summa
of Brazil, who epitomizes the ethnic roots as well as the qualities and defects of
an entire people. A composite of several heroes found in the Amerindian
legends which formed the basis of Mario's tale, even his name is oxymoronic,
since it is composed of the root "maku," (bad) and the suffix "ima" (great).
Macunaíma, the "hero without any character," lacks character not only in the
conventional moral sense but also in lacking all psychological coherence. His
character consists, as Mario de Andrade explained in a letter to Manuel
Bandeira, "in not having any character and his logic consists in not having any
logic." No *Pius Aeneas*, he is by turns selfish, generous, cruel, sensual, and
tender. If the authentic epic hero is all *sapientia et fortitudo*, Macunaíma is but
intermittently brave, and, frequently stupid. His most characteristic phrase is
"Ai! Que Preguiça!" (literally, What laziness!); laziness, in fact, serves as an
epic retarding device in *Macunaíma*. While occasionally crafty like Ulysses, he

is more often grossly egocentric like Ubu. He utters his epic challenges by telephone, and the telephone, symptomatically, is almost always busy. The logic of carnival is that of the world turned upside down, in which the powerful are mocked and ridiculous kings are enthroned and then dethroned in an atmosphere of gay relativity. The film proliferates in the sexual inversions common in carnivalesque literature as well as in carnival itself: Paulo José in drag giving birth to the protagonist; Macunaíma costumed as a French divorcée to trick Pietro out of the amulet; and Pietro himself in the kind of Hollywoodian bubblebath usually reserved for starlets. Ubuesque industrial magnate and big-time people-eater, Pietro Pietra is the most powerful figure in *Macunaíma*, and he, too, is dethroned. In his purple smoking jacket and green boxer shorts covering his padded buttocks, he looks very much like the *Rei Momo*, the burlesque King of the Revels of Brazil's carnival. Graced with multinational names and an Italian accent, he referred in the novel to the Italian *nouveaux riches* of the twenties and in the film to the dependant national bourgeoisie with its second-hand American technology. Pietro lives in the hybrid vulgarity of a palace where rococo clocks and breathing mannequins co-habit with neo-Egyptian sphynxes. He struggles with Macunaíma over an amulet—an amulet whose traditional folkloric role was to guarantee fishing and hunting (i.e., prosperity). As a millionaire who wants to eat Macunaíma, the hero of his people, he alludes to all the economic giants—Brazilian, in part, but especially North American—which devour Brazil and its resources. But even Macunaíma, though he defeats Pietro and wins the amulet, is enthroned and dethroned. After feeling the "immense satisfaction" of defeating the giant, he dissipates his advantage by returning to the jungle with the useless electronic bric-a-brac of consumer society.

Carnivalesque art, since it sees its characters not as flesh and blood people but as abstract puppet-like figures, laughs at beatings, dismemberment, and even death. The film is full of macabre humor and comic mutilations. When Macunaíma reports to his mother that he has lost a tooth, she responds by dropping dead, in literal respect for the proverb "caiu dente, é morte de parente" (a tooth falls, a relative dies). When Macunaíma becomes depressed over the loss of Ci, his brothers take him to a leper colony to cheer him up. (We see him kick a severed hand along the pavement, an homage to the hand poked at by the androgynous figure in *Chien Andalou*). One scene offers an orgy of dismemberment. Macunaíma goes to a wedding party for which the cannibalistically inclined Pietra has devised a festive game, a lottery in which the winners are thrown into a pool of fragmented bodies and voracious piranha fish. A close look at the contents of the pool reveals it to be an anthropophagic *feijoada* (the Brazilian national dish, consisting of sauce, black beans, and sausage) with human blood and limbs substituting for sauce and sausage. Macunaíma finally tricks Pietra into falling in, and as he is being devoured,

Pietra mutters that the *feijoada* needs more salt. The force of the sequence comes from the Godard-like dissociation between the gala setting, with its balloons and confetti and festively dressed guests, and the grisly events which take place within the setting, all clinched by Pietra's absurd final comment.

By focusing on bodily life—copulation, birth, eating, drinking, defecation—carnival offers human beings a temporary suspension of hierarchy and prohibition. The carnivalesque, for Bakhtin, is designed to transfer all that is spiritual, ideal, and abstract to the material level, to the sphere of earth and the body. Excrement (Ubu's *merdre*) as a literal expression of what Bakhtin calls the "lower bodily principle," forms part of this fecund imagery of the grotesque. Old time carnivals in Europe once featured "le jeu de la merde"(the shit game), in which revelers would sling manure at one another, a game later sublimated into more refined forms of slapstick: throwing talcum, water bottles, and other amiable aggressions. The excremental vision of Joaquim Pedro's film involves the protagonist being virtually shat into existence, in the opening sequence, and being shat on—by a vulture, by a goose—in his subsequent career. Urine, too, carries great prestige in the carnivalesque aesthetic. Gargantua urinates on the multitude, and the child Macunaíma would "piss hot on his old mother, frightening the mosquitoes." Copulating and feasting also abound in *Macunaíma*. The world is one of systematic orality, as if all its characters were fixed at what Freud called the "oral and cannibalistic phase."

The Politics of Carnival

However grotesque or fantastic, the carnivalesque esthetic retains a commitment to a certain realism (but not to illusionism) which addresses everyday life and speaks of contemporary events. Mennipean satire, as the journalistic genre of antiquity, was forever engaging in contemporary polemics. The novel *Macunaíma* mocked São Paulo politicians, intellectuals, libertines, and *nouveaux riches*. The popularity of the film version suggests that the Brazilian audience detected, below the surreal surface of the film, a carnivalized version of themselves and their situation. Allegorical and magical on first reading, *Macunaíma* becomes down-to-earth and quotidian on the second, developing, rather like surrealist painting, a tension between the realistic precision of the individual details and the apparent madness of the general conception.

What, then, does the carnivalized mimesis of *Macunaíma* show us? It shows us people going from the interior to the urban centers (thus recapitulating the trajectory of Cinema Novo) and becoming, for what are basically economic reasons, prostitutes like Sofará or hustlers like Macunaíma and Jigue. It also shows us the kind of political repression triggered by the 1968 coup-within-the-coup which handed power to the extreme right wing of the Brazilian military. "Suspicious attitude," explains the plainclothesman as he arrests the fleeing Macunaíma. The protagonist's speech in the public square denouncing the "evils of Brazil" elicits howls of anticommunist execration. The film also updates the novel by turning Ci, an Amazonian warrior in the novel—who, having sampled Macunaíma's "play," could not stop making love—into an urban guerilla and sexual activist in the film. Joaquim Pedro equips Ci's house with all the paraphernalia required by urban guerillas responding, in the late sixties, to the closing of Brazil's political system: a ditto machine for leaflets, materials for bombs, and money, presumably the booty from the kinds of bank robberies then practiced by the far Left.

Macunaíma also touches on another aspect of the political system, its structural rascism, something of which Mario de Andrade, as a mulatto, was doubtless aware. In the film, the passages in which Macunaíma turns from black to white reflect a sardonic consciousness of the absurdity of the "ideology of whitening" and the limitations of Brazil's "racial democracy." The white Manaape explains why his black brother Jigue was singled out for arrest: "A white man running is a champion; a black man running is a thief." When the white Macunaíma enters a magic fountain that turns hims black, the soundtrack plays the Portuguese version of "By a Waterfall," from Lloyd Bacon's musical *Footlight Parade* (1933) whose musical numbers were directed by Busby Berkeley. The choice seems especially apt when one recalls that the original inspiration for the "By a Waterfall" number was black children playing with the water spurting from a Harlem hydrant, a sight which suggests to the James Cagney character the spectacular possibilities of waterfalls splashing on *white* bodies. The allusion is rightly suggestive, evoking not only a complex play of black and white but also the relation between the American musical comedy and Brazil's carnivalized imitations of them in the *chanchada*, the genre in which Grande Otelo, the black actor who plays Macunaíma, was perhaps the most famous star.

Of the two "poles" of the cannibalist metaphor—the negative and the positive—Joaquim Pedro de Andrade clearly emphasizes the former. It is the notion of cannibalism as critique that he echoes in his "preface to Macunaíma:

Cannibalism is an exemplary mode of consumerism adopted by underdeveloped peoples. . . . The traditionally dominant, conservative social classes continue their control of the power structure—and we rediscover cannibalism. . . . The present work relationships, as well as the relationships between people—social, political, and economic—are still, basically, cannibalistic. Those who can, "eat" others through their consumption of products, or even more directly as in sexual relationships. Cannibalism has merely institutionalized and cleverly disguised itself. . . . Meanwhile, voraciously, nations devour their people. *Macunaíma*. . . is the story of a Brazilian devoured by Brazil.

The cannibalistic theme is treated in all its variations: people so hungry they eat themselves; an ogre who offers Macunaíma a piece of his leg; the guerrilla who devours him sexually; Pietra's wife who wants to cook him alive; Pietra himself with his anthropophagous soup; and finally the man-eating siren who lures him to his death. Brazil, practicing that "exemplary mode of consumerism," devours its own children and Brazil's poor, like Macunaíma, literally devour the Brazilian earth. The rich devour the poor, and the poor devour each other. We see the poor preying on each other when Macunaíma, tricked by a con man into buying a goose that defecates gold, goes on to steal from an already once-robbed shoeshine boy. The Left, meanwhile, while being devoured by the Right, purifies itself by eating itself—a practice which Joaquim Pedro calls the cannibalism of the weak.

Since the film version of *Macunaíma*, other Latin American filmmakers have elaborated the cannibals and the "carnivalist" metaphor. In *Como Era Gostoso meu Frances* (How Tasty was my Frenchman, 1971), Nelson Pereira dos Santos tells the story of a sixteenth-century Frenchman who is captured by Tupinamba Indians, who takes part in their tribal work, wars, and religious ceremonies, and who is finally cannibalized by them, incorporated, as it were, into the tribal body. Thus Dos Santos recycles the anticolonialist metaphor—the Tupinamba (read Brazil) must devour the European colonizer in order to appropriate his strength, but without being devoured in turn. The exiled Chilean filmmaker Raul Ruiz, similarly, develops the anthropophagic theme in *Le Territoire* (The Territory, 1981). The film's epigraph is from Mircea Eliade:

> Among all the inventions of the human spirit, anthrophagy impresses me the most. Outside of the moral question, the set of symbols which it gives rise to, and the psychological creativity which its practice implies, render it, for the historian of religion, a matter as complex, as harmonious and as worthy of respect as a Gothic cathedral.

In Ruiz's parable, a group of Americans ends up in a small Medieval town in Southern France, and later lose their way in the snow and are gradually converted to cannibalism. Western society, Ruiz suggests, is not as far from "savagery" as it likes to think.

In politicized carnivalesque films, the spirit of carnival is allied with the dynamics of class struggle in a process whereby the cheerful vulgarity of the powerless is made to shatter the pretense of the powerful. Arnaldo Jabor's *Tudo Bem* (Everything's Fine, 1978), for example, packs all of Brazil into a single bourgeois apartment. A couple, Juarez and Elvira, hire construction workers to remodel their apartment. The workers invite their impoverished relatives. The sick visit one of the maids, a mystic, in hopes of being healed. The other maid, a part-time prostitute, mocks her mistress's mannerisms and leads the workers in a carnival procession, using pots, pans, and construction tools

Figure 42.   The Cannabalistic Feijoado. *Macunaíma* (1969)

for percussion. The "slave quarters," in Glauber Rocha's felicitous phrase, "invade the Big House." As in *Viridiana*, the marginalized classes make an aristocratic home the scene of a carnivalesque degradation. The utopian energy of carnival overturns the "Order and Progress" of the bourgeois apartment. We see antagonistic classes, speaking irreconcilable languages and with radically opposed perspectives, in serio-comic confrontation within an abstract socially microcosmic space. How many social contradictions, we are led to ask, can fit into this space—i.e., Brazil—without a revolutionary explosion?

On the positive side, carnival suggests the joyful affirmation of becoming. It is ecstatic collectivity, the superseding of the individuating principle in what Nietzsche called "the glowing life of Dionysian revelers." (The primordial role of percussion comes from its unifying and tribalizing role.) On the negative, critical side, the carnivalesque suggests a demystificatory instrument for everything in the social formation which renders such collectivity difficult of access: class hierarchy, political manipulation, sexual repression, dogmatism, and paranoia. Carnival in this sense implies an attitude of creative disrespect, a radical opposition to the illegitimately powerful, to the morose and monological.

The carnivalesque has already demonstrated its usefulness in literary criticism. Bakhtin's revalorization of parody and carnival shifted the terms of the debate concerning the development of the novel. In a typically carnivalesque gesture, what had been considered marginal and eccentric—the parodic sport of a Sterne or Diderot—took over the center as a paradigm of dialogic textuality. The notion of the carnivalesque relativizes the overvaluation—often shared by bourgeois and Marxist critic alike—of the serious mimetic mode, suggesting the possibility of a realism which is not an illusionism, just as it suggests the possibility of a Left cultural critique which precludes neither laughter nor the pleasure principle.

5

The Pleasures of Subversion

If modernism, by placing all human beings in the quixotic predicament, represents a radical extension of the Cervantic critique of fictions, Marxism constitutes a politicization and historicization of that critique. I am not making the anachronistic suggestion that Cervantes was a Marxist, or that the reading of *Don Quixote* transformed Marx into a revolutionary thinker, but only that the Marxist critique of the ideological fictions of the bourgeois social order can be seen as a working out, a deepening, of certain features of the Cervantic critique. Ideology, after all, is essentially quixotic, a system of representation, according to Louis Althusser, based on "the imaginary relationship of individuals to their real conditions of existence.[1] Don Quixote's ideology does possess a certain logic and rigor; it consists of refracting social reality through the prism of chivalric literature. The real conditions of his life include windmills, prostitutes, and genteel poverty, but his "lived relation" to these conditions involves giants, courtly heroines, and a world unsoiled by material preoccupations.

Ideology, false consciousness, reification—these are diverse names for the veils of appearance that obscure the true face of class society. Demystification, for Marx, consists in stripping the conditions under which we live of their drapery of legalistic and moralistic concepts by confronting society's self image, its schemes of representation, its mystifications and idealizations, with its real-life processes. Too much of Marxist criticism, unfortunately, rather than clarifying the demystification process as it operates *within* art, has applied the strategy *to* art. Equating art with false consciousness, a certain Marxism deprives art of its liberatory force, falling into a facile reductionism. Art is not an economic category, and its productions cannot be reduced either to false consciousness or to the sublimate of class antagonism. Even reactionary classes, Marx recognized, can produce art which offers perennial delight. Although the class *qua* class may be destined for the dustbin of history, the artistic products of its members often wind up honoring the libraries and museums of the world. At its best art is itself, like Marxism, a critical instrument designed to lay bare the mechanisms of society even as it lays bare the devices of art.

Although often caricatured as merely quixotic, Marxism can be profoundly Cervantic, for it places in dialectical relation the earthbound materialism of a Sancho Panza and the utopian vision of a Don Quixote. Like Sancho Panza with his crude proverbial wisdom, Marx insists on the material behavior of human beings—"not men as narrated, thought of, imagined [but]...real, active men..."—but these reminders of human materiality represent only one side of the dialectic.[2] The other side involves the capacity to envision, beyond the degraded processes of the present, the lineaments of a future golden age free of alienation and oppression. While wandering through the arid landscapes of the kingdom of necessity, Marx could, like the knight of the sad countenance, catch intoxicating glimpses of the realm of freedom.[3]

The great utopians, the Manuels point out in their *Utopian Thought in the Western World,* have paradoxically often been the greatest realists, showing extraordinary comprehension of their time and place, offering penetrating analyses of the social, economic, and emotional conditions of their historical moment.[4] Don Quixote's vision of enchanters who frustrate the achievements of the virtuous and exalt those of the morally wretched can be taken as a shrewdly veiled account of real social forces that create an unfair distribution of the rewards of production. Quixote's utopianism operates in the nostalgic mode; he denies the present in the name of a golden age. But the utopian propensity can look backward or forward in its negation of the present, just as it can function positively or negatively, positing an ideal commonwealth or an inverted utopia. What will interest us here will be a kind of utopian realism, characterized by a double movement of revolutionary desire and hardheaded critique, celebration and demystification, utopia and dystopia, the sense of potential and the awareness of limits.

If the Marxist view, by stripping art of its mystical wrappings, constitutes a devaluation of art, it also redeems the very art it demystifies by granting it a potentially revolutionary use-value. Art loses what Benjamin calls its "aura," its overlay of magical and religious sanctifications, its residue of mystery.[5] Critics like Benjamin denounce the fetishization of art and deflate the romantic myth of artists as visionaries, sages, voyants, or "the unacknowledged legislators of mankind." At the same time, they forge a link between "high art" and the everyday mechanical and constructive crafts. The notion of art as "special" has been historically bound up with the idea of art as "useless." Art, for the idealist, frees human beings from the vulgar material pressures of life by fixing their gaze on the beautiful, thus unconsciously resuscitating for art the ideological function of medieval religion—used by the dominating class to legitimize its advantages and absorbed by the dominated class to numb its pain. But if art is simply another form of production—not inspiration, not genius, not the divine efflatus, but work—then artists can pay tribute to the element of craft in their work. In a wonderfully evocative passage, Benjamin describes how the art of storytelling was "woven thousands of years ago in the ambiance of the oldest forms of craftmanship."[6] Seized by the rhythm of weaving and spinning, the listener heard tales in such a way that the gift of retelling came easily. Artists, of course, have always paid tribute to the element of craft in their work. Cervantes, presenting the second part of *Don Quixote,* tells us that it was "cut by the same craftsman from the same cloth as the first." The Parnassian poets compared their work to that of silversmiths, and Yeats' *Sailing to Byzantium* implicitly compares poetry to "hammered gold." The relationship of the storyteller to his material, suggests Benjamin, is a craftsman's relationship." His task is "to fashion the raw material of experience, his own and that of others, in a solid, useful and unique way."[7] Films, Vertov suggested, should be as useful as shoes. There is no reason why art, whether in the form of a Grecian urn or a revolutionary film, should not be useful as well as beautiful and pleasurable.

The Lessons of Brecht

One thinker who rejected the false dichotomy of beauty and utility, pleasure and learning, was Bertolt Brecht. With Brecht, the distanciating manner is always closely tied to a dialectical analysis of alienation—the process by which human beings lose control of their labor power, their products, their institutions, and their lives. Although distanciating effects obviously pre-existed Brecht—indeed we have encountered them in Rabelais, Shakespeare, Cervantes—it was with Brecht that they became consciously directed toward a political goal: to shock the audience into an awareness that both social life and art are *human* creations and therefore can be changed, that the laws of a predatory society are not divinely inscribed but subject to human intervention.

Bourgeois ideology, for Brecht, masks the people's loss of real power by fostering certain illusions—the illusion of individual autonomy, of a free contractual relationship between labor and capital, producers and consumers, and so forth. This ideology is not a Machiavellian imposition by a dominating class, but rather a phenomenon generated by the social structure itself. It becomes our "lived world," in Althusserian terms, a kind of normal pathology, the moorings of the dominant system within the psychic and intellectual structures of *all* classes. It is precisely the normality of ideology that necessitates an art which makes things strange. Brecht believed that bourgeois normality numbs human perception and masks the contradictions between professed values and social realities; therefore he called for an art that would free socially conditioned phenomena from the "stamp of familiarity" and reveal them as striking, as calling for explanation, as other than "natural." "Behind the familiar," says the final couplet of *The Exception and the Rule,* "discover the surprising," and "behind the everyday, reveal the inexplicable."

Brecht speaks of the "alienation necessary to all understanding." Out of the ashes of social alienation—the alienation of the worker, the city dweller, the member of the oppressed minority, the emigrant, the exile, and the "internal émigré"—Brecht created the liberating alienation which leads to knowledge. His enterprise is one of deconditioning; he tries to make our daily myths and experiences "strange" to us in order to get rid of the false representations that we make of ourselves and of our society. Brecht put it this way in *Song of the Playwright:*

> Everything however I handed over to astonishment
> Even the most familiar
> That the mother gave her breast to the child
> That I reported as something which no one could believe.
> That the doorman closed the door to the freezing man
> As something which no one has ever seen.

"Astonishment," then, implies both a learned capacity and a capacity for learning. His theatre is didactic not so much in that it proselytizes on behalf of specific political ideas, but rather in that it communicates the process of learning.

Brecht does not refuse mimesis; rather he probes and investigates its nature. In this sense he offers a modernist and politicized version of the intermittent realism, the "partial magic," of Rabelais, Cervantes, and Shakespeare. His modernism, however, is not a radical formal aestheticism. His openness is not that of the "delirium of interpretation" or of infinite semiosis. His work is open, as Umberto Eco points out in *Role of the Reader*, in the same sense that a debate is open: a solution is seen as desirable and is concretely anticipated, but it must emerge from the collective collaboration of the audience. Brecht's goal was to demystify, to alert the public to the invisible codes not only of dramaturgy but also of political and economic power. His reflexivity is not innocuous or co-optable because he is less interested in denouncing the fact that art lies than in denouncing the fact that society lies, and that human beings can do something about it.

For the "West," the name Brecht, more than any other, evokes an alternative politicized dramaturgy to counter the reigning bourgeois conventions. But it must be emphasized that although Brechtian strategies were originally conceived in the context of Brecht's radical opposition to both fascism and bourgeois liberalism—which he saw as political variations on a theme—these strategies are not intrinsically tied to Brecht's historical moment or to his particular political options. What Brecht offers is a subversive *écriture* which can be employed in the demystification of any oppressive society or any reigning ideology. Raul Ruiz and Jean-Luc Godard, for example, are among the directors who use Brechtian techniques against Stalinism. In his *The Top of the Whale* (Het Dak Van de Walvis, 1983) Ruiz defamiliarizes Marxist dicta by inserting celebrated phrases such as "religion is the opium of the people" into passages of quotidian conversation, thus making them seem strange and formalistic. Jean-Luc Godard, as we shall see, uses Brechtian techniques to mock the ossified discourse of the French Communist Party in *Tout Va Bien*. A number of filmmakers from East European countries, similarly, have deployed Brechtian reflexivity to expose the bureaucratic corruption of Stalinist societies. Both Andrzej Wajda and Krysztof Kieslowski, for example, use the filmmaker-within-the-film format to expose official lies and manipulation. Wajda's filmmaker in *Man of Marble* unearths a number of specific abuses of the working class by the Stalinist power structure, even as it exposes the ossified and mendacious nature of the official media discourse. Kieslowski's *Amator* (inadequately rendered in English as "Camera Buff") centers on an aspiring worker-filmmaker who gets into trouble with the authorities for his revelations of bureaucratic ineptitude, thus revealing that he is an "amateur" in politics as well as in filmmaking.

Apart from the general goals of Brechtian theatre—laying bare the causal network of events, active spectatorship, defamiliarization—Brecht also proposed specific techniques to achieve these goals. (Indeed it is the divorcing of technique from general aim that leads to the innocuous self-referentiality of pseudo-Brechtianism.) In terms of *mythos* (plot), Brecht opposed his own "epic" theatre—whose narrative structure was interruptive, fractured, disgressive—to conventional "dramatic" theatre structured to build toward narrative climax or catharsis. In an epic text, Brecht suggested, one can cut up the work into individual pieces which remain fully capable of life. In terms of *ethos* (character), Brecht favored a play without heroes or stars, and rejected the theatrical tricks by which actors were turned into stars. In terms of acting, Brecht argued for a double distanciation—between the actor and the part, and between the characteʳ and the spectator—and suggested specific exercises, such as acting in the past tense or in the third person, to achieve this distanciation. Brecht believed in reflexivity, that art should reveal the principles of its own construction, to avoid the "swindle" of giving the impression that fictive events were not "worked at" but simply "happened."

Brecht also argued for the "radical separation of the elements," which meant not only that each scene was radically separated from every other scene, but also that each "track"—music, dialogue, lyric—was to exist in a certain tension with other tracks. Music, for example, was to be exploited not for its customary narcotic charm but rather for its potential for provocation. The songs, first of all, were set off from the dramatic action and the tone of the dramatic moment. Condemning the illustrative, culinary function of music, Brecht wanted music to express social attitudes and open up possibilities for contradiction. Music and lyrics were designed mutually to discredit rather than

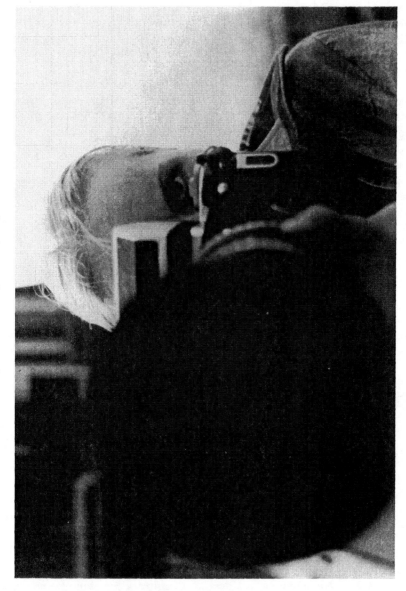

Figure 43. *Man of Marble* (1977)

complement each other. Bitter lyrics coincided with saccharine melodies and vice versa. Or there was discontinuity between the content of the lyrics and the tone of the singer. Senseless melodic accents and distortions of declamation contributed to a feeling of disorientation. The music itself, especially that written by Hanns Eisler and Paul Dessau, shocked by deliberate out-of-tune effects and sudden dissonances. Formal caesurae fractured the continuity and forced the listener to change his train of thought.

The Lessons Applied: *Tout Va Bien*

In an essay bearing the suggestive title "The Author as Producer," Walter Benjamin proposed that the artist be presented with "a single demand, the demand of *reflecting*, of thinking about his position in the process of production." Bertolt Brecht, meanwhile, speaking of the "apparatus" of stage, opera, and press, criticized the naiveté of intellectuals and artists, economically committed to the prevailing system but socially near-proletarian, who imagine that the apparatus is only concerned with the presentation of their work. This "muddled thinking," Brecht argues, has serious consequences: "For by imagining that they have got hold of an apparatus which in fact has got hold of them they are supporting an apparatus which is out of their control."[8] Brecht thus debunks a myth that art often entertains about itself, namely that in the cultural meritocracy of a nominally free society, talent and excellence rise naturally to the top through the free play of competition in the cultural marketplace. Brecht suggests, to the contrary, that the cultural apparatus, can "make" and "unmake" reputations, and that commodity-art depends for its promotion and distribution on the owners of capital.[9]

Godard and Gorin's *Tout Va Bien* (1972) thematizes these issues of production and consumption: the working class as producers and consumers of goods; artists and intellectuals as producers and consumers of information; filmmakers and audiences as the producers and consumers of films. The diegesis concerns Susan (Jane Fonda), an American journalist, and Jacques (Yves Montand), her new wave filmmaker husband now reduced by economic necessity to turning out tasteless commercials. Together they cover the story of a strike at a meat-processing plant. They interview the sequestered manager of the plant; he dismisses the strike as the work of a handful of misfits who have not yet come to understand the benign wisdom of neocapitalism. A spokesman for the CGT (the Communist party-dominated union), flanked by two doltish figures, discredits the strike by citing instructive statistics from a party newspaper. Then some young Leftists, speaking a more casual language, explain their position. They criticize the Communist party for its doctrinaire prudence and its unacknowledged complicity with the system. Finally we become acquainted with the couple. Politicized by the events of May 1968, subsequently forced to abandon political work, they have become newly energized by the strike. Their political reinvolvement, however, triggers a personal crisis between them, a crisis which provokes reflections on the links between their problems as a couple and the surrounding social malaise. Speaking directly to the camera, each of them in turn speaks of dissatisfaction with their work. Jacques makes commercials while postponing the political film he has long wanted to make. Susan, although without real ties to the working class, tries to represent them indirectly through her radio broadcasts; she ultimately quits, however, nauseated by the mediocrity of her own work. The film ends inconclusively, with a problematic reconciliation between them. A couple should be like Mao's "unity of opposites," we are told, but bourgeois society prevents people from living and working "as two."

Like Balzac in *Lost Illusions,* Godard in *Tout Va Bien* performs a materialist variation on reflexivity by reminding us of the cinema's economic base and institutional infrastructure. The opening credit sequence begins with a characteristic noise of filmmaking—the sound of a clapboard. The image track shows a process usually elided by credit sequences: the signing of checks to cover the film's various expenses, accompanied by the amplified sound of the checks being torn out of the checkbook. The superimposition of the sounds of money with the sounds of film production implies a necessary connection between finance and cinematic production, a connection made explicit by an off-screen dialogue: "I want to make a film," says one voice. "To make a film," responds another voice, "you need money." The checks, meanwhile—going for lighting, makeup, decor—call attention to the artifice of film. The fact that they are made out to "Transatlantic Bank" makes explicit the filmmaker's dependence on foreign capital.

Tout Va Bien unmasks the alienated nature of cultural work in class society. Jacques defines his work as "making films, finding new forms for new content," but in fact his new forms serve only to sell soap and razor blades. Susan tells journalistic anecdotes into the microphones of the American Broadcasting Corporation, but she ultimately finds it impossible to continue in the bourgeois media. Jacques and Susan represent a bifurcation of the filmmaking function into images and sounds; taken together they figure forth the *cinéaste* himself. Susan's dismissal of her former work as "crap" recalls Godard's severe judgments on his earlier films, while Jacques' self-characterization as a new wave director radicalized by May '68 corresponds to Godard's own political evolution at the time.

Godard places this cultural work in the context of productive work in general. The film examines, for example, all the stages in the production and consumption of food.[10] The first tracking shot in the film is of the meat-processing plant; the second runs alongside the cash registers in a supermarket where we see the workers paying for what they have themselves produced, the

Figure 44.   *Tout Va Bien* (1972)

parallelism of the shots underlining the "awful symmetry" of capitalist laws of production and consumption. Intellectuals, for their part, are defined as cultural workers, a definition which avoids the twin political pitfalls of elitist condescension toward workers on the one hand and self-deprecatory guilt on the other. Cultural workers are part of what Hans Enzensberger calls the "consciousness industry"; they are products of culture, of ideas, images, and sounds. Everything in the social atmosphere is their raw material; they digest this raw material, reproduce it, filter it, package it. Godard insists on the doubleness of the role of Leftist intellectuals in the media. On the one hand the media can digest and co-opt them, take their work and render it innocuous. On the other, the consciousness industry, to remain effective, needs women and men who can create new forms. It depends on people capable of innovation to supply all its channels; i.e., it depends on potential troublemakers like Jacques and Susan. His doubts and her quitting parallel, on an individual plane, the strike in the meat-processing plant.

The technique of the film underscores the socially exemplary side of events. The schematic decor, consisting of a double-deckered cutaway set, "signifies" the political and economic structure of society and shows the divisions between classes as well as their interdependence. Everything in the film—the posed portraits of social classes, the tripartite division of the sound track, the position statements—highlights the conflict of three political forces: capital, the Communist party, and the Leftists. Rather than treat the members of these groups as rounded personages, Godard has his characters read texts which expose their class positions: the boss speaks a passage from Saint Geour's *Vive la Société de Consommation;* the CGT members read from a Communist party newspaper *(La Vie Ouvrière);* and the Leftists read from the Maoist *Cause du Peuple.* The strike itself is exemplary, much as in Eisenstein's strike, although in the case of *Tout Va Bien* it is the contradictions, and not the triumphs, which are exemplary. Given the disunity of the Left, the strike necessarily dissipates its momentum. Rather than obscure such contradictions, the film highlights them. Rather than have us identify with the workers so as to participate vicariously in their triumph, the film leads us to understand the contradictions which preclude real victory.

Antiromance, *Tout Va Bien* is also antimimesis. Instead of critical realism à la Lukács, the film offers a critique of realism. Rather than offering a slice of life in its durée, the film presents a structural analysis of events. Unspectacular, the film resists uncritical consumption. Bright primary colors disposed in geometrical patterns flatten the visual space, as do the frontal angles and abstract framing. Instead of the affected disorder of naturalistic films, *Tout Va Bien* abstractly "layers" the image. One tri-leveled shot, for example, places a line of militant demonstrators at the bottom of the screen, a line of police with billy clubs above them (in terms of screen space), topped by a file of noisy cars and trucks streaming horizontally across a highway bridge in the background. The same kind of patterning takes place on a temporal level through the calculated repetition of certain images and sounds. Instead of a naturalistic "slice of life," we are given a critical *découpage* of social existence.

The Politics of Technique

Technique in *Tout Va Bien* is not something that exists in the service of the political message—it *is* the political message. The meat-processing plant is rendered exemplary through a technique that politicizes the spatial abstraction we encountered in *King Ubu* and *The Riflemen.* Calculated spatial discontinuities, reminiscent of *Last Year at Marienbad,* abstract the plant. The external shots of what appears to be a real factory do not match the shots of the studio factory—both of which differ from the photographs on the studio-factory walls. Thus Godard forces us to see the plant as typical—not in the sense of some statistical average but in the sense of the forces at work in present-day capitalism. The politicization of technique extends as well to the camera movements, which are restricted to fixed shots and beautifully executed tracking shots. Rather than simply accompany the movement, the tracking shots are autonomous; they call attention to themselves. Rather than merely register an event, they impose a political pattern on it. In the supermarket sequence, the camera tracks right to show the everyday processes of consumer society—people lining up at cash registers—then tracks left to record the disruption of these processes by rampaging Maoists, thus illustrating what Godard calls "the social use of the tracking shot."

The soundtrack of *Tout Va Bien* is also marked by discontinuity. In the supermarket sequence, the unnaturally amplified ding of cash registers alternates with an equally unnatural silence. At other times, words are divorced from their speakers: we see Jane Fonda's image and hear her voice on the soundtrack, but her lips do not move. Elsewhere, she monologues in English while her own voice intermittently dubs into French. At times the French overtakes the English and at times the reverse. The effect is to make us aware of the medium. Language—and cinema—no longer serve as the transparent conveyor of meaning; they become opaque. Another kind of dissociation is created by having Vittorio Caprioli (the boss) *say* a written text—Saint-Geour's *Vive la Société de Consommation.* The nervous tics and hesitations of method acting are applied to a passage whose rhetoric and style are transparently that of a written document. The comic effect is reminiscent of the dissociation created by pompously reciting the lyrics of popular songs—what is coherent when sung becomes absurd when recited.

Tout Va Bien is a film whose form says everything about itself. At the beginning of the film, two off-screen voices anticipate narrative strategies.

They'll need stars, they decide, and a story. "Do we really need a story?" one asks. "Certainly," replies the other—"a love story." There will be him, and then her, and they will have problems." This capsule summary, a quintessential precipitate of the thousands of cinematic love stories turned out by dream factories around the world, recalls Laurence Sterne's calculatedly schematic "Tale of Two Lovers" in *Tristram Shandy.* In the Sterne version is a him (Amandus) and her (Amanda) and problems (the Turks), thus offering a paradigm, as Robert Alter points out, of all the romances ever written. Godard, like Sterne, mocks our need for stories even while pretending to satisfy it. The film ends with a "reconciliation" written in cinematic narrative shorthand. We see Jacques sitting in a café while Susan crosses the street in his direction. Then we see the same shots, except that she is in the café and he crosses the street. In any case, the minimal frame fiction has come full circle, while the variant versions suggest the tenuous nature of filmic reconciliations, with their implicit promises of conjugal harmony. The film then closes with a parting shot at our need for fictions: an inscription saying, "Un conte pour ceux qui n'en tiennent aucun" (a tale for those who do not hold by them, or a tale for those who do not take account of things). Having decided on overall narrative strategy, the filmmaker's delegates then debate problems of character construction and setting. The story and the characters are not shown as pre-existing; rather, they are shown in the process of their invention.

This modernist self-consciousness is accompanied by Marxist self-criticism. The most sympathetic people in the film criticize themselves; only the manager and the Communist party members are rigid. More important, the film performs its own self-criticism by criticizing its own way of telling the story of class struggle. The workers at one point describe their working conditions to Jacques and Susan, while the film shows, in the realist style, what they are describing. Then someone objects that they must show the struggle and not simply exploit misery in an appeal for sympathy. The footage is rerun with this criticism in mind. Thus the film rehearses itself; like many of Godard's films, it is a "film en train de se faire" rather than a finished product. *Tout Va Bien* asks how one communicates the process of class struggle. Does one cite statistics and sell party books like potatoes in a supermarket? Does one recreate in the spectator the physical sensation of working in a meat-processing plant and thus elicit sympathy? Does one stage epic confrontations in the manner of the Odessa Steps sequence? Or does one show conflict through custard-pie slapstick in a supermarket? Do the workers themselves tell their story or does one tell it for them? Does one create a Brechtian opera and insert songs with aggressive lyrics ("The working class will kick the ass of the ruling class!")? Or does one adopt the mild yet persuasive charm of the popular French films of the thirties? All these approaches are essayed, and criticized, in the film. The cumulative effect is to make us realize that one cannot separate the politics of

Figure 45. *Tout Va Bien* (1972)

the story from the politics of the telling; the story itself changes as it is filtered through different methods of narration.

Many of Godard's films end with a kind of political stock-taking. *La Chinoise* ends with Véronique's realization that although she has not made a great leap forward, she has at least taken a small step. Susan and Jacques in *Tout Va Bien* learn to "think through their dissatisfaction" and "see themselves historically." The film tries to stimulate a critical vision in the spectator. The finished artistic product matters less than the process of struggle and collaboration. History, art, and individuals are shown as being "in process," "not finished." Godard struggles against the passivity bred of decades of manipulation. Instead of a cinema of vicarious experience to be consumed, he proposes, as the title of *Le Gai Savoir* suggests, a cinema of joyful learning. To Roquentin's "History is impossible," the off-screen narrator of *Tout Va Bien* responds: "Let each of us be his own historian."

After the at times masturbatory militancy of the Dziga Vertov period films, *Tout Va Bien* displays a kind of serenity. Godard feels confident enough to let the various political groups—even the advocates of consumer civilization—speak for themselves. The serenity comes as well from a new honesty about the filmmaker's relation to class struggle. Godard, after all, is *not* a Maoist peasant or a Latin American guerrilla—he is an artist-intellectual in the capitalist West. The intellectual, Godard seems to realize in *Tout Va Bien,* can only offer what Walter Benjamin called a "mediated solidarity" to the working-class oppressed of his own country. *Tout Va Bien* critically examines the role of intellectuals—especially those intellectuals who have access to the cultural and ideological *apparati*—within social relations as a whole. The cinetracts of the Dziga Vertov period, however essential in their search for a method, were at times irresponsible in their oracular Leftism. They indulged in a kind of tourism of revolutionary struggles—a few months in Italy, next to Prague, then over to the Chicago 8. *Tout Va Bien* retains the political bite of the earlier films, but is more accessible in its search for a peculiarly politicized kind of beauty.

Further Applications: *Numéro Deux*

Some of the recent films co-authored by Godard with Anne-Marie Miéville brilliantly realize the cinematic potential of the deconstructive techniques here under discussion. *Numéro Deux,* for example, extends the political and aesthetic logic of Godard's earlier work at the same time that it represents a radically new departure. His oeuvre as a whole displays a progressive discarding of narrative drama and spectacle in favor of the close scrutiny of the everyday. The subject of *Numéro Deux*—glimpses into the life of a working-class couple, the daily cadences of their existence, their relation to their own children and parents—represents a kind of ultimate banalization and proletarianization of what is conceivable as a cinematic subject. One can say of *Numéro Deux* what Flaubert said of *Madame Bovary,* that it is a "work in which nothing happens." But it is precisely because nothing happens, at least in the conventional sense of violence, intrigue, romance, and adventure, that the film enables us to see how much happens in the everyday. The "trivialized" subject of *Numéro Deux* constitutes a critique even of Godard's earlier antinarrative films, the characters of which retain, after all, a patina of romance. Beginning as poets or petty criminals, familyless Sartrean "bastards" who measure out their lives in espressoes, cigarettes, and films at the Cinémathèque, Godard's protagonists later become Left revolutionaries like Guillaume and Véronique in *La Chinoise.* In *Numéro Deux,* they are finally domesticated, linked to the common fate of marriage and family. They are situated in a home—not a suburban home suddenly invaded by terror (Hitchcock), not a bourgeois home torn by morbid desires (Bergman), and not a deluxe home temporarily vacated to make way for Maoist urban summer camp (late Godard), but simply an average working-class home.

Numéro Deux further elaborates the theme of production explored by *Tout Va Bien.* The film opens with a shot of Godard, profiled in semidarkness, in his video studio, while a television monitor shows him from another angle. His monologues, meanwhile, tells us in colloquial language how he came to make and finance the film. Then, in a series of punning associations, he introduces the crisscrossing themes of the film. The leitmotifs of work, production, factory keep coming up. Godard himself is a cultural worker, and the video studio a factory where he is both *patron* and *ouvrier.* Pierrot, the husband of the film, works in a factory, while for Sandrine *home* has become a kind of factory. The body, Sandrine points out, is also a factory, one that occasionally goes on strike through constipation (her) or temporary impotence (him). Marriage is a kind of co-production, and making love, she tells her husband, is often just a job. Childbearing is *re*production, while films are made by mechanical—and television programs by electronic—reproduction. Desire, according to the authors of *Anti-Oedipus,* is a form of production, part of libidinal economy, mobilizing an interplay of investments and overinvestments. Ideology, we remember from Althusser, is the reproduction of production relations within the individual psyche. All these dimensions of production and reproduction are alluded to and reflected on in the film.

The Video Subversion of Language

If, as we have seen, *Numéro Deux* subverts a popular form—pornography—it also subverts a popular medium: television. In a sense, the film simply extends Godard's longstanding interest in the print and electronic media. What is radically new in *Numéro Deux* is that Godard-Miéville do not merely allude to the media or incorporate certain aspects of its style or procedures. Nor do they simply allow the coexistence of fiction and television-style reportage within the same cinematic frame. Rather, they equate two specific media—cinema and television—as *languages.* They effect this equation in a number of ways. Shot largely in video and then transferred to film stock, the film integrates the technology of television into its process of production. Secondly, the television-style images (e.g., news broadcasts) and film-style images (Bruce Lee movies) are equated by being juxtaposed within the larger rectangle of the screen. And thirdly, certain effects associated with video (e.g., solarization) are superimposed on images which are felt to be photographic and cinematic. The naturalness with which these juxtapositions and equations take place makes us suspect that cinema and television function, as languages, in very similar ways. In fact, Godard has been implying as much for many years by insisting in interviews that the problem of cinema was inseparable from the problem of television, since both involved the production and distribution of image and sound. Godard's position parallels that of Christian Metz, who argues in *Language and Cinema* that television and film are so close as languages that they might as well be regarded, semiologically speaking, as one.[11] They are two versions, technologically and socially distinct, of the same language, one that combines moving images, phonetic sound, noises, music, and writing into a spatio-temporal configuration. The material traits and specific codifications of the two media are very largely identical. Although the origin of the images is electronic in one case and photographic in the other, the images are *perceived* as photographic in both media, and in any case such technological differences do not affect their status as languages.

Godard's previous incorporation of "lower" forms and genres pales in violence when compared to this irreverent "leveling" of cinema and television. Cinema, after all, has finally come to be surrounded by a halo of cultural prestige. Literary intellectuals, after their initial misgivings, have embraced it with enthusiasm and even honored it in articles and dissertations. Television, meanwhile, is regarded as almost a dirty subject by the literary intelligentsia, as hopelessly vulgar and congenitally tainted, a not surprising reaction when one reflects on the rude challenge that it offers to the traditional prerogatives of that intelligentsia.[12]

By virtually equating cinema and television, Godard-Miéville perform a veritable desacrilization of the filmic medium. If cinema, because it participates in mechanical reproduction, is in Walter Benjamin's terms relatively "aura-less," television lacks aura and mystique to a still greater degree. This lack of aura can be traced to three areas: 1) the conditions of production; 2) the technology of reproduction; and 3) the social conditions of reception. Cinematic production is surrounded by ritualistic reverence ("Silence!...

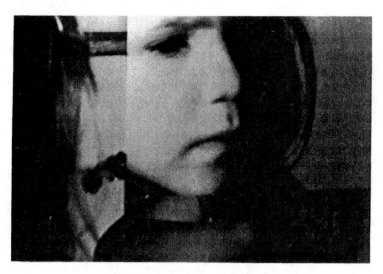

Figure 46.   *Numéro Deux* (1975)

Action...") aimed at getting something down on film; intensive work and preparation go into a brief final product, while in television there often exists (depending of course on the kind of program) a minimum of disproportion between the time of production and the time of the final discourse. Secondly, while filmic images are fixed forever in their motionless movement, rather like the figures on Keats' Grecian urn, the televised image can be erased and substituted. Cinema, consequently, forms an extendable collection of finished *works,* while telelvision consists of ephemeral, continuous *activity.* If cinema is a museum, television is a scene of work. If cinema is a series of artifacts, television is a process. Television perpetually exhausts new materials; it is an electronic monster, infinitely gluttonous, that continuously devours the provisions thrown into its rectangular maw. Repetition in cinema makes a classic; repetition in television makes a rerun. Thirdly, cinema, for a variety of social and historical reasons, takes place in the privileged space of theatre—latter-day heir of the sacred space of games, ritual, and ancient tragedy—while television takes place within the mundane surroundings of the average home. It accompanies our domestic routines and is available to almost everyone at the turn of a knob. For cinema we pay admission, but television comes for free, in fact, it is virtually crammed down our throats.

Given the rapid expansion of the electronic media, and given the key ideological role of those media—the media not only sell products, Enzensberger suggests, they also sell the existing order—any contemporary Brechtian approach to cinema must take into account all the *apparati* which have developed since Brecht's time. *Numéro Deux* develops a complex, dialectical view of the media, making us aware not only of its nefarious effects but also of the utopian possibilities it opens up. Godard-Miéville never let us forget who really controls the media. "The television screen," says Sandrine, "in front are the children, and behind—the government." One hopes to see images from one's own life, she complains, but in the end they are always other people's images. *Numéro Deux* repeatedly offers the images and sounds of television newscasters, with their bland faces, assured voices, and suave delivery. Inundating us with information, they deprive us of the means of decoding that information. In the sterile plenitude of a blizzard of news "items," the larger political configurations become unclear.

Television mediates our lives, colonizing our leisure hours and turning us into media junkies. The multiple images on the screen of *Numéro Deux* remind us that innumerable homes do in fact have multiple TV images. The media have provided the electronic furniture of our homes. The frequent superimposition of children's faces on the images of *Numéro Deux* alert us to the fact that children assimilate the world through television before they act or suffer in it themselves. What *Numéro Deux* does, above all, is to make all those media images and sounds "strange." The media drone in the background of our lives, the sounds of switched channels or a hastily displaced radio dial, the pseudo-intimate and pseudo-personal direct address of advertisements, the weird succession of smiling faces that introduce themselves and recommend some shampoo or dog food, the fabricated hilarity of game shows, the knowing omniscience of newscasters—all this our media-trained eyes and ears have become accustomed to, and all these *Numéro Deux* makes fundamentally strange.

At the same time Godard-Miéville do not see the media as some unredeemable wasteland. One might argue, in fact, that many of the revolutionary innovations in Godard's films come from television. The alternation of staged and improvised material in a film like *Une Femme Mariée* or *Masculin, Féminin,* for example, is quite "natural" to television. The atomization of the *récit* which characterizes Godard's films is also quite typical of television; the one-liners of a talk show, the two-sentence summaries of the news, or the suspense of a quiz or game show can be seen, on one level, as mininarratives. Advertisements, meanwhile, are miniature stories with built-in happy endings which come with the purchase of the product. If the media as presently constituted are in many ways oppressive, they are also potentially liberating. Television does participate in what Enzensberger calls "immaterial pauperization," but it could also, conceivably, democratize instruction. News programs do numb our consciousness; at the same time, however, they drag colonial wars into the heart of the imperial beast, and thus make us aware how policies impinge on the lives of people. All events become present and therefore, one hopes, come to "matter."

Split Writing/Split Screen

Godard said of *Numéro Deux* that the television for which it was conceived does not exist. The film, however, does exist, and opens up fascinating technical and aesthetic possibilities. Rarely in *Numéro Deux* does a single image fill the frame. Usually there are two images and often there are more. Since the images are "hung" on the screen like paintings in a gallery, we are forced to choose *which* image to contemplate, yet the very multiplicity of images makes it virtually impossible to "lose" ourselves in any one. Within the multiple images are embedded still other images—television screens, photographs—in an infinite regress of self-enclosed representations. Godard—Miéville set into interaction heterogenous series of images, thus alerting us to the fact of mediation. The simultaneous presence of images from 1) movie previews, 2) a Bruce Lee movie, and 3) soft-core porn, for example, highlights the mediation of *genre*. The juxtaposition of electronically produced images (television, video) and photographically produced images (film) makes us aware of the diverse visual codifications of different *media*. That we can recognize a video image as opposed to a filmic one renders both something other than "natural."

The effect of this proliferation of images within a single frame is reminiscent of that produced by the "split writing" of Jacques Derrida's *Glas.* In that book, Derrida juxtaposes two texts—one from Genet, the other from Hegel—continuously down each page throughout the book. This bifurcation of compositional units facilitates a joyous freeplay of textuality. The exorbitantly overfilled spaces of *Numéro Deux,* similarly, install a provocative textual dispersion. Poetically speaking, the juxtaposition of shots allows for a kind of instantaneous metaphysical poetry, a linking of incongruous images, a *discordia concors* whereby dissimilar entities are joined and occult resemblances suggested. The technique takes on a political dimension by suggesting certain ironic equations and contrasts. The co-presence of three images—a news program, a series of "coming attraction" previews, and a child copying a sentence on a blackboard—is open-ended in its suggestiveness. News programs, we may reflect, are designed to attract audiences and make a profit just like the previews. Children, for their part, absorb the world not only through school, but also through the films and television. Thus Godard-Miéville deploy but partially analyzed juxtapositions, leaving their inter-relations largely to the spectator's intelligence and imagination. At another point, the preview of a Bruce Lee film neighbors with a news report on a Leftist May Day parade. On the sound track we hear talk of "lutte" (in its physical sense) and "lutte" in its political sense. What does the juxtaposition signify? That Leftist demonstrations like the May Day parade have become mere spectacle, like Bruce Lee films, easily recuperable by the bourgeois media? That Leftists must struggle not only against the government but also against alienated forms of entertainment? The possible interpretations, multiple and open-ended, generate a fecund crisis of signification.

The whole question of spatial and temporal continuity (and the "matches" which help produce it) is rendered richly problematic by the "stereophonic" images of *Numéro Deux.* What if movement, direction, and position matches, for example, apply not to the relationship between successive shots but rather between two or even three images simultaneously present? What happens to the 30-degree rule, the 180-degree rule, and the axis match in the context of multiple images? Does not the very idea of a "cutaway" shot become meaningless in such a context? Would not parallel and alternate montage be possible not only by the traditional means of the alternation of two series of shots but also by the simultaneous co-presence of two series of shots? *Numéro Deux,* admittedly, opens up these possibilities rather than systematically exploring them, but we may reflect on some of the possible innovations. Reverse angle shots, usually dependent on a succession of shots, are made simultaneous in *Numéro Deux* by having two neighboring images offer both angles. Or the simultaneity is achieved within a single image through video superimposition; a shot of Sandrine turned away from the camera, for example, coincides with a superimposed close-up of her looking toward the camera. Diverse focal lengths are contrasted within single images and between or among neighboring images.

Christian Metz, lending semiotic precision to Eisenstein's intuitions concerning "vertical" and "horizontal" montage, points out in *Language and Cinema* that the syntagmatic dimension of cinema is deployed along two axes—the axis of consecution (the succession of shots within a sequence) and the axis of simultaneity (the reciprocal relations between image and sound and, more generally, between and among the five "tracks" or matters of expression of cinema).[13] The axis of consecution, corresponding generally to the duration of the film, includes four parallel and generally continuous series—the image track, the linguistic series, noises, and music. (Written elements, he notes, form another, generally more discontinuous series.) The axis of simultaneities, Metz continues, has itself two axes: first, the axis of spatial co-presence within the rectangle of the screen, and second, the simultaneous syntagms which may be established between or among the diverse series. Four of the series are temporal in nature. Language, music, and noise are clearly temporal, and the image, although initially spatial, is easily temporalized.

Any application of the Brechtian "separation of the elements" to the cinema must take Metz' analysis into account. The episodic nature of epic theatre implies a *horizontal* autonomy of syntagmatic segments whereby the burden of signification bears on each scene. There is no teleology, no causative necessity that binds the end to the beginning, no organic motivation but rather a series of segmentations, each with its own dialectically demonstrative power. The "separation of the elements" also suggests, however, a *vertical* layering or separating out. A vertical cross-section of the text will reveal early discriminated strata or autonomous tracks. These tracks can be discontinuous in their temporality. The temporal character of (at least) four of the tracks brings up the possibility that the heart of cinematic narrative is not simply one of a single story (however disjointed in its articulation) but rather of four (and I would suggest five) parallel but potentially discontinuous temporal series.

Although the Metz text considerably antedates *Numéro Deux*, only such an analysis can, I think, account for the semilogical complexity of the film. If we examine the two axes—simultaneity and consecution—along which the syntagmatic dimension is deployed, we discover that *Numéro Deux* brilliantly exploits the possibilities inherent in both. The film generally projects at least two images on a black background, so that our eye is forced to shuttle back and forth between them. Thus the single, centered perspective inherited from Renaissance humanism is relativized, the multiplicity of perspectives rendering identification with any one perspective difficult. The spatial co-presence of multiple images within the rectangle of the screen, furthermore, establishes syntagmatic possibilities denied to the single-image cinema. Since each spectator is forced to determine his own itinerary through the screen images, the narrative is relativized and, as it were, democratized. The movement within the screen is not linear or predetermined; each spectator makes his own syntagms. The spectator has to decide what the images have in common, or how they conflict; he/she has to effect the synthesis latent in the visual material.

If we consider the axis of the simultaneous syntagms established by the diverse tracks of the film, we find that *Numéro Deux* deploys five parallel but discontinuous temporal series—image, dialogue, music, noise, and written elements. These diverse series or tracks, to put it another way, pursue simultaneous but distinct trajectories in what amounts to a complexly spatialized tapestry of interwoven temporal threads. The diverse tracks fall behind, catch up, or overtake one another. The process of signification is displaced from one track to another, a sentence, for example, beginning as a written title and finishing, in an apparently aleatory but meaningful way, as a spoken utterance. Sandrine, the wife in the film, comments at one point that people always say "Once upon a time" when they could as well say "Twice upon a time." Her seemingly whimsical observation reminds us that it is in the nature of a linear narrative to evoke incidents in their uniqueness; the narrative events "happen" only once. In *Numéro Deux,* on the other hand, events repeat themselves for our contemplation. Or they happen partially, the rest of their happening deferred for a later syntagmatic moment. At one point, for example, we see Sandrine and her husband (Pierrot) fighting and gesticulating in one of the rectangles on the screen but we *hear* nothing. Subsequently, we hear the words exchanged in their quarrel, but we *see* nothing. Still later we both see and hear them in synchronous sound and image. The shifting aural and visual coordinates highlight the process of film as a matter of filling tracks and matching image with sound, sound with sound, and written word with both image and sound.

The rare occasions in which *Numéro Deux* returns to the single image give the spectator a feeling of anticlimax, of new possibilities and challenges suddenly closed off. Polysemic, multidimensional, and semioclastic, *Numéro Deux* elicits a new criticism because the old criticism is so transparently inadequate to it. The film makes us sensitive to the relative impoverishment of signification before it, leaving us not with a sense of closure but of new potentialities. At the same time, it makes us rethink pornography, rethink television, and rethink the cinema. Its title, finally, is as richly suggestive as the "elle" in *Deux ou Trois Choses que je sais d'elle. . . . Numéro Deux:* The second sex. *Numéro Deux:* Television as second-class cultural citizen. *Numéro Deux:* the second image in the frame. *Numéro Deux:* sound as subordinate to image. All these numéro deux's, the film suggests, deserve to find their true voice.

Realism, Reflexivity, Sexuality: *Sauve Qui Peut/(la Vie)*

Sauve Qui Peut/(la Vie)—mistranslated as *Every Man for Himself*—displays the two seemingly contradictory but in fact quite complementary trajectories that characterize Godard's work: a progressively more rigorous reflexivity coupled with an ever more inclusive and democratic realism. Anti-illusionist, Godard and Miéville show themselves to be unflaggingly realist both in the Brechtian sense of "laying bare the causal network" and in the phenomenological sense of precisely registering surface appearances and subjective impressions. While less technically innovative than *Numéro Deux,* their film brilliantly exemplifies this double movement toward reflexivity and verisimilitude.

Many of the reflexive devices, once again, echo Godard's earlier work. The penchant for inviting favored cineastes into the film itself—Samuel Fuller in *Pierrot le Fou,* Fritz Lang in *Contempt*—here takes the disembodied form of Marguerite Duras' off-screen voice. Godard himself, while not literally visible as in *Numéro Deux,* is present, as if at one remove, in the person of his fictive namesake and imperfect delegate Paul Godard. (Lacanian critics might be tempted to see in the protagonist's adoption of Godard's own father's name a kind of belated acquiescence in "Le nom de père.") The character triggers certain autobiographical resonances; like Godard, Paul is involved with video and television. Even his final car accident recalls Godard's own brush with death in 1970. At the same time, Godard exploits his surrogate to lampoon the groupies of the auteur cult. A doorman showers Paul with effusive declarations of love: "Je vous aime, Mr. Godard!" Absurdly literalizing the auterist love for its pantheon directors, the doorman specifies that it is not Mr. Godard's soul that he loves but his body.

Apart from occasional instances of homage *(Le Camion, City Lights),* and auto-pastiche *(Masculine, Feminine),* one is struck in *Sauve Qui Peut* by a relative paucity of intertextual allusion. The filmmakers seem to be speaking in their own voice rather than "through" other films. Instead of the cinephiliac winks of the earlier Godard films, *Sauve Qui Peut* offers a deeper kind of reflexivity. There is less of the bric-a-brac of reflexivity—movie posters, verbal references, photos of directors—and more of its substance. From *Two or Three Things* on, Godard is increasingly concerned with the mise-en-scene of the procedures of representation itself, with the paradigmatic and syntagmatic choices inherent in the elaboration of filmic discourse. *Ici et Ailleurs* neatly images the paradigmatic/syntagmatic nature of the filmic chain by aligning three video-cassette screens in a discursive "train" in which the individual cassette images form the "cars." Discourse ceases to be the transparent vehicle of *histoire;* it is pictured as a series of opaque objects, cinematic building blocks to be selected and combined. Instead of parody and homage, the rendering visible of discursive processes takes center stage.

Figure 47. *Sauve Qui Peut/ (la Vie)* (1980)

The five rubrics of *Sauve Qui Peut*—life, the imaginary, fear, commerce, music—apart from effecting a typically Brechtian "separation of the elements," highlight the cinema itself as the point of convergence of diverse regimes and a multiplicity of codes. The overall trajectory is from "life" to "music"—everyday experience transmogrified into art. "Life" is the starting point. "The imaginary" belongs to the director, the spectator, and to the film itself, the filmic experience corresponding to an exchange between these diverse imaginaries. "Fear" is the specific emotion which dominates the diegesis: fear of changing, of moving of solitude. "Commerce" conditions cinema at every point, inflecting choices and imposing solutions. "Music," finally, in this film "composed by Godard," constitutes the end point, the condition to which the film aspires, reconciling emotive richness with structural rigor.

In *Sauve Qui Peut,* music offers both a pretext for gags and a token of transcendent possibilities. The opening shot after the credits installs an aural hermeneutic which structures the entire film. We hear operatic singing, presumably coming from the other side of the wall of Paul's apartment. When the music continues despite a changed locale, we are led to speculate about its source. Subsequently, diverse characters, straining to catch a sourceless melody, ask "What is that music?" The enigma is resolved only in the final shot of musicians executing the hitherto off-screen score. The resolution of the enigma coincides with the moment of Paul's accident. Rather than use music to lubricate the spectator's emotions and elicit a feeling of tragedy, Godard-Miéville serve up a sound gag à la Mel Brooks. At the same time, Gabriel Yared's ethereal music serves a more serious purpose. It elicits a kind of Mallarmean *azur,* a beckoning utopia just out of range, an intermittently glimpsed realm of freedom where life and creativity are one, where life itself becomes music.

Godard's transgressions have always had the virtue of exposing the suffocating arbitrariness of dominant conventions. *Sauve Qui Peut* continues the temporal experimentation of *Numéro Deux,* but in a new direction. Godard-Miéville introduce 15 saccadic "skids"—variations on stop-action moments—which interrupt the more conventional 24-frames-per-second *défilement* of the rest of the film. These saccadic sequences, a novel form of slow motion, open up the possibilities of a truly polyrhythmic cinema. The slow-motion in question is not that derived from undercranking but rather a kind of variable velocity produced in the laboratory and often articulating several kinds of movement: that of people or objects in the shot (Denise on her bicycle), camera movement (the accompanying pan), and slow motion and freeze frames created, presumably, by an optical printer. Here the avant-garde draws inspiration from the archaic. Silent films, after all, were shown at variable speeds; rarely were they shown at the speed at which they were shot. Godard-Miéville's exploitation of the device, however, evokes the entire history of cinema and television—from Marey's *fusil photographique*, decomposing the flight of birds and the gait of men, through the intermittently slowed horses and athletes of *The Man with a Movie Camera*, to the freeze frames and instant playbacks of contemporary sports programs. The variable speeds correlate with character (Godard describes Denise as fast, Isabelle as average, Paul as slow) and with incident (why film a slap at the same speed as a kiss?). Just as Godard used "variorum" montage in *Pierrot le fou*—alternative versions of the same sequence—here he uses a kind of "conditional" velocity. The same shot modulates in texture and feeling, becoming heavy and ominous or lyrically playful depending on the speed of its execution. The possible permutations are infinite; they generate a form of cinematic relativity: Eisenstein meets Einstein.

The experimentation with variable speeds also promotes reflexivity in a number of ways. 1) The jerky succession of frame-by-frame movements highlights the normally obscured process of *"défilement"* (the progression of static frames through the projector), thus calling attention to the cinematic apparatus itself. 2) The appearance of "natural" movement, a key pillar in the conventional impression of reality, is disrupted. Paul's car accident, for example, is derealized by the protracted syncopated movement of his fall. 3) The experience of the film, in these privileged moments of altered velocity, coincides with its own analysis, as if the film were looking at itself on the Steenbeck. The usually unattainable text, when slowed or frozen in its fleeting progression, becomes available for closer scrutiny. At the same time, through this double movement of mimesis and deconstruction, life itself is put, as it were, through the movieola, opening up the perspective of a visual semiotics of everyday experience. While on one level a distancing device, the slow motion technique paradoxically brings us closer to sudden shifts of mood and details of facial expression. In an act of closely proffered attention, the temporal equivalent of a close-up, emotions and gestures are analyzed, exploded into tiny fragments to be examined as if under a microscope.

A striking proportion of the slowed segments has to do with relations between the sexes. Godard-Miéville probe the formulaic nature of conventional movie slaps, kisses, embraces. Usually stereotyped actions are revealed to cover a vast multiplicity of instances, each with its specific nuances. (One imagines a possible film devoted to a brief act of love, analyzed into an infinitude of tiny exchanges, minifoci of resistance and collaboration.) The filmmakers especially pinpoint the epidermic abrasiveness of contemporary sexual relations. At times this abrasiveness is explicit violent—Isabelle getting knocked around by her pimps—and at times more subtle and indirect. We see Paul advance toward Isabelle in pulsingly retarded movements, gradually occupying her space. As she watches warily, we seem to be witnessing a phallic incursion, a minirape. Later, Paul embraces, or, better, pounces upon Denise in a noisy slow motion collision, crystallizing a situation in which lovers find it virtually impossible to touch without bruising. The film, in such moments, dissects what Foucault would call the capillary forms of power, the ways that power seeps into the grain of everyday life and penetrates the smallest gestures.

Raymond Bellour suggests that the saccadic sequences fall into two groups, those that idealize woman and those that show aggression against her. Here we encounter again the double movement of celebration and critique, more specifically, the exaltation of woman and the denunciation of the sexism to which she is subject. Godard-Miéville here associate cinema and woman as the locus of utopian possibilities. The stop-motion sequences, associated with women, create an impossible temporal "elsewhere," the other place in which Godard, at least, has always lived. "Cinema is more important than life," Godard said in a recent interview: "I'm a representative of life. It's a life that doesn't exist. When Rimbaud said 'Real life is elsewhere,' he wasn't just playing with words—that 'elsewhere' is also the beauty of life. Cinema is in the means of communication, it is in this 'also.'"

Women in *Sauve Qui Peut* are more sympathetic than the men. They embody the possibilities of less alienated social relations. They are at the cutting edge of historical change, and it is they who speak the filmmaker's lines. Men are gently removed from the center to the periphery of the human sphere. Paul exhibits fossilized behavior: the vestigial sexism of a person who knows better but lapses into knee-jerk machismo in the crunch. The film communicates a certain male respect, tinged with envy, for feminine solidarity. While the women frequently speak to, and for, each other, there is virtually no significant converse between the men. Cecilia communicates easily with her mother, but she regards Paul with suspicion. *Sauve Qui Peut* conveys a pervasive feeling of men being judged by a disabused *regard des femmes,* inverting the partriarchal tradition of the male as sheltered voyeur. Women, if one excepts the sequences involving prostitution, constitute the active, initiating principle. Their voices virtually monopolize the sound track. They are the artists: Duras the cineaste, Denise the writer. The latter is always carrying her notebook, and we hear extracts from what is ambiguously defined as novel-essay-diary (all of which terms could be metaphorically applied to film) throughout *Sauve Qui Peut.* The new wave has come full-circle; Antoine from *400 Blows,* struggling with French composition, has become Denise; woman is now the practitioner of *écriture.* And the film's final shot carries a charge of feminine vengeance. Paul's ex-wife and daughter observe his accident with the same indifference with which men for centuries have observed violence directed against women.

At the same time, women are much abused in *Sauve Qui Peut.* What is the meaning of this obsessive return to images of degradation and humiliation? (Laura Mulvey and Colin MacCabe are certainly right to point out that

Figure 48. *Sauve Qui Peut/ (la Vie)* (1980)

Godard, even after becoming a kind of fellow-traveler of the women's movement, continually slides between an investigation of the images of women and an investigation which exploits those images.)[14] A clue to the meaning of such images in *Sauve Qui Peut* lies in their staging. The incidents of abuse are clearly presented as ritual humiliations, symptomatic instances of a general malaise. Their anti-illusionist mise-en-scène underlines their character as gestus. The emphasis throughout is on the nonreciprocity of the exchanges. Isabelle calls her clients "Monsieur"; they do not call her "Madame." The boss, exercising his male prerogative as arbiter of female beauty, obliges his secretary to say: "My tits aren't fantastic." She cannot oblige him to say: "My pot belly is grotesque." Isabelle's pimps spank her—a quintessential gesture of paternalistic infantalization—and force her to admit that no woman, be she duchess, secretary, or tennis champion, can be truly independent. One of the businessmen who rents Isabelle's body is named, significantly, "Mr. Personne." The john, the man with the cash, is a person, a subject; the prostitute is differentially defined as non-person, object.

Godard—if I may briefly separate him from his co-worker—is at once the most sophisticated and the most childlike of artists. He has the rare gift of looking at the world with a kind of infantile *ostranenie.* His misleadingly aloof authorial persona blinds us to the intense emotion distilled into his work. Miles Davis, accused of being "cold" to his public, once answered that "the love is in the music." We fail to recognize the emotion in Godard because it is not found in the usual places—the scenario and the acting. Godard might respond to the same charge of coldness by saying that the love is in the lighting, the editing, the music. *Sauve Qui Peut* is especially imbued with a painterly appreciation of natural and fabricated beauty: figures positioned in Millet-like landscapes, deep blues and lush greens straight out of Kandinsky or Klee, the action painting created by an intermittently frozen pan across a striated sky. Godard has been underappreciated as a purely visual artist. His images, at once geometrical and sensuous, crisp and surprising, indicate an impeccable sense of framing, composition, and color. In *Sauve Qui Peut,* he shows himself to be as sensitive to the beauty of Swiss landscapes as he was formerly to the formica-shiny beauty of Parisian cafés.

The Politics of Pleasure: *Jonah Who Will Be 25 in the Year 2000*

All of the texts we have discussed—from the ludic reflexivity of *Sherlock Jr.* to the carnivalesque disrespect of *L'Age d'Or* and the joyful learning of *Tout Va Bien*—have offered their quantum of pleasure. We have spoken a good deal of the subverting of voyeuristic pleasure, but we have spoken little of pleasure itself. Film criticism unfortunately has often demonstrated a problematic relationship to filmic pleasure, either endorsing entertainment uncritically and thus serving as unthinking accomplice to the film industry, or lamenting the delight that mass audiences take in vulgar (for the Arnoldian elite) or alienated (for Marxists) spectacles. On the Left, too many Marxists have thrown out the baby of pleasure with the bathwater of ideology. Even a certain Brechtianism's glorification of the rational and hard-working spectator becomes suspiciously reminiscent of the bourgeois work ethic. This refusal of pleasure and emotion has at times created an immense gap between Left cultural criticism and the popular reception of films. Indeed, the political implications of Left puritanism have been enormous. A Left that addresses its audience in moralistic terms, while advertising and mass culture speak directly to its desires and fantasies, not only shows severe theoretical limitations but also handicaps its own chances for efficacity in the world. The broad American hostility to socialism certainly has as much to do with the widespread impression that socialist societies are "gray" and "dreary"—recurrent adjectives in the lexicon of journalistic anticommunism—as with the notion that socialist theory is incorrect. A Left film analysis, it seems to me, should celebrate, rather then deplore, the fact of filmic pleasure, embracing it as a friend while exorcising its alienation.

A partial model for the subversive pleasure of which we have been speaking is *Jonah Who Will be 25 in the Year 2000* (1975), directed by Alain Tanner and coscripted by John Berger. The film explores the interwoven lives of eight characters struggling to retain their humanity in the face of alienation. *Mathieu* is a typesetter and union militant who has just lost his job. *Mathilde* works in a factory and looks forward to having a baby—the Jonah of the title. While searching for a new job, Mathieu encounters *Marguerite* and *Marcel,* two produce gardeners who hire him to collect the manure they use as fertilizer. Taken together, Marcel and Marguerite love the entire animate world; he discourses eloquently on the unfathomable mystery of animals and the horrors of imminent ecological disaster, while she adores organic farming. *Max,* meanwhile, is a disillusioned Trotskyist and gambler currently working as a proofreader. Although he has more or less relinquished political activity in despair, he does take action by disseminating information concerning an impending land speculation swindle and warning the potential victims— among whom are Marguerite and Marcel. Max meets *Madeleine,* a secretary by vocation and heretical tantric mystic by avocation. As an employee of the bank that is perpetuating the swindle, she consents to help Max thwart it by securing the necessary documents. *Marco* is a neighbor to Marguerite and Marcel. A dreamer and high school history teacher, a twentieth-century descendant of *philosophes* like Rousseau, he lectures on sausages and the "folds of time." He falls in love with *Marie,* a supermarket cashier who knowingly undercharges her elderly customers and is finally jailed by her managers for her generosity. Marco, for his part, is fired, presumably for having broached taboo sexual subjects in his classes, but really for daring to suggest that the capitalist system is not eternal and could, just conceivably, collapse.

Simultaneously integrated into society (if only by the work they perform) and outside of it, the liminal characters of *Jonah* work within capitalism and make it tick, yet they are torn creatures, traversed by revolt as well as acquiescence. Simultaneously at the center and on the periphery, few of them are explicitly Leftist, yet their words and deeds suggest both conscious and intuitive opposition to the reigning system, an opposition which takes diverse forms—Mathieu's union militancy, Marco's antiauthoritarian pedagogy, Marie's cash-register sabotage, Madeleine's "transgressions," Marguerite and Marcel's organic resistance to land grabbers, Mathieu's alternative school. The film implies the distant possibility of a linking of the diverse zones of resistance embodied by these characters and all those oppressed, excluded, or marginalized by the dominant system: the unemployed, the elderly treated like so much excess baggage, the third-world workers in their *bidonvilles*. It is this solidarity with the marginalized majority that makes *Jonah* a more politically responsible (albeit less culturally audacious) version of what we have elsewhere called the carnivalesque.

This implicit political strategy is marred, admittedly, by a somewhat condescending attitude toward a key group in this new majority: women. *Jonah's* female characters tend to the pallidly stereotypical (Mathilde the earth-mother, Madeleine the mystic) while the male characters are more rounded and politically assertive. The telling political lines go largely to the men, while the women are granted little feminist or Left consciousness. Marguerite is strong—she drives a tractor, hires and fires—but what Tanner gives her in strength he takes away in likeability.[15] Women in *Jonah* are associated with nature ("All is mystery in nature," Marcel says of Marguerite's pecadilloes) or nurture (Mathilde's breastfeeding and eagerness for pregnancy). They are not shown as potential agents of revolutionary change; they are not even shown to be oppressed *as women*.

Otherwise, however, *Jonah* offers an incisive fable concerning life in the afterwash of the radical sixties. Drawing on diverse intellectual sources—Rousseau's notion of the integration of individual ego into a "moi commun," the surrealist fervor to change life and transform the world, Marcuse's utopian synthesis of Marx and Freud—Tanner offers for our contemplation a kind of contemporary phalanstery, a radical cell meant to join with other cells in a vast federation of resistance. For Max the burned-out politico, it is the morning after the *fête revolutionnaire*, and the house is strewn with cultural debris: ersatz mysticism, macrobiotic foods, casual sex. For Tanner the director, however, the sixties are less an irretrievable golden age than a lesson for the future, the springboard for a new leap forward. In keeping with this optimism,

Figure 49. *Jonah Who Will Be 25 in the Year 2000* (1975)

the film moves, overall, from anonymity and isolation to community. As chance encounters burgeon into embryonic forms of solidarity, the characters begin to generate strong feelings of communality. The child Jonah, one feels, is mothered (which perhaps explains why all the names begin with MA) and fathered by the collectivity; and it is he who symbolically embodies their hopes and aspirations.

At the same time, *Jonah* never cultivates the counter-culture fantasy that capitalist society can be easily and painlessly "greened" by a modest planting of what was once called "Consciousness III." The repressive arsenal of that society is far too evident throughout the film. Marie is jailed. Marco and Mathieu are fired. Documentary footage of the Swiss Army put-down of unemployment demonstrations reminds us that peaceful, neutral Switzerland has its own heritage of repression. Where political and legal repression fail, economic pressure takes its toll. We spend most of our energy trying to survive, Mathieu points out, and some of us, with the little energy left over, try to fight the system.

Nor does Tanner hide the conflicts that rend the fragile community of *Jonah*. The group is divided by philosophical differences (Madeleine would dissolve all contradiction in Yin-Yang complementarity; Max objects that the capital-labor contradiction is irreconcilable) and tactical disputes (alternative versus public schools). Rather than obscure these tensions, the film makes of them a potential source of polyphonic diversity and strength. While forming a kind of community, the members of the group also play out certain polarities and complementarities: Marguerite mocks Mathieu's purist aversion to public education; Mathieu criticises Marco for not safeguarding his teaching position as a base for political work; Madeleine makes fun of Max's protestant asceticism and premature despair ("Men want history to go as fast as life. It doesn't work that way.") while he censures her naiveté concerning class struggle. But it is in this dialogic process of mutual and affectionate criticism that a kind of provisional truth emerges.

Jonah might be seen as a Rousseauist exercise in back-to-nature nostalgia, a communalist fantasy that nourishes the pipe-dream of small collectivist groups within the larger capitalist society, a kind of seventies *Our Daily Bread*. In fact, however, the film relativizes such solutions. The land speculators, we may assume, will eventually devour the produce farm, and the rebels' symbolic guerrilla-theatre victory over the banker (unseating him and substituting a pig) is clearly marked as a sepia fantasy. Mathieu ultimately returns to work and struggle, and his final words, addressed to Jonah and to us, anticipate the day when Jonah will be organizing strike committees. It is Mathieu the activist worker, rather than Max the pessimist or Marco the philosopher, who makes the comments on class-struggle that frame the film. Fired for militancy at the beginning of the film, he returns to militancy at the end. But the fundamental

Figure 50.   *Jonah Who Will Be 25 in the Year 2000* (1975)

project of *Jonah* is not so much to propose a fictive model for revolution as it is to politicize the desires and perceptions of its audience. The goal is to show oppression as systematic, in a society where "the better," as Mathieu puts it, "is systematically put aside." Rather than offer a sentimental endorsement of vague personal longings for a more humane existence, *Jonah* stresses the systematic nature of what at first glance seems merely personal and idiosyncratic. The film was not made for Leftists but for a mass audience. Its strategy is to appeal to whatever is revolutionary in the majority of people, in all those, at least, who have no direct stake in oppression. Tanner and Berger do not, however, practice a sugar-coated pill theory of political art, i.e., a strategy which offers the habitual dose of satisfactions in order to persuade spectators to swallow a progressive message. Rather, the film maintains contact with the spectator, by its charm, by its humor, and by a certain realism, while its process of construction favors a critical, distanced attitude on the spectator's part.

Rather than organize itself as a linear narrative, *Jonah* orchestrates, in the Menippean manner, a dialectical music of ideas. The leitmotifs of time, nature, work, and education are sounded early and resonate throughout the film. Marco's inaugural lecture to his class initiates many of the themes. Using blood sausages (an homage to his butcher father) and a metronome (his mother sang operettas) as visual aids, Marco offers a disquisition on the historical evolution of the notion of time. While agricultural societies were bound to the cycles and rhythms of the seasons, he says, capitalism brought with it the notion of time as a superhighway, a linear progression. Time became progress. But it was the "winners" of history—the conquerors—who first formulated the idea of progress. Then Marco imagistically evokes the historical horrors of emperial expansion into what we now call the "third world." The capitalists, turned into corkscrews, opened up the bottles of "interior" cultures and drank them to the dregs. (One need only think of the Spanish plundering Inca silver or the British taking African ivory). Their thirst satisfied, they broke the bottles. But the "winners" of history—and here we see a veiled allusion to the liberation struggles of the third world—fear that this past might come back to haunt them. While believing in the straight and inexorable superhighway of progress, they fear the savages displaced by its construction (one visualizes the Transamazonic Highway, where the image literally applies). Marco then links this idea of the past, weighing like a nightmare on the European brain, with the students' personal histories. They, too, are an evolving creation of their own past; they are now "reading" the messages stored in their own chromosomes, just as Marco himself is the synthesis, in some sense, of his father (the sausage) and his mother (the metronome). Marco ends the class by beating out a series of rhythms: opposition creates time, just as class struggle motivates history. Marco's lecture, far from being "woozy," constitutes a lyrical version of the dialectic wrapped in a philosophical meditation and expressed in images.

Jonah as a whole elaborates the leitmotifs of Marco's lecture. The banker Vendoeuvres (etymologically "seller of works" and phonetically "wind of works") and his agents, as the provisory winners of history, speak the language of progress and domination: "We are no longer in the Middle Ages. . . . You can't stop the economy. . . . The city is developing. . . ." Social Darwinists, they fancy themselves strong by intrinsic right. The produce farmers and their allies, on the other hand, are Europe's indigenous "savages" who besiege and harass the agents of capitalist progress. When the bank's agent visits Marguerite and Marcel in order to soften them up for an eventual land takeover, one of the farmhands—described by Marguerite as a "bit savage"—threatens to cannibalize him. Jonah, like the Emile of the film's closing Rousseau quotations, will be a new kind of savage: "a savage made to live in the cities."[16]

Marco's lecture, in which apparent discontinuities mask real continuities, microcosmically typifies the film's methods, for *Jonah* as a whole mocks the temporal strategies—the linear progression—of conventional fiction films. The opening sequences alert us to *Jonah*'s unorthodox narrative procedures: after the credits, we see a man (Max) enter a smoke shop and ask for cigarettes. He pays 1 Franc 90 for them and grumbles about inflation. An anachronistic intertitle—"The Next Afternoon"—is followed by a shot of a statue of Jean-Jacques Rousseau. An off-screen voice (if a mute statue can be said to be "off") recites the celebrated passage from Rousseau's *Social Contract* where the philosopher asserts that most people live and die in slavery: "As children they are wrapped in diapers and when they die they are nailed into a coffin. So long as they live they are enchained by institutions." With the absurd intertitle, Tanner incongruously couples the temporality of contemporary Geneva with the temporality of a Rousseau quotation. It is as meaningless to speak of the "day before a Rousseau quotation" as it is to imply, as occurs in *Chien Andalou* "eight years after once upon a time." In both cases, the intertitles pinpoint the artificiality of cinematic time—historical time and narrative time are as arbitrary in their slicing up as the links of a sausage—and bid us pay attention to something other than a linear story.

Bourgeois thought compartmentalizes experience into neatly ordered and immaculately separated categories—economics, politics, education, ecology—with the result that the sense of social totality is lost. *Jonah* shows such borders and frontiers to be oppressive. Marco, paraphrasing the French Leftist rallying cry for the German-born student leader Cohn-Bendit ("We are all German Jews") shouts: "We are all frontier cases!" *Jonah* violates frontiers. As if in illustration of Derrida's dictum that "No border is guaranteed," the film passes through borders as if they did not exist. Marie's situation as a Swiss worker obliged by citizenship law to sleep in France is in this sense emblematic of the arbitrary and unnatural nature of borders. But intellectual borders oppress as well, for example that which separates economics and sexuality. Marie tells

Marco's students that she occasionally hitchhikes to work to save money, but complains that the men who pick her up harass her sexually. When a student interjects "*some* men," Marie insists that it involves men generally, that it is systematic. Conclusion: economic necessity forces Marie to hitchhike; (male) capitalist power oppresses her in both the sexual and the economic realms. Men abuse her not because of "instinct" but because the sexual distribution of power favors such abuses.

Jonah displays an almost Melvillean awareness of the ecological interconnectedness of all phenomena. "O Nature, and O soul of man," Melville wrote in his whale story, "how far beyond all utterance are your linked analogies!" *Jonah* unearths the linked analogies of which Melville speaks. Marco, contemplating a halved cabbage, notes its resemblance to the twin lobes of the brain. Like Melville, Tanner creates a kind of metaphysical poetry whereby dissimilar entities are joined and occult resemblances suggested. Just as *Moby Dick* is supernatural and earthy, metaphysical and physical, full of Plato as well as whale sperm, so *Jonah* is whimsically fantastic *and* rooted in the Swiss earth, flush with vegetables, onions, manure. Whales, furthermore, swim ubiquitous in the film. Human beings kill them for lipstick, Marcel observes, while the shrimp that whales usually eat go uneaten, so that people, left with nothing but shrimp to eat, will eventually die of indigestion. Whales are not only material for lipstick, they are semioticians (sending out coded messages) and musicians (Mathieu's pupils sing along with their cries). Jonah, like his Biblical namesake, is to be vomited up by his whale of a century.

While "collapsing" conventionally separated realms, *Jonah* also overturns established hierarchies: adults over children, work over play, "high " art over "low" art. The carnivalization of roles has the adult Mathieu ask the children the "infantile" irrepressible why-questions that children usually ask: "Does the wind feel the clouds?" "Can water feel?" "Does the sun know it's called the sun?" The film suggests the transcendence of the work/play dichotomy by arguing the frivolity of work and the seriousness of play. The farm work is a kind of play ("I'm the king of shit," says Mathieu atop a mountain of manure) as is classwork, while art is both work and play, a paradigm of nonalienated labor. *Jonah* locates art everywhere—in a casual pun, a stylized gesture, an eloquent statement, a well-sung song. Rather than something special and exalted, frozen into monuments and artifacts, art forms part of the process of everyday life. Politicizing the surrealist vision of the artistic potentialities of all human beings, Tanner peoples his film with the artists of the everyday. Mathieu (borrowing from Pablo Neruda) sings the democratic virtues of the onion; Marguerite hawks her vegetables with poems; Mathilde poetizes her pregnancy; and Marie, with Charles the railroad man, re-enacts memories in song, dance, and sketch. Life constantly transforms itself into creative self-determining playfulness. Everything—a tick, a whale, a name, a word—yields the pretext for a story or a song.

Figure 51. *Jonah Who Will Be 25 in the Year 2000* (1975)

Figure 52.   *Jonah Who Will Be 25 in the Year 2000* (1975)

If *Jonah* democratizes art, it also demystifies history. Far from being the exclusive province of emperors and generals, history is shown to be the very stuff of our everyday experience. Charles is surprised that Marco is interested in his old train stories. "Of course," replies Marco, "I'm a history teacher." We are history, its subjects and its objects, and we should all be, to echo *Tout Va Bien,* our own historians. ("Imperial Rome is full of arcs of triumph," Brecht wrote in *A Worker Reads History;* "Who reared them up? Over whom did the Caesers triumph?") The film's title—*Jonah Who Will Be 25 in the Year 2000*—spotlights our own immersion in historical time. This period is our segment, our sausage-link, as it were, of history, and we will probably share it with Jonah. Mathieu wishes Marco's students, and indirectly the spectators, a long and happy life; he hopes they are all alive and well in the year 2000. His words are followed by a cut to the same classroom, this time in black and white, inhabited by elderly people, presumably the same students grown older. Our minds flash forward to the year 2000; time and history are deposited in our reluctant spectatorial laps. What will we, alone and together, have accompanied in the intervening years? The film encourages us not only to understand time but to seize it and change it.

A Brechtian ode to the thrill of comprehension and the joy of learning, *Jonah* shows people learning throughout their lives. Children learn to draw and sing; they master Boolean algebra and mimic the cries of whales. Everyone can learn, even the very old, and Marco, not accidentally, winds up teaching in a home for the elderly. Like Brecht, Tanner sees life "under the sign of" education, and *Jonah,* like many of Brecht's plays *(Galileo, The Mother)* proliferates in classroom scenes. In many shots, we find ourselves ranged as spectators-learners behind the students on the screen. But the film is designed less to inculcate specific didactic truths than to teach people *how to learn.* The classroom becomes the scene of two activities frowned upon in conventional schools—thought and laughter. Not only can anything be taught in class—Mathieu speaks of inflation, Marie of cashiering—but learning can take place anywhere, in a greenhouse, or even in the cinema. *Jonah* evokes the potentially inexhaustible charm of what Brecht called "cheerful and miltant learning."[16]

Brechtian theatre, as we have seen, advances by interruptions, juxtaposing scenes rather than developing causal narrative sequence. *Jonah* segments itself into over two-score sequences, sketches, quotations, and songs. The narrative line reflexively exhibits its own kinks and knots, the continuity disrupted not only by intertitles but also by the recurrent intrusion of black-and-white footage, often ushered in by minor jazz chords heralding a shift in mode. These monochrome interludes are very diversely used; often suggestive and occasionally unclear, they all show some oblique or fantasmatic relation to the real posited by the story; they realize a wish or name a fear. Some are brief excursions into life-as-it-should-be rather than as it is. Mathieu gets to look at the books of his employer. The adults get to play in the mud like so many happy porcine children. Marguerite gets to confront her banker-enemy with his ignoble double—a pig. The cold impersonality of a TV newscaster melts into relaxed gestures and warm personal words addressed to Mathilde seated before her set. Still other sequences constitute historical flashbacks—for example of the 1932 army occupation of Geneva—or fictional flash-forwards—when Mathieu wishes Marco's students long and happy lives. Our sequence is especially striking for its political ambiguities. Max's melancholy lament that "politics are finished" precedes shots of military parades in Moscow's Red Square. In Makavejev's *WR*, such footage slyly insinuates a link between militarism and sexual repression. Here, however, since we know Max has an elephantine memory for past political betrayals, we wonder if Tanner is not presenting a disenchanted Trotskyist's version of *why* politics are finished, i.e., because of Stalinism.

In still another black-white interlude, the hitchhiking Marie is picked up by a clean-cut young man who urges her to sit in the front seat. Marie bursts into a satirical cabaret-style ditty: "If you save your money you'll never be in debt/ Stay cold and never fall in love and you'll never burn to ash/ Kiss the ass of those who kick you and you won't have to worry about getting whipped/ Crawl close to the ground and there will be no danger of crashing." Her song burlesques the tight-fisted prudence of the *petit bourgeois* and her final query constitutes a sarcastically indirect refusal of an implied sexual proposition: "What made you think you could fly?"

The Brechtian theory of distanciation and the alienation effect form the basis of Tanner's film language. The episodic juxtaposition of sketches, each conceived as a theatrical "act," the fugue-like presentation of the characters and the alliterative stylization of their names, the archaic intertitles and the still photographs all form part of a Brechtian aesthetic. Many sequences recall both Godard and Brecht. Marie, home from jail, play-acts her prison experiences with Charles. When he plays a male prisonmate, she objects that there *were* no male prisoners. Then he mimes the ritual solemnity of a priest, but she complains that his gestures are all wrong. Charles finally opts for a Shakespearean solution; he plays the role of the prison itself by clasping his hands in front of his face in order to represent "wall." Brechtian in its minimalist approach to decor, Charles' solution implies that one need not literally reconstitute a wall; one need only "signify" it. More important the sequence—like the similar sequence in *Tout Va Bien* where the workers debate how to convey the visceral feelings associated with their everyday working lives—confronts us with the problematic narrative and esthetic choices involved in artistic representation. Indeed, in many ways Tanner does quietly what Godard does more obtrusively and audaciously. Tanner's reflexive techniques, like his colors, are more muted. "You don't see the camera," as

Tanner said of his own *Middle of the World,* "but you hear it running." The editing in *Jonah* is subtly "visible"; shots are held just a little too long or cut just a little too abruptly. The camera movements, rather than completely autonomous, are minutely displaced; the camera moves slightly when the personages do not, anticipating or trailing behind the movement in the shots. The passages between shots are often quietly startling; an extreme long shot of Mathieu on his bicycle, for example, cuts to alternating close-ups of his face and a red light.

Working with synchronous sound and long takes, Tanner gives his actors room to breathe and the space to interact. Jonah is structured around roughly 150 one-shot sequences plus a sprinkling of close-ups. Such sequences allow the actors to spread their wings, unlike conventional practice where an hour might pass (devoted to adjusting lighting, experimenting with set-ups) between the question of one character and the answer of another. At first glance, Tanner's method would seem to reinforce conventional Bazinian realism by avoiding the fragmentation that goes with montage. In fact, however, it has a contrary effect, precisely because spectators are accustomed to "invisible" montage and fabricated continuity so that shots which literally respect the spatial and temporal unity of the scene create, paradoxically, an effect of unreality and alienation.

Beyond Deconstruction

Tanner extends the lessons of Godard in very personal and in some ways, more sympathetic directions. We have spoken of the film's subversive qualities, but what about its charms? What are its strategies for winning people to a Left position. It is here that *Jonah* is most interesting, for it politicizes while it pleasures its audience. It refuses, and dialectically transcends, the sterile dilemma of a condescending populism on the one hand and an arid deconstruction on the other. Populism *(Burn! State of Siege, Missing)* wraps a radical message in Hollywood packaging in an attempt to be "accessible"; pure deconstruction *(Le Gai Savoir)* reflexively investigates textual processes, but tends to speak only to the intellect. *Jonah* explores new routes into the spectator's mind and psyche. In words superficially addressed to the other characters but really aimed at the spectator, Mathieu speaks of unifying the field of our desires, finding their common thread, and using them as levers. "Capitalism survives," John Berger wrote in *Ways of Seeing,* "by forcing the majority, whom it exploits, to define their own interests as narrowly as possible." Once achieved by extensive deprivation, this goal is now achieved in the developed world "by imposing a false standard of what is and what is not desirable." Psychoanalysis, meanwhile, has tended to lock desire into the category of the individual subject. *Jonah* attempts a redefinition of the desirable by appealing to deeply rooted but socially frustrated aspirations—for intimacy, for new modes of work, for solidarity, for festivity, for community, for freedom. Too many Leftist films play on guilt or appeal purely to the intelligence; *Jonah* tries to think through the social logic of our personal and collective desires, even while it demystifies the political and ideological structures that channel our desires in oppressive directions.

As the hegemonic formal expression of late capitalist society, Jameson argues, film drives the Utopian impulse, now reified, "back inside the monad, where it assumes the status of some merely psychological experience, private feeling, or relativized value.[17] *Jonah*, for its part, refuses this "monadic" pleasure. It does not encourage facile identification with idealized personages. It refuses the constant flow of identification via the ongoing exchange of glances by which conventional films suture us into the psychological and diegetic momentum of the story. Unlike "deconstruction" films, *Jonah* does favor a kind of identification, but it is neither with individual characters, on the one hand, or with anything so abstract as "the masses" on the other. Rather, we identify with a diverse collectivity groping toward communitas, and with the ideas they represent. We identify with eight characters and their children. We identify, in short, with a community of aspiration.

Deconstruction theory and deconstructed films performed an invaluable service by unmasking the ideology at work within cinematic forms themselves and denouncing the potential for exploitation in identification with streamlined plots and idealized characters. But as Metz points out, totally deconstructed films require a libidinal transfer whereby traditional satisfactions are replaced by the pleasures of intellectual mastery, by a "sadism of knowledge."[18] The pleasure in the toy is transmuted into the pleasure of breaking the toy. (The pleasure of breaking the toy, one might add, is not intrinsically less infantile than the pleasure of the toy.) While the work of deconstruction is invaluable and should continue, the cinema should also move beyond deconstruction into non-exploitative identification and self-critical narration. It is perfectly fine to denounce Hollywood escapism, but we must also recognize the desire that brings all of us to the cinema. For spectators are not corralled by force into the movie theatres; they go gladly to the slaughter.

A film like *Jonah* suggests, in an admittedly tentative and even problematic fashion, the possibility of the filmic channeling of social desire to generate a different kind of pleasure. Any film, to be effective, must offer a quantum of pleasure, something to know or see or feel. The challenge for liberatory films is to crystalize and actualize utopian hopes even while exposing their degraded expression. Distancing can only be effective, after all, if there is something—an emotion, a desire—to *be* distanced. It is of no value for films (or revolutions) to be "correct" if no one is interested in participating in them. The most successful reflexive texts conserve both diegesis and identification, but

Figure 53. *Jonah Who Will Be 25 in the Year 2000* (1975)

undermine them from within. While assuming the pleasures of conventional narrative, they mobilize the spectator to interrogate those pleasures and, furthermore, they make that interrogation *itself* pleasurable. They adopt the Cervantic strategy of playing with fictions rather than doing away with them altogether. They follow the way pointed by Brecht: to tell stories, but at the same time to step out of the story and question it. Unafraid of pleasure, the thrust of their interrupted spectacle is fundamentally comic, not in the sense of provoking hilarity but in the sense of maintaining a socialized distance between the desiring subject and the text. They articulate the play of desire and the pleasure principle *and* the obstacles to their realization.

The perennial comparison of the cinematic experience to the dream state points not only to its potential for alienation but also to its central utopian thrust. Dreams are not merely regressive; they are vital to human well-being. They are, as the surrealists emphasized, a sanctuary for desire, an intimation of the possible transcendence of stale dichotomies, and a source of a kind of knowledge denied cerebral rationality. It is as futile to condemn narrative as such—to pretend, for example, that narrative inevitably serves conservative ideologies—as it would be to condemn dreams. Human beings need both; both dream and narrative are arguably primordial functions of the human mind. Fabulating animals, we tell each other stories when we are awake and tell ourselves dreams when we are asleep. Without myths, Propp tells us, the tribe dies. Without the freedom of dreams, prisoners would die of despair. Story-collections such as *The Thousand and One Nights,* according to Todorov, allegorize the human obsession with stories, and in them, "narration equals life, the absence of narration, death."[19] Narration seems to be a genetic inheritance. Our very sentences, by their syntagmatic structure, form mininarratives. Narrative, for Barthes, is "international, transhistorical, transcultural: it is simply there, like life itself."[20]

Those who dismiss all narrative as intrinsically bourgeois and passivity inducing would do well to remember *Don Quixote.* Few books demonstrate so much love for fiction, for pure narrativity for its own sake, while at the same time providing reminders that we should not believe but only observe. Brecht's work, similarly, proliferates in tales and fables, but they are not stories to lose ourselves in but rather to learn from. The challenge for anti-illusionist fictions is how to respect the fabulating impulse, how to revel in the joys of storytelling and the delights of artifice, while maintaining a certain intellectual distance from the story. The subversive pleasure generated by a Cervantes, a Brecht, or a Godard consists in telling stories while comically undermining their authority. The enemy to be done away with, after all, is not fiction but socially generated illusion; not stories but alienated dreams.

Fredric Jameson, in *The Political Unconscious,* anticipates some collective and decentered cultural production of the future which would transcend the sterile dichotomy of realism and modernism alike. Brecht, if he did not himself fully realize such an idea, certainly pointed the way toward its realization. Implicit in his modernist realism is the assumption that the political and aesthetic avant-gardes, yoked by a common impulse of social and libidinal rebellion, concretely need each other. While revolutionary aesthetics without revolutionary politics is often futile ("They did away with grammar," said Brecht, "but they forgot to do away with capitalism"), revolutionary politics without revolutionary aesthetics is equally retrograde, pouring the new wine of social change into the old cracked bottles of conventional forms. Brecht, by warning against the twin traps of an empty and elitist iconoclasm on the one hand, and a formally nostalgic illusionism on the other, suggested the way toward the realization of that scandalously utopian and only apparently paradoxical idea—a majoritarian avant-garde.

Appendix

Reflexivity and the Specifically Cinematic

Reflexive strategies, while equally available to both literature and the cinema, have different materials to work with in the two media. Prose fiction, for example, is a purely verbal medium, while the "unattainable text" of film is a multitrack sensorial composite. Even films that literalize the idea of the film text, by limiting their profilmic material to written words—for example, Michael Snow's *So Is This*—are not strictly identical to a literary text. Snow's editing imposes a particular pace on the text; some words, such as the word "lengthy" are held on screen for a relatively long time, while others, such as "tits" and "ass" are held for only the few frames required for "legibility." The size of the letters varies from shot to shot, and patches of color and quick flares occasionally wander into frame. The mere fact of a text being read by an audience of spectator-readers, furthermore, changes the quality of the experience, and in the cinema, the "readers," at least in the conventional viewing experience, cannot personally vary the time of their "reading."

Our purpose here will be to examine what Metz would call the specifically cinematic dimension of reflexivity. Apart from the broader narrative and rhetorical strategies available to both novel and film, how can the cinema illuminate its specific textual processes? If the code of perspective is inherent in the individual photographs that make up a film, for example, how can the reflexive filmmaker subvert or call attention to this code? Rather than compose in depth, Godard "flattens" the image, arranging his profilmic subjects in a single spatial plane, without foreground or background or vanishing point to reinforce the impression of relief. Fixed 90° compositions make all planes parallel to the borders of the frame. Actors are posed against blank walls or schematic backgrounds which block perspectival lines. Rectilinear compositions and abstract framing force us to contemplate rather than "enter" the image, while the inclusion of two-dimensional materials—paintings, photographs, posters, newspapers, book covers—call attention to the screen as a two-dimensional surface.

One of the "subplots" of Michael Snow's *Wavelength* (1966-1967), a 45-minute film structured around a single zoom shot—or more accurately, around the analogue of a zoom movement, a series of shifts in focal length which cumulatively produce the effect of a progression from normal-lens to telephoto view—taken from a fixed camera position in a New York loft, has to do with the progressive emptying out of filmic illusions and depth. The film begins, at the wide-angle end of the progression, with Bazinian deep space and multiple spatial planes: foreground and middleground inside the loft and the background outside the loft in the street. Then the film moves inexorably toward two-dimensionality and flatness, finally obliterating the distinction between inside the loft and outside the loft, and putting us literally and figuratively "up against the wall." A similar emptying out occurs in relation to sound; the film begins with the synchronous "deep" sound of street noises and loft activities, then switches to an oscillator-generated sine-wave, a "flatter" more abstract kind of sound. But at the zenith of our claustrophobia, the final image, a photograph of waves, two-dimensional reminder of the primordial basis of the cinema in still photographs, opens up the space through its evocative power. In this Zen meditation of a film, we come to see the world in a loft, the universe within a photograph, flatness within depth and depth within flatness.

Reflexive filmmakers can also use color to either flatten the image or to call attention to the artificiality of filmic color. In *Wavelength,* Snow has his cameraman clumsily position filters in front of the lens. Godard insists on the presence of filters in the opening sequence of *Contempt,* developing a tripartite red-white-blue structure. In other films, following the lead of contemporary painting, Godard insisted on the two-dimensionality of the screen surface through the compositional use of color, arranging colors in blocks or in polar opposites. Godard's preference for sharply defined primary colors, meanwhile, reminded the spectator of the differences between natural and screen color. Whereas in nature color nuances are endless and inexhaustible, Godard closes off this inexhaustibility by rigorous selection. He manipulates advancing and receding colors, juxtaposing highly saturated reds and greens with blues, so that the contrasting colors rise to the screen surface as abstract patterns.

The perspectival "analogy" of the photographic image only partially accounts for film's "impression of reality." The photographs in a film exist sequentially, and the spectator, thanks to persistence of vision and the phi-effect (phenomenon of apparent movement) accepts shifting configurations of light as the equivalent of material tangible movement. In fact, the camera does not so much reproduce movement as analyze it, conserve it through mechanical reproduction, and then recompose it on demand with the aid of a projector. But the impression of real movement powerfully contributes to a feeling of depth and reality.

Reflexive filmmakers can exploit all kinds of film movement—movement within the shot, camera movement, optically produced movement, and the movement created by montage—for anti-illusionist as well as illusionist ends. Since movement, by detaching objects from their background, lends a feeling of corporality and depth to the image, one way of undercutting the persuasiveness of this conjunction is simply to minimize movement in the manner of Jean-Marie Straub, the Taviani Brothers, or late-manner Godard. Another way is to stylize and choreograph movement in antinaturalistic patterns, in the manner of Miklos Jansco or Glauber Rocha. In *Land in Anguish*, for example, Rocha has his actors move in choreographed figures that have more to do with the stylization of opera than the "naturalness" of dramatic realism.

Camera movement can be subordinated to the diegesis or can be autonomous and declare its independence from characters and plot. The opening camera movements of *Rear Window,* as we have seen, are pointedly unmotivated. After the shades of the windows are raised, as if without human intervention, the camera pans past a sleeping Jimmy Stewart, then moves out the windows, down into the courtyard, tilts up and pans around to introduce some of the neighbors and returns to Stewart sleeping in his apartment. There is no authorizing subject for the film's discourse at this point, only Hitchcock. In the final shot of Antonioni's *Passenger,* similarly, the camera shows a man in his apartment, then passes through a grated window, promenades around a patio, during which we hear a shot, only to return to the apartment with the man dead. Nothing "justifies" the camera movement except a desire to narrate the sequence in precisely that manner rather than another. In Rocha's *Land in Anguish,* the camera does not generally accompany the action; rather, it performs its own autonomous ballet of stylized, geometricized, and choreographed movements, creating a tension between the mobility of the camera and that of the characters.

Chris Marker's *La Jetée,* by depriving itself of movement in the shot, becomes a textbook demonstration of alternative means for producing movement. In what seems a perverse negation of the nature of the medium, whose primordial designations—cinema, motion pictures, movies—entail movement, Marker takes stasis as his point of departure. Even the title—"La Jetée"—evokes frozen activity, a verbal congealed into a substantive. The stasis takes us back to the primordial basis of film in the individual frames, but Marker's film also makes us realize that static images, when they are projected, are not completely static. There are always tiny tremors produced by the projection, infinitesimal changes of light on the screen and in the atmosphere.

Only one shot, six seconds in length, reproduces movement, but that shot's isolation and uniqueness in the film renders it strangely precious, as if we were seeing cinematic movement for the first time as a kind of miracle. But Marker exploits other kinds of movement: 1) *camera movement:* the camera performs a tilt pan over a photograph of the Arch of Triumph; 2) *optical camera movement:* the camera zooms out from a still of Orly airport and zooms in to the protagonist's face; 3) *optical movement created in the laboratory:* lap dissolves of the "destruction of Paris" evoke mists rising over ruins, dissolves of different positions of the woman asleep create a sense of graceful oneiric kinesis; 4) *movement evoked by editing:* simulated jump-cuts of the protagonist's face under experimentation evoke a man jerking in pain. *La Jetée* reminds us, finally, that the human mind is the ultimate source of cinematic movement. Our mind fills in the gaps between the static images, pressuring stasis into mental kinesis. *La Jetée* merely hyperbolizes this universal but generally obscured process.

Montage and Mimesis

All of these kinds of movement—movement in the shot, camera movement, optically produced movement—pale in significance compared to the narrative movement created by *montage.* It is through montage that discrete frames, individual shots and separate sequences are transformed into a psychologically persuasive fiction. Montage not only creates movement through the succession of angles and perspectives; it also "moves" in the emotional sense by involving the spectator in a story and creating an impression of *psychological,* rather than merely spatial depth. Although cinema initially convinced because of the unprecedented realism of its mimesis, it subsequently devised a kind of realism that went far beyond the analogical fascination of the individual shot. The individual shot, after all, furnishes but a schematic and truncated version of an isolated fragment of reality, while montage transforms these fragments into narrative discourse, and thus displaces the spectator's interest in the lifelikeness of individual images onto the lives lived *through* the images. It is this transfer of perspective, by which we come to share the feelings and impulses of imaginary characters, that simultaneously "moves" us and renders the movement of montage invisible.

Cinema invented a way of telling stories through a specifically cinematic organization of time and space. It devised what has become the esthetic cornerstone of dominant cinema—the reconstitution of a fictional world characterized by internal coherence and by the appearance of spatial and temporal continuity. Orthodox continuity implies a linear story, plausible causality, and psychological realism. It implies a film articulated into sequences which are coherent narrative wholes fitting into the larger coherent whole which is the film itself, with impeccably smooth transitions between sequences as between individual shots. This continuity is achieved—or was achieved in the classical period of the Hollywood film—by an etiquette for introducing new scenes (a choreographed progression from establishing shot to medium shot to close shot); conventional devices for evoking the passage of time (dissolves, iris effects); conventional techniques to render imperceptible the transition from shot to shot (the 30-degree rule, cutting on movement, position matches, direction matches, movement matches, and inserts to cover up unavoidable discontinuities); and devices for implying subjectivity (subjective shots, shot-reaction shots, eyeline matches). It was through this kind of montage that the classical fiction film acquired the emotional power and diegetic prestige of the nineteenth-century realistic novel.

Godard's career consists of a series of guerrilla raids on orthodox continuity, and his tactics have evolved as the enemy itself has evolved. A close look at either the overall narrative articulation or local editing of almost any Godard film will turn up innumerable violations of conventional continuity. Merely to catalogue his violations amounts indirectly to specifying the hidden and not-so-hidden codes of cinematic realism. In terms of the larger syntagmatic units, Godard's work presents an ongoing struggle against the tyranny of the conventional sequence. The very inapplicability of Metz's *Grande Syntagmatique de la Bande Image* points, in Godard's case, to all the ways in which his films depart from the *découpage classique* for which the Metzian schema was devised. A film like *Les Carabiniers,* by superimposing a childlike fable on diverse essayistic materials, throws the Metzian categories into disarray. A film like *One Plus One,* meanwhile, surprises because it exploits only one of the syntagmatic types delineated by Metz—the *plan-séquence.* The title, in fact, refers on one level precisely to this syntagmatic addition, one plus one, of ten *plans-séquences.* Whereas most filmmakers adroitly play on diverse syntagmatic types, much as a musician plays different keys in a harmonious whole, Godard plays here on only one cinematic key.

Conventional filmmakers, as everyone knows, employ continuity editors and "script girls" to watch over the little details of narrative consistency— clothing, weather conditions, relative positions of objects. Godard, for his part, makes a mockery of continuity even in this common everyday sense. The continuity of *Pierrot le Fou,* to take just one example, is blatantly and cheerfully inadequate. Marianne on leaving Paris is dressed like a *lycéenne;* after stopping for gasoline, she wears the uniform of a paratrooper; when they steal a Ford Galaxy, she has on a pale pink dress, and all this occurs without any narrative justification for the changes. When the fugitive couple perform agitprop theatre for American sailors, Godard does not bother to explain where they acquired the chalk, the uniform, and the Asiatic hat. In its blithe discontinuities, *Pierrot le Fou* resembles the comic strips to which it so often alludes; it takes advantage of the elipses between two images. Everything in the film—the characterization, the continuity, Ferdinand's journal—is full of holes.

In multiplying discontinuities, Godard simply foregrounds the primordial discontinuity of film itself. A filmic text is a discontinuous discourse, analyzable into discrete shots and individual frames. The process of film production, furthermore, is essentially discontinuous. Shots are selected from diverse takes made at different times. Editing involves physically collating separate pieces of film. The continuity of film, in sum, consists of a perpetual discontinuity. Montage normally imposes an apparent continuity on discontinuous materials. Godard merely underscores this discontinuity by emphasizing the individual frame ("22,337 frames tell you about Patricia and Emile," he informs us in *Le Gai Savoir*), or by making the transition from shot to shot jarringly abrupt (through *faux raccords,* movement and position mismatches, violent changes in scale) or simply obvious (the black leader for cuts in *Les Carabiniers*), or by insisting, in a Brechtian way, on the autonomy of individual sequences (the "douze tableaux" of *Vivre Sa Vie,* the "chapters" of *Pierrot,* the "quinze faits précis" of *Masculin, Féminin*).

The Parameters of Sound

We have so far stressed but one of cinema's matters of expression—the moving and sequential photographic images. The other four—recorded phonetic sound, recorded noises, recorded musical sound, and writing—are no less important to film as a signifying practice. Although sound tracks have become extremely sophisticated, film theory and criticism still tend to privilege the visual, as if sound were but an afterthought. Even the language we use to speak of the cinema reinforces this hegemony of the visual: we see ourselves as *spectators* (not auditors) *viewing* (not hearing) motion *pictures* (not sounds). Films like Malick's *Days of Heaven,* Coppola's *The Conversation,* and Altman's *The Wedding* reflect what has been called a "second sound revolution," but critics and theorists have been slow to respond to its challenge.

Sound, like any filmic resource, can be used to illusionist or anti-illusionist ends. In the illusionist film, sound intensifies and completes the impression of reality offered by the image; it reconstitutes a recognizable auditory world, lending sonorous depth—the aural equivalent to visual depth of field—to the image. The conventions of dramatic realism require that the image be accompanied by the natural sounds that such a sight would generate in everyday experience. Sound, then, amplifies the mimetic power of the medium, completing the image with its evocative powers, streamlining the narrative discourse, camouflaging discontinuity by the continuous flow of sound over cuts. It reinforces the impression of depth because it penetrates the space of the audience. Sensed as literally present rather than recreated, it fills out an imaginary third dimension lacking in silent cinema. The sound analogon, in some respects, has a higher coefficient of authenticity than the visual analogon. Unlike the image, it is not strictly localizable within the rectangular frame of the screen. While the photographic image records, for Barthes, a "having-been-there," the sound seems really there. Little distinguishes real from recorded sound: it is somehow both inside the screen and throughout the theatre, measurable in decibels and potentially capable of shattering glass or wounding eardrums. Whereas the image of a tiger could never hurt anyone, a recorded roar conceivably could.

Reflexive filmmakers prolong a cinematic tradition which appreciates sound as offering new combinatory possibilities of poetic and ideological juxtaposition, for counterpointing the image rather than underlining it. The tradition goes at least as far back as the famous statement signed by Eisenstein, Pudovkin, and Alexandrov calling for the "contrapuntal use of sound" and its "distinct nonsynchronization with the visual images." Many reflexive filmmakers have answered their call by exploiting sound to derealize rather than reinforce the image. Chris Marker demonstrates the ideologically informing power of sound in *Letter from Siberia* by accompanying the same footage—a shot of a moving bus, shots of workers paving a street—with three distinct commentaries, ranging from official communist to hostile anticommunist to neutral. The experience of the shots is radically modified by each version. Rocha, in *Land in Anguish,* uses recorded noises to contradict the image. Guns are omnipresent in the film but are never coordinated with their sounds. We see pistols, for example, but hear machine guns. In "The Encounter of a Leader with the People" sequence, we see a political militant fire a machine gun, but we hear nothing, yet the people quiet down as if *they* had heard it, as Rocha suspends the soundtrack to an unnaturally total silence.

Hollis Frampton in *(nostalgia)* brilliantly exploits the interplay of sound and image, of the iconic and the linguistic. The film consists of a series of photographs, successively burned to cinders on a hotplate, on which the filmmaker (dubbed by Michael Snow) makes digressive commentaries. The commentaries are displaced, applying not to the image we are seeing but to the image that we are about to see. The film bifurcates its spectator into an auditor and a spectator; we wonder whether we should trust our eyes or our ears, because we obviously cannot, at least initially, trust both. The film also demonstrates the anchoring function of words, their way, at times, of tying down the polysemy of the image, and at other times of opening the image up to polysemy. His gloss on a newspaper photo as showing a man contemplating his flood-destroyed grapefruit "anchors" its sense, although we might have found another explanation equally convincing. Elsewhere, however, the commentary forces us to re-see the iconic through the linguistic, as when the mention of the "central nervous system" coincides with the image of the coils of the hotplate, which we then see as evocative of the central nervous system.

The soundtrack in film has classically tended to privilege dialogue; that is why sound films were referred to as "the talkies" rather than the "noisies" or "the musicies." In the early sixties, however, Jean-Luc Godard and other new wave directors began to privilege noise. They abandoned directional microphones and selective amplification in favor of omnidirectional mikes and the inclusive "democratic" transcription of all ambiant sounds. By including sounds that the conventional decorum would have systematically eliminated or downplayed, these directors retroactively exposed the factitiousness of the old studio sound-conventions. Godard has ambiant noise intrude on lovers' conversations in *Masculine, Feminine;* pinball machines and traffic noises are granted access to the soundtrack. Apart from its thematic relevance—the effects of urban life on young love—the insistent noise makes a political point. It reminds us that lovers, and people generally, do not exist in a vacuum; the world is with them. Godard's use of sound, then, simultaneously criticises romanticism, which fosters the illusion that lovers can live in some ideal cinematic elsewhere, and the pseudo-humanism, privileging dialogue, which subtends studio sound practices.

Godard has transgressed, at one point or another, virtually all the taboos and conventions associated with studio sound practices—that all sounds must be "legible," that all dialogue should be comprehensible, that dialogue should not be repeated except for intentional emphasis, that swift changes in aural scale should be avoided, that "inaudible" sound matches should parallel "invisible" image matches, and that voices and lips should be synchronized with the image. Another convention stipulated that there should be no "holes" in the soundtrack, lest the spectators think that the loudspeakers are not functioning. But in *A Woman is a Woman,* Godard plays an Aznavour song intermittently, alternating full volume with total silence, and thus elicited precisely the feared reaction on the part of spectators, some of whom reportedly tore up the seats to protest what they thought was the theatre's inadequate sound system. Godard also spoofs the convention in *Band of Outsiders* by having Franz ask his friends for a minute of silence, a request which Godard obliges by turning off the entire soundtrack.

Ferdinand, in *Pierrot le Fou,* complains that he has one mechanism for seeing, another for listening, and still another for speaking, but they all go their separate ways: "There's no coordination. One should feel they are united. I feel they are deranged." Ferdinand's statement, a verbal echo of Rimbaud's "dérèglement de tous les sens," reflects precisely what happens in many Godard films, where each of the filmic tracks—image, dialogue, noise, music, writing— goes in a different direction. The film is dissociated into its separate matters of expression. The image tells one story; the dialogue another; the noise another; and the music still another. Godard uses all the elements in a concerted attack on the sensibility of the spectator and the conventions of illusionism. A disorienting sensory overload gives us too much to assimilate, as if the only way to understand the film would be literally to let the senses go their separate ways—viewing the film once for the images, once for the dialogue, once for the music, once for the background noises, and once for the titles. In some instances, not only do the sense go their separate ways, but each sense is asked to go in several directions at once. In *One Plus One* we are asked to listen simultaneously to dialogue, music, naturalistic noises, a novel being read by an off-screen voice, all while reading innumerable visual messages and written texts. And in *Numéro Deux* the problem is compounded by multiple images, each with its own assortment of sounds.

Music and Illusionism

Film music, like montage, is one of those devices which seem at first glance antinaturalistic, but which in fact came to be recuperated by a naturalist aesthetic. On superficial examination, all music which is not immediately "anchored" in the image (i.e., whose source is neither present nor implied to be present in the image) is by definition anti-illusionistic. Conventional cinema, however, often substitutes for the superficial realism of visual appearances the ultimately more persuasive realism of subjective response. The musical scores of Hollywood dramatic films lubricate the spectator's psyche and oil the wheels of narrative continuity. At the same time they direct our emotional responses in the manner of traffic cops; they regulate our sympathies, extract our tears, excite our glands, relax our pulses, and trigger our fears, always in strict conjunction with the image.

The style of film music which dominated the studios during the 1930s and '40s may be succinctly described as the symphonic style of late-nineteenth-century European romanticism. The composers who dominated the studios— Max Steiner, Dimitri Tiomkin, Franz Waxman, Miklos Rozsa—tended to be emmigrants from Europe steeped in a specific tradition of musical composition. The European education of these film composers within the Wagner-Strauss tradition inclined them to favor the lush sounds of rich orchestral scoring, with long-spanned melodies based on Wagnerian leitmotifs. The concept of the "Gesamtkunstwerk" was transmuted into a workable aesthetic for film music, one in which music fused with screen action, dialogue, and sound effect by providing the appropriate instrumental color.

Without slighting the brilliance of these composers, one can question the inevitability of their aesthetic as the only one for such a discontinuous medium as film. Their ideas, in lesser hands, were also susceptible to considerable vulgarization and standardization. The leitmotif became a rather mechanical system of allying particular themes to particular characters, themes which were returned to with only minimal variation during the course of the film. Film scores, at their most conventional, tended to be redundant, subliminal, hackneyed, and comfortably tonal. They were redundant because hyper-explicit, cheerful images redoubled with cheerful sounds, tragic moments underlined with "tragic" harmonics, and narrative climaxes carefully matched to swells and crescendos. The image was overstuffed with a pleonastically high coefficient of reality. (Lubitsch parodied such redundancy by having characters walk up stairs accompanied by an *escalier* of ascending musical notes.) Such scores are subliminal in that they are meant to be felt emotionally but not heard as music. To modify our traffic cop analogy, they are not uniformed policemen but plainclothesmen. The scores are hackneyed because they appeal to a series of petrified associations—flutes for love and meadows, martial drums for war, Mendelssohn for weddings, tremolos for the fantastic, and ominous chords to betray danger. The scores are comfortably and reassuringly tonal, finally, in being spiritually descended from the late romantic period. Often exploiting debased versions of Wagnerian leitmotifs, such music is emotionally effective, because easy to grasp, and subsequently marketable as albums. Returning the public to the lost paradise of tonality, melody, and final resolution, they rigorously avoid modernist dissonance and tension.

Conventional filmic music, in a sense, has never fundamentally departed from its original function in the days of silent cinema. The pianists and organists who accompanied silent films served a double function: their music 1) "covered" the noise of the projector, and 2) directed spectator response, underscoring the screen events with sound elements adopted to their mood and rhythm. Its function, then, was to efface the instruments of production of the cinematic illusion and to direct audience response. Although these two functions have been physically integrated into the filmic text and rendered more subtle, their purpose has not changed. The realistic effect of music is paradoxical in that music in itself is not representational. Music is polysemic, open to infinite association, and refractory (*Peter and the Wolf* and *Till Eulenspiegel* notwithstanding) to anecdote. But music, like montage, engages the psychic mechanisms of the spectator, substituting for literal visual mimesis the realism of subjectivity and the feel of thought. In realistic cinema well-chosen images and well-chosen musical sounds anchor each other. Music serves to carry the spectator over the rough spots of the diegesis—whence the importance of music during the opening credits, when the presence of written texts and the exposition of the facts of filmic production might definitely shatter the impression of reality.

Reflexive filmmakers play music *against* the image, against the dramatic moment, and often against other kinds of music in the same film. Bruce Conner's parodic *A Movie* (1958) begins with epic Hollywoodean music that makes us expect something heroic and grandiose; instead, we are given a disorienting sequence of film leader, found footage, and titles reading "start," "head," and "end of Part IV." Robbe-Grillet specified in his script that *Marienbad* should begin with "end of movie music." The Brazilian underground filmmaker Julio Bressane in *Killed the Family and Went to the Movies* superimposes Carmen Miranda's effervescent version of "What a great country for partying" on images of unredeemed squalor. Another Brazilian filmmaker, Rogerio Sganzerla, in *Red Light Bandit* constructs his soundtrack out of a veritable anthology of Hollywood programmatic music, classical symphonic pieces, and Brazilian and American camp materials, often making three or four pieces of music play simultaneously. Rocha's *Land in Anguish* frequently superimposes two very different kinds of music—the symphonies of Villa-Lobos and the Afro-Brazilian chants of candomblé. The superimposition, paradoxically, both amplifies the polysemy of the music and restricts it by suggesting hidden links between the two kinds of music. In all these instances, we become aware of music as music rather than simply being physically manipulated by it.

Although Godard often draws on the classical repertoire (Beethoven in *Une Femme Mariée*, Mozart in *Weekend* and *Masculine, Feminine*), his treatment of the music is modernist and Brechtian in its discontinuity. The music interrupts and is itself interrupted so that it can no longer serve as a subliminal guide for our emotions. Music in Godard struggles against the image and against a simplistic response. The emotional tone of the music clashes with the emotional tone of the image or dialogue. In *Pierrot le Fou*, sprightly music punctuates Ferdinand's discovery of a corpse in Marianne's bed. Whereas films traditionally form aesthetic wholes in which music, dialogue, and image elicit a single response, Godard works toward a complex multiple response. Véronique in *La Chinoise* demonstrates the point by telling Guillaume verbally that she no longer loves him, while telling him with music that she *does* still love him. Then she points to the conclusion: "Music and language; one must struggle on two fronts."

But perhaps more important than Godard's use *of* modernist music are the parallels *to* modernist music in his work. Godard, especially in his later films, redefines what constitutes music in a film. He organizes music, dialogue, naturalistic sound, silence (and even differently colored silences) into what amount to soundblocks composed into musical patterns. The music of *La Chinoise*, for example, not only "offends" from both ends of the respectability spectrum by including music by Stockhausen *and* some very ugly pop music, it also recalls serial music in its very structure as a film, developing a dialectical alternation of classical music, popular songs, background noise, and a kind of *musique concrète* produced by gongs and tinklers. Godard thus follows Noel Burch's suggestion that only through systematic exploration of the cinematic parameters can film liberate itself from narrative "tonality"—which if not strictly equatable with narrative illusionism certainly shares analogies with it— and develop more open forms resembling the formal strategies of post-Debussyan music. Godard, in a sense, has made the kind of decisive break in cinema that came with a Picasso in painting or a Schoenberg in music. With Picasso perspectival realism is shattered. With Schoenberg tonal depth and smooth aural texture give way to atonality and rupture. With Godard the codes of visual depth and narrative coherence are disintegrated in an attack on illusionistic representation.

Notes

Introduction

1. See Michel Foucault, *The Order of Things* (New York: Random House, 1973), pp. 46-49.

2. See Marthe Robert, *Roman des Origines et Origines du Roman* (Paris: Grasset, 1972).

3. Bertolt Brecht, *Galileo*, English Version by Charles Laughton (New York: Grove Press, 1966), p. 98.

4. Foucault, *Order*, p. 16.

5. Bertolt Brecht, *The Messingkauf Dialogues* (London: Methuen, 1964), p. 57.

6. Bertolt Brecht, *Brecht on Theatre* (New York: Hill and Wang, 1964), p. 66.

7. Peter Bürger has argued that one cannot simply equate modernism and the avant-garde, since modernism merely attacks traditional *écriture* while the avant-garde aims to alter the art institution. In my usage of the two terms, I will assume that the avant-garde assumes and gives political institutional bite to modernism; while the avant-garde is necessarily modernist, the converse is not necessarily true. For an exposition of Bürger's argument, see *Theory of the Avant-Garde* (Minneapolis: University of Minnesota Press, 1984).

8. Alfred Jarry, "Writings on the Theatre," in Roger Shattuck and Simon Watson Taylor, *Selected Works of Alfred Jarry* (New York: Grove Press, 1965), p. 84.

9. Jean-Paul Sartre, *La Nausée* (Paris: Gallimard, 1938), p. 60.

10. Jean-Louis Baudry, "Ideological Effects of the Basic Apparatus," (translated by Alan Williams), *Film Quarterly*, XXVII, No. 2 (Winter 1974-1975).

11. Some of the key essays in this debate are Jean-Louis Baudry, "Cinema: effets idéologiques produits par l'appareil de base," in Cinétique no. 7-8, 1970 (published in an English translation by Alan Williams in *Film Quarterly*, vol. 27, n. 2, Winter 1974-75) and "Le Dispositif: approches métapsychologiques de l'impression de réalité," in *Communications*, no. 23, May 1975 (published in English translation by Bertrand Augst and Jean Andrews in *Camera Obscura*, no. 1, Dec. 1976, as well as *L'Effet Cinéma* [Paris: Albatross, 1978]. See also Christian Metz, "Le Signifiant Imaginaire," *Communications*, no. 23, May 1975 published in English translation by Ben Brewster as "The Imaginary Signifier" in *Screen*, vol. 16, no. 2 Summer 1975, and "Le Film de Fiction et Son Spectateur," also in Communications no. 23 and translated by Alfred Guzzetti as "The Fiction Film and its Spectator" in *New Literary History*, Autumn, 1976. Comolli's "Machines of the Visible" is included in *The Cinematic Apparatus*, edited by Stephen Heath and Teresa de Lauretis, published by St. Martin's Press, 1980.

12. Erich Auerbach, *Mimesis: The Representation of Reality in Western Literature* (Princeton: Princeton University Press, 1953), p. 491.

13. For further discussion of realism and reflexivity in television, see my "Television News and its Spectator," in *Regarding Television* (ed. E. Ann Kaplan), AFI Monograph Series, Vol. II (Frederick, Maryland: University Publications of America, 1983).

14. See Brecht, *Brecht on Theatre*, p. 109.

15. For the details of the Bazin-Truffaut relationship, see Dudley Andrew, *André Bazin* (New York: Oxford University Press, 1978).

16. Jorge Luis Borges, *Ficciónes* (Buenos Aires: Emecé, 1965), p. 36.

17. Umberto Eco, *The Role of the Reader: Explorations in the Semiotics of Texts* (Bloomington: Indiana University Press, 1979), p. 21.

18. See *Godard on Godard*, ed. Jean Narboni, Tom Milne translator (New York: Viking, 1972), p. 201.

19. See Georg Lukács, *The Theory of the Novel: A Historico-Philosophical Essay on the Forms of Great Epic Literature*, Trans. Anna Bostock, (Cambridge: M.I.T. Press, 1975), p. 41.

20. See Fredric Jameson, *The Political Unconscious* (Ithaca: Cornell University Press, 1981), p. 146.

21. Gérard Genette, *Palimpsestes* (Paris: Seuil, 1982).

22. See "From *High Noon* to *Jaws:* Carnival and Parody in Brazilian Cinema," in Randal Johnson and Robert Stam, *Brazilian Cinema* (Cranbury: Associated University Presses, 1982), pp. 256-69.

23. See Noël Carroll, "The Future of Allusion: Hollywood in the Seventies (and Beyond), in *October*, Vol. 20 (Spring 1982), pp. 51-81.

Chapter 1

1. See *Partial Magic: The Novel as Self-Conscious Genre* (Berkeley: University of California Press, 1975), pp. 1-29.

2. Charles Musser has pointed out that *Uncle Josh at the Moving Picture Show* is itself a remake of a 1901 English film by Robert Paul called *The Countryman's First Sight of the Animated Pictures,* and part of a pattern of mutual theft between Paul and Edison. There is also a commercial aspect to the intertextuality of *Uncle Josh,* in the sense that it was calculated to show off segments from earlier Edison films along with the title "The Edison Projecting Kinetoscope." Indeed, the projector itself is dramatically revealed when the projectionist points to it in order to explain to Josh that he was only seeing a film. Here the apparatus advertises itself.

3. Christian Metz points out in "The Fiction Film and its Spectator" that a similarly paradoxical faith and scepticism characterizes certain "naive" publics of cinema, those who get up from their seats to shout encouragement to heroes. Their reaction would seem, at first glance, to reflect a naive faith in the filmic image but in reality, Metz argues, their active participation wakes them up from the "dream" of cinema. While expressing a ludic "encouragement du spectacle," the community celebrates its own existence as a community. The cinema as a scene for the projection of purely private dreams is more typical of the urban centers of the advanced capitalist countries.

4. See Jean-Louis Comolli, "Machines of the Visible," in Teresa de Lauretis and Stephen Heath's *The Cinematic Apparatus* (New York: St. Martin's Press, 1980).

5. Gérard Genette, "La Littérature selon Borges," *L'Herne* (Paris, 1964), pp. 323-27.

6. Bertolt Brecht, *The Messingkauf Dialogues,* trans. John Willet (London: Methuen, 1965), p. 51.

7. I would like to thank Roberta Pearson for allowing me to include here portions of an article we coauthored and which appeared in *Enclitic,* Vol. VII, Number i (Spring 1983) under the title: "Hitchcock's *Rear Window:* Reflexivity and the Critique of Voyeurism."

8. Jean Douchet, "Hitch et son public," *Cahiers du Cinema,* Vol. XIX, No. 3 (November 1960), p. 10.

9. Christian Metz, "History/Discourse: A Note on Two Voyeurisms," *Edinburgh Magazine* (1976), p. 23.

10. Although the cinema is founded on the pleasure of hearing (Lacan's *pulsion invocante* as well as on the pleasure of looking (scopophilia), Hitchcock generally emphasizes the visual rather than the aural dimension of voyeurism. Jeffries is granted access to music and noises but not to distant conversations staged as pantomimes. It should also be pointed out, however, that the soundtrack makes frequent allusion to voyeurism. The lyrics of Bing Crosby's "To See You is to Love You/and I See You Everywhere" (ironically superimposed on Jeffries' observation of Miss Lonelyhearts) are in this sense exemplary: "To see you is to want you/and I see you all the time/on the sidewalk/in the doorway/I see you everywhere/To see you is to love you/and I'll love you/and I'll see you/in the same old dreams tonight." A veritable ode to scopophilia, the song fuses sight and desire in its distant dream-like loving common to voyeur and spectator.

11. Christian Metz, "The Imaginary Signifier," *Screen,* Vol. XVI (Summer 1975), p. 60.

12. Michel Foucault, *Discipline and Punish: The Birth of the Prison* (New York: Vintage, 1979), p. 200.

13. For example, Donald Spoto writes in *The Art of Alfred Hitchcock* (New York: Hopkinson and Blake, 1976), p. 241, that "With the exception of one slow pan across the apartments, we see [the neighbors] only as Jeffries sees them." For Robin Wood in *Hitchcock's Films* (New York: Castle Books, 1969), p. 65, only once does Hitchcock grant the viewer information that Jeffries lacks. In all other cases, according to Wood, "we are allowed to see only what he sees, know only what he knows."

14. Metz has compared the spectator's situation generally to that of a child observing a "primal scene."

    For its spectator, the film unfolds in that simultaneously very close and definitively inaccessible "elsewhere" in which the child *sees* the amorous play of the parental couple, who are similarly ignorant of it and leave it alone, a pure onlooker whose participation is inconceivable. In this respect the cinematic signifier is not only "psychoanalytic"; it is more precisely Oedipal in type.—*The Imaginary Signifier* (Bloomington: Indiana University Press, 1982), p. 64.

15. Needless to say, my emphasis in this chapter is on films which confront the structures of male sexuality and what Teresa de Lauretis calls the "blind spots of [male] desire." For her discussion of "the operations by which narrative and cinema solicit women's consent and by a surplus of pleasure hope to seduce women into femininity," see *Alice Doesn't: Feminism, Semiotics, Cinema* (Bloomington: Indiana University Press, 1984).

16. In Buñuel's work, to speak more generally, interruptions and digressions are of the essence. "Digression," he tells us in his autobiography, "seems to be my natural way of telling a story..." (p. 166). One of Buñuel's earliest artistic endeavors, significantly, was a production of Falla's *El-Retablo de Maese Pedro,* based on the Master Pedro puppet show episode in *Don Quixote.* Buñuel's contribution was to add *four* real characters whose role was to interrupt the puppeteer's performance. See Luis Buñuel, *My Last Sigh* (New York: Alfred A. Knopf, 1983).

17. See Pascal Bruckner and Alain Finkielkraut, *Le Nouveau Désordre Amoureux* (Paris: Editions du Seuil, 1977).

Chapter 2

1. Although Marx never fulfilled his ambition of writing an extended study of *La Comédie Humaine,* he did make it clear that he regarded Balzac, along with Cervantes, as a supreme novelist. In a famous letter to Margaret Harkness, Engels wrote: "That Balzac was thus compelled to go against his own class sympathies and political prejudices, that he *saw* the necessity of the downfall of his favorite nobles and described them as people deserving no better fate: that he *saw* the real men of the future, where, for the time being, they alone were to be found—that I consider one of the greatest triumphs of realism, and one of the greatest features in old Balzac." In another letter to Harkness, Engels wrote that Balzac, with all his reactionary opinions, is worth a thousand Zolas, with all his democratic ones. One could learn more about French society from Balzac, Engels argued, than from "all the professional historians, economists, and statisticians of the period put together."

2. Jean-Paul Sartre, *Qu'est-ce que la Littérature* (Paris: Gallimard, 1948), pp. 154-55 (translation mine).

3. All references will be to Honoré de Balzac, *Illusions Perdues* (Paris: Garnier, 1961). All translations mine.

4. Walter Benjamin, *Illuminations* (New York: Schocken, 1969), p. 87.

5. Brecht implicitly compares film production to gold prospecting in his "Hollywood Elegies":

    By the sea stand the oil tanks. Up the ravines
    The gold prospectors; skeletons lie bleaching. Their sons
    Built the dream factories of Hollywood.
    The four cities
    Are filled with the oily smell
    Of films.

6. Quoted in Patrick Donald Anderson, *In Its Own Image: The Cinematic Vision of Hollywood* (New York: Arno Press, 1978), pp. 27-28.

7. Ibid., p. 28.

8. Walter Benjamin, "The Author as Producer," *New Left Review* (July-August 1970), p. 15.

9. Annette Michelson, "*The Man with a Movie Camera:* From Magician to Epistemologist," *Artforum* (March 1972), p. 66.

10. See Dziga Vertov, *Articles, journaux, projets* (Paris: Les Cahiers du Cinéma, 1972), p. 208.

11. Jane Feuer, *The Hollywood Musical* (Bloomington: Indiana University Press, 1982).

12. See Richard Dyer, "Entertainment and Utopia," included in Rick Altman, *Genre: The Musical* (London: Routledge & Kegan Paul, 1981).

13. Thomas Elsaesser, "'Vincente Minnelli,'" in Altman, *Genre: The Musical,* p. 16.

14. See Kristin Thompson, "Implications of the Cel Animation Technique," in Teresa de Lauretis and Stephen Heath's, *The Cinematic Apparatus* (New York: St. Martin's Press, 1980), pp. 106-20.

15. Dana Polan adopts a similar perspective on *Duck Amuck* in "Brecht and the Politics of Self-Reflexive Cinema," *Jump Cut,* no. 17 (1978), pp. 29-32.

16. See Elsaesser, "'Minelli,'" p. 16.

17. My discussion of *Two Weeks in Another Town* is partially indebted to Roger D. McNiven's unpublished paper "Self-reference as the Testament of a Director: Vincente Minelli's *Two Weeks in Another Town.*"

18. The Metz article forms part of Christian Metz, *Film Language: A Semiotics of the Cinema* (New York: Oxford, 1974).

19. See, for example, Ted Perry, *Film Guide to 8 1/2* (Bloomington: Indiana University Press, 1975), as well as the special issue of *Études Cinématographiques,* nos. 28-29, Fall 1963, devoted to the film.

20. See Kaja Silverman, *The Subject of Semiotics* (New York: Oxford, 1983), p. 244.

21. For an elaboration of this idea see Brian Henderson, "*Targets:* An Unshielding Darkness," in Roy Huss and T.J. Ross, *Focus on the Horror Film* (Englewood Cliffs: Prentice-Hall, 1972).

22. For Truffaut's account of the making of *Day for Night,* see F. Truffaut, *La Nuit Américaine* (Paris: Seghers, 1974).

Chapter 3

1. Susan Sontag, *Against Interpretation* (New York: Bell, 1961), pp. 242-43.

2. Robert Alter, *Partial Magic: The Novel as Self-Conscious Genre* (Berkeley: University of California Press, 1975), p. 6.

3. Henry Fielding, *Joseph Andrews* (New York: New American Library of World Literature, 1961), p. 61.

4. Ibid., p. 21.

5. For discussion of "story" and "discourse" see Gérard Gennette, *Narrative Discourse: An Essay in Method* (Ithaca: Cornell University Press, 1980) and Seymour Chatman, *Story and Discourse: Narrative Structure in Fiction and Film* (Ithaca: Cornell University Press, 1978).

6. Henry Fielding, *Tom Jones* (New York: Modern Library, 1950), p. 41.

7. Laurence Sterne, *Tristram Shandy* (New York: New American Library of World Literature, 1962), p. 86.

8. Ibid., pp. 230-31.

9. Vladimir Nabokov, *Lolita* (New York: Berkley Medallion, 1955), p. 91.

10. Emile Benveniste as quoted by Gérard Genette in "Boundaries of Narrative," *New Literary History* VIII, No. 1 (Autumn 1976), p. 9.

11. Wayne C. Booth, *The Rhetoric of Fiction* (Chicago: University of Chicago Press, 1961), p. 206.

12. Machado de Assis, *Memórias Póstumas de Brás Cubas* (São Paulo: Editora Cultrix, 1968), p. 25 (translation mine).

13. Machado de Assis, *Dom Casmurro* (Rio de Janeiro: Edições de Ouro, 1970), p. 243 (translation mine).

14. Tzvetan Todorov, *Littérature et Signification* (Paris: Larousse, 1967), p. 49.

15. De Assis, *Memórias Póstumas*, p. 29 (translation mine).

16. Ibid., p. 119.

17. See Umberto Eco, *The Role of the Reader: Explorations in the Semiotics of Texts* (Bloomington: Indiana University Press, 1979), pp. 47-66.

18. David Denby, "Woody's Poison-Pen Letter," *New York*, Oct 13, 1980.

19. Ibid.

20. Foster Hirsch, *Love, Sex, Death and the Meaning of Life: Woody Allen's Comedy* (New York: McGraw-Hill, 1981), p. 209.

21. John Fowles' "Foreward" to Harold Pinter, *The French Lieutenant's Woman: A Screenplay* (Boston-Toronto: Little Brown, 1981), p. ix.

22. Vladimir Nabokov, *Lolita* (New York: Berkley, 1955), p. 155.

23. Vladimir Nabokov, *The Real Life of Sebastian Knight* (Norfolk, Conn: New Directions, 1941), p. 95.

24. Meyer Abrams, "The Deconstructive Angel," *Critical Inquiry* Vol. III, No. 3 (1977), p. 431.

Chapter 4

1. Mallarmé: *Selected Prose Poems, Essays and Letters* (Baltimore: Johns Hopkins University Press, 1956), p. 10.

2. Alfred Jarry, "Writings on the Theatre," in Roger Shattuck and Simon Watson Taylor, *Selected Works of Alfred Jarry* (New York: Grove Press, 1965), p. 84.

3. Alfred Jarry, "De l'Inutilité du Théâtre au Théâtre," in *Tout Ubu* (Paris: Librairie Générale Française, 1962), p. 141 (translation mine).

4. Alfred Jarry, "Lettres à Lugné-Poe," *Tout Ubu*, p. 133.

5. Cited by Ado Kyrou, *Luis Buñuel* (Paris: Seghers, 1962), pp. 89-93.

6. Gérard Genette defines the pseudo-iterative as a presentation of narrative scenes in the imperfect, as iterative, when their concrete details ensure that no reader can seriously believe that such events would occur and reoccur in such a manner, several times, without variation. See Genette, *Narrative Discourse* (Ithaca: Cornell, 1972), p. 121.

7. Luis Buñuel, *L'Age d'Or* (New York: Simon and Schuster, 1968), p. 69.

8. Both the overheated moralism of the title and the anachronistic juxtaposition of personages from diverse historical epochs recall, in a parodic mode, certain films of D.W. Griffith. The historical leaps and bounds parallel the improbable temporal shifts in Griffith's *Intolerance,*

where parallel montage shuttles us back and forth between Biblical Babylon, the France of Charles IX, and the present. Subtitled "Love's Struggles through the Ages," the Griffith film was lampooned by Keaton, one of Buñuel's cinematic heroes, in *The Three Ages* (1923), which traces an identical love triangle in prehistoric, Roman, and modern times. Keaton sprinkles his parody with hilarious anachronisms—dice bearing Roman numerals, Ben Hur style chariots with "spare" dogs in the "trunk." Buñuel, by making Christ contemporaneous with eighteenth-century Frenchmen and twentieth-century Romans (through the linkage of "at that exact moment") draws out the aggressive potential of the comic techniques developed by silent cinema's brilliant farceur.

9. Jean-Luc Godard, *Godard on Godard* (London: Secker & Warburg, 1972), p. 190.

10. Antonin Artaud, *The Theatre and Its Double* (New York: Grove Press, 1958), p. 93.

11. *Godard on Godard*, p. 198

12. Buñuel's "as-told-to" autobiography, *My Last Sigh* (New York: Knopf, 1983), offers ample evidence of his carnivalesque propensities, whether in his taste for mock rituals (p. 72), his love of disguise (p. 227), or his carnivalesque laughing at death by plotting a final practical joke—pretending to convert to Catholicism—in front of his atheist friends—for his deathbed. He also makes interesting observations on the "art" of blasphemy:

> Now the Spanish language is capable of more scathing blasphemies than any other language I know. Curses elsewhere are typically brief and punctuated by other comments, but the Spanish curse tends to take the form of a long speech in which extraordinary vulgarities—referring chiefly to the Virgin Mary, the Apostles, God, Christ, and the Holy Spirit, not to mention the Pope—are strung end to end in a series of impressive scatological exclamations. (p. 159)

13. Jarry's letter is quoted in Roger Shattuck, *The Banquet Years* (New York: Vintage, 1955), p. 220.

14. In his discussion of *A la Recherche du Temps Perdu*, Genette defines (p. 85, *Narrative Discourse*) syllepses as follows:

> Having christened the anachronies by retrospection and anticipation *analepses* and *prolepses*, we would give the name *syllepses* (the fact of taking together)—temporal or other—to those anachronic groupings governed by one or another kinship (spatial, temporal, or other).

15. See Alejo Carpentier, "De lo Real Maravilloso Americano," *Cine Cubano*, No. 102 (1982), pp. 12-14.

16. Brazilian modernist Oswald de Andrade describes Carnival as follows: "Carnival in Rio is the religious happening of the Brazil-wood race. Wagner is submerged by the Carnival revellers of Botafogo. Barbarousness is ours. Rich ethnic formation. Vegetative wealth. Minerals. Cuisine. Vatapá, gold, dance." "Manifesto da Poesia Pau-Brasil," in *Do Pau-Brasil à Antropofagia e às Utopias* (Rio de Janeiro: Civilização Brasileira, 1972), p. 5.

17. See Roberto da Matta, *Ensaios de Antropologia Estrutural: O Carnaval Como Rito de Passagem* (Petropolis: Vozes, 1973) and *Carnavais, Malandros, e Heróis* (Rio de Janeiro: Zahar, 1978).

18. See João Luiz Vieira, "From *High Noon* to *Jaws:* Carnival and Parody in Brazilian Cinema," in Randal Johnson and Robert Stam, *Brazilian Cinema* (East Brunswick: Associated University Presses, 1982).

19. See Emir Rodriquez Monegal, "Carnaval, Antropofagia, Paródia," in *Paródia* (Rio de Janeiro: Paz e Terra, 1981).

20. In "Des Cannibales," Montaigne reports that the "Brazilian" Indians asked him three questions, only two of which he could remember—why some Europeans were rich and others poor, and why Europeans worshipped men called kings who were no taller than they were. Lévi-Strauss, writing more than three centuries later, claims to have been asked the same questions by Indians in Brazil.

21. Oswald de Andrade's diverse manifestoes are collected in *Do Pau-Brasil à Antropofagia a às Utopias* (from Brazil-Wood to Anthropology and to the Utopias: Rio de Janeiro: Civilização Brasileira, 1972) (translations mine).

22. Haroldo de Campos, *Morfologia de Macunaíma* (São Paulo: Editora Perspectiva, 1973).

23. One of the anomalous features of *Ubu Roi, Les Carabiniers,* and *Macunaíma* is their common tendancy to posit highly unorthodox kinship patterns. In *Ubu Roi* we are never quite sure whether Mere and Pere Ubu are husband and wife or mother and child. In *Les Carabiniers,* we never know whether Michelangelo, Ulysses, Venus, and Cleopatra are brothers and sisters, husbands and wives, or parents and children. Venus calls Cleopatra "Mama" at one point, for example, even though they appear to be around the same age.

Chapter 5

1. Louis Althusser, *For Marx* (New York: Vintage, 1970), p. 231.

2. Karl Marx, *Capital,* trans. Edward Aveling and Samuel Moore (New York: International Publishers, 1967 Vol. I, p. 82n.

3. It might be objected that Don Quixote's golden age is laid in the past while that of Marx is envisioned for the future. But while it is true that Don Quixote overtly condemns the new middle class life in the name of feudal aristocratic values, at the same time he demands change in the direction of what he sees as justice. Here the nostalgic mode serves as auxiliary to utopia.

4. See Frank E. Manuel and Fritzie P. Manuel, *Utopian Thought in the Western World* (Cambridge, Mass: Belknap/Harvard, 1979).

5. Walter Benjamin, "The Work of Art in the Age of Mechanical Reproduction," in Gerald Mast and Marshall Cohen, *Film Theory and Criticism* (New York: Oxford, 1974).

6. Walter Benjamin, "The Storyteller," in *Illuminations* (New York: Schocken Books, 1969), p. 91.

7. Ibid., p. 108.

8. Bertolt Brecht, *Brecht on Theatre* (New York: Hill & Wang, 1964), p. 34.

9. Brecht expressed his bitterness toward the "owners" of culture in a poem, "Deliver your merchandise!"

> Without cease
> When in my course I traverse their cities
> I hear them say!
> Show us what you have in your stomach!
> Spread it out on the table!
> Deliver your merchandise!

Say something to excite us!
Speak to us of our grandeur!
Guess our secret desires!
Show us the way!
Make yourself useful!
Deliver your merchandise!

. . . .

Show yourself one of ours
And we will name you the best among us.
We can pay, we have the means.
No one else can.
Deliver your merchandise!

Know that our great prophets
Are those who lead us where we want to go.
Become a master by serving us!
Last by helping us last.
Play our game, share the booty.
Deliver your merchandise! Be good to us.
Deliver your merchandise!

When I see their rotting faces,
I lose my appetite.

Translation mine from the French of Bernard Lortholary. The poem is included in Bertolt Brecht, *Poèmes* (Paris: L'Arche, 1967), VI, pp. 5859.

10. Godard's film has a precedent in Vertov's *Kino Glaz*, where Vertov not only showed all the stages in the production and consumption of food but also made a strikingly visual demonstration of the idea that workers literally produce everything. He shows a peasant woman going to market to buy meat. Then her motion is reversed, followed by a sequence showing, also in reverse, the processing and distribution of meat. The intertitles read: "Kino-eye turns the clock back. 22: What was in iceboxes at the market. 23: What was a bull twenty minutes ago. 24: We give back the bull its innards. 25: We put his hide back on him. 26: The bull revives. 27: In the slaughter room. 28: Into cattlecars. 29: Back again in the herd." In another sequence, Vertov applies the same productive logic to the process of production and distribution of bread, again shown in reverse motion. Explaining his intention, Vertov wrote: "By revealing the origin of objects and bread the camera graphically demonstrates to every worker that he himself produces everything, and consequently, that they belong to him." Quoted by Masha Enzensberger, "Dziga Vertov," *Screen* Vol. 13, No. 4 (Winter 1972/73), p. 103.

11. See Christian Metz, *Language and Cinema* (The Hague: Mouton, 1974), especially sec. X.5.

12. See Hans Magnus Enzensberger, *The Consciousness Industry* (New York: Seabury Press, 1974).

13. See Metz, *Language and Cinema*, sec. VIII.5.

14. See Laura Mulvey and Colin MacCabe, "Images of Woman, Images of Sexuality," *Godard: Images, Sounds, Politics* (Bloomington: Indiana University Press, 1980).

15. In having Marguerite combine economic with sexual independence, Tanner and Berger perhaps allude to a suggestion advanced by Rousseau in his *Emile*, to wit that true

independence for women would be dangerous because it would inexorably lead to the unrestrained expression of her supposedly insatiable sexual appetite. If the authors are alluding to this idea, they would have done better to make the allusion clear and to distance themselves from Rousseau's conception.

16.   *Jonah* at times recalls another "school film," Vigo's anarchist masterpiece *Zéro for Conduct.* Marco's classroom is graced with a wall poster of Chaplin, whose cake-walk the sympathetic teacher Huguet mimics in the Vigo film. In a microcosmic world of oppressive hierarchy, Chaplinesque comedy evokes freedom from arbitrary authority. Tanner even "quotes," twice, a Vigo camera movement. In the Vigo film, the camera tracks around the class as the midget-principal declaims with demented fervor. Tanner deploys the same tracking movement during two "Left" lectures: Marco's on time, and Mathieu's on inflation. The shots point up a contrast—the students seem less bored and hostile than in Vigo—but also a parallel. The situation satirized in the Vigo film has not radically changed as long as the structure remains the same, with teachers pontificating to students arranged in rows.

17.   Fredric Jameson, *The Political Unconscious* (Ithaca: Cornell University Press, 1981), p. 160.

18.   See "Entretien avec Christian Metz," *Ca* 7/8 (May 1975), p. 23.

19.   See Tzvetan Todorov, *Grammaire du Décaméron* (The Hague: Mouton, 1969), p. 92.

20.   Roland Barthes, "Introduction to the Structural Analysis of Narratives" in *Image-Music-Text*, trans. Stephen Heath (New York: Hill and Wang, 1977), p. 79.

Selected Bibliography for the 1985 Edition

This is a partial and selective bibliography which emphasizes full-length books rather than articles. In hopes of being useful, I have updated the original bibliography to include more recent books not referred to in the text nor incorporated but which are nevertheless relevant to the subject.

Adorno, T.W. *Negative Dialectics*. London: Routledge & Kegan Paul, 1973.

Alea, Tomas Gutierrez. *Dialectica del Espectador*. Havana Cadernos de la Revista Union, 1982.

Alter, Robert, *Partial Magic: The Novel as a Self-Conscious Genre*. Berkeley: University of California Press, 1975.

Althusser, Louis. *For Man*. New York: Pantheon, 1969.

Altman, Rick, ed. *Genre: The Musical*. London: Routledge & Kegan Paul, 1981.

———, ed. *Cinema/Sound*. *Yale French Studies*, No. 60 (Spring 1980).

Anderson, Patrick Donald. *In its Own Image: The Cinematic Vision of Hollywood*. New York: Arno Press, 1978.

Andrew, Dudley. *Concepts in Film Theory*. New York: Oxford, 1984.

Appel, Alfred Jr. *Nabokov's Dark Cinema*. New York: Oxford University Press, 1974.

Auerbach, Erich. *Mimesis: The Representation of Reality in Western Literature*. Trans. Willard Trask. Princeton: Princeton University Press, 1953.

Augst, Bertrand. "The Apparatus: An Introduction." *Camera Obscura*, No. 1 (1976): pp. 97-100.

Bakhtin, Mikhail M. *Rabelais and His World*. Cambridge: M.I.T. Press, 1968.

———. *Problems of Dostoevski's Poetics*. Ann Arbor, Mich: Ardis, 1973.

———. *The Dialogic Imagination*. Austin: University of Texas Press, 1981.

Banu, Georges. *Bertolt Brecht ou le petit contre le grand*. Paris: Aubiers Montaigne, 1982.

Barthes, Roland. *Camera Lucida: Reflections on Photography*. New York: Hill and Wang, 1980.

———. *Elements of Semiology/Writing Degree Zero*. Boston: Beacon, 1968.

———. *Image, Music, Text*. Trans. Stephen Heath. New York: Hill and Wang, 1980.

———. *Mythologies*. New York: Hill and Wang, 1972.

———. *S/Z*.

Baudry, Jean-Louis. "The Apparatus." *Camera Obscura* No. 1 (Fall 1976).

———. "Ideological Effects of the Basic Cinematographic Apparatus." *Film Quarterly* XXVIII, No. 2 (Winter 1974-75), pp. 39-47.

———. *L'Effet Cinema*. Paris: Albatross, 1978.

Bazin, Andre. *What is Cinema?* 2 vols. Berkeley: University of California, 1967.

Becker, George, ed. *Documents of Modern Literary Realism*. Princeton: Princeton University Press, 1963.

Bellour, Raymond. *L'Analyse du Film*. Paris: Albatross, 1979.

———. *Le Cinéma Américain*. Paris: Flammarion, 1980.

————. "Hitchcock, the Enunciator." *Camera Obscura* No. 2.

————. "Psychosis, Neurosis, Perversion." *Camera Obscura* No. 3/4 (Summer 1979).

————. "The Unattainable Text." *Screen*, Vol. 16, No. 3 (Autumn, 1975).

Benjamin Walter. *Illuminations.* New York: Schocken Books, 1969.

Bernadet, Jean-Claude. *O Que e Cinema?* São Paulo: Brasiliense, 1980.

Berger, John. *Ways of Seeing.* London: Penguin, 1972.

Bergstrom, Janet. "Enunciation and Sexual Difference." (Part I). *Camera Obscura* No. 2 (1977).

Bonitzer, Pascal. *Le Champs Aveugle.* Paris: Cahiers/Gallimard, 1972.

————. *Le Regard et la Voix.* Paris: Union Générale d'Editions, 1976.

Booth, Wayne C. *The Rhetoric of Fiction.* Chicago: University of Chicago Press, 1961.

Bordwell, David, and Thompson Kristin, *Film Art: An Introduction.* Reading, Mass.: Addison Wesley, 1979.

Brecht, Bertolt. *Brecht on Theatre.* New York: Hill and Wang, 1964.

Burch, Noel. *Theory of Film Practice.* New York: Praeger, 1973.

Burch, Noel, and Dana, Jorge. "Propositions." *Afterimage*, No. 5 (Spring 1974).

Burger, Peter. *Theory of the Avant-Garde.* Minneapolis: University of Minnesota, 1984.

Burgin, Victor, ed. *Thinking Photography.* London: Macmillan, 1982.

Caughie, John, ed. *Theories of Authorship.* London: Routledge & Kegan Paul, 1981.

Chatman, Seymour. *Story and Discourse.* Ithaca: Cornell University Press, 1978.

Chiampi, Irlemar. *O Realismo Maravilhoso.* São Paulo: Perspectiva, 1980.

Chion, Michel. *La Voix au Cinéma.* Paris: Cahiers du Cinéma, 1982.

Corrigan, Timothy. *New German Film: The Displaced Image.* Austin: University of Texas Press, 1983.

Coward, Rosalind, and Ellis, John. *Language and Materialism.* London: Routledge & Kegan Paul, 1977.

Culler, Jonathon. *Structuralist Poetics.* Ithaca: Cornell University Press, 1981.

————. *The Pursuit of Signs: Semiotics, Literature, Deconstruction.* Ithaca: Cornell University Press, 1981.

————. *On Deconstruction: Theory and Criticism after Structuralism.* Ithaca: Cornell University Press, 1982.

de Lauretis, Teresa and Stephen Heath. *The Cinematic Apparatus.* New York: St. Martin's Press, 1981.

Delleuze, Gilles. *L'Image-Mouvement.* Paris: Editions de Minuit, 1983.

Delleuze, Gilles, and Guattare, Felix. *Anti-Oedipus.* New York: Viking, 1976.

Derrida, Jacques. *L'Ecriture et la Différence.* Paris: Seuil, 1967.

————. *Of Grammatology.* Baltimore: Johns Hopkins Press, 1974.

Dort, Bernard. *Lecture de Brecht.* Paris: Seuil, 1960.

————. *Theatre Public: Essais de Critique.* Paris: Seuil, 1967.

Eagle, Herbert. *Russian Formalist Film Theory.* Ann Arbor: Michigan Slavic Productions, 1981.

Eagleton, Terry. *Marxism and Literary Criticism.* Berkeley: University of California Press, 1976.

————. *Literary Theory: An Introduction.* Minneapolis: University of Minnesota Press, 1983.

Eco, Umberto. *A Theory of Semiotics.* Bloomington: Indiana University Press, 1976.

Ellis, John. *Visible Fictions.* London: Routledge & Kegan Paul, 1983.

Enzensberger, Hans Magnus. *The Consciousness Industry.* New York: Seabury Books, 1974.

Feuer, Jane. *The Hollywood Musical.* Bloomington: Indiana University Press, 1982.

Flitterman, Sandy. "Woman, Desire and the Look: Feminism and the Enunciative Apparatus in the Cinema." *Cine-Tracts*, Vol. II, No. 1 (1978), pp. 63-83.

Foster, Hal, ed. *The Anti-Aesthetic: Essays on Postmodern Culture.* Port Townsend, Washington: Bay Press, 1983.

Foucault, Michel. *The Order of Things: An Archaeology of the Human Sciences.* New York: Pantheon, 1971.

_____. *The History of Sexuality.* New York: Pantheon, 1978.

_____. *Discipline and Punishment: Birth of the Prison.* New York: Vintage, 1979.

Frye, Northrop. *Anatomy of Criticism.* New York: Athanaeum, 1968.

Garroni, Emilio. *Provecto de Semiotica.* Barcelona: Gustavo Gil, 1975.

Genette, Gérard. *Narrative Discourse.* Ithaca: Cornell University Press, 1980.

_____. *Palimpsestes: La Littérature au Second Degre.* Paris: Seuil, 1982.

Girard, René. *Deceit, Desire, and the Novel.* Baltimore: Johns Hopkins University Press, 1965.

Godard, Jean-Luc. *Introduction à une Véritable Histoire du Cinéma.* Paris: Albatross, 1980.

_____. *Godard on Godard.* New York: Viking, 1972.

Gombrich, E.H. *Art and Illusion.* Princeton: Princeton University Press, 1961.

Goodman, Nelson. *Languages of Art.* Indianapolis and New York: Bobs-Merril, 1968.

Harvey, Sylvia. *May 1968 and Film Culture.* London: British Film Institute, 1978.

Heath, Stephen. *Questions of Cinema.* Bloomington: Indiana University Press, 1981.

_____, ed. *Signs of the Times.* Cambridge: Granta, 1971.

Hebdige, Dick. *Subculture: The Meaning of Style.* London and New York: Methuen: 1979.

Henderson, Brian. *Critique of Film Theory.* New York: Dutton, 1980.

Huizinga, Johan. *Homo Ludens: A Study of the Play Element in Culture.* Boston: Beacon, 1950.

Hutcheon, Linda. *Narcissistic Narrative: The Metafictional Paradox.* London: Methuen, 1984.

Jameson, Fredric. *Marxism and Form: Twentieth Century Dialectical Theories of Literature.* Princeton: Princeton University Press, 1971.

_____. *The Prison-House of Language.* Princton: Princeton University Press, 1972.

_____. *The Political Unconscious: Narrative as a Socially Symbolic Act.* Ithaca: Cornell University Press, 1981.

Johnston, Claire, ed. *Notes on Women's Cinema.* London: Society for Education in Film and Television, n.d.

Kawin, Bruce. *Mindscreen: Bergman, Godard and First-Person Film.* Princeton: Princeton University Press, 1978.

_____. *The Mind of the Novel.* Princeton: Princeton University Press, 1982.

Kinder, Marsha, and Houston, Beverle. *Close-Up: A Critical Perspective on Film.* New York: Harcourt Brace Jovanovich, 1972.

Kristeva, Julia. *Desire in Language.* New York: Columbia University Press, 1980.

_____. *Semiotike: Recherches pour une semanalyse.* Paris: Seuil, 1969.

Kuhn, Annette. *Women's Pictures: Feminism and Cinema.* London: Routledge & Kegan Paul, 1982.

Lacan, Jacques. *The Language of the Self: The Function of Language in Psycho-analysis.* Trans. Anthony Wilden. New York: Dell, 1968.

_____. *Ecrits.* Paris: Seuil, 1966.

Lebel, Jean-Patrick. *Cinéma et Idéologie.* Paris: Editions Sociales, 1972.

Lellis, George. *Bertolt Brecht, Cahiers du Cinéma and Contemporary Film Theory.* Ann Arbor: UMI Research Press, 1982.

Lemon, Lee T. and Reis, Marion J., trans. and ed. *Russian Formalist Criticism: Four Essays.* Lincoln: University of Nebraska Press, 1965.

Lentricchia, Frank. *After the New Criticism.* Chicago: University of Chicago, 1980.

Levin, Harry. *Contexts of Criticism.* Cambridge: Harvard University Press, 1957.

_____. *The Gates of Horn: A Study of Five French Realists.* New York: Oxford University Press, 1963.

Lovell, Terry. *Pictures of Reality: Aesthetics, Politics, and Pleasure.* London: British Film Institute, 1978.

MacCabe, Colin. "Realism and the Cinema: Notes on Some Brechtian Theses." *Screen,* Vol. 15, No. 2 (Summer 1974).

———. *Godard: Images, Sounds, Politics.* Bloomington: Indiana University Press, 1980.

Manuel, Frank E., and Manuel, Fritzie P. *Utopian Thought in the Western World.* Cambridge: Harvard/Belknap, 1979.

Matejka, Ladislav, and Titunik, Irwin R., eds. *Semiotics of Art: Prague School Contributions.* Cambridge: M.I.T. Press, 1976.

Metz, Christian. *Film Language: A Semiotics of the Cinema.* New York: Oxford University Press, 1974.

———. *Language and Cinema.* The Hague: Mouton, 1974.

———. *The Imaginary Signifier.* Indiana University Press, 1981.

Michelson, Annette. "Camera Lucida/Camera Obscura." *Artforum.* January 1973.

———. "From Magician to Epistemologist," in P. Adams Sitney *The Essential Cinema.* New York: N.Y.U. Press, 1975.

Mulvey, Laura. "Visual Pleasure and Narrative Cinema," *Screen.* Vol. XVI. No. 3, (Fall 1975).

Nichols, Bill. *Ideology and the Image.* Bloomington: Indiana University Press, 1981.

Noguez, Dominique, ed. *Cinéma, Théorie, Lectures.* Paris: Klincksieck, 1973.

Oudart, Jean-Pierre. "Cinema and Suture," *Screen,* Vol. 18, No. 4 (Winter 1977-78).

Penley, Constance. "The Avant-Garde and its Imaginary," *Camera Obscura* No. 2, Fall 1977.

Place, Janey, and Burton, Julianne. "Feminist Film Criticism," *Movie,* No. 22 (1976).

Poggioli, Renato. *The Theory of the Avant-Garde.* New York: Harper and Row, 1968.

Polan, Dana. "Brecht and the Politics of Self-Reflexive Cinema," *Jump Cut* No. 17 (1978).

Ropars-Wuilleumier, Marie-Claire. *De la Littérature au Cinéma.* Paris: Armand Colin, 1970.

———. *Le Texte Divise.* Paris: Ecriture, 1981.

Scharf, Aaron. *Art and Photography.* London: Penguin, 1968.

Scholes, Robert. *Fabulation and Metafiction.* Urbana: University of Illinois Press, 1979.

Shattuck, Roger. *The Banquet Years.* New York: Vintage, 1958.

Silverman, Kaja. *The Subject of Semiotics.* New York: Oxford University Press, 1983.

Simon, William G. *The Films of Jean Vigo.* Ann Arbor, UMI Research Press, 1981.

Todorov, Tzvetan. *The Poetics of Prose.* Ithaca: Cornell University Press, 1977.

Walsh, Martin. *Brechtian Aspects of Radical Cinema.* London: British Film Institute, 1981.

Williams, Christopher, ed. *Realism and the Cinema.* London: Routledge & Kegan Paul, 1980.

Williams, Linda. *Figures of Desire.* Urbana: University of Illinois Press, 1981.

Wollen, Peter. *Signs and Meaning in the Cinema.* Bloomington: Indiana University Press, 1972.

Xavier, Ismail. *Discurso Cinematografico.* Rio de Janeiro: Paz e Terra, 1981.

———. *A Experiencia do Cinema.* Rio de Janeiro: Graal, 1983.

Index